Prayer and Practice in the American Catholic Community

American Catholic Identities
A Documentary History
Christopher J. Kauffman, General Editor

American Catholic Identities is a nine-volume series that makes available to the general reader, the student, and the scholar seminal documents in the history of American Catholicism. Subjects are wide-ranging and topically ordered within periods to encounter the richly textured experiences of American Catholics from the earliest years to the present day. The twenty-six editors of these volumes reveal a command of trends in historiography since the publication of John Tracy Ellis's three-volume work, *Documents of American Catholic History*. Hence the American Catholic Identities series shows developments in our understanding of social history — the significance of gender, race, regionalism, ethnicity, and spirituality, as well as Catholic thought and practice before and since the Second Vatican Council.

The series elucidates myriad meanings of the American Catholic experience by working with the marker of religious identity. It brings into relief the historical formations of religious self-understandings of a wide variety of Catholics in a society characterized by the principles of religious liberty, separation of church and state, religious pluralism, and voluntarism.

American Catholic Identities is united by such dominant factors in American history as waves of immigration, nativism, anti-Catholicism, racism, sexism, and several other social and ideological trends. Other aspects of unity are derived from American Catholic history: styles of episcopal leadership, multiple and various types of Catholic institutions, and the dynamic intellectual interaction between the United States and various national centers of Catholic thought. Woven into the themes of this documentary history are the protean meanings of what constitutes being American and Catholic in relation to the formations of religious identities.

Titles of books in the series are:

Public Voices: Catholics in the American Context, Steven M. Avella and Elizabeth McKeown

The Frontiers and Catholic Identities, Anne M. Butler, Michael E. Engh, S.J., and Thomas W. Spalding, C.F.X.

Creative Fidelity: U.S. Catholic Intellectual Identities, Scott Appleby, Patricia Byrne, C.S.J., and William Portier

Keeping Faith: European and Asian Catholic Immigrants, Jeffrey M. Burns, Ellen Skerrett, and Joseph M. White

Prayer and Practice in the American Catholic Community, Joseph P. Chinnici, O.F.M., and Angelyn Dries, O.S.F.

Gender Identities in American Catholicism, Paula Kane, James Kenneally, and Karen Kennelly, C.S.J.

"Stamped with the Image of God": African-Americans as God's Image in Black, Cyprian Davis, O.S.B., and Jamie Phelps, O.P.

¡Presente! Latino Catholics from Colonial Origins to the Present, Timothy Matovina and Gerald E. Poyo, in collaboration with Jaime Vidal, Cecilia González, and Steven Rodríguez

The Crossing of Two Roads: Being Catholic and Native in the United States, Marie Therese Archambault, O.S.F., Mark Thiel, and Christopher Vecsey

A workshop for the editors of these books was entirely funded by a generous grant from the Louisville Institute.

American Catholic Identities
A Documentary History
Christopher J. Kauffman, General Editor

Prayer and Practice
in the American
Catholic Community

Joseph P. Chinnici, OFM
Angelyn Dries, OSF
Editors

ORBIS BOOKS
Maryknoll, New York 10545

#44592604

The Catholic Foreign Mission Society of America (Maryknoll) recruits and trains people for overseas missionary service. Through Orbis Books, Maryknoll aims to foster the international dialogue that is essential to mission. The books published, however, reflect the opinions of their authors and are not meant to represent the official position of the society. To obtain more information about Maryknoll and Orbis Books, visit our website at www.maryknoll.org.

Library of Congress Cataloging-in-Publication Data

Prayer and practice in the American Catholic community / Joseph P. Chinnici, Angelyn Dries, editors.
    p. cm. – (American Catholic identities)
   Includes bibliographical references.
   ISBN 1-57075-342-3
   1. Spirituality – Catholic Church – History – Sources. 2. Spirituality – United States – History – Sources. 3. Catholic Church – United States – History – Sources. 4. United States – Church history – Sources. I. Chinnici, Joseph P. II. Dries, Angelyn. III. Series.

BX1407.S66 P73 2000
248.4'82–dc21

00–058443

In gratitude for Lucile Rogers Chinnici,
whose example and life combined faith and learning,
prayer and practice in an extraordinary way.
In the company of the saints, may she read this work with joy.

With gratitude to my parents,
Jerome Francis Dries (1909–1999),
for his inquisitive spirit and searching faith,
and Marion Cronin Dries,
both of whom were my first teachers in prayer.

CONTENTS

Part 2
CONSTRUCTION OF AN AMERICAN CATHOLIC IDENTITY: 1866–1917

Contents   ix

Part 4
FRUITION OF EARLY REFORMS: 1946–79

FOREWORD
Christopher J. Kauffman

To contextualize this book within the literature of American Catholic studies is to underscore its originality. There are documentary histories of spirituality, but they fall into categories remote from the themes and thesis of this work. They feature texts of heroic adepts committed to an ascent of the ladder of perfection or texts on elite models of heroic virtue. Though this book includes ecclesiology and other areas of theology, they are rendered historically in contexts rather than used as proof-texts for theological categories.

There is only one other collection of documents in American spirituality, the Paulist series edited by John Farina. Structured on one person, theme, or school associated with the general topic, each of these books has a lengthy introduction on the historical significances of the documents, such as Joseph P. Chinnici's nearly one-hundred-page elucidation of the historical meanings of the documents in his book, *Devotion to the Holy Spirit*. Since the Paulist series includes books related to spiritualities of several faith traditions, themes emerge which are not easily congenial with the American Catholic identities of prayer and practice. However, both the Paulist works and this Orbis book are dedicated to mining the rich veins of primary sources on American spirituality and are predicated on the need for lengthy introductions emblematic of their common interdisciplinary methodology. One laments that the Paulist series has been discontinued as an ongoing project.

The paucity of secondary literature related to American Catholic spirituality is another mark of this book's unique qualities. Robert Orsi's *Madonna of 115th Street* and *Devotion to St. Jude* are foundational to any contemporary interdisciplinary exploration of topics in this field. Orsi's anthropological methodology and his elucidation of the religious meanings of everyday people, symbolized by his "theology of the streets," have led one reviewer to designate his work as vernacular religion. In its introductions and in many of its documents, the present work depicts the religious experiences of people in the pews and in processions on the streets, portraits that fit into vernacular religion.

Among the secondary works there is actually only one book-length study of American Catholic spirituality, Joseph P. Chinnici's *Living Stones: The History and Structure of Catholic Spiritual Life in the United States,* also an Orbis book. Essential reading for students and scholars committed to an understanding of the interdisciplinary study of American Catholic spirituality, the book has thirty-five pages of endnotes, a virtual bibliography for the field. Like the present work, *Living Stones* is organized according to discrete topics and reflects its commitment to an interdisciplinary methodology with the stress upon anthropology. However, the present book includes footnotes that feature the important secondary works, not only in American Catholic studies but also in anthropology, American religion, material culture, and studies of sodalities, popular devotions, and other areas congenial with its identity as a multidisciplinary study of primary sources in several spheres of American Catholic history.

The introductory material of *Prayer and Practice,* representing nearly 20 percent of the book, is another mark of its originality. The General Introduction opens with a very brief description of three historical documents on sanctity, symbolic of the historical development of the topic, illustrating the "basic premise of our book." What a splendid device to immediately engage the reader on a journey through the introductory material: its explanation of the principles for selecting documents, its eight themes, its descriptions of the four periods, and an overview of its thesis in the concluding section. At the end of this journey the reader encounters a roadmap of eight topics, each of which has several subtopics listed vertically on the side of the page. At the top of the page are the four periods listed horizontally; numbers of documents related to the subtopic in each of the four periods are listed under the dates of the four periods. For example, under the topic "Handing on the Faith" there are eight subtopics; next to "Liturgy" there are numbers of fifteen documents, ten of which are located in the two twentieth-century periods, 1918–45 and 1946–79. This chart clearly signifies the originality of this book.

The editors' key metaphor — the kaleidoscope — conveys the relationships that form shifting historical patterns shaped by contexts in the American experience: for example, religious pluralism, immigrant experiences, and Catholic history (the sacraments, liturgy, images of church, etc.).

The introductions to the particular documents identify them in relationship to the particular period, as well as comment on their anthropological, ethnic, or other meanings. This introductory material is congenial with the editors' commitment to allow the documents to speak for themselves as distinctively fresh voices of prayers and practices in American Catholic life.

In the compilation of each of the documents and the composition of introductory material the editors draw upon their own research, publications, and teaching experience. Angelyn Dries's work *The Missionary Movement in American Catholic History* is based on research in thirty-two archives in the United States as well as in two Vatican archives. This experience with primary sources is evident in the selection of documents for this volume. Her introduction to the earlier book runs parallel to that of *Prayer and Practice* with its emphasis upon themes, a multidisciplinary methodology, and the command of contexts for establishing relationships in shifting patterns of historical development. Actually, the kaleidoscope metaphor originates in her introduction to *The Missionary Movement.* A former student of Joseph Chinnici, Angelyn Dries is a seasoned scholar and an easy collaborator.

Joseph P. Chinnici's principal publication, *Living Stones,* is, as I previously remarked, also based upon a wide array of primary sources, many of which are incorporated into this documentary history. His introduction to the earlier work in part resembles that of *Prayer and Practice* in its attention to the significance of anthropology, sociology, and psychology to the religious historian in "search of the history of meaning." However, the periodization of *Prayer and Practice* represents considerable refinements of the periods of *Living Stones.*

Joseph P. Chinnici and Angelyn Dries have clearly sorted out the significances of the primary source material and have crafted fine introductions to what is clearly an original and useful book. Students and their teachers are treated to distinctive voices of prayer and practice that will enliven the classroom and stimulate scholarly publications.

ACKNOWLEDGMENTS

Over the years, our contacts with archivists, historians, religious congregations, and colleagues around the country have provided a rich background from which we were able to draw the documents for this book. This volume was possible because of their assistance. We thank Thomas Wangler for his insightful conversation and direction toward several eighteenth- and early-nineteenth-century documents. Robert Carbonneau, CP, generously provided us with several Barnabas Ahern documents from which to make our selection. Sister Ruth Boedigheimer, Archivist for St. Benedict's Monastery collection, St. Joseph, Minnesota, provided both the materials printed here and also valuable access to the history of the sodality at the college. Anne Butler guided us to the Sister St. Pierre document and to Sister Francisca Eiken, CCVI, Archivist for the Sisters of Charity of the Incarnate Word of San Antonio. Sister Maria E. McCall graciously corresponded about the Katherine Drexel papers. We are grateful to Sister Mary Rose Krupp, Archivist for the Ursuline Convent of the Sacred Heart, Toledo; Sister Marita Maschmann, OSF, Archivist of the Sisters of St. Francis of Assisi, Milwaukee; Anne E. Chester, IHM, and Jane Farrell, IHM, who assisted us with material on the House of Prayer Movement; Sister Jeremy Quinn, CSA, Congregation of the Sisters of St. Agnes, Fond du Lac, Wisconsin; and John Lynch, CSP.

We further acknowledge the assistance of Patrick Jordan and Gregory Wilpert of the Commonweal Foundation; Ann Luther of Retreats International; Columban Crotty, SSCC, the National Director for the Enthronement of the Sacred Heart Center, Fairhaven, Massachusetts; William J. Riley, Vice President of Operations, Family Rosary, Inc.; William E. Graf, Director of Archives, Diocese of Rochester, New York; Dan Brosnan, Archivist, Diocese of Tucson, Arizona; John Treanor of the Archdiocese of Chicago's Joseph Cardinal Bernardin Archives and Records Center; and Anne C. Edwards, Chancellor of the Catholic Diocese of Richmond. In addition, special thanks are due to Kay Aitchison, the Executive Director of the Christian Family Movement; Mary Benard of the Unitarian Universalist Association of Congregations, Boston; Joanne J. Kuffel and the Apostolate of Suffering; Todd Brennan of the Thomas More Association; William Kevin Cawley, the Archivist and Curator of Manuscripts at the Archives of the University of Notre Dame; and Barbara Henry, who helped a great deal by making the pamphlet collection of Catholic Americana available from the rare books and special collections department at the Catholic University of America.

Among those in the publishing field, we wish to thank Mary Elizabeth Sperry, the Permissions Manager for the United States Catholic Conference

Publishing and Promotion Services. She could not have been more cooperative. We are also grateful to Rita Conallaro, Contract/Licensing Administrator
for the World Library Publication of J. S. Paluch Co., Inc.; Patricia A. Koss-
mann, Literary Editor, America Press, Inc.; the Rights and Permissions Office
of the New York Times; Diana Harrington, Assistant at the Copyright and
Permissions Office at Random House, Inc.; Gordon A. Conner, Permissions
Manager for the Catholic University of America Press; Fran Hurt, Editorial
Assistant for U.S. Catholic; Karen Ryan, Executive Researcher, William H.
Sadlier, Inc.; Kevin Seasoltz, OSB, Editor of *Worship;* Susana J. Kelly, Per-
missions Editor for Ave Maria Press; and Doris Goodnough, Rights and
Permissions, Orbis Books, Maryknoll, New York. Unless otherwise noted,
the illustrations are taken from Joseph P. Chinnici's holy card collection.

    We each would like to add a personal note of thanks. Joseph to his research
assistant for the past ten years, Kristeen Bruun, who worked extensively at
Notre Dame and the Catholic University of America to provide documents
which have influenced the interpretation present in the book. Her footprints
appear here and there in the twentieth-century materials. Jeffrey M. Burns, his
colleague at the Franciscan School of Theology, Berkeley, fellow historian, and
Archivist for the Archdiocese of San Francisco, has provided encouragement,
historical knowledge, and official access to those rich archives. Our present
work would not have been possible without the invaluable help of a number of women and men religious. Long association with them and exposure
to the rich sources of their heritage have made the history of prayer and
practice in the community possible. Joseph thanks Sister Mary Martha Blan-
ford of the Poor Clare Monastery, Evansville, Indiana, who made the papers
of their foundress, Magdalen Bentivoglio, available. Sister Kathryn Lawlor,
an expert in the history of her community of the Sisters of Charity of the
Blessed Virgin Mary, although her documents do not appear here, provided
very significant interpretive materials and insights into the historical development of religious practice in the United States. Throughout Joseph's scholarly
study of American Catholic prayer and practice, Sister Constance Fitzgerald
of the Carmelite Monastery, Baltimore, has provided inspiration, scholarly
example, and an accessibility to sources which have made this present work
possible. Years ago Father Vincent Tegeder granted full access to the Virgil
Michel papers at St. John's Abbey, Collegeville, Minnesota, and the present
Archivist, Brother David, and Abbot Timothy Kelly facilitated their publication here. Father Jeremy Harrington of St. Anthony Messenger Press has
provided both personal inspiration and now official permission to present
the origins of St. Anthony devotion to the public. Joseph's colleague, Angelyn Dries, OSF, has been, at the same time, teacher and scholar, pioneer
leader to new areas of investigation, student, companion in research, fellow
laborer, patient collaborator, and great friend. What have we that we have not
received?

    Angelyn finds herself beholden to Tim Cary, Archivist for the Archdio-
cese of Milwaukee, for his prompt and gracious service directing us to the
Clara Tiry materials and for providing some photographs; Stephanie Mor-

ris, Archivist of the Medical Mission Sisters, Philadelphia, for her continued assistance over the years; Robert Johnson-Lally, Archivist/Records Manager for the Archdiocese of Boston; Father Denis L. St. Marie and the St. Francis Xavier Mission Association, Diocese of Cleveland; Carl Hoegerl, CSSR, Archivist for the Redemptorist Provincial Archives, Baltimore Province; and Mary Jeanne Michels, OSF, who proofread the manuscript before we sent it to the publisher and who assisted us in a variety of ways to ease our work in the last few days of the project. Mentor, friend, and teacher extraordinaire, Joseph Chinnici, OFM, remains a continual inspiration personally and professionally. He is an ideas artist, whose bursts of inspiration and intuition are undergirded by a lightning-quick mind simultaneously tuned to pastoral and historical sensitivities.

Finally, throughout it all, Christopher Kauffman has been the moving force and inspiration for a project which lay dormant, like an unrealized hope, in the recesses of our imaginations. Bill Burrows of Orbis Books had the courage to embark on a very large project. The Franciscan community at Arch Street in Berkeley provided hospitality and patiently supported their greatly dependent confrere and friend; the favor was reciprocated a hundredfold by the local community of the Sisters of St. Francis in Milwaukee.

JOSEPH P. CHINNICI, OFM	ANGELYN DRIES, OSF
Franciscan School of Theology	Cardinal Stritch University
Berkeley, California	Milwaukee, Wisconsin

GENERAL INTRODUCTION

Joseph P. Chinnici, OFM, and Angelyn Dries, OSF

Martin John Spalding (1810–72) stood in the pulpit in his cathedral in Louis-ville, Kentucky, in 1845 and lectured on the topic "Sanctity, a Mark of the Church." What distinguished Catholics from Protestants, he claimed, was that while Protestants lived good, just, and moral lives, possessed great civic and social virtues, and were filled with zeal and learning, they did not promote the values Spalding aligned with sanctity: an active daily and hourly prayer and not simply a passive keeping of the "Sabbath," the gospel preached to the poor, and the promotion of the value of self-sacrifice. Ninety years later, in 1935, the proponents of Catholic Action presented another view of sanctity, one focused on the life of grace in the person, his or her share in baptism, and the role of the Christian in shaping society. Still again, in the wake of the Second Vatican Council, a more ecumenical and global portrayal of the life of holiness influenced the community. These different portrayals of holiness, set within local, national, and global contexts and in dialogue with citizens of many religious persuasions and of none, express the basic premise of our book: in the experience of the American Catholic community, prayer, practice, doc-trine, and social change act in kaleidoscopic relationship with one another.[1]

---

1. For an overview of American religious history since 1893, see Martin E. Marty, *Modern American Religion,* 3 vols. (Chicago: University of Chicago Press, 1989–96). For interpretations of American spirituality, see Gustave Weigel, "Etats-Unis," *Dictionnaire de spiritualité* (Paris: G. Beauchesne, 1961), 4/2:1428–45; Joseph P. Chinnici, OFM, *Living Stones* (New York: Mac-millan, 1989; reprint, Maryknoll, N.Y.: Orbis Books, 1996); William L. Portier, "Spirituality in America: Selected Sources," *Horizons* 23, no. 1 (spring 1996): 140–61, which reviews pertinent vol-umes related to pre-twentieth-century American religious figures in the Paulist Press series Sources of American Spirituality; Aidan Kavanagh, OSB, "Spirituality in the American Church: An Eval-uative Essay," in Philip Gleason, ed., *Contemporary Catholicism in the United States* (Notre Dame, Ind.: University of Notre Dame Press, 1969), 197–214; Bruce Lescher, "American Catholic Spir-ituality," in Michael Glazer and Thomas J. Shelley, eds., *The Encyclopedia of American Catholic History* (Collegeville, Minn.: Liturgical Press, 1997), 45–53; Joseph P. Chinnici, OFM, "The His-tory of Spirituality and the Catholic Community in the United States: An Agenda for the Future," in Nelson H. Minnich, Robert B. Eno, and Robert N. Trisco, eds., *Studies in Church History in Honor of John Tracy Ellis* (Wilmington, Del.: Michael Glazier, 1985), 392–416; David Tracy, "Traditions of Spiritual Practice and the Practice of Theology," *Theology Today* 55 (1998): 235–41, which identifies the split in theology between theory and practice and the need for a com-munity and a holistic-centered approach to the process of theologizing; Robert Bellah, "Religion and the Shape of National Culture," *America* 181, no. 3 (31 July 1999): 9–14.

A living faith community modulates and adapts as it meets new social, political, and ecclesial realities in extraordinary times of trauma, such as war and economic depression or illness, in rites of passage heralding significant steps in life, and in everyday happenings and decisions. American Catholic spirituality both followed and challenged the course of the culture; it was shaped by contact with Protestants, Jews, and new immigrants, was impacted through the geography of rural and urban life, and was formed by major historical events and changing socioeconomic patterns. American Catholic prayer and practice were further modulated by the demands of the unique political realities of the United States: pluralism, democracy, individual rights, the common good, and the fact that no one religion was dominant in the country.

We have gathered our documents at a productive period in historical theory. Since the advent of immigration studies, the field of American history has broken open to reveal an ever more impressive and colorful portrait of what the stresses and strains of life have been for a people thrown together from around the globe. Subsequent historical interpretations have drawn from the work of scholars in cultural anthropology, feminism, regionalism and geography, devotional life, material culture, and popular religion,[2] against which background we unfold the formation of the religious, intellectual, and social

---

2. On cultural anthropology, see as starting points Catherine Bell, *Ritual, Perspectives, and Dimensions* (New York: Oxford University Press, 1997); Nathan D. Mitchell, *Liturgy and the Social Sciences* (Collegeville, Minn.: Liturgical Press, 1999); the classic works by Mary Douglass, *Purity and Danger: An Analysis of Concepts of Pollution and Taboo* (New York: Frederick A. Praeger, 1966); idem, *Natural Symbols: Explorations in Cosmology* (Sarasota, Fla.: Cresset Press, 1970); Clifford Geertz, *The Interpretation of Cultures* (New York: Basic Books, 1973); and Victor Turner, *The Ritual Process: Structure and Anti-structure* (Ithaca, N.Y.: Cornell University Press, 1969); idem, *Dramas, Fields, and Metaphors: Symbolic Action in Human Society* (Ithaca, N.Y.: Cornell University Press, 1974).

As to feminism: the experience of women religious and women's role and leadership in labor unions were among the first areas investigated in the wake of feminist perspectives in the 1970s. See, for example, Mary Ewens, *The Role of the Nun in Nineteenth-Century America* (New York: Arno Press, 1981); Barbara Misner, *Highly Respectable and Accomplished Ladies: Catholic Women Religious in America, 1790–1850* (New York: Garland Press, 1988), which is based on her 1982 dissertation; Janet Wilson James, ed., *Women in American Religion* (Philadelphia: University of Pennsylvania Press, 1980); Rosemary Radford Ruether and Rosemary Skinner Keller, eds., *Women and Religion in America*, 3 vols. (New York: Harper and Row, 1981, 1983, 1986); Karen Kennelly, CSJ, ed., *American Catholic Women: A Historical Exploration* (New York: Macmillan, 1989); James J. Kenneally, *The History of American Catholic Women* (New York: Crossroad, 1990).

On regionalism and geography, see, for example, Belden Lane, *Landscapes of the Sacred: Geography and Narrative in American Spirituality* (New York: Paulist Press, 1988); Belden Lane, ed., *The Solace of Fierce Landscapes: Exploring Desert and Mountain Spirituality* (New York: Oxford University Press, 1998), makes more explicit the theoretical framework for this perspective; Robert Orsi, ed., *Gods of the City: Religion and the American Urban Landscape* (Bloomington: Indiana University Press, 1999); Peter W. Williams, "The Iconography of the American City; or, A Gothic Tale of Modern Times," *Church History* 68, no. 2 (June 1999): 373–97.

On devotional life, in addition to the studies on particular devotions cited in footnote 4 of the introduction to part 3, see also Ann Taves, *The Household of Faith: Roman Catholic Devotions in Mid-Nineteenth-Century America* (Notre Dame, Ind.: University of Notre Dame Press, 1986); C. Gilbert Romero, *Hispanic Devotional Piety: Tracing the Biblical Roots* (Maryknoll, N.Y.: Orbis Books, 1991); Jay P. Dolan and Gilberto M. Hinojosa, eds., *Mexican Americans and the Catholic Church, 1900–1965* (Notre Dame, Ind.: University of Notre Dame Press, 1994); Ana Maria Diaz-Stevens, *Oxcart Catholicism on Fifth Avenue: The Impact of the Puerto Rican Migration upon the Archdiocese of New York* (Notre Dame, Ind.: University of Notre Dame Press, 1993).

worldviews of those who have preceded us. Historians of American Catholic life have benefited from and advanced many of these approaches.

Our book will be of interest to a diverse group of readers. In addition to historians of religion in America, scholars in the phenomenology and anthropology of religion, persons interested in the roots of the spiritual quest in this country, people in parishes who would like to learn about the faith of those who have gone before them, those who more formally pursue the study of spirituality, and those responsible for liturgical direction will find ample material for study and reflection. Seminaries and universities will find the book constructed for useful employment in course curricula related to Catholic studies, liturgy, church history, and world Christianity. Mission scholars can note the dynamics of adaptation and inculturation of "Roman" Catholicism in local settings.

Criteria for Selection

Any selection process presupposes particular criteria for inclusion and exclusion. As our goal was to expose the broad range of American Catholic spirituality, we asked, How do people shape their religious environment and give significance to what they do? Thus, our documents emphasize human interaction and how people put their lives together to make meaning, both personally and institutionally.

We also chose documents keeping in mind current European and American historiographical approaches which emphasize material culture, practice, and rites of passage, as these unfold in "ordinary" people's lives.[3] This enables us to see not necessarily how Catholic spirituality is presented but rather how it is received and acted upon. Current scholarship also notes the close correlation between prayer and practice and the construction of people's symbolic universe.[4] We view the texts as literary rhetorical devices which necessarily imply a particular audience and context, even as they draw upon common symbols.

We have used traditional sources for spiritual development which were common to many groups, not just those which emphasized ethnicity or a specific characteristic of religious identity. Realizing that the black, Native

---

On material culture, see, for example, Colleen McDannell, *Material Christianity: Religious and Popular Culture in America* (New Haven, Conn.: Yale University Press, 1995).

On popular religion, see, for example, Robert W. Scribner, "Elements of Popular Belief," in Thomas A. Brady Jr., Heiko A. Oberman, and James D. Tracy, eds., *Handbook of European History 1400–1500, Late Middle Ages, Renaissance and Reformation I: Structures and Assertions* (New York: E. J. Brill, 1994), 231–62; Craig Harline, "Official Religion — Popular Religion in Recent Historiography of the Catholic Reformation," *Archive for Reformation History* 81 (1990): 239–63; Natalie Zemon Davis, "From Popular Religion to Religious Cultures," in Steven Ozment, ed., *Reformation Europe: A Guide to Research* (St. Louis: Center for Reformation Research, 1982), 321–42.

3. See, for example, Michel de Certeau, *The Practice of Everyday Life* (Berkeley: University of California Press, 1984); and Arnold Van Gennep, *The Rites of Passage* (Chicago: University of Chicago Press, 1960).

4. See in particular the groundbreaking work by Robert Orsi, "Everyday Miracles: The Study of Lived Religion," in David D. Hall, ed., *Lived Religion in America: Toward a History of Practice* (Princeton, N.J.: Princeton University Press, 1997), 3–21; and Orsi, ed., *Gods of the City.*

American, and Hispanic traditions would receive fuller treatment in other volumes of this same series, we have included mainly Euro-American ethnic and regional sources: English, Irish, German, French, Italian, and samples from most parts of the United States. We have not traced the growth of "schools" of spirituality, such as the Benedictine, Mercedarian, Dominican, Franciscan, or Jesuit spiritualities, for example, nor have we examined a "states of life" spirituality (clerical, lay), nor traced the fluxes of "popular religiosity." Our major interpretive lens has not been that of gender. Rather, we move spirituality beyond its devotional and role elements and look at the universal call to holiness. We do not highlight individuals like Dorothy Day and Thomas Merton, traditional spiritual figures associated with American Catholicism, but do provide the context for why these persons became popular. Our documents, which are weighted in the direction of the twentieth century, and even more so in the direction of the post–World War II era, attempt to provide new primary sources to enhance current scholarship on the liturgical movement, women's studies, religion in America, and the phenomenology and anthropology of religion.[5] The introductions to the sections and the documents, taken as a whole, provide an overall interpretive framework.

We provide many sources for categories of religious experience identified in the phenomenology of religion, such as spiritual discipline or way of life, rituals, and creeds. Intensification of religious living is demonstrated in ethical choices in "real" life using appropriate religious "tools" to enable the choice to fit into the person's understanding of the ideal. Bishop Verot's pastoral on peace written from Savannah, Georgia, in the midst of the Civil War, wealthy Katharine Drexel's decision-making process to enter religious life, and Clara Westropp's mission women in her living room make us aware that handing on the faith and its practice was the purview not only of the hierarchy but of the whole community.

Common Themes

As we selected our sources, we saw eight common patterns in American Catholic prayer and practice.

1. Competing ecclesiological emphases draw out different dimensions of spirituality. The community's use of sacred symbols and images for Christ, the Eucharist, Mary, and the church provided for a variety of perspectives which affected the enfleshment of the transcendent and consequent development of interior prayer, social bonds with each other and with God, and the establishment, lessening, or shoring up of ecclesiastical authority. Symbols and images also allowed for an examination of what people shared in common as well as how they perceived their diversity. For example, as we view devotion to the Sacred Heart over the two hundred plus years we have surveyed, we

---

5. One example of the potential for this area of research can be found in Victor Turner, "Ritual: Tribal and Catholic," *Worship* 50 (November 1976): 504–26; see Catherine Bell, "Ritual: Change and Changing Rituals," *Worship* 63 (January 1989): 31–41, for a critique of Turner.

find the 1792 *Pious Guide* (doc. 2; hereafter document numbers will be in parentheses) and Mother Bentivoglio's personalist and affective appropriation (27) quite a contrast to the 1873 New York bishops' (26) moralistic emphasis on the devotion as an antidote to the social problems of the age; still another interpretation of the image of the Sacred Heart and a slightly different ecclesiological emphasis emerged from the community in the 1950s (66). Similar patterns can be discerned in the interpretation of the Eucharist (16, 37, 40, 50, 91), the image of Mary (13, 63), and the Body of Christ (10, 54, 67, 90). In this way a symbol and image reflected both continuity and change in the community.

2. When ecclesiastical structures began to harden and constrict, people found ways in which to express spiritual release. This can be noted, for example, in John J. Keane's sermon on holiness of life (30) and the sisters at the motherhouse in Milwaukee (46). The latter text comes from the late 1920s, after religious life became more organized canonically and tended to be more homogenized. We observe these women who employed their religious imagination to move them beyond the strictures of their convent to be in mission to the whole world.

3. American Catholics, from their beginnings in an established country, have recognized scripture as a part of their spiritual inheritance. We see this in the 1805 Confraternity of the Holy Cross (4), which began with an appropriate scripture passage, and the 1810 meeting in Baltimore where bishops promoted a good English translation of scripture (5). The concern continued in the First Council of Baltimore in 1829 (7), and numerous religious practices throughout the different periods reflected the use of and meditation upon scripture (11, 15, 30, 35, 51, 59). The formation of the Catholic Biblical Association (1936) and the 1941 publication of the confraternity's version of the New Testament began the repositioning of scripture to the center of Catholic prayer and practice (60, 65, 70, 76). Increasingly, Catholics in the United States valued scripture, and, as they had better access to it, they continued to use it as a formative tool in their spiritual life. This goes against the myth sometimes held that only with the Second Vatican Council did Catholics develop an interest in the Bible.

4. Sacraments, the traditional rites of passage for Catholics, were frequently performed with Protestants and others in attendance. At these critical intersections of life and the holy, of Catholic practice and the pastoral need to catechize, we find a remarkable consistency in the expressed need to have the rites conveyed in a comprehensible manner (5, 7, 71). It is rather fascinating that 1960s Catholics requested some of the same liturgical modifications as their counterparts in the Carroll era. At the same time the rites of passage displayed the interchange and mutual appropriation which occurred between the teachings of the hierarchy and the customs and aspirations of the laity in the formation of a single community (6, 7, 33, 71). Not surprisingly, and probably because of a basic sacramentality in all of Catholicism (i.e., the expression of the holy through that which we see, touch, etc. [15, 28]), we find a holistic approach to prayer. Prayer appealed to the imagination and to all the senses in

things like holy water, oil, candles, and bodily movement, and to the mind and will, as Catholics lived out the consequences of their belief in the Incarnation and participation in a sacramental religion (16, 36, 39, 57, 80, 86, 90, 91).

5. We find a kind of ubiquity to prayer and practice expressed in homes, churches, and public places. The drama of incarnation and redemption appears everywhere and is expressed in personal and communal prayer, in rural processions and city dramas, in one's sick room and family room, in small chapels and high cathedrals (2, 3, 23, 25, 45, 46, 61, 68, 74, 76). The pervasiveness of prayer was aided considerably by the adroit use of the media of the day. We find in the late eighteenth and nineteenth centuries the use of good acoustics of a church for parish missions (26), printed circulars (36), and pamphlets (4, 41, 62). In the twentieth century we find workbooks (51, 76), drama and processions (39, 57, 80), and radio, movies, and television (56, 68, 72).

6. Catholic prayer and practice, oriented toward others, become increasingly global in outlook and intent, as does the society at large. We see that prayer is never simply "private," but has either implicit or explicit social consequences. Prayer expresses itself in various visible and invisible affiliations and takes shape in liturgy, confraternities, associations, and sodalities. Connections are made with saints and holy persons and with each other (12, 43) and often are related to mission (45, 51, 58, 62, 75). The descriptions of sanctity (12, 56) portray the bonds holy people form, as do suggestions for intensified prayer (42, 63, 87, 88). Boundaries grow larger in the twentieth century, especially after World War I and World War II placed Americans all over the globe. We see the relational intent widen from the conversion of America (38), to ecumenism (83), to Latin America and the East (92, 93), to world mission (46, 63, 75, 77, 91).

7. Catholic prayer and practice of devotions have developed and changed considerably in response to the community's posture toward and participation in society. Thus, various stages of devotionalism have been reflected in the movement from the largely ethnic and neighborhood-based communal devotions of the immigrant period (23, 24) to a more mobile and national devotional network which emerged in the depression era (49), to a 1950s sectarian devotionalism reflective of a socially accommodated community focused more on family issues and desirous of establishing specific practices which would religiously differentiate its members from their Protestant neighbors (66, 68, 73). It was this sectarian form of devotionalism which collapsed in the 1960s (81, 82, 85), as new types of contemplative, ecumenical, and socially involved devotional aspirations called for expression (80, 86, 87, 88, 89).

8. We have included a view "from the outside," a reflection illustrating how Protestants and Jews and the broader public perceived American Catholic practice. We are aware of various broadsides against Catholics (47), but our documents indicate that Protestants and Jews also called Catholics to be truly "Catholic" in their spirituality. Such a view identifies one aspect of the public and, we might add, prophetic impact of Catholic spirituality. Eliza Allen Starr identified her search for an "authorized faith" (9) as a home wherein to

develop the spirituality begun in her youth. In 1868 (23) Catholics were at home with a public prayer which was comprehensive, full-bodied, and expressive in posture, sound, and silence. In 1931 Catholics were praised for catholic values which enriched the religious life of all persons: "reverence for God, beauty, one's inner spiritual self," self-sacrifice, regular worship, and prayer (52). Will Herberg criticized confident 1950s American Catholics (73) who, while they had come through difficult times and had strong social teachings and respect for the human person, also possessed an air of "practical secularism," which separated religion from other aspects of life. Theoretically Catholicism is universal in outlook, but Herberg found American Catholics sectarian in practice. By the mid-1970s the prominent religious correspondent of the *New York Times,* Kenneth Briggs, could identify the convergences between the Catholic mystical tradition, Eastern religious practices, and new spiritual movements in the community (92). These views from outsiders provide a glimpse into the different tendencies in Catholic life and spirituality during each period.

Overview of the Periods

The documents we have chosen illustrate a trend, an orientation, or exemplify an era. The sources manifest a continuity in the need to be connected to others in a community and the use of scripture and tradition in the formation of a personal and communal spirituality, even though the public face of the church will change.

Part 1. Foundations: 1785–1865. This period is associated with institution building after the arrival of increasing numbers of immigrants. We have a series of texts which relate to episcopal decisions and provincial councils directed to the use of scripture, liturgical practices, and rites of passages in an American, missionary setting. During this period there was a very clear intention to make an alliance between popular aspirations, the need for tight community formation, and symbolic expressions of the faith.

Part 2. Construction of an American Catholic Identity: 1866–1917. This part relates the experience of a geographically diverse Catholicism. We note the development of frontier prayer styles of missionaries and farming parishes and the growth of devotions and religious affiliations in various societies to foster community formation. At the same time we notice an institutionalization of religious forms and practice through the Second and Third Plenary Councils of Baltimore and a defense of authority in the New York pastoral on the Sacred Heart.

Part 3. The Era of Catholic Action: 1918–45. It was during this time that Catholic constituencies aligned themselves with more developed national church structures. The nationalization of devotion to St. Anthony (49) in the 1930s exemplified the direction taken by other devotions, such as St. Jude (Claretian Fathers) and Our Lady of Perpetual Help (Redemptorists), to establish national headquarters for adherents from around the country. The retreat movement, especially for laity, which had its modern origins in the first decade of the twentieth century, by the 1930s supported two national organizations, one for men and one for women. Catechesis, especially of children, became more organized through the establishment of the National Confraternity of Christian Doctrine, which aligned itself with various groups using the principles of Catholic Action. The biblical and liturgical movements also became more organized through the establishment of the Catholic Biblical Association and through the Benedictine support for national liturgical conferences and the Jesuit sponsorship of the Sodality of Mary. During this period, when Catholics found themselves more well placed in the social and economic world, they also tended to create a separate religious culture. Modernization and professionalization were reflected in the increased role-segmentation within the community (hierarchy, priest, religious, and lay vocations were all separate), and more pronounced specific elements of Catholic identity (fasting practices, devotions, Mary, Eucharist, and penance) became unifying elements indicative of a single community. The image of the Mystical Body, which carried much of the theological weight of the period, served as a balance to this organizational and practical emphasis and evoked a universal call to holiness.

Part 4. Fruition of Early Reforms: 1946–79. The period saw the further development and interconnection of the liturgical, scriptural, and catechetical movements. Popularization of scripture through Bible histories, missals, Bible vigils, and Bible reflections as part of individual and corporate gatherings was the result of the combined efforts of national groups, religious communities, and local parishes. Scripture and liturgy were also explicitly intertwined in ever-wider circles with the experience of globalization. By the 1960s contemplation came to be considered as a "normal" approach to prayer for all, rather than as a specialized prayer of those in the "state" of cloistered religious life. The fruition of reform was not painless, however, and soon various groups surfaced to reclaim what they saw as "universal," unchanging Catholic practice.[6] This polarization over Catholic prayer and identity, in its depth and intensity a new development in the community, would grow and become a public force shaping the future development of the community after 1979. As historians, we see a new era of Catholic prayer and practice emerging in the late 1970s and early 1980s, one more shaped by internal division, the advent of new immigrant groups, and a changing dynamic in the society at large. Our book thus ends with the completion of the first phase of the conciliar reform and leaves further commentary to contemporary sociologists and another historical study. We are confident, however, that this new era also reflects

---

6. Michael W. Cuneo, *The Smoke of Satan: Conservative and Traditionalist Dissent in Contemporary American Catholicism* (New York: Oxford University Press, 1997); William D. Dinges, "Resistance to Liturgical Change," *Liturgy: Journal of the Liturgical Conference* 6 (fall 1986): 67–73; idem, "Roman Catholic Traditionalism," in Martin E. Marty and R. Scott Appleby, eds., *Fundamentalisms Observed* (Chicago: University of Chicago Press, 1991), 66–101; and John Seidler and Katherine Meyer, *Conflict and Change in the Catholic Church* (New Brunswick, N.J.: Rutgers University Press, 1989).

the kaleidoscopic relationship between Catholic prayer, practice, doctrine, and social change which has marked the periods we have studied.

We conclude by inquiring, What is "American" about Catholic prayer and practice in the United States?[7] First, not unlike all spirituality, American Catholic spirituality has been shaped from within by drawing upon multiple traditional sources — doctrine, liturgy, scripture, an appeal to earlier holy persons, and personal and communal prayer — and by outside factors, especially civic, economic, social, and political forces. In practice, we find an ecclesiastical spirituality, which includes the sacramental, various forms of Eucharistic devotion, holy "material," and "role" spirituality: priestly and lay. We also have a social and civic spirituality demonstrated in the use of Sorrowful Mother devotions and prayer to St. Michael the Archangel in time of war and in the use of prayer for public figures and for peace to meet present exigencies. Both types of spirituality are frequently found in the same person. As will be seen in the following pages, the American political settlement, its social and economic and religious culture, has distinctively influenced traditional European forms of prayer and practice and reshaped them in new ways.

Second, American Catholics have sought a type of holiness and sanctification in their ordinary lives that is in constant dialogue with their daily environment. Jean-Louis Cheverus's instructions to the Hanley family of Boston (3); Mother St. Pierre's need for money to support the mission to Hispanic children (34); the men and women devoted to St. Anthony, seeking his assistance to obtain food or jobs (49); and Clara Tiry's interaction with those who suffered physical affliction (45) — all bespeak a premise that God and the holy meet in daily life. At other times, heroic models of sanctity provided the inspiration for engagement in more mundane tasks.

Third, American Catholic spirituality tends to be self-consciously inclusive. All strata of the Catholic community were concerned that everyone (children, adolescents, and adults; married, single, and religious; the sick and those in good health; the rich and poor) had resources available to meet their spiritual needs. The liturgical movement in this country gave witness to a potent mix between social reform, participation in the sacrifice of the Mass, and the priesthood of all believers; in the postconciliar period, contemplation has been held out as an ideal practice available to every Christian and Catholic. In this we see a kind of democratization of Catholic prayer and practice, a tendency increased by the great organizational infrastructure of parishes and schools in the United States.

Fourth, American Catholics have not developed a theoretical structure or "school" from which to start. Rather, they are empirical, entrepreneurial, eclectic, practical, adaptive, and diverse, all signs of a living community of faith in the context of a socially and religiously pluralistic country. While American *periti* provided insightful interventions at the Second Vatican Council, pastoral

---

7. For some other approaches to this question, see Jean Leclercq, OSB, "The Distinctive Characteristics of Roman Catholic American Spirituality," *Louvain Studies* 9 (spring 1983): 295–306; and Theodore Maynard, "The Spiritual Heritage of America," *Spiritual Life* 2 (December 1956): 235–44.

implementation of prayer and liturgy, though uneven around the country, came from the continuing focus to have Catholics who were knowledgeable, informed, and active in their religious practice.

Fifth, throughout the volume, we see the pervasive power of strong images, such as Body of Christ, Mystical Body, and Mary, and specific practices, such as forms of penance and affiliations, to engage masses of people and connect them to each other and to the transcendent, as they interact with their environments and circumstances. The multivalency of symbols and practices draws together groups which might philosophically be divergent in their thoughts, and in a pluralistic country this use of symbolization becomes all that much more significant. Because the Incarnation, the enfleshment of God in human form, is so central to Catholicism, adherents have had to examine the consequences of the belief, not just as a theological position but as one which intersects every aspect of life.

In conclusion, we have found that repeated reading of each section and of the whole set of documents continues to disclose the manifold richness of prayer and practice of a large segment of the population of the United States. We hope you will find the documents an opening to further research on a vibrant, living community, multiform in its religious expression, yet drawing upon common symbols and traditions.

How to Use This Book

We have included a chart that will help the reader compare and contrast the various dimensions of the documents which we have highlighted, thus observing common areas we have presented in each period. These areas include rituals (rites of passage, liturgy, processions, calendars), handing on the faith (tradition, scripture, catechetics, family life), material culture (sacramentals, rosaries, holy cards, statues, and images), models of holiness, sacred disciplines (feasting and fasting, mortification, penance, retreats), spiritual companionship, prayer, affiliations (confraternities, societies, sodalities), images and symbols (Eucharist, Mary, Sacred Heart), mission, and an "outsider's" view of Catholic prayer and practice.

We can examine each of these categories vertically by the year of the document to note similarities and differences in each category and in the relation of categories one to the other. We can also view sources horizontally within a time frame and note the interaction of themes in each of the four periods. By so doing, we are able to note recurring themes, continuities, and discontinuities and to uncover the process of change in the community. Each document can also be illustrative of a circle of intersection of themes, such as dialogue with society, models of holiness, and anthropological presuppositions. Or we can ask, for example, How do Catholics approach suffering and what role do religious models play in the process? We have a range of answers in our documents, from direction of the suffering toward communion with other suffering persons, to motivation toward reconciliation, with an expected result of discipleship, endurance, or release from suffering.

TOPIC	1785–1865	1866–1917	1918–45	1946–79
Handing on the Faith				
Scripture			60	65, 70, 76
Liturgy	5, 7	23, 25, 37	43, 48, 50, 51, 53	67, 74, 76, 78, 79
Creed	1		93	
Church				
In Synod, Council	5, 7	21, 32		83
As Teacher	1, 6, 7, 9, 14, 16, 18	26	41	64, 91
Mystical Body	10		48, 53	67, 74, 76,
Ethical Choices	18	27, 31	47, 52, 59	69, 73
Prayer Books	2	32, 40		
Catechetics	1, 3	32	51	70, 83
Family Life	3		61	65, 76, 79
Key Symbols/Beliefs				
Holy Spirit		30		86
Eucharist	12, 16	23, 24, 37, 40	50	82, 90, 91
Sacred Heart	2	24, 26, 27		66
Mary	13	20, 22		63, 68
Rituals				
Rites of Passage	5, 6, 7, 10	33		71
Processions		25	57	80
Calendar Year		22, 25		
Models of Holiness				
Exemplars, Saints		29, 31	44, 56	63
Theoretical Models	14	30	54	67, 72, 89
Mission in Society and World				
Social Challenges	18, 19	35	41, 55, 59	62, 80, 91, 93
Protestants	5, 8	23, 38	47, 52	62, 83
Catholic Action			42, 51, 54, 55, 58	62, 74, 76, 77
Missionary Outreach		29, 38	46	62, 63, 75, 77, 93
View from the Outside	9	23	47, 52	73, 92
Religious Practices				
Sunday Observance	3, 8	23		
Fasting/Feasting	17	34		69, 84
Retreats	11		42	82, 87, 89
Personal Prayer	2, 12, 19	27, 30, 33, 34, 40	45, 57	68, 75, 87
Contemplation	2, 12			68, 88, 92
Affiliations				
Confraternities	2, 4, 10			77
Sodalities		20, 22	48, 58	74
Penance	17	30, 34	41	64, 72, 84
Spiritual Companionship	2, 10	21, 31	45, 46	87, 88
Devotions	2, 4, 10, 16	23, 24, 26, 27, 39, 40	49, 57	66, 68, 78, 80, 81, 82, 85
Material Culture				
Sacramentals	15	28		
Images		36, 39		
Use of Media			56	62, 68, 72
States of Life				
Bishops	1, 5, 6, 7, 12, 13	29, 36	41, 56	69, 72, 90
Priests	8, 16	29, 37	59	62
Religious	14, 19	27, 31, 33, 34	46	63, 75, 78, 87, 88, 93
Laity	2, 3, 4, 8, 9, 11	23, 24, 25	42, 43, 45, 54, 58, 61	64, 65, 67, 70, 74, 76, 77, 86, 89

Part 1

FOUNDATIONS
1785–1865

Introduction

"These Catholics," Alexis de Tocqueville (1805–59) wrote in *Democracy in America*, "are faithful to the observances of their religion; they are fervent and zealous in the belief of their doctrines. Yet they constitute the most republican and the most democratic class in the United States."[1] When these words were first published in 1835 by the famous French commentator on the politics, customs, and mores of the United States, the Catholic community was in the middle of a great transition. Beginning as a small, fairly prosperous group practicing a minority religion, some twenty-five thousand as estimated by Bishop John Carroll in his first report to Propaganda Fide in 1785, the community would grow through mostly Irish and German immigration to three and a half million by the end of the Civil War, the largest single denomination in the United States.[2] The social changes themselves were reflected in the lives of the major exemplars of holiness, now canonized saints, who lived in this period: Elizabeth Seton (1774–1821), Rose Philippine Duchesne (1769–1852), and John Nepomucene Neumann (1811–60) (see docs. 13, 44; document numbers cited hereafter in parentheses).[3] The history of the community's prayer

---

1. Alexis de Tocqueville, *Democracy in America*, the Henry Reeve text as revised by Francis Bowen and Phillips Bradley (New York: Vintage Books, 1945), 1:311.

2. See for background Jay P. Dolan, *The Immigrant Church: New York's Irish and German Catholics, 1815–1865* (Baltimore: Johns Hopkins University Press, 1975); and idem, "A Critical Period in American Catholicism," *Review of Politics* 35 (October 1975): 523–36, for a good overview. For a comparison of the changes in prayer and practice, see Thomas E. Wangler, "Daily Religious Exercises of the American Catholic Laity in the Late Eighteenth Century," *Records of the American Catholic Historical Society of Philadelphia* 108 (fall–winter 1997–98): 1–21; Joseph C. Linck, CO, "'The Example of Your Crucified Savior': The Spiritual Counsel of Catholic Homilists in Anglo-Colonial America," in Joseph C. Linck, CO, and Raymond J. Kupke, eds., *Building the Church in America: Studies in Honor of Monsignor Robert F. Trisco on the Occasion of His Seventieth Birthday* (Washington, D.C.: Catholic University of America Press, 1999), 13–29; Ann Taves, *The Household of Faith: Roman Catholic Devotions in Mid-Nineteenth-Century America* (Notre Dame, Ind.: University of Notre Dame Press, 1986); and idem, "Context and Meaning: Roman Catholic Devotion to the Blessed Sacrament in Mid-Nineteenth Century America," *Church History* 54 (1985): 482–95. For the use of the Carroll catechism, see Charles J. Carmody, "The 'Carroll Catechism' — a Primary Component of the American Catholic Catechetical Tradition," *Notre Dame Journal of Education* 7 (spring 1976): 76–95.

3. For some documentation, see Ellin Kelly and Anabelle Melville, *Elizabeth Seton: Selected Writings*, Sources of American Spirituality series (New York: Paulist Press, 1987); Sister Mary Celeste, SC, ed., *Elizabeth Ann Seton, a Woman of Prayer: Meditations, Reflections, Prayers, and*

and practice cannot be divorced from the developments which accompanied this emergence from a small colony of English inheritance, centered mostly in Maryland and the Eastern seaboard (2, 3, 4, 10), to one covering the huge area from Boston to New Orleans, New York to Louisville, and beyond (6, 12, 14, 19). Numerous adjustments accompanied the journey, adjustments dictated by the movement of a largely European, rurally formed, post-Tridentine confessional Church to a modern Catholicism in a new land, one marked by the free exercise of religion, constitutionalism, and a burgeoning market capitalism and industrialism (8, 13, 24).[4] After Catholic immigration began to rise and the immigrants' piety became influenced by Continental romanticism in the late 1820s, an anti-Catholicism associated with the evangelical awakening also entered as a primary shaping force on the identity of the Catholic community, giving its prayer and piety a tighter ethical, devotional, communitarian, and hierarchical structure (6, 7, 8, 9, 14).[5] Throughout the whole period, the prayer and practice of the community reflected the continuing struggle both to define boundaries with Protestants and to find a place and make a contribution to society in order to atone for its ills, intercede for its leaders, develop its moral life, and prevent its self-destruction in the Civil War (6, 7, 11, 16, 17, 18, 19). As these developments are reviewed in this foundational period of Catholic prayer and practice in the United States, the reader might take note of the following specific trends which would give shape to a distinctive American Catholic spirituality that would continue throughout U.S. history.

1. The prayer and practice of the Catholic community have been largely shaped by the handing on of the faith through key sources of tradition: scripture, liturgy, and the communication of the tradition through creeds, cat-

---

Poems, Taken from Her Writings (New York: Alba House, 1993); Louise Callan, RSCJ, *Philippine Duchesne: Frontier Missionary of the Sacred Heart, 1769–1852* (Westminster, Md.: Newman Press, 1965); and Alfred C. Rush, CSSR, *The Autobiography of St. John Neumann, C.SS.R., Fourth Bishop of Philadelphia* (Boston: Daughters of St. Paul, 1977).

4. For the importance of these elements in the shaping of prayer and piety, see Louis Chatellier, *The Religion of the Poor: Rural Missions in Europe and the Formation of Modern Catholicism, c. 1500–1800* (Cambridge: Cambridge University Press, 1997); R. Po-Chia Hsia, *The World of Catholic Renewal, 1540–1770* (Cambridge: Cambridge University Press, 1998); Hugh McLeod, *Religion and the People of Western Europe, 1789–1989* (Oxford: Oxford University Press, 1997); R. Laurence Moore, "What Religious Pluralism Meant: Insiders and Outsiders in American Historical Narrative and American History," in Jon Butler and Harry S. Stout, eds., *Religion in American History: A Reader* (New York: Oxford University Press, 1998), 198–221; Joseph P. Chinnici, OFM, "Spiritual Capitalism and the Culture of American Catholicism," *U.S. Catholic Historian* 5, no. 2 (1986): 131–61.

5. For the romantic change in piety and the ever-increasing impact of anti-Catholicism, see Robert Emmett Curran, SJ, " 'The Finger of God Is Here': The Advent of the Miraculous in the Nineteenth-Century American Catholic Community," *Catholic Historical Review* 83 (January 1987): 41–61; idem, ed., *American Jesuit Spirituality: The Maryland Tradition, 1634–1900*, Sources of American Spirituality series (New York: Paulist Press, 1988); Robert R. Grimes, *How Shall We Sing in a Foreign Land? Music of Irish-Catholic Immigrants in the Antebellum United States* (Notre Dame, Ind.: University of Notre Dame Press, 1996); Jenny Franchot, *Roads to Rome: The Antebellum Protestant Encounter with Catholicism* (Berkeley: University of California Press, 1994); Barbara Welter, "From Maria Monk to Paul Blanshard: A Century of Protestant Anti-Catholicism," in Robert N. Bellah and Frederick E. Greenspahn, eds., *Uncivil Religion: Interreligious Hostility in America* (New York: Crossroad, 1987), 43–71; Jay P. Dolan, "Catholic Attitudes toward Protestants," in ibid., 72–85.

echisms, and the teaching of the pope and bishops. In this initial period of formation all of these sources played a key role in shaping the communal culture and ethos (1, 3, 5, 7, 13). The documents show an increasing desire to establish a common scriptural translation, liturgical ritual, and catechism. Much of this nineteenth-century legislation would come to fruition with the plenary councils of 1866 and 1884 (22, 32).

2. The desire to shape the boundaries of the community in a pluralistic country — to answer the key question, How do Catholics behave in their relationships with Protestants and in a land of religious pluralism especially during key religious rituals symbolic of religious identity? — is reflected clearly in the legislation surrounding the liturgical celebration of the Eucharist and the rites of passage (5, 6, 7, 8). The use of English in the sacraments, the presence of Protestants at marriages and funerals, the religious care of the unbaptized, and the importance of Sunday obligation show the interplay between Catholic communal formation and the religious culture of the United States. Martin John Spalding's "model of sanctity" presented in document 14, in carefully comparing Protestant and Catholic marks of sanctity, shows both the distinctiveness of the Catholic consciousness and its accommodating argument for the social usefulness of holiness.

3. While this foundational era necessarily saw the implanting of hierarchical structures and the importance of the organs of the tradition of the faith, a strong horizontal sense of communal identity ran throughout the period. The importance of family prayer, affiliations created through confraternities, and popular practices which portrayed the Church as one Body of Christ went hand in hand with the emphasis on hierarchy and legislation (3, 4, 10, 15, 19).

4. This period saw the emergence of what historians would later call American "immigrant moralism." Closely aligned with the inheritance of social Puritanism, this attitude toward life stressed correct action and behavior, moral propriety, duties, and obligations. The broader cultural ethos was reflected in the Catholic community's focus on legislation that would govern behavior, its attitude toward Sunday, and emphasis on self-denying asceticism (7, 8, 14).

5. Two very vital traditions of prayer are represented in the Anglo-American inheritance associated with devotion to the Sacred Heart (2), a good example of Jesuit affective contemplation, and the French tradition of interior prayer, represented in the description of Benedict Joseph Flaget (12). Together they symbolize key streams of the European contemplative tradition and its movement during this period into the United States. These forms, more centered on personal transformation and the interiorization of the life of Christ, often existed side by side and in the same person with a devotional spirituality more focused on the sacraments, obedience to the laws of the Church, devotional images, and correct behavior (13, 15, 16).

1. Handing on the Faith: The Catechetical Tradition, 1785–93

An emphasis on the formation of the community in the truth of the Catho-
lic faith through the development of popular catechisms grew throughout the
seventeenth and eighteenth centuries both in Europe and in England. Father
Robert Molyneaux (1738-1808), an English Jesuit educated in Bruges, probably
composed the first indigenous catechism building on the English Catholic tra-
dition of Laurence Vaux (1519-84), Henry Turberville (1609-78), and Richard
Challoner (1691-1781). Published frequently with the approbation of John Car-
roll (1735-1815), A Short Abridgement of Christian Doctrine first appeared in
1785, and later editions claimed to be "newly revised...for use in the United
States." The "Carroll catechism," as it came to be called, became a fundamental
reference point for subsequent catechisms in the United States (see doc. 32).
The following selections, taken from chapters 2 and 5 of the 1793 edition, deal
primarily with the understanding of the church and the practices which consti-
tute Catholic identity; they can be compared with other images and practices
which emerged from other sources in this foundational period (see docs. 8, 10,
11, 14, 15, 16, 17).

Chap. II: Of The Apostles Creed

Q. Which is the ninth article?

A. The holy Catholic Church, the communion of saints.

Q. What is the Catholic Church?

A. All of the faithful under one head.

Q. Who is the head?

A. Christ Jesus our Lord.

Q. Has the Church any visible head on earth?

A. Yes; the Bishop of Rome, who is the Successor of St. Peter, and commonly called the Pope.

Q. Has the Church of Christ any mark by which we may know it?

A. Yes; it has these four marks; it is One, it is Holy, it is Catholic and Apostolical.

Q. How is the Church one?

A. Because all of its members agree in one faith, are all in one communion; and are all under one head.

Q. How is the Church holy?

A. By teaching a holy doctrine, by inviting all to a holy life, and by the eminent holiness of so many thousands of her children.

Q. How is the Church catholic or universal?

A. Because she subsists in all ages; teaches all nations, and maintains all truths.

Q. How is the Church apostolical?

A. Because she comes down by a perpetual succession from the apostles of Christ; and has her doctrine, her orders, and her mission from them.

Q. Can the Church err in what she teaches?

A. No; she cannot err in matters of faith.

Q. Why so?

A. Because Christ has promised, that *the gates of hell shall not prevail* against his Church, and that the Holy Ghost shall teach her all truth, and he himself will abide with her for ever.

Q. What is meant by the communion of saints?

A. That in the Church of God, there is a communion of all holy persons in all holy things. . . .

Chapter V: Of the Commandments of the Church

Q. Are we bound to obey the commandments of the Church?

A. Yes; because Christ has said to the pastors of his Church, *he that hears you hears me; and he that despises you despises me,* Luke XVI 10.

Q. How many are the commandments of the Church?

A. Chiefly six.

Q. Which are they?

A. 1. To keep certain appointed days holy; with obligation of resting from servile works.

2. To hear mass on Sundays and holidays of obligation.

3. To keep fast in lent, the Ember days, and Wednesdays and Fridays in advent, and eves of certain festivals; and to abstain from flesh on Fridays and Saturdays, excepting, in this Diocese, the Saturdays between Christmas and candlemass; and on other appointed days of abstinence.

4. To confess our sins to our pastor or other priest duly authorized, at least once a year.

5. To receive the blessed Sacrament, and that at Easter, or thereabouts.

6. Not to marry within certain degrees of kindred, nor privately without witnesses, nor to solemnise marriage at certain prohibited times.

Q. Why does the Church command us to fast?

A. That by fasting we may satisfy God for our sins.

Q. At what age do persons begin to be obliged to confession?

A. When they come to the use of reason, so as to be capable of mortal sin; which is generally supposed to be about the age of seven years.

Q. At what time do they begin to be obliged to communion?

A. When they are sufficiently capable of knowing these sacred mysteries, and of discerning the body of our Lord.

> *A Short Abridgment of Christian Doctrine, Newly Revised for the Use of the Catholic Church in the United States of America, to Which Is Added a Short Daily Exercise* (Georgetown [Washington, D.C.]: James Doyle, 1793), 8–10, 20–21. This text was furnished through the courtesy of Thomas Wangler.

2. Devotion to the Sacred Heart of Jesus, 1792

Probably compiled by both the sisters of the Carmelite monastery, Port Tobacco, Maryland, and the Jesuits at Georgetown (Washington, D.C.), The Pious Guide to Prayer and Devotion may be considered the first popular prayer book origi- nating in the newly formed United States. The compendium contained many of the favorite devotions of the English Catholic community (e.g., Litany of Jesus, the Jesus Psalter), a method of hearing Mass, reflections on the Ten Command- ments, and numerous examples of litanies and indulgenced prayers. Subsequent editions (1808, 1815, 1825, 1834, 1845, 1846, 1847, 1851) added numerous prayers and devotions and reflected the movement in the community from the more sober English style of the eighteenth century to the baroque Counter- Reformation spirituality of the immigrant church (see docs. 13, 15, 16). In the first section presented below, the seventeenth-century inheritance of interior affective prayer typical of the English Jesuit tradition is evident. The preface, notable for its refutation of the Jansenist critique of the devotion, was omitted from subsequent editions of The Pious Guide. *"A Practice of Devotion for a Secular Family," the second section, shows the easy convergence between this style of prayer and the early American republicanism of the John Carroll era. Both selections can be compared and contrasted with other images of the Sa- cred Heart emerging in both the nineteenth and twentieth centuries (see docs. 26, 27, 66).*

Devotion to the Sacred Heart of Jesus

"I will speak to his Heart, and from it obtain whatever I shall desire." St. Bonavent[ure], in *stimulo amoris,* p. I, cap. I

I. Part the First
The Nature and Excellence of This Devotion

The devotion to the sacred Heart of Jesus has Jesus Christ himself for its author; it is he that planned the project thereof, he explained the nature of it and foretold its future progress. The Church has at all times considered the sacred Heart of Jesus as an object worthy of her veneration; for whilst she honoured, as she ever did, his sacred humanity, doubtless the heart which is the principal part thereof, must have deserved her adoration. However, this devotion, (tho' ever holy in itself) has not always been solemnized alike. It is only in these latter days, that the time appointed by the eternal decrees of

Providence being come, Almighty God was pleased to disclose to the whole world the inestimable treasures of the sacred Heart of his divine Son. Such ever was the conduct of God over his Church; from time to time in order to rouse and stir up the piety of the faithful, he sets up devotions, which tho' not new in themselves as to the substance and groundwork, are yet so in their solemnity and respective circumstances. Thus has he established the devotion to the most adorable Sacrament of the Altar; thus again the devotion to the sacred Name, to his sacred Wounds, etc.

But to give a more clear idea of this devotion, let us trace it back quite up to its source, and see on what occasion it came forth.

In the year 1680, there lived in the Diocese of Autun, in the town called Paroi le Monial, in the monastery of the Visitation, a young woman unknown to the world, but favoured with the most strict communications with Almighty God, a worthy spouse of the spotless lamb. Her life was a series of the most eminent virtues, and her soul was filled with the most distinguished graces. For many years, this devout soul had been inceilantly [sic] engaged in the meditation of the immense riches of the adorable Heart of Jesus Christ: For many years, she glowed with the holy extasies of a divine and uninterrupted love at the sight of its perfection; she had long sighed after that happy moment, when she might see this amiable heart known, honoured and loved throughout the whole world. She then little knew that she was to be the happy person chosen by Almighty God to bring about this great work. On a certain day, within the Octave of Corpus Christi, finding herself more than ordinarily burning with this ardent desire, Jesus Christ appeared, and spoke thus to her. (a) "You cannot, says he, testify your love for me better, than by doing what I have so often asked at your hands," and disclosing his sacred heart, he said: "Behold this Heart, which has loved mankind so tenderly, and spared nothing even to the wasting and consuming itself in testimony of its love, and yet in return I generally meet with nothing but ingratitude, contempt, sacrileges, irreverences and coldness, even in the very sacrament of my love; and still what more sensibly affects me, is, that I receive this usage from hearts peculiarly consecrated to my service. Wherefore I demand of them, that the first Friday after the octave of the blessed Sacrament, be consecrated to a special feast in honour of my Heart, that a solemn reparation of honour and a public act of atonement be offered to it on that day, and holy communion received, with an intent to repair by it, as far as possible, all the injuries and affronts it has received, when exposed on the altars, and I promise it shall dilate itself, to pour profusely the gifts of its divine love on all such persons, as shall pay to it this homage, and induce others to the performance of the same religious office."

These are the words of Jesus Christ himself, and from them daily weighed, as from a most copious spring, flow such truths, as most properly belong to this devotion, and are the fittest to convey a distinct notion of the nature of it. They will be more fully unfolded in the following queries.

As the Church does not pronounce on the authenticity of this revelation, or the sanctity of the person to whom it was made, in order to conform as we ought, to the wise regulations of the Holy See, we only relate this as an historical fact, yet so certain and so averred as to challenge deservedly our belief and adherence. We speak here as formerly the faithful spoke of the revelation of St. Juliana, which gave rise to the solemnity of the feast of Corpus Christi.

First Query: What is the Object of this Devotion?

A. The object thereof is the heart of Jesus Christ, an object of all others evidently the noblest, the holiest, the greatest, the most divine and altogether the most sweet and most amiable that can possibly be conceived. Hence it follows, that devotion relating to it, bears with it that particular mark of sanctity, dignity, grandeur, sweetness and loveliness, which no other can come up to. The dignity of this adorable Heart arises 1. From its union with the most perfect and most compleat soul that ever was, whereof this divine heart has been the organ in the production of its sensible affections. From this close union of the heart with the soul, that universal notion among all polite nations is sprung, whereby they are induced to pay to the hearts of great men, after their death, honours suitable to the merits of the soul they were united to. If so, what shall we say of the sacred Heart of Jesus, since it was united to such a soul? 2. To what a pitch of grandeur and infinite merit, is it not raised by its union with the second person of the blessed Trinity? Whatever belongs to the adorable person of Jesus Christ, claims all our veneration in an infinite degree; the least part of his sacred body, a drop of his blood, a hair of his head, deserves our utmost adoration. Everything that has but touched his sacred body, becomes thereby venerable, as the cross, the nails, the lance, the thorns. If the lance, which pierced the Heart of Jesus, is by that very touch become an object of veneration to the whole Church, what shall we say of the Heart itself, which has imparted so much dignity to the contemptible flesh?

3. A farther proof of the dignity of the Heart of Jesus is taken from the divine function it was formed for, I mean that of burning incessantly with the purest and most ardent flames of the love of God. From the very first instant of its production, it glowed with that divine and uninterrupted fire to the last instant of its mortal life, and will ever thus burn for all eternity. By one single act of the love of God produced by it, the divine Majesty is infinitely more honoured, than it could possibly be by the united love of all creatures even possible during a whole eternity. How noble then must that Heart be, the function whereof is to receive continually the impressions of this sacred love, and produce the highest acts thereof uninterruptedly for all eternity? Hence the complacency of the eternal Father for this divine object, since nothing can be more acceptable in his eyes, than the never ceasing love of his only Son.

It is plain from all this, that we do not mean to honour the sacred Heart of Jesus barely as an inanimate and lifeless Heart, but we consider it as united to the divine person and as the chief instrument of the most holy soul that ever was. This undoubtedly was not sufficiently attended to by those who at first seemed to attack this devotion. They considered the sacred Heart merely as an inanimate and lifeless Heart, but we consider it as united to the divine person and as the chief instrument of the operations of the most holy soul that ever was. They considered the sacred Heart merely as an inanimate piece of flesh without life or feeling, as a holy relick purely material, without paying any attention to its union with the divinity, and to such spiritual and divine riches, as are annexed to it, and which impart to it life and motion.

Second Query: What is the End of this Devotion?

We are to consider the sacred Heart of Jesus under two different aspects; on the one side, as a Heart full of love and breathing nothing but the salvation of mankind; on the other side as a Heart that is offended, insulted and defiled by unthinking man, by sinners void of all sense of gratitude and unaffected by his love. The inclination of this adorable Heart to reconcile man to God, and Earth to Heaven, must raise in us sentiments of the most ardent love and feelings of the greatest sorrow, to dispose of us for a reparation of the wrongs and outrages it daily suffers. The end thereof proposed by this devotion, to which the faithful are earnestly invited, is in the first place to honour by frequent acts of love and adoration, and by all manner of submission and homage the unbounded love of Jesus throughout the whole course of his mortal life, but chiefly in the Sacrament of the holy Eucharist, the sum and abridgment of all his wonders, where he still burns with the love of us. In the next place it is to share in his grief and to make amends on our part of those many insults his love for us exposed him to during his mortal life, and still exposes him to every day in the blessed Sacrament, where he is so little loved by men, so little known, and oftentimes so outrageously abused even by those, who know him.

Third Query: What are the Advantages of this Devotion?

They are numberless, and unspeakable....

Do you desire, pious souls, to attain the very summit of perfection? Behold here a safe and easy road to it. I say a safe road: in matters of devotion nothing is so much to be feared as illusion. Whatever is uncommon and singular, is deservedly to be mistrusted. Now this devotion steers clear of any such danger; the object it honours is of all objets the most worthy, the Heart of a Man-God; the end it proposes is quite divine; the practical duties performed therein, are agreeable to the spirit of the church; and since Jesus Christ speaking of himself, says, that he is the way, that leads to life, and the gate, thro' which we must enter heaven, how can we fear being misled by penetrating into the most august Sanctuary of his sacred Heart in order to partake of that fullness of grace and sanctity, abiding therein as in its centre?...

There is still another benefit entailed on this devotion, and it is this. It is not confined merely to some select and privileged souls, more versed in spiritual matters, and more enlightened than the common. No: it lies within the reach of all degrees of people, the unlearned as well as the most learned. The great ones and the rich of the world have here no superior advantage over the poor, and those of the common sort, because it rests wholly on the dispositions of the heart, and all have a heart to give to God, and may find one in Jesus Christ, ever ready to receive their gift. Cheer up therefor, ye afflicted souls, narrow geniuses, indigent and forlorn creatures. If you be not allowed to enjoy, in this world, neither the pleasures of life, the splendour of honours, nor the treasures of wealth, yet you may be admitted into the sacred Heart of Jesus Christ, and therein you will find abundantly, whatever the world has denied you: happy, if you but know, how to improve this great treasure, where you may provide yourselves with riches for time and eternity itself.

What then remains, but that we enter into the adorable Heart of Jesus Christ! He came down on earth chiefly for this end, to bring with him the sacred flames of divine love, which ought to fire all hearts. Let us then throw ourselves into that burning furnace, to glow with its heavenly heat; repair into that sacred asylum, to be under shelter from all the dangers of salvation; to that spring of living water, to find comfort in our troubles; to that model of all virtues, to transcribe them into our lives; in a word to that place of delights, to commence there our heaven on earth....

Part the Second
The Practice of This Devotion

In general, by the practice of this devotion nothing more is meant, than the use of such means as are best calculated to render us true adorers and faithful imitators of the sacred Heart of Jesus Christ. Now, this practice is both interior and exterior. The interior practice consists in the inward acts of faith, adoration, love, hope, confidence, gratitude, and the like. The exterior practice consists in outward and visible acts, such as are means to denote outwardly the inward devotion. Of this sort are prayers, novenas, confessions, visits to Jesus Christ in the blessed Sacrament, associations, confraternities, fasting, penances, and generally all pious and edifying acts which are performed to honour the adorable Heart of our blessed Redeemer. Whereupon it is not amiss to observe, that we must not so rest and depend on these outward practices, as to persuade ourselves, that if we have but performed them, we have thereby fulfilled all justice. This would be confining the whole system of devotions to bare and empty ceremonies. Much less ought they to be considered as a claim to impunity for one's faults, or as a security of a future conversion, after having long slighted Almighty God's grace. This would be a gross illusion and a fatal abuse, ever disavowed by all true devotion. But on the other hand, because devotion is misused, it is no reason why it should be condemned or suppressed; for the best things are liable to be misused. The abuse indeed ought to be checked, but the devotion itself, wholly saintly and solid, should ever be preserved....

II. A Practice of Devotion
for a Secular Family, &c.

This practice consists in an agreement of some pious and virtuous people, of whom one daily at his convenience visits the Heart of Jesus, as ever remaining in the holy Eucharist, and therein his own, and the name of the others his associates, honours this sacred Heart by the recital of that act of virtue, as hereafter expressed, which in particular has fallen to his lot or choice for that month. These acts of virtue in general, are five [*sic*]: *Adoration, thanksgiving, atonement for sin,* and *petition.*

2. The number of devout persons composing it, may be greater or less, as occasions serve. Though only five are appointed, for the duty of reciting the five acts, yet this ought not to hinder every particular [*sic*] from joining in the daily reciting of the said acts. Even it is advisable they should, each one, for example, choosing that particular act for himself, which his own devotion shall suggest.

3. The five chosen by lot, engage themselves to recite daily, in the name of the whole association, the respective act, which falls to their charge. They are, if we may call them so, public deputies or ambassadors to the throne of heaven, in order to obtain favours for the rest, and to draw down particular blessings upon each one of this association.

4. The choice of these five deputies, may be made in the following manner. Let there be as many billets, as there are persons, who are to draw for this honourable preferment: on five only of these shall be written the particular acts, which are to be said, as the *Act of Adoration,* the *Act of Thanksgiving,* and so on. The other billets are blanks. The whole being mixed together, each draws one billet for himself. Those who draw the billets written upon, charge themselves with offering up, during the following month, to the sacred Heart, in the name of the rest, that act, which has fallen to his lot.

5. A draught must be made for the absent, within any competent distance, and if a lot, or one of the five endorsed, falls to any one of them, notice should be given immediately that no time be lost, where so great an interest of the association is at stake.

6. This choice should be made twelve times a year, and the most proper time for it would be towards the end of each month.

7. Every associate should have in his house or chamber, a picture of the Sacred Heart. The advantage amongst others is this. Should any particular be hindered from visiting the blessed Sacrament, he may before this picture, acquit himself of the obligation, he has voluntarily taken upon himself....

8. The virtues of the greatest estimation, as most dear to the sacred Heart of Jesus among the associates, must ever be Meekness and Humility, and the vices opposite to these must be had in equal detestation.

If then, devout Reader, this sacred Heart of Jesus, is really an object of your affections, as no doubt it ought to be, make up amongst those, with whom you live, your family, friends and domestics, a small association of this nature, and take my word for it, Almighty God will look with a propitious eye both on you, and this your Assembly.

The Pious Guide to Prayer and Devotion, Containing Various Practices of Piety Calculated to Answer the Various Demands of the Different Devout Members of the Roman Catholic Church (Georgetown [Washington, D.C.]: James Doyle, 1792), 13–22, 24–26, 38–40.

3. Sunday Obligation without a Priest, 1798

Jean-Louis Cheverus (1768–1836), a French émigré priest, arrived in Boston on 3 October 1796 and began ministering to the Catholic peoples in New England, an area of the church which was then part of the Diocese of Baltimore. The community was scattered and priests were few, a missionary situation not untypical in the sprawling church in the nascent United States. Cheverus composed numerous instructions for the people on how to keep Sunday holy in the absence of a priest (see docs. 1, 8). The following directives, dated from Boston 20 July 1798, were sent to the Roger Hanley family. The practices enabled the minority Catholics to keep distinct from their Protestant neighbors yet also allowed them to be models of virtue and holiness. Cheverus's concern for family prayer would be a constant throughout the history of the community (see docs. 2, 27, 61, 65, 66, 76).

Directions on Family Prayer

Have charity for all men, pray for the salvation of all, do good to everyone, according to your power, whatever may be his religious persuasion, but never forget that you belong to the Roman Catholic Church, that is to say, to the true Church of Jesus Christ, & that it is unlawful for you to attend the public worship of any other persuasion. Obey, like dutiful children, the laws of your mother the Holy Church; keep the days of fasting & abstinence etc.

Every day say your prayers on your knees morning & night with attention and devotion.

Every Sunday, meet all together, if possible, read in the morning the prayers & instructions for Mass with at least one chapter in the poor man's catechism,[1] & in the afternoon some of the prayers appointed for Sundays with another chapter in the same book.

Moreover let everyone of you learn & recite every Sunday something out of your Christian Doctrine,[2] so that you may know the whole of it perfectly & never forget it. Take care to be well prepared for confession and for receiving the blessed Sacrament, against the next time that you will have a Catholic priest with you. Besides the above, you will read every Lord's day in the Manual[3]

Morning, What every Christian must believe. p. 3–8

Afternoon, What every Christian must do. p. 8–10

---

1. J. Mannock, *The Poor Man's Catechism; or, The Christian Doctrine Explained* (cf. the edition of Baltimore: Dorin, 1815).

2. *A Short Abridgment of Christian Doctrine, Newly Revised for the Use of the Catholic Church in the United States of America; to Which Is Added a Short Daily Exercise,* 12th ed. (Georgetown [Washington, D.C.]: James Doyle, 1793).

3. The term "manual" clearly refers to Richard Challoner's *The Garden of the Soul; or, A Manual of Spiritual Exercises, and Instructions, for Christians, Who Living in the World Aspire to Devotion* (London: J. P. Coghlan, 1793), which opens with a section titled "What Every Christian Must Believe," followed by "What Every Christian Must Do."

Love God and serve him with all your heart, obey your parents, live friendly with one another, & avoid sin as the most dreadful of all evils. Remember me in your prayers, I assure you I shall not forget you in mine.

Reprinted through the courtesy of the Archives, Archdiocese of Boston, Cheverus Papers, box 1:12, 1797–1835, with reference and footnotes courtesy of Thomas Wangler.

4. Confraternal Prayer, 1805

The formation of devotional societies or confraternities was one of the strongest expressions of communal piety characteristic of Catholic life after the Council of Trent (1545–63). This tendency toward affiliation took shape in the early church in the United States in the formation of groups dedicated particularly to the mysteries of Christ's life and to a happy death (see doc. 10). The "rules of life," emphasizing participation in the church's liturgical life, catechetical instruction, mutual support, moral reform, and outreach to the poor, played an important role in community formation and identity. Confraternal prayer and practice have remained a constant feature of Catholic piety in the United States and provide an important religious bridge in accommodation to American voluntarism (see docs. 20, 22, 35, 58, 74, 77). The following document, Rules of the Confraternity, or Association of the Holy Cross, *was written in Boston, whose Holy Cross Church became the center of Catholicism in New England when the diocese was established in 1808.*

God forbid that I should Glory, save in the Cross of our Lord Jesus Christ. Gal vi 14

The Cross is the Altar on which Jesus Christ the Son of God has accomplished the great work of our redemption. From an instrument of ignominy, he has made it the throne of his love, the glory and sign of a Christian, the badge of his servants, the banner under which they fight, the terror of the devils, the high-way to Heaven, the school and incentive to all virtue. It is by meditation at the foot of the Cross on the sufferings of a God-man, that we learn the enormity of sin, the severity of divine Justice, the incomprehensible love of Jesus for us, the value which he sets on our souls, the return of love which we owe him, the happiness of suffering with him and for him. There we learn patience, resignation, obedience, humility, forgiveness of injuries, love of our enemies, how to conquer our passions, to die to ourselves, and to live to God alone. By such meditations innumerable souls have been raised to the highest sanctity. The knowledge of Jesus crucified is the whole science of the saints, *I know nothing but Jesus Christ, and him crucified,* I Cor. 2,2.

To encourage and spread this excellent devotion and knowledge of Jesus crucified, is the design of the association or *Confraternity of the Holy Cross.* It is designed to honour in a particular manner the passion and death of our Divine Savior, to recall frequently to mind all that he has suffered for us, to study the lessons which he preached from his Cross, and to put them in practice.

Its object is to excite and maintain among the Catholics of this town and diocese (of which the Catholic Church has been dedicated under the title of the Holy Cross), an emulation of piety, to strengthen them against the multiplied temptations to which they are exposed; and to procure by the good example of the members, the propagation of our holy faith among our dissenting brethren.

The means to be used are, the frequentation of the holy sacrament, the communion of prayers, pious instructions, and a great union among the members.

The following are the practices and Rules recommended to the members. But they must always bear in mind that no exterior practices of religion, however excellent in themselves, are of any avail before God, unless they be accompanied by an interior spirit of piety.

1. Every Friday of the year will be to the associates a particular day of devotion — on which they will recall to remembrance the passion and death of Jesus Christ. To that purpose they will recite on that day the *prayers to Jesus suffering* (page 176 of the manual, or the *litanies*, page 290);[1] or at least five *our Father*, and five *Hail Mary*, which they will terminate by the short prayers, (page 99), which they are exhorted to recite every day: *We adore and worship thee, O Christ, with all praise and benediction; because by thy bitter death thou has redeemed our souls. Have mercy on us Dear Jesus, have mercy on us.* And the verse: *Christ became obedient unto death, even the death of the Cross.* They will also hear Mass on that day to the same intention, if consistent with their occupations.

2. They will come to confession once a month, and if fit, receive the blessed communion on first Sunday of each month, and, besides the greatest festivals, on the days of *the finding* and the *exaltation of the holy Cross*, or Sundays following; and also on the festivals of *St. John the Evangelist*, and *St. Mary Magdalen*, who stood at the foot of the Cross with the holy Mother of Jesus.

3. On the Friday preceding the first Sunday of the month they will meet in the Church at five in the afternoon in summer, and half past three in the winter; and there recite or sing the above prayers, the vexilla, and stabat, hear a short exhortation, and end by some prayers according to the season, or preparatory for the next communion.

4. On Good Friday they will spend at least an hour in the Church, in fervent adoration, exclusive of the hours of the divine office, which hour however they may anticipate from the end of Mass on holy Thursday, after the blessed sacrament has been deposited on the little altar.

5. One hour also in the course of every year, or oftener according to the number and devotion of the associates, will be allotted to each one, to be spent in the Church in acts of adoration of Jesus on the Cross, and really present in the Blessed Sacrament, and other pious exercises; which hour and day will be recorded together with his or her name in the book of the Confraternity.

---

1. See Richard Challoner, *The Garden of the Soul; or, A Manual of Spiritual Exercises, and Instructions, for Christians, Who Living in the World Aspire to Devotion* (Philadelphia: Matthew Carey, 1792).

6. As a token of the present association, and to excite to a perpetual remembrance of the passion of Jesus Christ, each member will constantly wear a little cross, or crucifix, which will be visible on the breast, at least on communion days, and at all the meetings of the Confraternity.

7. When the number of the associates will be sufficient, there will be a general meeting of the Associates twice a year, in May; and November; the men however meeting separately and on a different day from the women, to deliberate upon whatever may promote the design of the Association, make collections for the poor, choose some trustees or others, whose duties shall be to visit during the six months of their appointment, the sick of the Association, or other sick, principally the poor, to assist and comfort them, to inquire about the instruction of the children, and perform every other work of charity, corporal and spiritual, according to their abilities.

8. These meetings will always be presided by the chief Pastor, or another clergyman in his room; or if they cannot be present, by the oldest Trustee, or other person appointed by the Pastor.

9. After the death of any one of the associates, the Association will cause a Mass to be celebrated for his soul, at which all the associates will endeavor to be present, the same shall be done also on the first anniversary day of the death. They will also offer their next communion for the soul of the departed member.

10. All persons desiring to become members, will apply to their respective Pastors, who after sufficient examination, will inscribe their names in a book kept for that purpose.

11. Previous to their admission they will promise to refrain from the frequentation of the theatre, of every house or place of bad fame; from gambling or dangerous companies; from spreading evil reports, from every word of cursing and swearing, and to suppress this last wicked habit in their families, and check it in others as much as they are able.

12. Any person who, after having been received in the Association, shall indulge in the habit of the following practices, or other equally scandalous, shall be liable to admonition, and even expulsion:

1. Dangerous and scandalous familiarities with persons of a different sex:

2. Habitual or frequent intemperance in drinking:

3. Gambling, or frequenting gambling houses:

4. Frequenting the theatre:

5. Selling liquors on Sundays, out of cases of necessity:

6. Quarrelling, fighting, cursing, swearing, irreligious or immodest discourses:

7. Usury:

8. Detraction or backbiting:

9. Membership with, or attending at the lodge, or lodges of free-masons.

13. The virtues to be particularly cherished by the Association are:

1. A lively devotion to the passion of Jesus Christ.

2. A frequent adoration of that divine Savior in the blessed Sacrament.

3. A particular respect and veneration for the blessed Virgin Mother of God, which they will manifest on all occasions, and promote by word and example.

4. A great care for the good order of their families, if they have any; instructing their children, sending them to catechism and instructions, having family prayers every night, being early at home, cherishing peace and concord, avoiding quarrels, banishing from their houses dangerous companies, swearers, tale-bearers, and whatever is contrary to decency, and mutual edification.

5. Brotherly love and union among the members. Brotherly love was the distinctive character of the first Christians, of whom it is written that *they were but one heart and one soul.* Acts 4,32. Such also must be the character of this Association, whose members are called brothers or sisters for that particular purpose. Hence they will be prompt to assist one another according to their abilities, both in spiritual and corporal necessities. Their mutual charity must be manifested, not by words alone, but by deeds. *My little children,* says the beloved apostle, *Let us not love in word, nor in tongue, but in deed and in truth.* I John 3,18.

Preliminary Questions for Admission

1. Are you sincerely attached to the faith and practices of the Roman Catholic Church?

2. Do you desire admission to this confraternity from a pure motive of promoting the glory of God, your own sanctification, and of the edification of your neighbor?

3. Are you determined, with the help of divine grace, to avoid all scandalous and sinful practices, and to live in habits of regularity and piety?

4. Are you resolved to observe with fidelity the rules of the association, even such as do not bind under any kind of sin?

5. Are you disposed to contribute to the best of your power to the welfare of the association, and of every one of its members?

6. After an affirmative answer made to each of the above questions, made kneeling at the railing of the sanctuary, the clergyman will pronounce on the new member the following blessing:

May our divine Lord and Savior Jesus Christ, through the merits of his holy passion, bless you, and grant you grace to persevere in the faithful observance of these holy resolutions. Amen.

With Christ I am nailed to the Cross... who loved me, and delivered himself for me. Gal. 11,19 and 20.

> Rules of the Confraternity, or Association of the Holy Cross Established at Boston, with the Approbation of the Right Rev. Bishop. Document courtesy of Thomas Wangler.

5. Ecclesiastical Discipline and Community Formation, 1810

Throughout the nineteenth century, meetings of the bishops with their priests or meetings of bishops themselves established legislation governing Catholic prayer and practice (see docs. 7, 21, 32). The legislation itself was an important indicator of the growth of the community, its internal difficulties, and its perceived relationship with the world. The first synod of John Carroll and the clergy was held in 1791, and after the Diocese of Baltimore was divided in 1808, Carroll met with his suffragan bishops of Philadelphia, Boston, and Bardstown in November 1810. The following selections from this meeting show the concern of the bishops to establish guidelines in the American church for the reading of scripture, celebration of the liturgy, and entrance into and development of the community (baptism and marriage). The focus on the rites of passage as key areas of community formation continues to the present day (see docs. 6, 7, 33, 71).

8. Holy Scripture

The translation of the old and new testament, commonly called *The Douay Bible,* is to be literally followed and copied, whenever any part of the holy Scripture is inserted in any prayer-book, or book of devotion, and no private or other translation is to be made use of in those books.

9. Vernacular languages

It being made known to the Archbishop & Bishops that there exists a difference of opinion & practice among some of the clergy of the United States concerning the use of the vernacular language in any part of the public service, & in the administration of the Sacraments, it is hereby enjoined on all Priests not only to celebrate the whole Mass in the Latin language, but likewise, when they administer Baptism, the Holy Eucharist, Penance & Extreme Unction to express the necessary & essential forms of those Sacraments in the Same tongue, according to the Roman Ritual; but it does not appear to be contrary to the injunctions of the Church to say in the vernacular language the prayers previous and subsequent to those sacred forms, provided however, that no translation of those prayers shall be made use of, except one authorised by the concurrent approbation of the Bishops of this Ecclesiastical Province; which translation will be printed as soon as it can be prepared under their inspiration. In the mean time the translation of the late Venerable Bishop Challoner may be made use of.

11. Baptisms

Conformably to the Spirit of the Church, & its general practice, the Sacrament of Baptism shall be administered in the church in all towns where churches are created.

12. Sponsors

When a Sponsor for a child to be baptized cannot be procured, the child is not to be solemnly baptized with the usual ceremonies, but only receive what is called private Baptism, or baptism without the ceremonies.

14. Marriages

Many difficulties having arisen in regard to the forming of a general Rule, that all Marriages should be celebrated in the church, as a practice most conformable to the general discipline, it was judged premature to make now an ordinance on that subject; but all Pastors are directed to recommend this usage generally, and prepare the minds of their flock for its adoption in a short time.

> "Decisions of the Archbishop and Bishops of the Ecclesiastical Province Established in the United States in Council Assembled at Baltimore," 15 November 1810; original text in Archives of the Archdiocese of Baltimore; reprinted in Peter Guilday, *The Life and Times of John Carroll, Archbishop of Baltimore (1735–1815)* (New York: Encyclopedia Press, 1922), 592–93.

6. Early Rites of Passage, 1826

The establishment of regular ecclesiastical discipline and the curtailment of the excesses of folk religiosity were constant concerns of church leadership in the European Catholicism of the early modern period. When John Dubois (1764–1842) was installed as the third bishop of New York in November 1826, he inherited this approach and also faced the difficult challenges of a large diocese, few priests, little instruction, and large numbers of immigrants. These selections from the conclusion of Dubois's first Lenten pastoral reflect the common tensions between folk custom and church discipline, home and church services, and civil and religious jurisdictions which continually shaped the community's prayer and practice in the nineteenth century (see docs. 5, 7, 21, 27).

Pastoral Directives

After having thus, dearly beloved brethren, glanced over some of the obstacles which oppose the growth of Religion and Virtue in your hearts, and having pointed out the probable means of removing them, permit us to turn your attention to abuses which, although they may appear of minor importance, are calculated to undermine, gradually, your religious principles. To Catholics, faithful to the commands of their Church, it might be sufficient to observe, that they are contrary to its general discipline: We allude to the administration of the Sacrament of Baptism and Matrimony, and to the Funeral Service. Our habitual intercourse with our dissenting brethren has introduced amongst us practices which, although they may flow naturally from their religious principles, are repugnant to the spirit of our Church. It has been the practice,

from the remotest antiquity, to have children brought to the Church to be
baptised. There they were offered to Our Lord in his Holy Temple; there
their names were enrolled as members of the Church Militant. This holy
practice was not dispensed with even for the persons of potentates. The Ritual of the Church itself designates in what part of the Temple the different
ceremonies are to be performed. The majesty of the place, the sacred vest-
ments, the baptismal fonts, and above all, the presence of the adorable victim,
from whose blood all the Sacraments derive their virtue, are calculated to excite the gravity, the grateful respect which the regeneration of man ought to
excite in the believers[;]...that temple in which the child was baptized became particularly venerable to him as he gazes up. Now this adoption of a
child in the great Christian family, has become a simple meeting of a few
friends, in a private room, where refreshments are prepared for the invited
guests, and so little do the people appear sensible of its impropriety, that the
same practice is observed by those who live at the very door of the Church.
The consequence of it is, that no other records of births and baptisms are
kept, but a few notes sometimes hastily taken by the Priests, who go to those
houses to baptize the child; or, by the parents, when they think of it, and
know how to write in a family Bible or Testament, exposed to the depre-
dations of the children. The difficulties, which may arise from this, when,
for civil purposes, the day of the birth of the child, its legitimacy, its ge-
nealogy, must be ascertained at law, are obvious; whilst, if the children are
brought to a church to be baptized, the Sexton, for a small compensation,
not burthensome to the poorer parents, could be appointed to keep a regular register, signed by the officiating Clergyman and some of the witnesses of
the ceremony, from which, in cases of necessity, extracts might be obtained,
to obviate those difficulties. The same observations can be made on the administration of the Sacrament of Marriage, which, administered as it is, in
private houses, looks more like a civil contract, than a religious ceremony;
sometimes attended with a levity, a coarseness of behaviour, to be reprobated,
even before a civil magistrate; whilst this Sacrament, which ought to be received in a state of Grace, should be preceded with Confession, and even, if
possible, with Communion, whilst unexperienced youths should apply, before hand, for advice to their Pastor, in an engagement, on which depends,
in some measure, their temporal and eternal welfare: the Priest is suddenly
called upon to administer this Sacrament to people, whom he knows nothing
of, who have been whole years, perhaps, without receiving the Sacraments,
and even never received them, and is placed thereby in the alternative, either
of affixing that sacred seal to guilty sinners, or, by refusing his ministry, to
put them under a kind of necessity, in order to avoid scandal, to add a new
sin to the former, by seeking the nuptial rites out of the Church. Hence the
danger of marrying minors; people who are already married to others: hence
are many marriages contracted without reflection or advice; hence so many
improper matches, or many quarrels, divisions, regrets after marriage, and
separations — the ordinary consequence of unions which have not been ce-
mented by Religion, or rather have begun in sacrilege. We are not ignorant,

dearly beloved brethren, that there are some cases where it is proper, and even necessary, particularly in the country, to administer these Sacraments in private houses, in case of danger on the part of the children, at a great distance from the Church, and when the weather is very severe — when the mother is too infirm to expose herself and her child to a long journey, but these are exceptions to the rule — they do not abrogate it, nor must you think that we need to bring you back, all at once, to the old discipline, by reforming suddenly an abuse which has been so long tolerated. We prefer appealing to your piety, religion, and good sense, for its gradual abolition. Let the most virtuous and respectable members of our Church here, give the first example in bringing their children to the Church to be baptized, or receiving the Holy Sacrament of Marriage at the foot of the Altar, and the rule will soon prevail. A time will come, when the ancient discipline may be prudently insisted on.

The same deviation from the spirit of the Church seems to prevail at our funerals. Among our forefathers, no sooner was a soul separated from the body, than notice of it was sent to the Pastor, that Divine Sacrifice might be offered for it, the parish bell was tolled to invite all charitable persons to unite in humble supplication to the throne of mercy on behalf of a departed brother: The body was exposed, not so much to satisfy the curiosity as to invite the charity of the beholders to pray for him: the visits then were so many acts of religion: the corpse was respectfully ushered into that church which had so often witnessed the piety of the deceased — it was placed at the foot of the altar, where the All-saving Victim resides — the Holy Sacrifice was offered if it was morning — the evening service was read or sung, if in the afternoon. The mournful apparel of the church, the solemnity of the place, of the ceremonies, of the Holy Canticles, excited the people to prayer, and reminded them of that awful judgment at which the soul of that departed Christian had appeared, and for which each of the assistants must prepare himself. The holy water, the burning incense were so many tokens of the respect paid to the precious relics of a Christian destined to a happy resurrection, and of the purity required for it. All that springs from our faith in Purgatory and the necessity of helping our brethren with our prayers, and was calculated to revive that faith in our dissipated minds. What has been substituted in the city for those edifying rites? Pride, dissipation, and gluttony seem to preside over our funerals. A wake is kept where frequent libations of liquor are used instead of Holy Water, idle conversation instead of the prayers formerly said. And would to God these wakes were not enkindling those passions which the sight of a corpse ought to smother! Would to God that the guests invited to that funeral banquet would not betray in their behavior on the road to the grave the excesses of the preceding night. What follows corresponds with this preparation. No expense is spared to give the funeral procession all the show which may gratify the pride of the survivors, and overburden the often distressed family. Carriages, and often scarfs and gloves are lavished. But here terminates the respect intended for the dead. A few words of prayer hastily and indistinctly pronounced over the grave by a Priest, dressed in his common clothes, are all the marks of Religion shown on the occasion. The corpse is interdicted from admission into the church under a penalty of twenty dollars, for fear the floor or the pews should be injured by the attendants; and as if the whole of a Catholic burial consisted in the corpse being admitted into the church ground, there is a by-law sanctioned formerly by the trustees, which seems to leave it to the choice of the family of the deceased to call in the minister of religion or not. In justice to the present trustees we ought to observe that the irregularity escaped their notice, and that on the first representation they showed a praise-worthy zeal to correct those abuses. In noticing them we only wish to point out to you how custom can reconcile us to inconsistencies. We have no doubt that we shall obtain from their piety their concurrence in suppressing these anti-Catholic regulations. But is it a wonder that under such a discipline, the necessity of praying for the dead should be forgotten, that with very few exceptions, that sweet intercourse of prayers called the Communion of Saints, which unites the Militant Church with the Church Suffering, as well as with the Church Triumphant, should be stopt among us, and that as soon as the body has disappeared, the soul should be forgotten? Is it a wonder that we should lose our faith, or rather are these not signs of expiring faith[?] We will not dwell upon the frequent practice of calling in the minister of religion at the last extremity, when the sick are no longer capable of being prepared for the dreadful account, particularly after a long succession of sinful habits, and the total neglect of the sacraments — so that the whole attendance of the Pastor is reduced to the annointing [*sic*] of an almost inanimate carcase, without previous confession, and without communion. Such abuses need only to be mentioned to strike those with horror in whom faith is not extinguished. This and other points will be the subject of future observations to our venerable Brethren, the Clergy, and of other instructions to you, Dearly Beloved Brethren.

> "John, by Divine Permission, and with the Approbation of the Holy See, Bishop of New York to Our Venerable Brethren, the Clergy, and to the Faithful of the Diocese," pp. 9–11. In Archives, the Archbishop's House, Westminster, England.

7. The First Council of Baltimore, 1829

By 1829 the Catholic population in the United States had expanded to approximately five hundred thousand, and dioceses stretched from as far west as St. Louis to as far south as New Orleans. From 3 to 18 October 1829, Archbishop James Whitfield (1770–1834) of Baltimore met with his fellow bishops and others to discuss the state of the church and legislate for its future development. Throughout the nineteenth century the community grappled with similar concerns: the challenges of Protestantism, the inheritance of regional customs, the intelligibility of the liturgy, the jurisdiction of the church gathered in council and the jurisdiction of the local ordinary, and the tensions between a domestic-based missionary church and a more developed diocesan parochial church (see docs. 3, 5, 6, 21, 32). Among the many decrees which were eventually issued after Roman approval in 1831, five in particular reflected these difficulties.

IX. [On Scripture]

Since the faithful protection of the deposit of sacred scripture, committed to the Church by the Lord, requires from the bishops that they strive with all their powers that the Word of God not be presented to the faithful contaminated by the deceits or negligence of people, we exhort most strongly all the pastors of souls of this Province that at all times, they have always before their eyes what has been decreed by the Council of Trent, by the supreme pontiff, especially what is recommended in the encyclical letters of Leo XII and Pius VIII, and by the Most Illustrious and Reverend John Carroll, Archbishop of Baltimore, one with the other bishops of his province, gathered in a meeting in 1810. Let them guard their flock from bibles spoiled by non-Catholics and permit them to be nourished with the untainted food of the Word of God as found in approved versions and editions. Therefore, we decree that the Douay version, which is accepted in all the churches where English is spoken, and which has been properly prepared by our predecessors, must by all means be retained. Likewise, the bishops should take care that, according to the most approved exemplar designated by them, in the future all editions of both the new and old testaments of the Douay version be amended. Annotations may be chosen only from the Fathers of the Church or from learned Catholic teachers.

XVI. [On Baptism]

Since it is of great importance that a general law — Baptism in the Church — be immediately kept in the regions to which the law is contrary to regional custom, nevertheless we leave it to the judgment of Bishops and Missionaries, [and emphasize] that whenever possible they support [the custom] urging the Faithful to bring infants to the church in order that Baptism can be conferred on them.

XVII. [Baptism of Non-Catholics]

We believe infants of non-Catholics who are brought by their parents are to be baptized as long as there is a probable hope of their Catholic education. Moreover, they [the priests] must certainly be solicitous that the sponsors be Catholic. Let the priest remember that whenever there is danger of death all infants not only may but must be baptized.

XX. [On Burials]

We have decided, according to the prescribed Roman Rituals, that in administering the sacraments, and in performing burials, the priests are obliged, at all times, to use the Latin language. If they think it appropriate for the sake of instruction to translate into English, only that version which has been approved by the ordinary may be used. Wherever some other custom has arisen contrary to this decree, we wish its immediate abrogation.

XXIII. [Location of Eucharistic Service]

We decree that no priest, by force of general faculties that will apply to him for celebrating Mass in "any decent place," may do so in private buildings, unless in private stations, and in those buildings which the Ordinary will have designated or where there is need to give attention to the Missions, which are far from some churches. But if, at another time, the Ordinaries grant permission to celebrate in private buildings because of special circumstances, we recommend to them to grant this for one time or another.

> *Concilia Provincialia, Baltimori Habita Ab anno 1829 usque ad annum 1849,* Editio Altera (Baltimore: John Murphy and Company, 1851), 76–77, 79–81. Translation from the Latin by Francis Dombrowski, OFM Cap, and Margaret Klotz, OSF.

8. Sunday Observance in Protestant and Catholic America, 1840

Certainly an adversarial relationship with Protestant neighbors shaped the Catholic community's prayer and practice, giving it a strong internal cohesion and clear definition in the nineteenth century (see docs. 14, 23, 27, 32, 37). However, both groups of Christians also shared common cultural problems and a desire to bring some moral order into the crowded city streets and open frontier of the new land. Augustus J. Thébaud (1807–85), a Frenchman, member of the Society of Jesus, and well educated in both theology and the natural sciences, came to frontier Kentucky to teach at St. Mary's College, Marion County, in 1839. He became the president of St. John's College (later Fordham University), New York City, and spent the rest of his life working in education or pastoral ministry in New York State and Canada. Thébaud observed at first hand several convergences between Protestantism and Catholicism and in his memoirs noted how both groups emphasized Sunday observance and a strict code of behavior, characteristic traits of American Christianity. Until the 1960s, his irenic tone represented another, albeit minor, strand in the theological and cultural formation of American Catholicism (see docs. 30, 52, 83).

...Hence the morality of the sects in the United States, at least, was still essentially Christian; and in 1840 strangers saw at once that this was not a pagan nation, nor yet a people composed mainly of indifferentists.

This was manifest firstly in the number of churches and Christian schools erected everywhere. Steeples, in many instances surmounted by the sign of the cross, met the eye in nearly every street; the smallest villages counted generally four or five; nay, sometimes you were surprised by a church in the midst of forests, a central point having been chosen for the farmers' families scattered around. They were mostly modest edifices without pretension to architectural beauty. Still they had cost money — the total amount must have been enormous; and Americans were not the men to throw away their money; so they must have believed in religion.

The schools also were Christian schools. In 1840 no one had yet spoken of non-sectarian schools. They were all *denominational,* though this expression was not used. Each sect — except a few insignificant ones like the Unitarians — having so far preserved at least the essentials of Christianity, the belief in one God and three Persons, the dogmas of the Incarnation and Redemption through Christ, that of the indwelling of the Holy Ghost through grace, and finally the belief in a hereafter, in an eternity of happiness or punishment in heaven or in hell, — all this being a solemn fact throughout the country, the schools where religion was always taught to children were Christian schools. This great source of pure morality, therefore, existed in the United States.

In the second place, public opinion was openly in favor of religious practice, and of a moral life among the citizens. It is sufficient to mention here the universal observance of the Sunday, and the sacredness of the marriage tie. In all the States and territories the *laws* enforced absolute rest and the most decent behavior on the first day of the week; but public opinion was so decided that the practice of it would have been universal if there had been no state laws enforcing it. Puritanism even had not then entirely disappeared. The Catholic Church has never exacted so strict an observance of the Sunday as was then customary in all states of the Union. When we took charge of the College of St. Mary's the rigor of the religious code on this point was unknown to us, because we were all Frenchmen; accordingly when the service in the church had been performed, we allowed some boys to practise on musical instruments out of doors, while some of the other pupils were permitted to take a rifle and hunt squirrels and rabbits in the woods. As there were no farmhouses in our neighborhood, and nobody could hear what was going on, we heard of no strictures for some time. But several of our own parishioners who came every Sunday to the church of St. Charles, distant two miles from the college, became aware at last that there was both music and gun-practice on our grounds. One of them, a member of the grand jury of the county, came to inform our worthy president that "unless both breaches of the law were instantly discontinued, he would be bound by his oath to denounce us at the next meeting of the grand jury."

The remarks regard only the exterior observance of the Sunday. As to the necessity of going to church, the laws in vigor did not impose any obligation on the citizens, as was formerly the case, I think, in Connecticut; but public opinion was not favorable to a total disregard of this holy precept, and any family whose members were never seen at *meeting* would not have enjoyed a good reputation among their neighbors. Though it be needless to give any description of the absolute stillness prevailing all over the country on Sunday, still a few words will not be amiss. It is doubtful whether the same hushed solemnity had ever before prevailed among the most devoted Christian nations. Trade was totally suspended, and artisans completely rested from their labors. All stores and shops were closed except dispensaries and pharmacies; the noise of wagons and carts was unheard on the granite pavements; the only sound was that of the bells calling people to prayer; a few carriages only appeared in the deserted streets. In New York a stroll in the lower part of the city (for instance, in Duane, Beaver, and Front streets) offered one of the most remarkable spectacles a stranger could witness. All the wholesale establishments, full of life during the week, became spectres rising in solitary grandeur. Not only the counting-rooms, on a level with the sidewalk, were closed and bolted, presenting only a front of hard iron shutters; but all the windows of the upper stories, to the very roof, were also hermetically closed, as if the whole buildings [*sic*] had been suddenly abandoned, never to be opened again. The streets in that part of the city were as completely deserted as are now those of Thebes and Memphis in the country of the Pharaos. A few steps farther, along the wharves and piers, it was still more awful and weird; the dingy stores on one side and the stately ships and barks on the other looked like two long rows of phantoms scarcely kept alive by the presence of a few sailors perched here and there on the top of masts or at the end of the spars. Yet a few hours before, in the afternoon of Saturday, no district of New York had presented such an appearance of life, bustle, and confusion. Was not the idea of Sunday, that is, of Christ, of God, of religion itself, powerful and paramount among that multitude of human beings which formed the busy population of the great commercial metropolis? And so it was in all other large cities of the United States.

But in the villages, in the fields, in the woods, even, the tranquillity and repose was, if possible, still more striking. Only the light of the sun, the brilliant drops of dew, the flight and songs of birds, gave life to the landscape. Never was a husbandman seen sowing, reaping, or harvesting on Sunday. The horses and bullocks were free from the heavy weight of the yoke; the cows and sheep, safely parked in well-enclosed pastures, were allowed to graze without a shepherd or a shepherdess. Scarcely did the girls take time to fill their milk-pails in the fields and carry them to the dairy. The simple-minded farmer would have feared a complete failure of his crops, if he had dared to disobey the third commandment. Inside of the house peace and quiet reigned supreme; the boys were restrained from boisterous games on that day, and the girls, on returning from church with the family, abstained from their usual rambles in the neighborhood.

God from the heights of heaven saw the millions of people newly settled in the Western Hemisphere, bent on worshipping Him as the tradition of their forefathers had taught them to do. If the voice of the true Church was not heard among them, it was not their fault; their ancestors had been deceived by pretended reformers. They at least intended to obey God who had spoken in the Old Law; and the heart of the Creator was moved by their prayers, and showered His temporal blessings over them.

But their obedience to God was not confined to one of His precepts. It has been said that the schools of the country were still Christian; and all the children of the land were faithfully taught to commit to memory the text of the decalogue, and they were commanded to show it in their daily life. This is the best, nay, the only way to practise morality; and when the sacred text is explained by the apostolic teaching preserved in Catholicism, the highest degree of holiness can be attained in this world. To this obedience to God's commandments must be ascribed the purity of morals which then prevailed in the United States, and powerfully contributed to knit together in the same uniformity of conduct the various elements which composed this great nation.

I do not, of course, pretend that there was no sin. The Americans, like all other men, have inherited from the first Adam the moral stain caused by his disobedience. Many of them, even at that time, had never been baptized, and consequently were unregenerated. Human passions too often made them swerve from the right path; and they were liable to evil habits — the greatest curse of mankind. Not only the eye of God followed the reckless career of wicked men among them, in order to punish them at the proper moment, but human justice had from the beginning of the colonies published a stern code of retribution against evil deeds. There were in the country criminal courts, jails, scaffolds, and hangmen.

Augustus J. Thébaud, SJ, *Forty Years in the United States of America (1839–1885)*, ed. Charles George Herbermann (New York: United States Catholic Historical Society, 1904), 152–57.

9. The Story of a Conversion, 1845–54

Eliza Allen Starr (1824–1901), descended from a leading Protestant family in New England, became a lecturer on art, an author, poet, and eventual recipient of Notre Dame's Laetare Medal. In the last portion of the nineteenth century, her Pilgrims and Saints *(1885) toured the reader through the European church and the geographical locations important to the Catholic heritage. In the following selection from her letters to her cousin, she tells the story of her conversion. With its emphasis on an authoritative basis of belief and the finding of an intellectual home in Catholicism, the narration illustrates both the popular conception of the Catholic faith (see doc. 14) and the attraction Catholic prayer and practice have provided for generations of converts (see doc. 64).*

Descended from a Puritan New England family which had helped to rock the cradle of Harvard University, born of Unitarian parents, educated by Unitarian teachers in Unitarian schools, surrounded by the choicest artistic, literary, and social influences under Unitarian auspices, a girlhood inspired by William Cullen Bryant, ripening into womanhood when Carlyle, Emerson, Longfellow, were the philosophers, essayists, poets of the day — how is it that I became a Catholic — a Roman Catholic?

On my first visit to Boston, in 1845, friends took me on my first Sunday to the music hall to hear their favorite preacher, Theodore Parker. Around me was the brilliant talent of the American Athens — an imposing array to the eyes of the country girl who knew them all, as they were pointed out to her, through the glorifying medium of books, and whose reverent imagination had exalted them to a plane of heroic merit. Placed between my artist friend and her husband, who was the author of one of the standard histories of the United States, I was prepared for an intellectual and spiritual banquet which would mark an era in my life. It certainly did so mark it, but in a way how different from that which I had anticipated! For as sentence after sentence came from the lips of the renowned preacher, first a tremor, then an actual chill came over me, as with smoothly flowing language, but irresistible logic, I found him demolishing every foundation-stone of my religious faith, and even hope. There was nothing left for me but to find other premises, other starting-points, or forego all the beautiful intellectual as well as spiritual life which had come to me as a child from the sacred scriptures; the Old Testament story of man, the New Testament story of a Child born to save the world from its sins, Who was crucified, died, rose again from the dead, ascended into heaven, from whence He would come to judge the living and the dead — all this I had believed on the authority of the Scriptures themselves, and this, too, while theological discussions were rife in old Deerfield, where Dr. Samuel Willard had raised the Unitarian standard, and among his most zealous supporters were my own family.

The shock was a severe one; nor did I recover from it when we left the music hall and walked along the quiet — Sunday quiet — streets of Boston to the home of my friends. Nor did I recover from it all the weeks of my visit nor when I met in genial conversation the lions of intellectual Boston. The question had been started, and would not be laid to rest. "What authority have I for the faith that is in me?" for faith I had in these great Christian facts, nor did I intend to resign it without evidence to the contrary....

From the moment I left the music hall of old Boston on that bright June morning in 1845 this quest for an authorized faith was the quest of my life. It was useless to talk, to argue; but I could keep my ears open, my eyes open, every intellectual sense open; and as far as in me lay I did this; and yet, read current history as I would, read or listen to theological discussions as I would — at least to those around me — the questions of an authorized faith remained unsolved.

In 1848 I went to Philadelphia. For the first time in my life I came in contact with educated Catholics; for the first time in my life set foot in a Catholic church, but very, very seldom caring to attend a service, and without the slightest intention of becoming a Catholic. Why should I? And yet, week after week, month after month, was being solved, without discussion, the question of an authorized faith in the Holy Scriptures; above all, in the four gospels. For behind these gospels I saw the church which had produced them, along with the epistles, evangelists, apostles, united under one divine head, the promise of our Lord Himself — "Lo, I am with you all days, even to the consummation of the world" — being fulfilled by transmitting His own authority to St. Peter, whom He had declared to be the corner-stone of His church; this authority to be transmitted by him to his successors to the end of time, so that these eighteen hundred and forty-eight years had been bound together by ties as strong as God could make them, even while working through the medium of His own creatures, made capable, as they were, of receiving and executing His will as perfectly as the winds, the seasons, the very stars that obey Him.

All this dawned upon me by degrees — very slowly but very clearly — until after nine years of mental struggle the Roman Catholic Church rose before me as an authorized teacher of divine truth, the depository of the Christian traditions, as she had been of the ancient scriptures venerated by the Hebrews and of those of which she was herself the author and expounder under the title of the new. To accept her instruction, then, was to understand aright the revelation of God to man; to follow her guidance was to walk in the way of salvation. Never has my confidence in the Catholic Church as a teacher, a guide, wavered for one instant. Intellectually, as well as spiritually, I have been more than satisfied with the nourishment afforded my by this "mother of fair love, of knowledge, and of holy hope," my only anxiety having been, still being, so to use the treasures put at my disposal as to hear at last the sentence, "Well done, good and faithful servant; enter thou into the joy of thy Lord."

> *The Life and Letters of Eliza Allen Starr,* ed. James J. McGovern (Chicago: Lakeside, 1905), 33–36.

10. A Popular Image of the Church, 1846

> *First established in the church of the professed house of the Society of Jesus in Rome in 1648, the association of the* bona mors, *or "good death," became one of the most popular devotional practices of early modern Catholicism (see doc. 4). The "society for the promotion of the grace of dying well" spread quickly and widely in early American Catholicism. Composed of men and women, priests and laity, slaves and free citizens, this association, which connected with the basic human experience of death and dying, emphasized the communal and interdependent character of Catholicism (see docs. 1, 4). Along with the growth of other associations particularly prominent in the nineteenth century, the* bona mors *both shaped the community and reflected its spiritual self-understanding (see docs. 20, 22, 28, 37). The following is taken from a small pamphlet describing the association.*

Chapter III
The Advantages of the Association
The first Advantage is drawn from the nature of Pious Associations, which are so many societies of God's faithful servants gathered together in the name of Christ. Therefore the Associates have a firm and lively confidence that Christ is in the midst of them, when they meet together, to dispense His Heavenly Treasures according to the preparation they bring to receive them; for His Presence being a token of His love, there is no doubt that He will give ear to their Pious Petitions; He will behold their spiritual wants with an eye of Pity and enrich them with grace, to carry them through all the dangers of this present Life.

A second Advantage may be illustrated from the comparison of a Pious Confraternity with the human Body; to which the Members receive a mutual assistance from each other: the Eyes guide, the Feet support the whole Body; each Member labors not for himself alone, but to supply the respective necessities of the other Members.

So, in this mystical Body each one's good works will be available, and by a participation of merits, prove advantageous to all.

For, if God, in His Justice, for the private faults of Achan, punished His Chosen People, by permitting their armies to be routed by His and their enemies; we may piously hope, since God is pleased to glory in His Mercy above all His other Divine Perfections, that for the Pious Deeds of some individuals, He will bestow favors upon others who have united themselves, in this Pious

Association, to the Adorers of His Sacred Passion. A third Advantage arises from the Prayers of the whole Body of the Associates which are offered up for all the Members in general.

It may truly be said that, by the communication of Good Works mentioned above, and by this particular application of Prayers for the Members of the Association, there are as many Solicitors for the good of each one and as many Intercessors to obtain it, as there are persons enrolled in the Confraternity: and the Graces and Favors God bestows on each one on this account, are like the Precious Ointment poured upon Aaron's head, which descends to the very hem of his garment, to refresh the whole body with the fragrant odor of Virtue and Sanctity.

This Participation of Prayers will be most advantageous and comforting in your Agony, on which your Eternal welfare depends; for, you will be sure, when that Hour comes, that there will be many Associates actually pleading your cause at the Throne of Mercy.

Neither will their Charitable Assistance cease with your life; because you will leave behind you an Assembly who will daily pray for the Repose of your Soul, and solicit Jesus Christ as long as you are retarded, to hasten your Entrance into Eternal Bliss, which is the Final End of this Association.

Oh! Pious Reader! who knows but your Eternal Salvation depends on your joining it? for since it affords the Best Means to obtain a Good Death, you may not have that Blessing, if you neglect to avail yourself of its inestimable advantages!

The fourth Advantage proceeds from the Treasures of the Holy Church, the Faithful Depository of Christ's Merits, which it has pleased his Holiness, the Vicar of Jesus Christ on earth, to open in favor of each Member of this Holy Association, by granting to every one who joins it, many Plenary and Partial Indulgences.

> *A Pious Association of the Devout Servants of Our Lord Jesus Christ, Dying on the Cross, and the Most Blessed Virgin Mary, Commonly Called Bona Mors, in Order to Obtain a Good Death* (Baltimore: Lucas Brothers, 1846), 20–22. Original found in RGIX, AISQ, Series 1–4, file 22, Archives of the Baltimore Carmel.

11. The Practice of Retreat, 1846

The members of the Catholic community had been encouraged from the early colonial period onward to take some time away from the activities of family life and work and devote themselves to recollection, prayer, and moral improvement (see doc. 4). Popular missionaries such as John Baptist David (1761–1841) preached retreats in established and frontier areas, and eventually the practice became one of the most significant shapers of the piety of the community. Less emotional and communal than the revival mission, the retreat as a "therapy for the soul" emphasized the more interior dimensions of Christian life. The following excerpt, directed to the laity in 1846, is notable for its emphasis on the discernment of God's will, its presentation of both a personal and social morality, and its references to scripture and the popular spiritual writing of The

Imitation of Christ. *Its general outline of retreat practices constituted one of the backbones of popular piety (see docs. 42, 89).*

Thoughts on a Spiritual Retreat

A Retreat is a blessing which the Almighty sends us because he loves us.

It will recall to our mind that we have a God to serve, a soul to save, a hell to avoid, a heaven to secure.

God wishes, during the Retreat, to restore peace to our agitated souls, and to pardon those sins which are the source of our interior troubles.

Is not this peace, this pardon, deserving of our utmost and most serious efforts?

It is the will of God that we should assist at the exercises of this Retreat, and perform them with a sincere and upright heart. He, by his grace, will do the rest, and perfect the work that he has begun.

Prayer of St. Francis Xavier for the Conversion of Sinners

Eternal God! Creator of all things, remember that the souls of those who are in a state of sin are the work of thy hands, and made to thy image and likeness. To thy dishonor, O Lord! the flames of hell are daily receiving new victims. Remember that for the salvation of these unhappy souls thy Son, Jesus Christ, suffered a most cruel death. Permit not, we beseech thee, that he be any longer despised by his rebellious children. Graciously hearken to the prayers of thy faithful servants, and to those of thy Church, the beloved Spouse of thy divine Son; be mindful of thy mercy; forget their past infidelity, and bring them all to the knowledge and service of our Lord Jesus Christ, whom thou has sent into the world, who is our salvation, our life, our resurrection, who has rescued us from the pains of hell, and to whom be glory for ever and ever. Amen. Hail Mary, etc.

Readings Suited to the Time of a Retreat

1st day: Acts of the Apostles, ch. ix, Following of Christ, b. 1, ch. xxv.

2nd day: St. Matt. ch. v, Following of Christ, b. 1, ch. xxii.

3rd day: St. Matt. ch. xx, Following of Christ, b. 1, ch. xxiii.

4th day: St. John, ch. xiv and xv, Following of Christ, b. 1, ch. xxiv.

5th day: 1 Cor. ch. xi, Following of Christ, b. 2, ch. x.

6th day: St. James, ch. i and iii, Following of Christ, b. 3, ch. xxxix.

7th day: 2 Cor. ch. vi, Following of Christ, b. 2, ch. xii.

Practices for the Time of a Retreat

Assist faithfully at all the exercises of the Retreat.

Perform them with attention, and a sincere desire to profit by them.

Observe as strict a silence in going to, and returning from the church, as circumstances will permit, endeavoring to keep your thoughts fixed on some pious subject.

Perform daily some act of charity or mortification.

Withdraw, as much as possible, from secular business.

Implore frequently the grace and light of the Holy Ghost.

Make a review of your conscience since the time of the last Retreat.

Consult your director in regard to all matters that disturb the mind, or which require his advice.

Often say to yourself: this Retreat is a signal favor from heaven. How will I wish, at the hour of my death, to have performed it?

"I do not know," says St. Ignatius, "nor can I conceive a more effectual means of sanctifying oneself than the exercises of a Spiritual Retreat."

Resolutions at the Close of the Retreat

I will always remember that I have to serve God, to save my soul, to fear an evil death, to undergo a rigorous judgment, to avoid hell fire, and to secure the happiness of heaven. These thoughts must at all times predominate in my mind.

I will reflect often upon the vanity of earthly things, the emptiness of worldly pleasures, and the brevity of human life.

I will mingle in social amusements and entertainments only so far as the laws of charity or courtesy may require.

Remembering that the wisdom of this world is folly before God, I will never suffer its distracting cares or occupations to interfere with my obligations to God.

I will guard against the influence of human respect, and discharge every duty despite the observation of men.

In the practice of piety, I will endeavor to prevent that offensive character which it might assume from the indulgence of humor or singularity.

I will be careful not to contract debts beyond my means, and will observe the most scrupulous justice towards my neighbor.

In regard to the poor and suffering members of society, I will consider it a happiness to relieve their wants according to the means which I possess.

I will approach the sacraments frequently, and shun the occasions of sin.

The resolutions, and others of a more particular nature, which I have formed during the Retreat, I will read once a month, and animate myself to a faithful observance of them.

Prayer

O Lord! finish in me the work thou hast begun. Aid me in fulfilling the good resolutions which thou hast inspired; for without thee I can do nothing. O holy Virgin! the powerful help of Christians, obtain for me the grace to accomplish what I have resolved for the honor of thy divine Son. Amen.

The Catholic Almanac for 1846 (Baltimore: F. Lucas Jr., 1846), 24–26.

12. A Bishop's Interior Life, 1850

Nineteenth-century sources afford only a few glimpses into the interior life of the episcopal leaders of the community. Benedict Joseph Flaget (1763–1850), born in France and ordained for the Society of St. Sulpice, emigrated in 1792 and became one of the shapers of the community, especially after his consecration in 1810 as the first bishop of Bardstown, a see transferred to Louisville, Kentucky, in 1841. He greatly influenced Martin John Spalding (1810–1872), and when the latter compiled a history of Flaget's life, he included in the appendix a brief description of the pioneer bishop's character and spirit. Originally written in French, the following passage is indicative of Flaget's emphasis on interior communion with Jesus, the centrality of the Eucharist, and his love of nature, three characteristics he shared with many other men and women of the era. If The Pious Guide to Prayer and Devotion (see doc. 2) represented the best of the English Jesuit tradition of affective prayer, Flaget incarnated the interior riches of the French tradition.

While sojourning in Europe, his time was so engrossed by visits which he was compelled to make or receive, by sermons which he was constantly requested to deliver in parishes, communities, and houses of education, that his patient condescension was constantly put to most severe trials. But, on all occasions, an unalterable serenity and affability appeared in his words and manner. Those who had the happiness of approaching him, were charmed as soon as they beheld him. His speech, the expression of his countenance, all bespoke the union of his soul with God. For he began each day by fervent prayers, and by meditation prepared his heart for the duties and struggles of his office. He habitually rose at a very early hour, in order to enjoy uninterrupted communion with God, and when I repaired to his room, in order to obtain his first blessing, his reception had in it something so paternal and touching, that it was easy to perceive that he had been conversing with the Most High.

Being one day much indisposed, I urged him to sleep later the next day. "O no!" he replied immediately, with unwonted vivacity, "it is only at that time that I can speak to God as I should. Deprive me not of this happiness."

The life of our Lord Jesus Christ was the habitual subject of his meditations. I once inquired of him, whether he was in the habit of using a book when meditating. "Yes," said he; "but when I meditate on the passion of the Lord, and I generally do so, I have no need of one. I know all that by heart."

More than once I surprised him, while engaged in this holy exercise. It is impossible for me to describe his humble and respectful attitude, or the expression of profound recollection which was stamped on his features. He seemed to have entirely forgotten his fatigues and sufferings; the presence of God engrossed his thoughts. But, at the approach of certain festivals, his fervor redoubled. In 1838, he was at Turin during the Christmas solemnities. The missionaries of St. Vincent of Paul having courteously offered him hospitality, he was permitted to repair to a little oratory, where he might adore the Blessed Sacrament. The cold was excessive, and the Bishop was laboring under an indisposition which terminated in a dangerous illness; but he continued to repair to his cherished oratory, where, it was evident to all, he received signal favors. His prayer seemed the overflowing of a heart burning with divine love. At times, profound sighs expressed the emotions of his soul; and, unable to speak, his eyes were bedewed with tears. "God," he observed to me, at this period, "has given me the grace, from my youth, to meditate on those mysteries with an especial relish. To contemplate this divine Savior in the manger, has ever afforded me a singular pleasure. I have interrogated our Americans, in order to ascertain the attentions which are bestowed upon the children of the savages and slaves at the moment of their birth; and I have discovered that they are far better treated than was this divine Infant! Oh! God of love! and, after that, dare I complain of anything?"

He loved also to reflect on the parable, in which the Sovereign Master compares himself to a vine, of which his disciples are the branches. "I have never," he said, "meditated on this text without profit. Oh! my God, grant that this little branch may ever remain attached to the divine trunk. Ah! my child, it is from this sacred trunk that all life proceeds." These last words were accompanied by one of those expressive looks, he so often cast towards heaven.

It may be said that the remembrance of our Lord, in some of the mysteries of His holy life, was ever present to the mind of the venerable Bishop; and that he thence derived strength and consolation. "Truly," he was wont to say, "when we consider the mystery of the incarnation, we are led almost to rejoice for the sin of our first parents. To have a God for Father and Redeemer! *Felix culpa!* — happy fault!!"

But, of all the mysteries, the one in which he most delighted, was that of the Holy Eucharist; it is not possible to describe the piety with which he offered up the divine Sacrifice. All present were profoundly impressed by his manner. I remember a distinguished Archbishop, who respectfully carried away the sacred linens of which Bishop Flaget had made use; and the Archbishop's secretary afterwards remarked to me: "I am very sure it was to preserve them as relics." As to his thanksgiving, it may be asserted that it lasted the entire day; for everything reminded him of the happiness he had enjoyed in the morning. He often spoke to me of it, and invited me to think of it also; and, having one day said to him: "My Lord, you would have been happy to repose, like St. John, on the bosom of our Lord Jesus Christ, would you not?" "Alas!" he replied, with that accent of faith which animated all his words, "I might do so every day; for this good Savior comes daily to me. What grieves me is, that I think not sufficiently of Him. I think of Him often, it is true, but I ought never to forget Him...."

It was not merely at certain stated periods, that Bishop Flaget practiced this holy recollection and spirit of prayer. He never lost sight of the presence of God; and the different objects he beheld, instead of proving sources of distraction to him, tended to promote recollection. From his American correspondence, it is evident that, for many years, he had contracted the habit of being ever mindful of the presence of God. Some extracts from this correspondence will prove our assertion:

In 1805, the prelate had retired for some time to the country, in order to recover from the effects of a long illness. From his solitude, he wrote thus to his family: "Often I plunge into the depths of those immense forests, where are seen trees coeval with time. Far away from the noise and confusion of cities, nothing interrupts my solitary walks. Even the sun seems to respect these retreats; for his rays reach me not. Amid this repose of nature, I remember with pleasure what history relates of the ancient Germans, that they made a deity of the silence of the forests; and, extending my view higher than those poor barbarians, I adore the Author of this silence, and the Source of all Peace. What pious thoughts have come to my mind! What contempt do I not conceive for the world, and all it contains! Happy, could I only learn to contemn myself, and to desire that others should also contemn me!"

At a later period, the duties of the ministry having led him to the famous Falls of Niagara, he wrote to his brothers as follows: "This spectacle, perhaps the greatest and most magnificent which the universe presents, furnished me with subjects of meditation, which I shall never forget. After having passed three or four hours in contemplating those volumes of water, which are precipitated with a prodigious velocity, from a height of one hundred and fifty feet, it seemed to me I had been there but a moment; my eyes still desired to rest upon this scene. But night cast over it her sombre veil, and I reluctantly retraced my way to the hotel. As I walked on, I repeated often to myself: Alas! torrents of grace are daily flowing upon the hearts of men, and upon mine in particular, and, like those rocks over which this immense river rolls, we are not penetrated by them; and grace returns again into the infinite abyss whence it proceeds, without having produced any fruit."

It is said of St. Francis of Assisium [*sic*], that he loved to behold impenetrable forests, lofty rocks, harvest fields and smiling vineyards, the beauty of the wide extended meadow, the freshness of fountains, the verdure of gardens, earth and fire, air and winds; and that he exhorted them to remain pure in order to honor God and serve Him. Bishop Flaget evinced similarly elevated tastes. Every thing in nature spoke to him of God, and his active mind saw in each creature a motive for praising and blessing the Creator. Thus, when the time of prayer came, he had no effort to make in order to recollect himself; it might rather be said that he then entered into his proper element. Prayer was his life; and it has been already seen that, although age deprived him of all else, it could not take from him this precious treasure.

We may hence affirm that this holy Bishop was truly a man of prayer; and, amid the labors and turmoils of a life constantly agitated, he was able to maintain the spirit of prayer. This it was that enabled him to perform such great actions; for, though of ourselves we can do nothing, if God be with us, we can do all things.

Martin John Spalding, *Sketches of the Life, Times, and Character of the Rt. Rev. Benedict Joseph Flaget, First Bishop of Louisville* (Louisville: Webb and Levering, 1852), 367–73.

13. Pastoral on the Immaculate Conception, 1854

With the great influx of immigrants and the rise of nineteenth-century European devotionalism, the American Catholic community developed a strong practical piety centered on Mary. Especially after 1840, the proliferation of Marian prayers during the month of May, the celebration of feasts, the spread of the miraculous medal, and the recitation of the rosary indicated a significant shift from the Christ-centered piety of the early colonial community in Maryland (see docs. 2, 4). In 1847, after the request of the Sixth Provincial Council of Baltimore in the previous year, Pope Pius IX declared Mary, under the title of the Immaculate Conception, the patroness of the United States. Several American prelates participated in the meetings previous to the papal declaration of December 1854 which proclaimed the Immaculate Conception as a truth of the Catholic faith. As a symbol for the church, this nineteenth-century image of Mary provided a strong counterpoint to the perceived evils of the day and would remain dominant until the post–World War II era (cf. docs. 63, 68, 85). John Nepomucene Neumann (1811–60), the fourth bishop of Philadelphia, 1852–60, and future saint of the church, issued the following reflections on the Immaculate Conception just before he departed for Rome in October 1854.

Although the Church has not yet declared the Immaculate Conception to be an article of faith, nevertheless it is evident she cherishes this most just and pious belief with a loving constancy second only to that infallible certainty with which she maintains the truth of all those doctrines the acceptance of which is necessary for salvation. With a zeal probably never surpassed in former ages, the subject has been investigated by many of the most gifted and holy men now living; and with such a munificent outlay of ancient and modern learning, of profound argument and soul-stirring eloquence have they treated it, as to leave not only the more devout clients of Mary, but every unbiased mind convinced beyond the possibility of doubt, that if there be anything certainly true, next to the defined doctrines of faith, it is this apostolic and therefore ancient and beautiful belief.

Hence it is not surprising that, wherever enlightened piety exists, hardly a moment's hesitation on this subject will be entertained. *"Caro Jesu! Caro Mariae!"* "The flesh of Jesus is the flesh of Mary!" they will exclaim with the great St. Augustine. How can it be that the God of all purity, to whom even the least shadow of sin is an object of eternal abhorrence, should have suffered His Virgin Mother to be, even for an instant, such an object in His sight? From her He received that flesh and blood — that human nature in which, made one with the Divinity, He redeemed the world: and can we believe that the same in Mary's person, in any possible degree, was ever sullied by the demon's breath, dishonored by the taint of guilt? Or, again, with St. Cyril the pious Catholic will ask, "Who hath ever heard that an architect built a glorious dwelling for himself and once gave it over to be possessed by his most cruel and hated enemy?"

If there were no other words of Holy Writ on this topic than these — "Mary, of whom was born Jesus, who is called Christ" (St. Matt. i. 16) —

they would be amply sufficient. Behold the divine fact that overthrows every difficulty, the inspired oracle that sweeps away every objection.

Never, Christian brethren, never can we admit that she was for one moment the slave of the devil; the Virgin who was destined to be the Mother of God, the Spouse of the Holy Spirit, the Ark of the New Covenant, the Mediatrix of Mankind, the Terror of the Powers of Darkness, the Queen of all the Heavenly Hosts.

Purer than heaven's purest angel, brighter than its brightest seraph, Mary, after her Creator, God, who made and gave her all, is the most perfect of beings, the masterpiece of Infinite Wisdom, Almighty Power, and Eternal Love.

To such a being we cannot reasonably suppose that a perfection was denied which had been already gratuitously bestowed on inferior creatures — on the Angelic Spirits, for example, some of whom afterward fell away from God and are lost forever. And again, the first man and the first woman were created sinless — pure as the virgin world on which the Almighty had just looked down with infinite delight and declared it to be *valde bona! — exceeding good!* How just and natural, therefore, — may we not add, how unavoidable? — is the conclusion that this sublime privilege was not withheld from Mary, set apart as she was from all eternity for an office and for honors in the kingdom of God, to which no other created being ever will or can be exalted! The more so since profound divines do not hesitate to assert that, rather than be without the grace conferred upon her in her Immaculate Conception, and thus, though only for an instant, an object of God's displeasure, Mary would have preferred to forfeit forever the infinite dignity of being the Mother of Jesus Christ.

Gladly would we dwell more at length on the subject, but as you may yourselves observe the occasion does not allow it. The few thoughts we have uttered are but the echo of Christian antiquity, of the faith, the filial love, the confidence in Mary, when apostles and evangelists were still on earth and revered her name.

How profound should be our gratitude in being able to say, that name we also reverence, their confidence in Mary we cherish, their filial love we share, their faith is ours! Could the Martyrs and Virgins, the heroic confessors of the faith, the renowned Fathers and Doctors of the Church, "beloved of God and men, and whose memory is in benediction" (Eccles. xlv) — could these arise and unite their voices to those of their successors now around the Chair of Peter, what would be their testimony? They would point to their immortal writings, and in the language of St. Augustine, so worthy a representative of the genius, wisdom, and piety of the primitive Church, they would remind us that when they speak of the law by which all the children of Adam are born children of wrath, *"they speak not of Mary,"* with regard to whom, on account of the honor due to our Lord, when they discourse of sin they wish to raise no question whatsoever. (*Lib. de nat. et grat.*) Nay, with an *Amen,* loud as that which St. Jerome tells us rolled through the magnificent churches of Rome like the thunder of heaven, they would respond to the following declaration of the Council of Trent (Sess. V.): "This Holy Synod declares that it is not its intention to include in this decree, where original sin is spoken of, the Blessed and Immaculate Mother of God."

May the day soon dawn upon the world — whether it be in our unhappy times or not — when with one mind and heart Christendom will acknowledge and proclaim this her most honorable privilege! Meanwhile, submitting every thought, word, and wish to the judgment of the Church, we shall continue to confess her power, regarding Mary as that "great sign" which St. John saw in heaven — a woman so resplendent with light, grace, and dignity that he describes her as "a woman clothed with the sun; with the moon beneath her feet, and on her head a crown of twelve stars; whose Son shall rule the nations with an iron rod: and her Son was taken up to God, and to His throne." (Apoc. xii)

And should the Dragon of Impiety spoken of in the same mysterious vision, whose power to seduce the nations is but too evident, still continue to make war on God and His Church; should the fearful days of wide-spread unbelief foretold by the Apostles prove to be *our own*, when men will no longer endure sound doctrine, but, according to their own desires, will heap up to themselves teachers having lying lips; turning away their hearing from the truth to give heed to fables; speaking proud words of vain philosophy; despising government and all majesty; audacious, self-willed; fearing not to bring in sects; promising their followers *liberty,* whereas they themselves are the slaves of corruption — days of calamity in which, the same inspired teachers warn us, men will blaspheme whatever things they know not, that is, the unsearchable ways of God and mysteries of religion; and what things soever they naturally do know, in these they will be corrupted mockers, murmurers, full of complaints, inventors of evil things; disobedient to parents; without affection, without fidelity; walking according to their own desires in ungodliness; filled with avarice and envy; counting for a pleasure the delights of a day; sporting themselves to excess; rioting in their feasts with you, having their eyes full of adultery and never-ceasing sin; alluring unstable souls who have lost their faith and, leaving the right way, will in the end discover that they have been following "wandering stars to whom the storm of darkness is reserved forever;" Christian brethren, if these be the times in store for the already afflicted Church of Jesus Christ, in the midst of which, with fear and trembling, we her children are to work out our salvation, to whom can we turn with more confidence than to His Divine Mother, whom the Church has never invoked in vain?

Hail! Holy Queen, Mother of Mercy! Guard the kingdom of the Christ-loving Pius, our chief Bishop. Pray for the people. Intercede for the clergy. Protect the consecrated virgins. Unto us all give strength against our enemies and thine, courage to the fearful, joy to those that mourn, peace to the contrite of heart, perseverance to the just. Let all experience thy protection, Virgin and Mother! through whom the nations are brought to penitence, the demons are put to flight, and they that sit in darkness and the shadow of death are filled with the knowledge and the love of thy Son!

Given under our hand, at our residence in Philadelphia, on the Feast of St. Charles Borromeo, in the year of our Lord eighteen hundred and fifty-four.

John Nepomucene,
Bishop of Philadelphia

Life of Right Rev. John N. Neumann, D.D., of the Congregation of the Most Holy
Redeemer; Fourth Bishop of Philadelphia, trans. John A. Berger, CSSR (New York:
Benziger Brothers, 1884), 388–92.

14. A Model of Sanctity, 1857

During each stage of its development in the United States, the Catholic community has possessed some "model of holiness" which captured its imagination and supported its actions (see docs. 26, 30, 54, 67, 89). Martin John Spalding (1810–72), the foremost apologist and most influential churchman of the nineteenth-century immigrant church, first preached his vision in the cathedral of Louisville in 1844–45. Evidences of Catholicity went through several editions (1847, 1857, 1870), and its approach, much of it enshrined in Spalding's later legislative work as archbishop of Baltimore, became the foundation upon which subsequent generations built their arguments for the sanctity of the church. The following selection, taken from the revised 1857 edition of Evidences, *is notable for its rhetorical image of Protestantism, the use of scripture, the description of "cockle" and "good grain" in the church, the conception of "the church of the poor," and the focus on the role of vowed religious men and women as an argument for the church's sanctity. Only with the Catholic Action model of the mid–twentieth century would the community significantly depart from this basic orientation (see doc. 54).*

There can be no doubt, my Dear Brethren, that Sanctity is an essential and a distinctive Mark of the Church, necessarily growing out of her very origin and nature, and intimately connected with the ends for which she was established. The Church is a *divine* institution; she is the work of the great Man-God, the masterpiece of His infinite wisdom and holiness; and she was established for promoting the glory of God and the salvation of mankind. Her origin is most holy, her objects are most holy; and therefore must she be herself holy. Viewing her in the light of a divinely established and therefore adequate instrument for promoting the salvation of men, her doctrines, her moral principles, and her sacramental ordinances, must necessarily possess two qualities: first, they must contain in themselves all that is requisite and suitable for the blotting out of sin, the bestowal of grace, and the full carrying out of the atonement; and second, they must be practical in their influence on men, producing at all times abundant fruits of Holiness. In other words, the Church must be holy in all her institutions; and she must have been conspicuous, in all ages of her existence, for the holy lives of many among her members; so conspicuous, that all men might by this Mark, in combination with the others, easily recognize her, and distinguish her from all other societies.

I say, *of many among her members;* for it is certainly not a necessary consequence of Sanctity; considered as a distinctive characteristic of the Church, that all those who belong to her outward communion should be distinguished for holiness of life. There was a Judas even among the twelve who were trained to piety under the eyes of Jesus Christ Himself, and who were destined to become his instruments for sanctifying the world. Our blessed Lord foretold that scandals should come; and He contented Himself with pronouncing a wo [*sic*] upon the authors of them: "Wo to the world because of scandals. For it must needs be that scandals come; nevertheless wo to that man by whom the scandal cometh." [Mt. 18.7] Human nature is corrupt and prone to evil; the Church was instituted to remedy this corruption, and to lead mankind to holiness; but she was to discharge this heavenly office chiefly by moral suasion and by the winning attractives of divine grace, without infringing the free exercise of free will. Men were to be earnestly invited to holiness, not compelled to embrace it; the boon of sanctification and salvation was to be freely tendered to all, none were to be constrained to receive it, whether they would or not.

There was to be cockle as well as good grain in the field of the Church; and it was the will of the divine Husbandman that "both should grow until the harvest" of the general judgment, lest those who would seek "to gather up the cockle should root up the wheat also together with it." [Mt. 13.29–30] Jesus Christ himself ate and drank and associated with the publicans and sinners, while He severely rebuked the hypocrisy of the self-righteous Pharisees, who censured Him for this merciful condescension to human weakness. He had no words of harshness for the adulteress and for poor Magdalene; He denounced, with all the strength and energy of His divine eloquence, the sanctimoniousness of those who wore long faces, uttered long prayers at the corners of the streets that they might be seen by men, boasted of their high reverence for the sabbath, and bitterly sneered at others reputed less holy than themselves. [Mt. 23]

I dwell upon this consideration, because it is essential to a right understanding of Holiness considered as a characteristic of the Church; and because those who have not paid sufficient attention to the merciful character and conduct of Jesus Christ, as everywhere set forth in the gospel, are in the habit of entertaining very erroneous ideas on the subject. They conceive that the Church is necessarily composed only of the holy and the elect, and that publicans and sinners should be excluded from its saving influences, as objects of loathing and totally unworthy of the Christian profession. They seem to vaunt the superior holiness of their own peculiar church organizations in this respect, and thereby virtually censure the conduct of Christ himself, as did the Pharisees of old. Surely the Church is not more holy than her divine Founder; and if His holiness was not sullied by contact with sinners, neither is that of His Church by a conduct growing out of a similar spirit of divine mercy and condescension. In fixing the standard of Holiness, as a distinctive Mark of the Church, we must look, not so much to the current notions of the days, as to the words and example of Christ; and then we cannot go astray....

1. And first, let us examine what are the claims to Sanctity and doctrine and of practice put forth by our dissenting brethren, and how far those claims warrant the belief, that any or all of their many conflicting denominations

really possess the attribute of Holiness, stamped by Christ upon His true Church, as distinctive of its character. Have the peculiar doctrines of Protestantism any special adaptation to the promotion of Sanctity; have they really produced saints worthy [of] the name? For three centuries those principles have been exerting their legitimate influence on large masses of Christian population; and surely we should now be able to look back, and estimate aright their tendency in the practical development of Holiness.

It is deemed almost unnecessary to remark, that, in pursuing this line of investigation, I mean no disrespect whatever to Protestants, much less do I intend wantonly to wound the feelings of those who sincerely and conscientiously dissent from the Catholic Church. I hope to conduct the inquiry in no invidious or uncharitable spirit, and with proper Christian candor and fairness. Cheerfully do I admit, that our Protestant brethren exert themselves, in their own way, to promote piety, and to inculcate certain principles of morality among their followers; and that they number among their various denominations many men distinguished for talent, learning, zeal, and for religion as they understand it, as well as for all the civil and social virtues.

But still, for all this, I cannot think that their distinctive doctrines possess any features peculiarly conducive to Holiness and vital piety, or that their influence has ever produced many persons conspicuous for Christian Sanctity, according to the meaning of this term as laid down in the gospel. Some of you may probably think that I am wrong in this opinion, and that the expression of it is an evidence of prejudice and illiberality, rather than of Christian candor; but, at least, you will do me the justice to listen patiently and attentively to the reasons I shall have to produce in its support. I may tell you in the language of that bold man [Luther], whom not a few profess so much to reverence — "Strike, but hear!" . . .

2. Among the evidences of His divine mission which Christ gave to the disciples, was this: "That the poor have the gospel preached to them." [Mt 14.5] Now, I do not say that the gospel is never preached to the poor among our separated brethren; but every candid observer will admit that, at least among many of their denominations, the wealthy are much more sought after and more cared for than those who are deficient in this world's goods. Who are usually the most respectable and the most influential members in the various Protestant Churches? Who are generally elevated to the rank of deacons and elders? Who occupy the first seats? Who manage the concerns and control the destinies of the denomination? Are they not most generally the rich and the influential in society? Do not these often claim, as a sort of right, the principal influence in church deliberations and enactments? Is not the pastor himself often made to feel their influence? Does he dare rebuke their vices with the same freedom and boldness as he does those of the poorer members?

Again, who cause the principal dissensions and divisions in the Protestant Churches? Is it not usually the richer members, whose *dignity* is not sufficiently respected, or whose opinion is neglected in the administration of affairs? Christ pronounced a blessing upon the poor, and denounced a woe against the rich; do our separated friends imitate His example and copy His spirit in this respect? He said, "It is easier for a camel to pass through the eye of a needle, than for a rich man to enter into the kingdom of heaven:" [Mt. 19.24] Do not many of the Protestant denominations in our midst practically annul this declaration, by promising heaven to the rich on easier terms than they do to the poor? Is not this palpably and lamentably true? (As will be shown a little later, the Catholic Church does not neglect the poor, nor pay inordinate court to the rich, in her heavenly ministrations. We think all candid persons will be prepared to admit this.)...

4. Is it not, moreover, more or less customary among Protestants, especially in our cities, to inquire which is the most respectable and *fashionable* church? Where it is that those who move in the first ranks of society are in the habit of meeting for worship? Where it is, that one may hope to hear the most popular preacher, and to meet the most fashionable circles? And, on the contrary, are you not often shocked at seeing the bitter sneer curl upon the lips, and on hearing the withering and unchristian taunt thrown out against particular churches frequented only by the poor, the ill-dressed, and those who are held in contempt by the world? What is all this but sheer pride and worldly-mindedness? Does it betoken aught of the spirit of Christ? Aught of the unearthly character of His gospel? Does it not, on the contrary, give evidence of a disposition to unite the service of God with that of mammon, though Christ proclaimed that these two services were wholly incompatible: "You can not serve God and mammon." [Mt. 6.24]...

9. Again, there is much talk among our separated brethren about the Sabbath. A particular manner of keeping this day holy has always been a main staple of Protestantism; and we often hear the bitter taunt uttered against those who do not keep it as holily as themselves! Is there not, to say the least, much exaggeration in all this? Is there not a manifest tendency to make this day one of mourning rather than of holy rejoicing, as it was always viewed by the Christian Church from the beginning? Was not the day changed from Saturday to Sunday, with a special view of making it commemorative of Christ's resurrection, the most joyous of all Christian mysteries? Were the Scribes and Pharisees the more holy on account of their exaggerated reverence for this day, or in consequence of the accusations against our blessed Saviour and His disciples for alleged violations of its sanctity?

And do not our Protestant friends, in their mistaken zeal on this subject, obviously imitate the Pharisees and Jews, more than they do Christ and His followers? Is not the very word *Sabbath* evidently more Jewish than Christian, the name of the Jewish *Sabbath* or Saturday, rather than of the Christian *Sunday* or Lord's day? And are not Protestant churches generally kept locked during the six days of the week, and opened for worship only on the *Sabbath,* and then only during the hours of service? Is this any peculiar evidence of that Christian Sanctity which manifests itself at all times in daily and hourly prayer? How different is this practice from that of Catholic countries, in which all the principal churches are constantly kept open from sunrise to sunset, and from that even in this country, where the Catholic churches with a resident pastor are thrown open every morning for divine service?...

But perhaps we shall be more fortunate in detecting among our dissenting brethren, the practical fruits of Holiness, than we have been in discovering principles leading thereto. Let us see. I would not willingly detract from the merits of our Protestant friends, much less would I, for a moment, question their sincerity. I will even grant, that they have produced as many fruits of Holiness as their very defective religious system would possibly allow; nay, that they have often overstepped their theory in their practice. I am not speaking of mere social or civic virtues, for which I cheerfully acknowledge that they have been always distinguished; but I am speaking of that high order of Christian virtue, which is usually called Sanctity or Holiness. I am discussing principles and their necessary logical development and tendency as evidenced by history, not men, in their moral character and religious sincerity, of which God only can judge, because He alone is fully acquainted with the heart and the motives of human action.

This distinction being carefully borne in mind, I may ask, where are the practical fruits of Christian Holiness which Protestantism has yielded during the three hundred years of its feverish existence? Where are the Christian men and its holy women, who have cheerfully "denied themselves, taken up their cross, and followed Christ"? [Mt. 16.24] Where its holy virgins and celibataries, who trampling upon the world and conquering the flesh, according to the exhortation of Christ, "have made themselves eunuchs for the kingdom of heaven's sake"? [Mt. 19.12] Where its lovers of holy poverty, who, despising riches and panting after higher perfection, have complied with the advice of the Saviour to the young man of the gospel: "If thou wilt be perfect, go, sell what thou hast, and give to the poor, and thou shalt have a treasure in heaven; and come, follow me"[?] [Mt. 19.21] Where its noble heroes, who, entering upon the service of Christ with all their hearts, have broken every earthly tie for His love, and have merited the reward promised by Him in the following remarkable words: "And every one that hath left house, or brethren, or sisters, or father, or mother, or wife, or children, or lands, for my name's sake, shall receive a hundred-fold and life everlasting"? [Mt. 19.29] Has Protestantism produced many such heroes; has it produced even one in the entire period of its history, who has given to the world an example of all these exalted virtues?

M. J. Spalding, *Lectures on the Evidences of Catholicity; Delivered in the Cathedral of Louisville* (Louisville: Webb and Levering, 1857), 195–97, 199–200, 202–3, 207–8, 210–11.

15. The Sacramental: Universal Access to the Holy, 1858

The nineteenth-century immigrant Catholic surrounded himself or herself with ordinary objects which enlivened an interior faith and provided an almost constant reminder of the provident power and protection of God as an intimate companion. Candles, wax, water, ashes, food, clothing material, palms, and oils, when blessed by the church, became visible reminders of the relationship between heaven and earth, the spiritual and the material elements of life. Part and parcel of the immigrant church's high devotionalism and its lively awareness of God's presence, "sacramentals," as they were known, became significant fea-

tures of Catholic faith (see docs. 28, 36). The following introduction to a book published in Cincinnati in 1858 describes the relationship between the life of Jesus, the understanding of the church, and the popularization of sacramental objects in the faith of the Catholic community.

The Gospel presents to us the record of our Saviour's birth and public life, but passes over, in almost total silence, the years of His Egyptian exile and His abode at Nazareth. His childhood's days wherein His little hands assisted His dear Mother in easy household work, or, with the unskillfulness of His age, used the plane and chisel of St. Joseph — the glorious evenings of the Jewish Summer, when, in early manhood, He went to the brow of the cliff that overhung Nazareth, and gazed wistfully to the South, towards Jerusalem, and wept to think that, whilst all round was so fair, the hearts of His countrymen should be curtained by the shades of sin — the moonlight nights He passed on that same mountain's top in the "prayer of God," — all have been hidden from our view. This mystic period is the "sealed fountain" and the "closed garden" of the Canticles. Many a bright stream of grace that flows over the green fields of the Church springs from that hidden fount, and many a zephyr, richly laden with the perfume of lowliest yet sweetest flowers, blows from that mysterious garden. Even in our Lord's public life, much He said in familiar converse with His disciples which the multitude never heard. Not that He would conceal His heavenly doctrine, but because of the hardness of the Jews' hearts, and, that having eyes, they saw not and ears, and heard not, as He Himself declared. The meanest and most sinful among them might have gone, if he had so chosen, to our Lord, in His retirement, as did Nicodemus, to hear from His divine lips the explanation of each holy saying and parable, as far as it was for his soul's good.

The Church is a perfect copy of Jesus. She is the Incarnation continued, and, if Jesus lived a hidden life, and taught in public and in private and suffered, she has imitated and still imitates Him in all. Jesus "spoke to the multitude in parables things hidden from the foundation of the world," and so, in the first ages the Church explained the great mysteries of the Blessed Eucharist and the Trinity to the children of the household only, whilst to the scoffing Jew and Heathen, she spoke not at all of them, or in guarded and mystic language. And why? — to exclude them forever from the fountains of life-giving grace? Little would we know of the tenderness of her motherly heart towards the erring children, bought by the Blood of Christ her Spouse if such were our thought. She but obeyed the divine injunction, "cast not your pearls before swine;" she was waiting until, by her holy preaching and holy life, she would soften those hard hearts to receive the impress of love from the Ever Blessed Three and the mystery of Christ's Body and Blood.

The discipline of the secret is no longer in force, but still there are many beautiful doctrines and practices of our religion hidden alike from infidel and Catholic, not that the Church conceals them, but because they will not seek them. We may compare the Church to a glorious temple, whose exterior beauty is a type of the interior. We enter, and the font at the door tells us that, by baptism, we are buried with Christ unto death, and rise with Him unto life, members of His mystic Body. The statues of the Apostles and other Saints tell us that the Church is Apostolic and holy. The sacrifice going on at the altar, the Bishop administering Confirmation, the penitent leaving the sacred tribunal, the calm on his countenance but a faint image of that in his heart, the priest proceeding quickly, yet reverently, down the aisle, bearing the Viaticum and the Blessed Oils, the white-robed Levites, like worshiping Angels in the sanctuary, the bride and bridegroom kneeling for the nuptial benediction, all tell us that the Church has the Seven Sacraments, the seven streams of Precious Blood that flow from the Sacred Heart of Jesus. We admire and love and then go our way. But if we had looked closer we might have noticed many rich draperies along the walls. They conceal small yet most beauteous chapels wherein we might have seen many a rite performed, full of sweet symbolism, yet which has been excluded from the main edifice, reserved as that is for statelier functions.

Now let us apply our comparison. The leading articles of faith, especially the doctrine of the Sacraments, form the great temple itself, whilst what Cardinal Wiseman has called the "Minor Rites and Offices" under which is included our present subject, "Sacramentals," are the side chapels. These minor points of teaching and practice are today what the discipline of the secret was in the Apostolic times, and the familiar discourse of our Saviour to the little circle of His disciples in the time of His public ministry. The lukewarmness of the faithful has made them so. Unlike the Jews, they receive, with respect and love, Christ's public instruction delivered by His priests, but like them, they do not care to join the company of the disciples, and talk with our Lord as a Friend and a Father. They are guests in the household of faith rather than children. They pay their homage to Jesus in the grand reception room, but they do not accept his invitation to repair to the inner apartment, and, by examining the beautiful treasures He keeps concealed therein, to have love's dying embers kindled into a bright flame.

We shall love our religion in proportion as we study it. Much study will beget charity, and charity, we know, blotteth out many sins.

> Love is a flower pleasing to the eye,
> Sweet to the smell, but Love can droop and die;
> Let streams of prayer and study cease to flow
> The root from which Love springs will cease to grow.

Our love for Jesus and Holy Mother Church will become warmer and purer if we examine the minor articles of our belief as well as the more important. Let us endeavor, with the assistance of God, and by following approved Catholic authors, to perform this labor of love in regard to the Sacramentals of the Church.

What Is a Sacramental?

These things make a Sacrament: the conferring of inward grace by an outward sign, in virtue of divine institution. Thus in Baptism the pouring of water is the outward sign, and by it habitual, or sanctifying, grace is infused into the soul, because of Christ's institution. Now the Sacramentals, like the Sacraments, have an outward sign or sensible element, but unlike them, they are mostly of ecclesiastical origin, and do not, of their own power, infuse grace into the soul, but only excite it to desire whereby it may obtain from God's gratuitous mercy that grace or its increase. Holy Water is a Sacramental, but, of its own nature, it washes not the soul from sin and pours not grace into it, as do the waters of Baptism. If, however, a person uses it devoutly, it will, on account of the Church's blessing attached to it, assist his will in forming pious desires.

> William J. Barry, *The Sacramentals of the Holy Catholic Church, or Flowers from the Garden of the Liturgy* (Cincinnati: John P. Walsh, 1858), 9–15.

16. The Exposition of the Blessed Sacrament and Peace, 1860

The practice of Forty Hours Devotion in the presence of the Blessed Sacrament was begun in Philadelphia in 1853 by Bishop John Neumann (1811–60). By the time Francis Patrick Kenrick (1797–1863), the archbishop of Baltimore, proposed in his Lenten pastoral the practice of the exposition of the Blessed Sacrament, the devotion had begun to spread. Devotion to the Blessed Sacrament would thus begin to join the image of the Sacred Heart and the image of Mary as one of the most popular symbolic carriers of the community's identity until the mid–twentieth century (see docs. 13, 22, 24, 27, 37, 40, 68). In the following passage, Kenrick explains the historical and theological foundations of the Eucharistic practice and indicates appropriate religious sentiments of worship, awe, thanksgiving, and supplication. He suggests that the latter aspiration be directed toward warding off the impending civil war.

To the Clergy and Faithful of the Diocese of Baltimore:

Grace to you, and peace from God our Father, and the Lord Jesus Christ.

Venerable brethren of the clergy, beloved children of the laity, at the approach of the penitential season of Lent, we address you, not to lay again the foundation of penance from dead works, but proceeding to more perfect things, to excite your devotion towards our Lord Jesus Christ in the most holy Sacrament of the Eucharist. "Having loved His own who were in the world, He loved them to the end," and on the eve of His death for our redemption, He gave us the most precious legacy of His Body and Blood, veiled under the Sacramental species. The church, grateful for the Divine Gift, has always rendered most profound homage to her Spouse concealed in this mystery, and has sought to express her faith in His presence by every solemn act of worship. In the sixteenth century, when with many revealed truths, it was rejected and blasphemed, the zeal of St. Charles Borromeo prompted him to institute at Milan public exercises, continued during two entire days, in honor of the Blessed Sacrament, whereby he sought to attract to the churches faithful and devout worshippers, whilst the votaries of the world were engaged in the vain amusements and criminal excesses of the Carnival. Pope Pius IV encouraged this devotion by the grant of indulgences, which several Pontiffs have since enlarged, and which our present holy Father has vouchsafed to extend to this diocese. It soon became a favorite exercise, and was promoted with great zeal by St. Philip Neri at Rome, and by St. Francis de Sales in his Apostolic missions in Chablais, where it powerfully contributed to the conversion of the population. Throughout Italy, Spain, Germany, France and other countries it has long been practised with great advantage to religion, as also in various parts of these United States. We feel happy in introducing it into this diocese, being firmly persuaded that it will be attended with a great increase of piety and devotion.

This exercise chiefly consists in the public exposition of the Blessed Sacrament during two days, amidst a brilliant display of lights, intended to represent in a sensible manner that Christ our Lord is the light of the world, and to raise our minds to the contemplation of His glory in the heavenly Jerusalem, the Lamb being the lamp thereof. The exposition takes place after the celebration of Mass, and a procession made preparatory to the replacing of the Sacrament in the tabernacle. The Litanies of the Saints with other prescribed prayers, are recited on the first and third days. It is the spirit of the church that the entire devotion of the faithful during this whole time should be concentrated in this mystery, and that their minds should be employed in holy meditation on the goodness, love and mercy of our Lord Jesus Christ.

The homage which we owe to our Lord in this mystery is that of supreme adoration, since His Body and Blood are truly present, and subsist in His Divine Person. As God He is one with the Father; as man, His Human Nature having a divine subsistence is likewise adored. The angels were commanded to adore Him at His birth, in the apparent helplessness of infancy: and in reward of His humiliations, every knee must bend to His name, of those who are in heaven, on earth, or beneath the earth. His presence in the sacraments, although not to be conceived in a carnal manner, is nevertheless true, real and substantial: His Body, which was offered on the cross, being there, His Blood, which was poured out for our sins, being in the sacred chalice. "No one eateth this Flesh," writes St. Augustine, "without first adoring it, so that not only are we free from sin in worshipping it, but we should be guilty of sin, were we to fail to worship it." St. Chrysostom addressing the torpid christian, who, insensible to the attractions of his Lord, neglects to receive or worship Him, cries: "Consider, I beseech thee, the royal banquet is prepared: angels minister at the table: the King himself is present: and dost thou remain listless? Adore and communicate." Faith in the divine presence gave rise to those impressive rites which have come down to us from the early ages — the prostrations before the altar, the burning of incense, the cries for mercy. Hence we borrow the song of the Cherubs: "Holy, Holy, Holy Lord God of hosts: the heavens and the earth are full of Thy glory." With the devout Israelites we greet our Redeemer: "Blessed be He that cometh in the name of the Lord." With holy Fervor, brethren, you should invite all creatures to join in homage: "Blessed be the name of His majesty for ever, and the whole earth shall be filled with His majesty. So be it. So be it." With the glorified spirits you should say: "Blessing, and glory, and wisdom, and thanksgiving, honor and power, and strength to our God for ever and ever. Amen."

Worship, praise, thanksgiving, and supplication best suit this exercise. Controversial discussion, or even moral instruction is not appropriate. This devotion supposes a lively faith in the presence of our Lord in the sacrament, and is intended as a reparation for the neglect of many to worship Him, and for the sacrileges committed by unworthy communicants, who crucify again the Son of God, and make a mockery of Him. Mary, at the feet of Jesus, pondering on His words, is the model to be imitated by those who come to our temples on this occasion. The Israelites terrified by the thunders of Sinai would not have the Lord to speak to them, lest they should die: but we, encouraged by the condescension of our Lord, who conceals His majesty and glory under the sacramental veils, approach Him, that we may be enlightened. We should invoke Him with earnest desire to know His will, like the child Samuel: "Speak, for Thy servant heareth." The splendor of the heavenly vision blinded Saul, who subdued by the divine display, and stung with remorse at the approach made to him of having persecuted his Lord, cried out: "Lord, what wilt Thou have me do?" We also should eagerly inquire, what we must do to repair our delinquencies: how we must atone for our irreverences: how we must expiate our sacrileges. The mild splendor of the altar is calculated to impress us sensibly with His presence, without overwhelming us. It should inspire us with awe, tempered with affection, so that like the beloved disciple, on witnessing the miraculous draught of fishes, we may say with lively faith: "It is the Lord." With the prophet we should say: "The Lord is in His holy temple: let all the earth be silent before Him." With the psalmist we may invite others to join in worship: "Come, let us adore and fall down, and weep before the Lord that made us. For He is the Lord our God: and we are the people of His pasture, and the sheep of His hand." A lively sense of the presence of our Lord will enable us to meditate on His maxims with great profit to our souls: it will recall to our minds His sufferings in a manner to excite our deepest gratitude and tenderest love: it will inflame our hearts with zeal for His glory. Like the apostle, we shall be ready to exclaim: "If any one love not our Lord Jesus Christ, let him be anathema."

Whilst we give homage to our Divine Redeemer, we should call on Him with confidence for all those graces and blessings which we need for our sanctification and salvation. He is Lord of all, rich towards all who invoke Him. By directing the Mass of the second day of the exercise to be offered for peace, the Church sufficiently intimates that this should be the special object of our most earnest supplications. In the celebration of the holy sacrifice she daily asks this blessing with marked solicitude: "Direct our days in Thy peace." "Mercifully give peace in our days:" and changing the prayer for mercy twice uttered, she cries: "Lamb of God, who takest away the sins of the world, grant us peace." Doubtless she desires for each one that "peace of God which surpasseth all understanding:" but she is not indifferent with regard to social harmony and the friendly relations of nations. Dreading the calamities of war and civil discord, she implores God to take away all causes of dissension, and unite all hearts in bonds of friendship. We, brethren, should specially seek these blessings. Although hitherto as citizens of this great confederation, we have enjoyed temporal prosperity with much peace, the seeds of dissension are scattered abroad, the social relations are disturbed, and even the tocsin of civil war has already sounded within our borders. Our very christian civilization is placed in jeopardy. Pray then that Christ, the Prince of peace, may vouchsafe to come to our assistance, and establish in all hearts the reign of His grace and love, that His will may be for all the supreme law, and His revelation the great rule by which every understanding may be directed. "Let the mountains receive peace for the people, and the hills justice." Let us implore Him to unite all in faith and love, and to bless, perfect, and perpetuate our civil institutions. With entire devotedness let us offer homage to His justice, power, and majesty, which none can resist with impunity. Then "shall He come down like rain upon the fleece, and as showers falling gently upon the earth. In His days justice shall spring up, and abundance of peace until the moon be taken away."

> *Pastoral of the Most Reverend Archbishop of Baltimore* (Baltimore: Kelly, Hedian and Piet, 1860).

17. The Practice of Lenten Penance, 1862

The Lenten pastoral letter of the diocesan bishop has always served as a primary tool both reflecting the views of the community and shaping its belief. In the nineteenth century, practices of penance and mortification, fasting and abstinence from meat, varied from region to region, depending on the inherited tradition (English, French, Spanish) and the demands of daily life (see doc. 21). These excerpts from the 1862 Lenten pastoral of Jean-Marie Odin (1800–1870), successively vicar apostolic of Texas (1840), bishop of Galveston (1847), and then second archbishop of New Orleans (1861), reflect a typical regional variation and explanation of the importance of penance in the life of the Catholic Christian at the time of the Civil War. Other interpretations of fasting and abstinence in the community would indicate their changing relationship to society and a different view of spirituality (see docs. 30, 41, 69, 84).

The law of penance, D[early] B[eloved] B[rethren], is strictly obligatory for all men. Penance is the penalty of sin, the safeguard of virtue, the proper condition of the christian.

If we have sinned, our offence, says St. Augustine, must necessarily be punished, either by the sinner himself offering in atonement the voluntary severities of penance, or by Almighty God revenging on the sinner his outraged Majesty. Such is the unchangeable decree of divine justice.

And for that reason, the Holy Scripture, almost in every page, recalls to our minds this most important truth, that penance is an essential condition to forgiveness: "If we do not penance, says the Wise Man, we shall fall into the hands of the Lord, and not into the hands of men." — "Do penance for all your iniquities," saith Ezechiel, and iniquity "shall not be your ruin." "Be converted to me with all your heart, in fasting, in weeping, and in mourning, says the Lord" by the Prophet Joel. It was by fasting that the inhabitants of

Niniveh, deploring their transgressions, averted the wrath of Almighty God. By submitting his flesh to the austerities of a severe penance, by interrupting his sleep to pray with fervor and humility, by moistening his bread with his tears, David truly penitent, manifested his repentance, and obtained to rise from his dreadful fall. In a word, we do not find in the Scripture one single sinner sincerely converted, who, while renouncing his sins, did not submit himself to the practice of penance. Let us then acknowledge that penance is an essential condition to be reconciled with Almighty God.

Could we say that we have no sins to atone for? Alas! B[eloved] B[rethren], let us listen to the voice of our conscience, and it will remind us of our numerous transgressions, of our multiplied revolts. It will reproach us the neglect of our duties, so many feelings of pride, so many revengeful designs, so many acts of injustice, so many falsehoods, detractions and slanders, so many fits of anger, blasphemies, profanations of the Lord's day, and other sins we have been guilty of, not to speak of those shameful sins which should not even be named among christians! how many days lost in indifference and forgetfulness of Religion, in vicious habits, or at least in the excess of pleasures or the uselessness of an indolent life! Let us then confess, with humble and profound confusion, that we are all sinners, great sinners, and since there be no forgiveness without penance, let us devote ourselves to the practice of that virtue, with courage and generosity of heart.

And even had we already atoned for all our sins penance would still be necessary to us; for while it is an essential condition of conversion for the sinner, it is also a preventive needed by the just. The enemies of our salvation surround us on all sides. Dangers threaten us at every step. The devil, bent on our ruin, assails us without ceasing. The world is a raging sea covered with shipwrecks; it leads us astray by its maxims, it seduces us by its pomp; it corrupts us by its perfidious pleasures and pestiferous examples. Our own heart, carried away by that concupiscence, which is in us the effect of the original stain, allures us continually, inflames our imagination, darkens our intellect, weakens and perverts our will, and smothers in us the voice of religion and of duty. The flesh rebels against the spirit, and the law of sin, according to the teaching of the Apostle, taking the place of the law of God, averts us even from the good we approve and draws us into the evil which we do reprove and condemn.

How will we escape all those dangers, and overcome the devil? By penance. "Be sober and watch," says the prince of the Apostles, "because your adversary, the devil, as a roaring lion, goeth about, seeking whom he may devour." That is to say, have recourse to mortification and penance, and you will triumphantly repel the assaults and artful wiles of the devil. How will we escape the snares and seductions of the world? By penance, through which, being crucified to that corrupt and corrupting world, we will trample under foot its pomps and vanities, and we will despise its delusions. Penance will expel from our heart bad thoughts and guilty desires, and by mastering, with the spirit of mortification, the power of the flesh, it will give us a glorious victory over the assaults of our sinful body and will preserve in us the life of grace. It is by penance that the Saints, withdrawing from the satisfactions, allurements and pleasures of the earth, have secured their salvation. Let us then follow their footsteps, in order to arrive at the same end, remembering that penance is an essential character of the christian.

For we cannot suppose, Beloved Brethren, that Our Lord, in suffering for us, intended to exonerate us from the obligation of doing penance. He came to enable us to give efficacy to our expiration by uniting it to his; but for this very reason we are more strictly bound to follow our Master, our Chief, our Model, in the path of penance. And we see, in fact, that the gospel reminds us, at every page, of the obligation of self-denial, the necessity of doing violence to ourselves, of carrying our cross, of taking heaven by storm, and all those maxims imply the practice of penance. Therefore to refuse to practise that virtue, would be equal to renouncing our title of disciples of Christ, and our right of reigning with him hereafter, since according to the formal teaching of the Apostle, it is only after we will have been partakers of the sufferings of Our Lord by the practice of penance, that we will partake of his glory for all eternity.

To-day, B[eloved] B[rethren], we have a more pressing motive to humble ourselves profoundly before Almighty God, to pray with renewed fervor, and to draw down upon ourselves, by the holy severities of penance, the mercies of the Lord. Our country, which heretofore had enjoyed such undisturbed prosperity, has become involved in a bloody war. An implacable foe endeavours to desolate with fire and sword our cities and our whole land. Your fathers, your husbands, your sons, your brothers have already shed their blood for the defence of the country. It is not easy to foresee the end of this disastrous war, which, in its vicissitudes, is for us the source of such deep emotions. Although we look with perfect confidence on the result of this conflict in which justice is on our side, we ought not to cease raising our supplicant hands to heaven. It is not by frivolity and pleasures, but by prayer and penance, we will secure for ourselves the protection of the Almighty. While our brethren are nobly exposing their breasts to the weapons of the enemy, let us fervently beseech the Lord that he may be pleased to shield them with his powerful arm, to protect our rights, and to preserve our liberties untouched. . . .

Wherefore, having previously invoked the holy name of God, and consulted our Council, we have ordained and do ordain as follows:

1. The use of meat is allowed every day during Lent, except Fridays. Those who are fasting are allowed on the days they keep fast, to eat meat at one meal only. Those who are dispensed with the fast, by reason of their age, health, or labor, are allowed to eat meat at every meal.

2. The use of every kind of fish is forbidden at those meals at which the use of meat is allowed.

3. Persons who think that they may have claims to a dispensation, either partial or entire, from the aforesaid regulations with regard to fasting and abstinence, should consult their pastors or confessors, on all doubts regarding this matter, and act in accordance with their advice.

4. The time granted for the fulfillment of the Easter duty will commence on the first Sunday in Lent, and end on Trinity Sunday.

5. In every church, during Lent, instructions will be given, as much as possible, calculated to enlighten the faithful on the duties of a christian life, and to make them relish the practice of the same.

6. The faithful are exhorted to be assiduous in assisting at these instructions, in order that those graces which God in his mercy has prepared for them, be not entirely lost.

7. The clergy, when announcing to their parishioners the collection to be made at Easter for the seminary, will insist on the importance of this work and on the obligation for the faithful to contribute thereto according to their means.

> *Pastoral Letter of the Most Reverend Archbishop of New Orleans for the Lent of 1862, pp. 2–5, 10–11. American Catholic Pamphlet Collection, the Catholic University of America.*

18. Praying for Peace during the Civil War, 1863

While the Catholic community and its leaders sadly supported slavery as a public institution, there was open disagreement about the Civil War. On all sides ethical choices had to be made and some judgment brought to bear upon the justice involved on both the Union and Confederate sides. The archbishops of New York and Cincinnati, John Hughes (1797–1864) and John Baptist Purcell (1783–1883), respectively, spoke forcefully for the Union side. Augustin Verot (1805–76), the bishop of Confederate Florida and Georgia, by defending both slavery and the justness of the Southern cause, showed the close relationship between moral judgments and cultural presuppositions in interpreting Catholic prayer and practice (cf. docs. 41, 80). In November 1863 he published a pastoral letter which reflected the anguish of the people and the need to search for an image of God capable of assimilating the moral division in the community.

...But although we feel confident of the justice of our cause, and speak of it boldly and warmly, still we must add a remark explanatory of the course which some of our fellow brothers in the episcopate have, or seem to have taken. Catholic divines discussing the topic of *war,* unanimously declare that war may sometimes be lawful, in spite of the assertions of some sectarians to the contrary, and that the first condition for the legitimacy of a war, is that the cause for which it is waged be a good and just one. From this they conclude that as a general rule a war can be just only on one side, as justice cannot be contradictory to itself; or, in other words, if one party be right the other must be wrong, and hence in the eyes of God a war can be just only on one side. But the same divines observe that in some cases a war may be just on both sides; for one party may be in the wrong truly and really, and still not perceive it — not be conscious of it. This must be the natural and necessary consequence of the imperfection of the human mind, which may and does, in many instances, make excusable and unimputable mistakes. This may very easily happen in obscure rights, and indeed, it occurs every day in lawsuits, which require all the prudence and learning of an able judge to decide points in which one party only is, but both believe they are, in the right. In like manner it may happen, that the reasons which seem to us so true and evident of the justice of our cause in the present war will not appear to others in the same light, and other reasons apparently strong in their estimation may lead them to a different conclusion, and so we are to remain satisfied, or at least abstain from injurious recriminations, insults and imprecations if others do not embrace our own views, and if they think they are fighting for justice by fighting against us. There is no tribunal on earth to decide such questions. At a certain period well defined in history, christian nations had recourse to the common Father of the Faithful, the Pope, who was likely to render a disinterested and equitable decision, but such ages have been styled *dark*. In the present age of light and progress, nations deem it a more enlightened process to drown their quarrels in rivers of blood. But happily the providence of God extends to all times and places, and he comes to his ends by means suited to his wisdom, justice and mercy, in spite of the folly or malice of men.

After these explanations, which the nature of the subject required, we return to the great object for which we address you, a union of fervent and worthy prayers in behalf of peace — to arrest the further effusion of blood which has already deluged our land, and rescue thousands from grief, distress, privations and sufferings which language is inadequate to describe. God has a thousand ways of granting to us the boon we desire so ardently. We do not ask for a miracle, although even miracles are promised to prayer proceeding from a heart full of faith and confidence. God, in his ordinary providence, can remove all impediments to peace. He may grant victories to our armies which will dishearten our enemies and make them desist. He may enlighten those who rule over our destines so as to make them conceive, mature and execute counsels of peace. He may change the minds and dispositions of our adversaries and make them desire peace and become afraid of the horrors of war; he may cause the abettors and authors of this war to appear by a premature death, at the bar of his justice; he may suggest to foreign nations sympathy for our cause, and incline them to become our protectors and allies. He has the hearts of all men in his hands, *cor regis in manu Domini*, and no one can execute a project without his permission, consent and participation. Nothing is hard or impossible to God, and he can even by the apparently natural course of human events defeat the best contrived plans of crafty politicians, profound statesmen and invincible warriors. . . .

We ought, then, to remain deeply impressed with the idea that all things are in the hands of the Lord, and that in spite of statesmen, and of armies, and of political craftiness, he can, and will do what he likes. Now it is a truth not less consoling, that in some respect he has placed all the treasures of his mercy and power at our disposal, because he has promised to hear our prayers whenever presented to him in a proper manner and with due dispositions. "Amen, I say to you, if you ask anything of the Father in my name, he will grant it to you." John 16. By this magnificent promise he has, in some measure, resigned over his omnipotence into our hands; since he promises to do whatever we ask in the name of the Saviour. It is true that the things which he promises to prayer absolutely and unconditionally are those that relate to our salvation, and are, properly speaking, the only ones which we ask in the name of the Saviour, as St. Augustine explains this passage. But the Saviour, himself has taught us, in the very prayer which he has left unto us, to pray not only for the things of the next life but also for those of the present; he has directed us to ask for our daily bread, under which are included all the things necessary to our souls and to our bodies; he has also instructed us to pray for deliverance from evil, and although the chief evil we ought to desire to be delivered from is sin, still other calamities, especially war, which is a concentration of all calamities, and also an abundant and prolific occasion of sin, is assuredly one of these evils that we may well ask to be delivered from. We should, however, ask for those temporal blessings with a heart resigned to his holy will; leaving to his infinite wisdom the time and the means of coming to our aid.

It is our duty to consider attentively the conditions that secure efficacy to our prayers, and to guard against the defects that would rob them of their power and credit before God. "You ask and you receive not, because you ask amiss." James 4. And this is the answer to the complaint so many persons make that they have asked for peace, and peace seems to be as far off as ever. Those persons who complain of the barrenness of their prayers have, perhaps, good reason to impute to themselves that they pray without humility, without confidence, without purity of intention, without perseverance. All these are conditions essential to a good prayer. It seems likewise meet that a blessing common to all, and in which all are interested, should be asked by all; and this is the reason why we should place great confidence in union of prayers throughout the length and breadth of the land. Our Lord himself has said: "Where there are two or three assembled in my name, there am I in the midst of them." A fervent communion seems to be the best way of securing all the conditions of a good prayer. Communion supposes you to have become the friends of God, and strengthens the bonds of that friendship you have contracted with God. Many hitherto have prayed for peace, and they have not been heard. Is it not because they prayed, being in the state of mortal sin? Reflect, my christian friend, whether you have good reasons to expect that you are entitled to be heard in your prayers for peace, when you are in the state of mortal sin. Is the enemy of a man welcome to ask a favour of that man without first being reconciled with him? If you ask peace of God, being yourself his enemy by your mortal sins, will he not tacitly answer you: How do you dare present yourself before me, being full of transgressions which provoke my anger and dishonor my majesty? How do you expect to receive a favor from me, when you continue to offend me? How do you expect that I will free you from the evils of temporal war, when by your sins you continue to wage an impious war against me? Make your peace with me, that I may put you at peace with mankind....

Right Rev. A. Verot, Bishop of Savannah, Administrator Apostolic of Florida, *Peace Pastoral, November, 1863* (Augusta, Ga.: F. H. Singer, 1863), 8–12. American Catholic Pamphlet Collection, the Catholic University of America.

19. Prayer and Charity during the Civil War, 1865

The cloistered French Ursuline nuns, an order founded by Angela Merici (1474–1540), first came to the United States in 1727, and the community, with various foundations from Ireland and Germany, spread throughout the United States. Even though enclosed, the community had a long history of education and care for the sick. As this memoir of an Ursuline community member in Illinois indicates, during the Civil War the communion of those who were enclosed with their relatives and those suffering on the battlefield matched those sisters of more active orders who distinguished themselves as nurses on the battlefields. Together the prayer and active charity of all the sisters served greatly to ameliorate Protestant views of Catholicism. Recourse to silent intercession for the neighbor and devotional prayer in a limit-situation has been characteristic of the community (see docs. 16, 33, 45, 46, 64b).

One event which drew the eyes of the world on the little corner occupied by the city of Springfield, was the burial of the immortal Abraham Lincoln on May 4th, 1865. All the houses along the route of the funeral cortege were draped in mourning. Feeling was intense and some persons foolishly thought that the Ursulines, being from the south, even South Carolina, would not show sufficient sympathy in the nation's woe. General McClernand therefore sent word to the Convent to have the house extra heavily draped. This was done. Little they knew, these ardent Abolitionists, how even Convent walls could not prevent the tears of anguish flowing from the Nuns' eyes at every battle lost or won during that awful War of Brothers. Politics and war were forbidden subjects of conversation. It was only to the silent watcher in the Tabernacle that the anguish of imagining a father or brother lying cold and dead on the silent battlefield, or languishing in some loathsome prison, was told. Nothing but prayer could help. Party issues were forgotten when the telegraph wire flashed or the daily paper told of one who would answer the roll call, never again. After the war Mother Charles's mother and her nieces found in the Convent the home and shelter from which they had been driven by "battle's fierce alarms." Oh! those dark days! What a price was paid for the blessings we enjoy under that starry flag which stands for Liberty and Union! I anticipate, but the subject naturally suggests itself here.

When Lincoln's statue, crowning his monument in Oak Ridge Cemetery was completed, a committee of gentlemen waited on Mother Joseph to tender her the honor of unveiling it, Oct. 15, 1874, in recognition of the valued services rendered the country, in its hour of trial, in the hospitals and on the battlefield, by the Sisterhoods of the Catholic Church. Poor Mother Joseph! She appreciated the offer, but she was dismayed beyond measure, for after her long, cloistered life, she could not bring herself to do anything so conspicuous. With thanks she declined, and told the gentlemen that other Sisterhoods whose life work lay in the direction of public services of charity — in a word, some Sister who had actually stood and served where shot and shell had made a wide swath of death and destruction, would be better suited. Such Sisters were found.

A Member of the Community, *Half a Century's Record of the Springfield Ursulines* (Springfield, Ill.: H. W. Rokker, 1909), 104–5.

Part 2

CONSTRUCTION OF AN AMERICAN CATHOLIC IDENTITY 1866–1917

Introduction

After the Civil War, the country set about rebuilding itself as a nation. Protestants in the North extolled an active Christianity in response to the ebb and flow of poverty and depression while Southern congregations maintained a degree of insular regionalism. Surges of patriotism, piety, and social reform engulfed the religious communities.[1] Although Catholics had participated on both sides of the war, the church itself maintained national unity and achieved a new public respectability in the wake of the charity of the hundreds of American women religious who had nursed the wounded and dying. Some in the Catholic community reached middle-class status, and a few became wealthy, but the continued influx of European immigrants swelled the cities, shifted the balance of Catholic presence to the urban areas, and occasioned the growth of new social projects.[2] In periodic bursts of nativism, Protestants suspected that Catholics had a dual allegiance to Rome and to the U.S. government, and, hence, were dangerous to a democratic republic, an idea fueled by Thomas Nast's cartoons in *Harper's Weekly* and by popular evangelist Josiah Strong. Many immigrant Catholics identified with a beleaguered papacy and supported a strong Roman allegiance.[3] In this respect affiliation groups and devotional life both strengthened hierarchical authority and provided a source of communal identity for workers in industrialized towns and cities against

1. For recent studies, see Randall M. Miller, Harry S. Stout, and Charles Reagan Wilson, eds., *Religion and the American Civil War* (New York: Oxford University Press, 1998), especially Samuel S. Hill, "Religion and the Results of the Civil War," 360–82, and Randall M. Miller, "Catholic Religion, Irish Ethnicity, and the Civil War," 261–96.
2. For a good overview of specific issues, see Robert Emmet Curran, SJ, *Michael Augustine Corrigan and the Shaping of Conservative Catholicism in America, 1878–1902* (New York: Arno Press, 1978). The philanthropic spirit which this age evoked is found in Katharine Drexel's family. She used her father's inheritance to fund many of the expenses of the Catholic Bureau of Indian Missions. See Anne Butler, "Mother Katharine Drexel: Spiritual Visionary of the West," in Glenda Riley and Richard W. Etulain, eds., *By Grit and Grace: Eleven Women Who Shaped the American West* (Golden, Colo.: Fulcrum Publishing, 1997), 198–220; Mary J. Oates, *The Catholic Philanthropic Tradition in America* (Bloomington: Indiana University Press, 1995), 66–70, 150–51.
3. The standard account of nativism is John Higham, *Strangers in the Land: Patterns of American Nativism, 1860–1925* (New Brunswick, N.J.: Rutgers University Press, 1963).

the increasingly secular and materialistic society (see docs. 20, 21; hereafter document numbers will be in parentheses) epitomized in the "Gilded Age."[4]

The Catholic community itself continued to manifest the diversity, regionalism, and drive toward unity characteristic of the earlier foundational period. The variety of European sources of spirituality can be seen, for example, in French (29, 34), Irish (23, 26), German (25, 39), and Italian (27) roots, as well as in more indigenous and inculturated sources (30, 31, 33, 35).[5] The bishops felt a need to stabilize and standardize religious practice among faithful adherents of such wide racial and ethnic origins. The Second Plenary Council of Baltimore (1866, doc. 21) and, more so, the Third Plenary Council of Baltimore (1884, doc. 32) attempted a uniform, doctrinally sound practice of prayer and knowledge, as public Catholicism became a larger institutional presence in the country.[6] Toward the end of the century, communal identity was further expressed in large national gatherings, many of which were led by a confident laity or in which laity took an active part: five Catholic Afro-American Congresses (1889–94), the Lay Congress (1889), the Columbian Congress (1893), the National Eucharistic Congress (1895), and the 1909 and 1913 American Catholic Missionary Congresses.[7] Nevertheless, the church still retained its

---

4. For general developments in Catholic prayer and practice, see Joseph P. Chinnici, OFM, ed., *Devotion to the Holy Spirit in American Catholicism* (New York: Paulist Press, 1985); Jay P. Dolan, *Catholic Revivalism: The American Experience 1830–1900* (Notre Dame, Ind.: University of Notre Dame Press, 1978); idem, "American Catholics and Revival Religion, 1850–1900," *Horizons* 3 (spring 1976): 39–57; Thomas E. Wangler, "Catholic Religious Life in Boston in the Era of Cardinal O'Connell," in Robert E. Sullivan and James O'Toole, eds., *Catholic Boston: Studies in Religion and Community 1870–1970* (Boston: Roman Catholic Archbishop of Boston, 1985), 239–72.

5. For the significant impact of the immigrant experience on religious identity, see Timothy Smith, "Religion and Ethnicity in America," *American Historical Review* 83 (December 1978): 1155–85; and for some specific examples, Hugh McLeod, "Catholicism and the New York Irish 1880–1910," in Jim Obelkevich, Lyndal Roper, and Raphael Samuel, eds., *Disciplines of Faith: Studies in Religion, Politics, and Patriarchy* (New York: Routledge and Kegan Paul, 1987), 337–50; Jay Dolan, "Philadelphia and the German Catholic Community," in Randall M. Miller and Thomas D. Marzik, eds., *Immigrants and Religion in Urban America* (Philadelphia: Temple University Press, 1977), 69–83; Joseph M. White, "Cincinnati's German Catholic Life: A Heritage of Lay Participation," *U.S. Catholic Historian* 12 (summer 1994): 1–16; Robert Anthony Orsi, *The Madonna of 115th Street: Faith and Community in Italian Harlem, 1880–1950* (New Haven, Conn.: Yale University Press, 1985); Rudolph J. Vecoli, "Cult and Occult in Italian-American Culture: The Persistence of a Religious Heritage," in Miller and Marzik, *Immigrants and Religion*, 25–47; Michael E. Engh, SJ, "From *Frontera* Faith to Roman Rubrics: Altering Hispanic Religious Customs in Los Angeles, 1855–1880," *U.S. Catholic Historian* 12 (fall 1994): 85–105. For some reflections on black spirituality as background to document 35, see Albert J. Raboteau, "Down at the Cross: Afro-American Spirituality," *U.S. Catholic Historian* 8 (winter-spring 1989): 33–38; and Cyprian Davis, OSB, "Black Spirituality," *U.S. Catholic Historian* 8 (winter-spring 1989): 39–46.

6. On the councils, see *Sermons on Subjects of the Day, Delivered by Distinguished Catholic Prelates and Theologians, at the Second Plenary Council of Baltimore, United States, October 1866* (Dublin: W. B. Kelly, 1868); and *The Memorial Volume: A History of the Third Plenary Council of Baltimore* (Baltimore: Baltimore Publishing Co., 1885).

7. See for examples Rev. John Henry Barrows, DD, ed., *The World's Parliament of Religions: The Columbian Exposition of 1893* (Chicago: Parliament Publishing Co., 1893); *The World's Columbian Catholic Congresses with an Epitome of Church Progress* (Chicago: J. S. Hyland and Co., n.d.); *Three Catholic Afro-American Congresses* (Cincinnati: American Catholic Tribune, 1893); Francis C. Kelley, ed., *The First American Catholic Missionary Congress* (Chicago: J. S. Hyland and Co., 1909).

diverse regional spiritual practices among the European immigrants, Native Americans (33), Hispanics (34), and African Americans (35), as well as among a few Asian Catholics.

We see descriptions of Sunday Masses that suggest a pervasive Catholic atmosphere "in the bones," so to speak (23). Silent liturgies, or "Low Masses," which heightened the sense of mystery and transcendence in the Latin liturgy, were often accompanied by catechetical instruction and the moralism of temperance societies. But sung "High Masses" and afternoon vespers were also to be found. By the mid-1870s, German congregations were initiating a reform in liturgical music through the Caecilia Society (25, 43), which protested operatic-style music at Mass and emphasized a return to the Ratisbon version of Gregorian chant, simplified music for a choir, congregational singing, and a focus on the liturgical year.[8] Reflecting somewhat the excesses of the Gilded Age, high religious art was available to rich and poor alike in paintings, statuary, church architecture, and the proliferation of religious pictures. Church buildings, especially in the cities, could be favorably compared with those of other denominations. James Cardinal Gibbons (1834–1921), who compared the role of religious images to those of patriotic figures in the United States, guided Catholics toward interiority and correct doctrine in the use of religious material culture (36).[9] At the end of the century, John Lancaster Spalding (1840–1916), bishop of Peoria, Illinois, commenting on the growth of the church and its institutions of service, raised the need both of a Catholic university and of thoughtful, pragmatic sanctity in the United States: "Whoever at any time, in any place, might have been sage, saint, or hero, may be so here and now; and though he had the heart of Francis, and the mind of Augustine, and the courage of Hildebrand, here is work for him to do."[10] But in the meantime, a new wave of immigrants, along with their particular devotions and other religious practices, arrived from northern Mediterranean areas and Eastern Europe. The saint who represented them was Frances Xavier Cabrini (1850–1917, doc. 56).[11]

During the post–Civil War period, the spiritual issues raised by Orestes Brownson (1803–76), Isaac Hecker (1819–88), the Americanists, and the Paulists achieved some degree of public importance (30). Their hopes for the

8. For similar attempts at liturgical reform, see William Busch, "From Other Times: A Voice of a Plenary Council," *Orate Fratres* 21 (September 1941): 452–58; Thomas O'Gorman, "From Other Times: Worship and Grace in Religion," *Orate Fratres* 20 (October 1946): 495–502; Alfred Young, "From Other Times: An American Prelude to Pius X: On Congregational Singing," *Orate Fratres* 21 (June 1947): 356–62.

9. See James Emmett Ryan, "Sentimental Catechism: Archbishop James Gibbons, Mass-Print Culture, and American Literary History," *Religion and American Culture* 7 (winter 1997): 81–119. Most basic on material culture is Colleen McDannell, *Material Christianity: Religion and Popular Culture in America* (New Haven, Conn.: Yale University Press, 1995).

10. J. L. Spalding, *Means and Ends of Education* (Chicago: A. D. McClurg and Co., 1897), 223, quoted in John Tracy Ellis, *Documents of American Catholic History* (Wilmington, Del.: Michael Glazier, 1987), 2:417.

11. Frances Xavier Cabrini, *Travels of Mother Frances Xavier Cabrini: Foundress of the Missionary Sisters of the Sacred Heart of Jesus* (Chicago: Missionary Sisters of the Sacred Heart of Jesus, ca. 1944); Stephen Michael DiGiovanni, "Mother Cabrini's Early Years in New York," *Catholic Historical Review* 77 (January 1991): 56–77.

conversion of America to Catholicism and the adoption by Catholics of a new, vigorous piety coincided in the 1890s with a rise in nationalism.[12] Overall, this type of active and optimistic program in the American church was tempered both by the condemnation of "Americanism" (1899) and the edict against Modernism (1907), just when the United States was becoming a world power. The conversion of America could be thought of by those confident enough to see the compatibility of Catholic and American values (38).

Toward the end of this era, *The Catholic Encyclopedia* (1911) defined prayer as "an act of the virtue of religion which consists in asking proper gifts or graces from God."[13] In fact, though, the prayer and practice of American Catholics went far beyond petitionary prayer, vocal prayer, and forms of meditation suggested by the writer. In this period, the reader will note several distinctive emphases in prayer and practice.

1. Devotional life and sodalities remained strong and emphasized both a union with God (27) and a supportive Catholic identity for immigrants who experienced a hostile world. Devotional prayer of the church militant could help regenerate even the political world (20, 22, 26, 38).[14] The reception of Communion at Mass was infrequent, but Eucharistic devotion was promoted through Forty Hours, Benediction, visits to the Blessed Sacrament, and the Eucharistic League (24, 37, 40). The Mass was one devotion among many (37), wherein a kind of democracy reigned among the worshipers, who came from various socioeconomic backgrounds and were united in prayer (23).

2. Geographically, a large part of the United States remained a frontier, even into the twentieth century. Prayer in this context, where the church was far less organized than along the Eastern Seaboard, tended to highlight heroism (29), a lively interaction with the saints who interceded for daily needs (28, 34), and a community gathered especially during key points in the liturgical year (25).

3. The move toward institutionalization in the church and a uniformity of practice was a way to make the Catholic Church a visible element in society. But the uniformity of practice and discipline suggested by the Second and Third Plenary Councils of Baltimore (21, 32) had to cover quite a variety of circumstances. A contrast, for example, can be seen between a New York parish of twenty-five thousand (a veritable beehive of spiritual activity [23] centered on the factory whistle of industry, shop girls, house maids, and

---

12. The literature on this distinctive issue of Americanism and its spirituality is vast, but in addition to numerous studies mentioned above see as starting points, John Farina, *An American Experience of God: The Spirituality of Isaac Hecker* (New York: Paulist Press, 1981); idem, "Nineteenth-Century American Interest in Saint Catherine of Genoa," *Catholic Historical Review* 70 (April 1984): 251–62; *The Americanist Controversy: Recent Historical and Theological Perspectives*, entire issue of *U.S. Catholic Historian* 11 (spring 1993); Thomas Wangler, "The Birth of Americanism: Westward the Apocalyptic Candlestick," *Harvard Theological Review* 65 (July 1972): 415–36.

13. John J. Wynne, "Prayer," in *The Catholic Encyclopedia* (New York: Robert Appleton, 1907–12), 12:345–50, with quotation from 345.

14. See Kenneth Moss, "St. Patrick's Day Celebrations and the Formation of Irish-American Identity, 1845–1875," *Journal of Social History* 29 (fall 1995): 125–48, for background on docs. 23 and 24.

tanners) and a rural congregation in Ohio (composed mainly of farmers who had cleared the wilderness to establish their farms and whose spiritual clock centered on nature and rogation days [25]). At the same time as the solidification and move toward uniform practice, we see a "homey," unitive spirituality based on a life of grace, attention to the Holy Spirit, interior prayer, and personal decision making (30, 40). Both dimensions attempted to shepherd the masses and make their spirituality informed, holistic, and participative (32, 37).

4. In spite of an abundance of clergy-written advice books for women stressing docility, humility, purity, and women's role in the home,[15] we also see Marian devotion expressed in more militant terms. Women themselves are pictured in a vigorous, prayerful, decision-making manner (20, 31, 33, 34) and form the majority of the active participants in religious activities. We also see examples of spiritual companionship between men and women (27, 31).

20. The Work of the Association of the Perpetual Rosary, 1866

Ave Maria *was one of the most popular devotional magazines in American Catholicism for over one hundred years. Begun in 1865 (and ending in 1968), just as communities started to recover from the ravages of the Civil War, its volumes reflected a concern for the course of contemporary society and a revival in practices of prayer. On a popular level, especially among Irish Catholics, the recitation of the "Hail Mary" in a sequence of five decades of ten beads each, the decades being separated by an "Our Father," had traditionally served as a meditative device to enliven people's participation in the joyful, sorrowful, and glorious mysteries of Christ's life as experienced by his mother. The following selection, a translation by the editors of* Ave Maria, *combines this traditional prayer with both the tendency toward associationism and the increasing ideological linkage in European and American Catholicism between pious practices, allegiance to Rome, and a religious defensiveness with respect to modern society.*

The first quality of a work is its *actuality*. It is by this that it takes root in society, that it lives and does good there. Now it is not difficult to see in the Perpetual Rosary, a work which is all actuality.

1st. *It is a prayer for the multitude that prays no more.* "That which maintains the world in its balance," writes a well known author, "is a certain equipoise between *prayer* and *action*, between the suppliant voices of fearful or grateful humanity, and the incessant din of their passions and their occupations. When this equipoise is disturbed, all is disturbed, as well in souls as in society. Let us not examine to what degree this trouble exists in our modern world. It would be too sad to enumerate all the points of the globe where prayer is silent, and where God listens for, without hearing, the voices of man."

The Perpetual Rosary is intended as a counterpoise to all this multitude that prays no longer. And who does not see how these ever active and ever

---

15. On "domestic" spirituality in the nineteenth century, see Colleen McDannell, *The Christian Home in Victorian America* (Bloomington: Indiana University Press, 1986).

fervent supplications, these torrents of tears poured without ceasing at the feet of God by faithful souls, must be powerful to turn away His anger, to lighten the weight of our iniquities, and to re-establish in the midst of us, that balance so necessary between the empire of Heaven and the empire of earth?

2d. *It is a source of grace to regenerate the present morbid state of society.* The most violent diseases of our modern society are *indifference* and *materialism.* What numbers of men we see around us who still bear the name of living, but who are in reality dead! No more Christian sentiments, no more instinct for the supernatural life, men of the moment, who live for the present only, who obstinately seek the things of this world, as if it were the only one; indifferent toward God, indifferent to every form of belief as to every religious duty, indifferent to their eternity! How shall we reinstate these fallen natures; how raise these burdened hearts? How resuscitate to the supernatural world of grace these souls completely buried and lost in nature and sin? Man by himself can do nothing. To give life to these corpses, a miracle of grace is wanted; and miracles of grace are worked by prayer — prayer fervent, persevering, perpetual, like that of our dear associates.

3d. *It spreads the knowledge of Mary.* The world in general knows little of the Blessed Virgin. It does not even suspect the place which she occupies in the divine plan. For the world, Mary is altogether a secondary personage, the devotion to her an accessory to Christianity. One must be a devotee to go and kneel at the foot of her altar. This error, unfortunately too common, tends to nothing less than to ruin the economy of our redemption, and to sap the foundations of Christianity.

4th. *It glorifies Mary.* It seems the design of Providence that Mary should now be better known and honored in the Church. We are evidently moving toward this exaltation and glorifying of the ever Blessed Virgin. Much of the road is traveled already, and still we have not reached the end. The dogmatic definition of her Immaculate Conception is only a dawn which must be the herald of a purer and more brilliant day, for Mary will not leave unrewarded the honor and glory which the Church on earth has decreed to her in this matter. Many souls have a certain presentiment of an era of greatness and prosperity about to rise upon the earth, and which will be the reign of Mary. It is this hope which rejoices the soul of our Holy Father, Pius IX, and which, in the midst of his bitterness, makes him ever full of joy.

Now who does not see how admirable the Perpetual Rosary comes in to harmonize with the hopes of the august Pontiff and of the Church? Does it not lead most naturally to this new *era* of the glories of Mary in the world?

5th. *It affords Mary a Guard of Honor to defend her against her enemies.* Hell is not ignorant that Mary is a channel of grace. Its chief method, therefore, of working for the loss of souls, is to separate them from Mary, that they may be separated from Jesus, *out of whom there is no salvation.* Behold the heresies of our days; no one is particular now about systems of belief; Protestantism takes another way: *it buys souls for money; it destroys in them the veneration of Mary,* and by these two diabolical means it makes prodigious ravages in the Holy Church of God.

The Association of Saint Francis of Sales has undertaken the combat against the first of these maneuvers; the Perpetual Rosary is providentially designed to make war against the second. Whilst the associates of Saint Francis of Sales form a rampart around souls to preserve them against the double seduction of heresy and money, the associates of the Perpetual Rosary form an impenetrable fortress round Mary to defend and avenge her honor. They are her *guard of honor;* her *knights* watch night and day at her feet, their Rosaries in hand, like those *strong men* of whom the Scripture speaks, who, with their swords drawn, stand continually around the throne of Solomon, to render homage to him, and to defend him against the perils of the night.

Oh! who would not take part in this guard of honor of the august Queen of Heaven? Every Christian is a soldier of Jesus Christ. Every Christian may and should be, by this fact alone, a soldier of Mary; for the cause of the Mother is inseparable from that of the Son — it is one and the same cause. If then we ought to clothe ourselves in the armor of God, that is to say, in the *girdle of truth,* in the *breastplate of justice,* in the *buckler of faith,* in the *helmet of salvation,* and take in our hands the spiritual sword of the Word of God, praying at ALL TIMES in spirit, WATCHING AND PERSISTING IN PRAYER (Eph. ch vi), ought we not also, as soldiers of Mary, to clothe ourselves in the armor which she has prepared for us, that is to say, to take the *Rosary* which contains within itself all the arms of which Saint Paul speaks[?] All, without distinction of sex, of age, of rank, of science, of fortune, or of condition, all can be *armed knights* of Mary, our divine Queen; all can bless her, praise her, with Rosary in hand, and thus defend her worship and avenge her against her enemies, save souls from hell, extend her reign, and obtain new subjects for her empire.

6th. *It defends the Holy Church Militant.* The Church is at the present day attacked with violence. One might think that hell was trying to take revenge on Pius the Ninth, and make him expiate the mortal displeasure occasioned to it by his promulgation of the dogma of the Immaculate Conception.

Now, who does not remember that the holy Rosary has saved the Church many times already? In the thirteenth century, from the Albigenses; in the sixteenth, from the Mussulman invasions. Why should it not be destined now to save her again from the perfidious and sacrilegious schemes of all the agents of hell?

7th. *It is a solace to the Church suffering.* The souls in purgatory, who form the Church suffering, have never, perhaps, been so much neglected as at the present epoch. The groanings of our brothers and sisters buried in flames can no longer be heard; the noise of the passions of the world drowns their voices; the cares of a selfish life leave no room for the remembrance of the dead. But the *Perpetual* Rosary prays for the dead; it is a fruitful mine of indulgences, all applicable to the dead. Who would not unite in this stream of prayers and indulgences for the solace of so many souls, who, for centuries perhaps, stretch vainly toward us their suppliant hands?

8th. Finally, the Perpetual Rosary not only obtains all these precious results by its own proper efficacy, it obtains them in a still greater degree in causing, by its consolidated and regular organization, the practice, alas, too neglected, of the duties of the confraternity of the Grand Rosary to flourish; for to enter into Mary's guard of honor, the applicant must belong to a canonical confraternity of the Rosary and fulfill its obligations.

The Perpetual *Rosary* considered under all these points of view, is then a work, truly *beautiful, eminently Catholic,* and of an *incontestable actuality.* These considerations ought to be a powerful motive for *every good Christian* to attach himself to it, and for the *ministers of the Lord in particular* to look favorably upon it and extend it.

> "Object of the Association of the Perpetual Rosary," *Ave Maria* 2, no. 12 (24 March 1866): 189–90.

21. Promotion of Uniformity of Discipline, 1866

By 1866 the Catholic population of the United States numbered almost two million, and on 7 October of that year, seven archbishops, thirty-eight bishops, three abbots, and numerous theological consultors gathered in Baltimore to set the juridical course of the church during the era of reconstruction. The Second Plenary Council of Baltimore, as the gathering was called, summarized previous legislation, published both doctrinal and disciplinary decrees, and provided the foundation for a strong institutional presence in society. Its legislation reflected the continued application to the United States of the decrees of the Council of Trent, the importance of unity with Rome, and the desire to differentiate Catholic from Protestant belief and practice. The following selection, while recognizing the inheritance of different practices in the western and southwestern United States, argues for as great a uniformity as possible with respect to fasting, abstinence, and the celebration of feasts.

381. It is clearly manifest that the Catholic Faith, since it depends totally on the authority of God who teaches, commands or forbids, at no time in its history or the variety of its places, has ever been able to be diminished, outdated or in any way changed. Holy Mother the Church everywhere and in every way chooses and seeks to preserve her discipline always the same, although that discipline is of human origin, and at times is wisely to be altered or changed; therefore care must be taken, as far as is in our power, that our discipline in no way is at variance with that of the universal Church, or if that cannot be, that it conform as closely as possible to it. It is mainly for this reason that we advise uniformity, which we very much want to see existing in all the churches of these provinces.

382. First let us speak about what pertains to church precepts. It is greatly to be regretted that so much discrepancy can be found among us in feasts and fasts. In some places there are seven or eight feasts, while in others only four. The observance of the Lenten Fast is different in different regions. It would indeed not be difficult to introduce a certain uniformity by reducing the number of feasts to a minimum, and by seeking an easier law of fasting. But, by all means, care must be taken, that we do not become different from the universal Church by a false type of uniformity among ourselves.

383. The Fathers are of the opinion that the feast days which are observed

in each Province are to be retained. However, the Patronal Feast of the Blessed Virgin Mary Conceived without Stain should be celebrated in all the Provinces on the eighth day of December as a feast of precept. As regards the Provinces of St. Francis, Oregon, and the Diocese of the Holy Faith, we think that the Holy See should be asked that for those five feast days, that differ from those of the Baltimore Province, that there be granted a dispensation as regards the precept of hearing Mass and abstaining from servile work, not however as regards devotion and external solemnity. We also think that by authority of the Holy See they should be allowed to conform to the Baltimore Province in the observance of days of fast.

384. Furthermore it is our wish that from now on the Patronal Feast of each consecrated church be celebrated with due solemnity. Since this can be easily done in the cities, there is no excuse for its being neglected. The same should be done even if the church is only blessed. However, in rural areas and in small towns, where it would be difficult to gather the people during the week, it will be possible to transfer the feast for the external solemnity to the following Sunday.

> *Concilii Plenarii Baltimorensis II in Ecclesia Metropolitana Baltimorensi, A Die VII. Ad Diem XXI. Octobris, A.D., MDCCCLXVI., Habiti, et a Sede Apostolica Recogniti, Acta et Decreta* (Baltimore: 1868), *Titulus* VII, 198–99, trans. Reverend Peter Krieg, OFM.

22. "History of the Sodalities," 1866

A continued feature of Catholic prayer and practice in the post–Civil War period, sodalities provided the relational space where religious belief, personal need, communal formation, and social challenges intersected. Deeply rooted in the ethnic neighborhoods and aligned with parish structures, these popular organizations generally recognized the community's hierarchical and role divisions and aimed to unite special-interest groupings (men or women, adults or youth). In many instances, however, the communal nature of the societies cut across the role and gender divisions prominent in society and church and emphasized a universally shared call to holiness. Typically, a group began with a small circle of laypeople, met monthly for prayers and perhaps a sermon from the priest-director, formed their own elected leadership, and adopted a social (mutual aid society, care for the sick), literary (the promotion of good literature), or devotional (the frequentation of the sacraments, mutual support through prayers) purpose (cf. doc. 28). The following selection from Ave Maria, *a magazine, provided the introduction to a long series on various societies throughout the country.*

There seems, just now, to pervade the whole country, a general tendency towards the formation of "unions" of every kind. Indeed the hour is favorable to such notions. It is not then out of place to propose the union of Sodalists. This, if accomplished, will not only afford pleasure and benefit to themselves, but be, besides, a means under God, of extending and strengthening the influence of "Holy Church." But in order to bring about an actual union, as it were, of hands, it will be necessary to bring about a unison of hearts, of sympathies, of souls. They must become aware of each other's existence, whereabouts, aims, hopes, and condition. This it is proposed to accomplish by the "History of the Sodalities."

Nor is our title intended to embrace only the articles that will follow from our hand; for these can only refer to our own city, but it is hoped that our present words will form the "Introduction" to a complete series of such articles from the pens of as many correspondents as there are cities, towns and villages with Sodalities established in their midst.

By Sodalities we mean to include all societies of that kind: not only those of the Immaculate Conception — which, of course, has a right to the particular attachment of America's sons who are under the patronage of the Immaculate Conception — but also those of the Holy Angels, of which there are so many, and of the Holy Infancy, and Sacred Passion, and of the Most Holy Sacrament, etc., the last mentioned claiming ever our chief reverence and respect.

Our introduction would be incomplete without some allusion to the general aims of the Sodalities, and their successes so far. This not so much for the Sodalists themselves, though some of these doubtless have forgotten them, as for those who will read the AVE MARIA, but who know not the object of Sodalities. A Sodality, as the word itself makes known, is a collection of persons, be they young or old, and the word, of late days, is only applied to a collection of persons having as the aim of their association, the extending of particular devotion either to the Holy Angels, or to the Immaculate Queen, or to our Lord Himself. Thus we have the Sodalities of the Holy Angels, of the Immaculate Conception, and of the Sacred Passion as alluded to above.

Having in mind the extension of devotion, the members are expected to be particularly devout, and hence are only admitted after a sufficient probation, and then required publicly, that is in presence of the meeting, to express their resolution to follow the rules laid down for their guidance.

It is readily perceived then that such associations produce much good in a community. And indeed we have no doubt that it would take volumes to recount the many extraordinary favors and blessings gained from heaven wherever they exist. It is enough to soften the hardest heart to listen to one good priest whom we once conversed with, as he details the wondrous influence of his Sodalities. The poor girl, for instance, who earns her daily bread, in the factory or public store, who has to endure the searching looks, the unscrupulous words of the idlers who dot her homeward and shopward path, and all day long mingles with companions whose ways are not always the best; such an one finds in her companions of the Sodality a solace, in the Sunday meetings, a pleasure to look forward to and draw her mind from evil, and in the pious practices of the Sodality an encouragement and spiritual strength.

And so with the boy and the young man, sons of the toiling millions whose life goes on amid the lowlier occupations of mankind. And the sons and daughters of the rich, and highly stationed, too, whether assembling by themselves, or mingling in holy unison with their less favored brethren, are formed to virtue. But oh, the glorious picture on communion day! Beautiful bright morning! which smiles upon the youthful train as it goes on towards the altar there to kneel and to receive the Bread of Angels. And to witness all this in America! America, on some of whose statute books doubtless are yet remaining those once dreaded blue laws; America, where but a short time ago Catholicism was so little known and Catholics so severely used. Most assuredly our Blessed Patroness is taking possession of her realm. Her armies are forming; let them all unite, and, with one accord stand ready to obey her least command.

"History of the Sodalities," *Ave Maria* 2 (24 November 1866): 741–42.

23. Sunday Morning at St. Stephen's, New York, 1868

By 1865 the Catholic community in New York City boasted of thirty-two churches, numerous parochial schools, and a host of extraparochial institutions such as hospitals, orphanages, and academies. Catholics of German and Irish heritage dominated, and the city church had begun to take on the ethnic character and "immigrant moralism" which would mark its life for the next eighty years. One of the most prominent churches was St. Stephen's, the pastor of which was Edward McGlynn (1837–1900), a priest who would become well known for his liberal views on church practice and social reform. Described here in the pages of Atlantic Monthly *in 1868, the worshiping community at St. Stephen's embodied the different economic strata present in the community at large and reflected the social cohesion encouraged by both the Latin liturgy with its accompanying rituals and a strong program of catechetical formation (cf. docs. 3, 8, 25, 48, 51, 67, 76, 79, 91).*

It was a very cold and brilliant morning, stars glittering, moon resplendent, pavement icy, roofs snowy, wind north-northwest, and, of course, cutting right into the faces of people bound up the Third Avenue. An empty car went rattling over the frozen-in rails with an astonishing noise, the conductor trotting alongside, and the miserable driver beating his breast with one hand and pounding the floor with one foot. The highly ornamental policeman on the first corner was singing to keep himself warm; but, seeing a solitary wayfarer in a cloak scudding along on the ice, he conceived a suspicion of that untimely seeker after knowledge; he paused in his song; he stooped and eyed him closely, evidently unable to settle upon a rational explanation of his presence; and only resumed his song when the suspected person was five houses off. There was scarcely any one astir to keep an adventurer in countenance, and I began to think it was all a delusion about the six-o'clock mass. At ten minutes to six, when I stood in front of the spacious St. Stephen's Church in Twenty-Eighth Street, there seemed to be no one going in; and, the vestibule being unlighted, I was confirmed in the impression that early mass did not take place on such cold mornings. To be quite sure of the fact, however, I did just go up the steps and push at the door. It yielded to pressure, and its opening disclosed a vast interior, dimly lighted at the altar end, where knelt or sat, scattered about one or two in a pew, about a hundred women and ten men, all well muffled up in hoods, shawls, and overcoats, and breathing visibly. There was just light enough to see the new blue ceiling and its silver stars; but the sexton was busy lighting the gas, and got on with his work about as fast as the church filled. That church extends through the block, and has two fronts. As six o'clock approached, female figures in increasing numbers crept silently in by several doors, all making the usual courtesy, and all kneeling as soon as they reached a pew. At last the lower part of the church was pretty well filled, and there were some people in the galleries; in all, about one thousand women and about one hundred men. Nearly all the women were servant-girls, and all of them were dressed properly and abundantly for such a morning. There was not a squalid or miserable looking person present. Most of the men appeared to be grooms and coachmen. Among these occupants of the kitchen, the nursery, and the stable there were a few persons from the parlor, evidently of the class whom Voltaire speaks of with so much wrath and contempt as *dé vots et dé votes*. There were two or three men near me who might or might not have been ecclesiastics or theological students; upon the pale and luminous face of each was most legibly written, This man prays continually, and enjoys it.

There is a difference between Catholics and Protestants in this matter of praying. When a Protestant prays in public, he is apt to hide his face, and bend low in an awkward, uncomfortable attitude; and, when he would pray in private, he retires into some secret place, where, if any one should catch him at it, he would blush like a guilty thing. It is not so with our Roman Catholic brethren. They kneel, it is true, but the body above the knees is bolt upright, and the face is never hidden; and, as if this were not enough, they make certain movements of the hand which distinctly announce their purpose to every beholder. The same freedom and boldness are observable in Catholic children when they say their nightly prayers. Your little Protestant buries its face in the bed, and whispers its prayer to the counterpane; but our small Catholic brethren and sisters kneel upright, make the sign of the cross, and are not in the least ashamed or disturbed if anyone sees them. Another thing strikes a Protestant spectator of Catholic worship, the whole congregation, without exception, observe the etiquette of the occasion. When kneeling is in order, all kneel; when it is the etiquette to stand, all stand; when the prayer book says bow, every head is low. These two peculiarities are cause and effect. A Protestant child often has some reason to doubt whether saying its prayers is, after all, "the thing," since it is aware that some of its most valued friends and relations do not say theirs. But among Catholics there is not the distinction (*so* familiar to us) between believers and unbelievers. From the hour of baptism, every Catholic is a member of the church, and he is expected to behave as such. This is evidently one reason for that open, matter-of-course manner in which all the requirements of their religion are fulfilled. No one is ashamed of doing what is done by every one in the world whom he respects, and what he has himself been in the habit of doing from the time of his earliest recollection. A Catholic appears to be no more ashamed of saying his prayers than he is of eating his dinner, and he appears to think one quite as natural an action as the other.

On this cold morning the priest was not as punctual as the people. The congregation continued to increase till ten minutes past six; after which no sound was heard but the coughing of the chilled worshippers. It was not till seventeen minutes past six that the priest entered, accompanied by two slender, graceful boys, clad in long red robes, and walked to his place, and knelt before the altar. All present, except one poor heathen, in the middle aisle, shuffled to their knees with a pleasant noise, and remained kneeling for some time. The silence was complete, and I waited to hear it broken by the sound of the priest's voice. But not a sound came from his lips. He rose, he knelt, he ascended the steps of the altar, he came down again, he turned his back to the people, he turned his face to them, he changed from one side of the altar to the other, he made various gestures with his hands, but he uttered not an audible word. The two graceful lads in crimson garb moved about him, and performed the usual service, and the people sat, stood, knelt, bowed, and crossed themselves in accordance with the ritual. But still not a word was spoken. At the usual time the collection was taken, to which few gave more than a cent, but to which *every one* gave a cent. A little later, the priest uttered the only words that were audible during the whole service. Standing on the left side of the altar, he said, in an agreeable, educated voice: "The Society of the Holy Rosary will meet this afternoon after vespers. Prayers are requested for the repose of the souls of — "; then followed the names of three persons. The service was continued, and the silence was only broken again by the gong-like bell, which announced by a single stroke the most solemn acts of the mass, and which, toward the close of the service, summoned those to the altar who wished to commune. During the intense stillness which usually followed the sound of the bell, a low, eager whisper of prayer could occasionally be heard, and the whole assembly was lost in devotion. About twenty women and five men knelt round the altar to receive the communion. Soon after this had been administered some of the women began to hurry away, as if fearing the family at home might be ready for breakfast before breakfast was ready for them. At ten minutes to seven the priest put on his black cap, and withdrew; and soon the congregation was in full retreat. But by this time another congregation was assembling for the seven-o'clock mass; the people were pouring in at every door, and hurrying along all the adjacent streets towards the church. Seven o'clock being a much more convenient time than six, the church is usually filled at that hour; as it is, also, at the nine-o'clock mass. At half past ten the grand mass of the day occurs, and no one who is in the habit of passing a Catholic church on Sunday mornings at that hour needs to be informed that the kneeling suppliants who cannot get in would make a tolerable congregation of themselves.

What an economy is this! The parish of St. Stephen's contains a Catholic population of twenty-five thousand, of whom twenty thousand, perhaps, are old enough and well enough to go to church. As the church will seat four thousand persons, all this multitude can hear mass every Sunday morning. As many as usually desire it can attend the vespers in the afternoon. The church, too, in the intervals of service, and during the week, stands hospitably open, and is usually fulfilling in some way the end of its erection. How different with our churches! There is St. George's, for example, the twin steeples of which are visible to the home-returning son of Gotham as soon as the Sound steamer has brought him past Blackwell's Island. In that stately edifice half a million dollars have been invested, and it is in use only four hours a week. No more; for the smaller occasional meetings are held in another building, a chapel in the rear. Half a million dollars is a large sum of money, even in Wall Street, where it figures merely as part of the working capital of the country; but think what a sum it is when viewed as a portion of the small, sacred treasure set apart for the higher purposes of human nature! And yet the building which has cost so much money stands there a dead and empty thing; except for four hours on Sunday! Our Roman Catholic brethren manage these things better. When *they* have invested half a million in a building, they put that building to a use which justifies and returns the expenditure. Even their grand cathedrals are good investments; since, besides being always open, always in use, always cheering and comforting their people, they are splendid illustrations of their religion to every passer-by, to every reader of books, and to every collector of engravings. Such edifices as St. Peter's, the cathedrals of Milan and of Cologne, do actually cheer and exalt the solitary priest toiling on the outskirts of civilization. Lonely as he is, insignificant, perhaps despised and shunned, he feels that he has a property in those grandeurs, and that an indissoluble tie connects him with the system which created them, and which will one day erect a gorgeous temple upon the site of the shanty in which now he celebrates the rites of his church in the presence of a few railroad workers.

While these successive multitudes have been gathering and dispersing something has been going on in the basement of St. Stephen's, a long, low room, extending from street to street, and fitted up for a children's chapel and Sunday-school room. The Protestant reader, it is safe to say, has never attended a Catholic Sunday school, but he shall now have the pleasure of doing so. It ought to be a pleasure only to see two or three thousand children gathered together; but there is a particular reason why a Protestant should be pleased at a Catholic Sunday school. Imitation is the sincerest homage. The notion of the Sunday school is one of several which our Roman Catholic brethren have borrowed from us. This church, hoary and wrinkled with age, does not disdain to learn from the young and bustling churches to which it has given all they have. The Catholic Church, however, claims a share in the invention, since for many ages it has employed boys in the celebration of its worship, and has given those boys a certain training to enable them to fulfil their vocation. Still, the Sunday school, as now constituted, is essentially of Protestant origin. Indeed, the energetic and truly catholic superintendent of St. Stephen's school, Mr. Thomas E. S. Dwyer, informed me, that, before beginning this school, he visited all the noted Sunday schools in New York, Protestant, Catholic, and Jewish, and endeavored to get from each whatever he found in it suitable to his purpose.

James Parton, "Our Roman Catholic Brethren," *Atlantic Monthly* (21 April 1868): 432–35.

24. Devotional Life in the Gilded Age, 1870–85

John Talbot Smith (1855–1923), a priest-chaplain who served both the Christian Brothers and the Sisters of Mercy in New York City in the last decade of the nineteenth century, observed at first hand the subtle changes and prominent development of Catholic prayer and practice in the large metropolitan community. The selection below is from "The People and Their Parishes," which is one chapter of his much larger history of the church in New York. The chapter describes the development of the church in the Diocese of New York during the tenure of John Cardinal McCloskey (1810–85). In addition to painting a picture of Catholicism as a public force, the text presented here acknowledges the significant contribution of Jesuit, Redemptorist, Franciscan, Dominican, and Paulist preachers in shaping the faith of the community, the changes in popular devotions, and the wide influence of prominent women authors.

The celebration of the Mass and other church services became more beautiful and more attractive as the means to carry out the liturgy became more abundant. Marble altars of artistic quality, decorated sanctuaries well furnished, well-heated churches and comfortable pews, capable choirs with good organists and good music to deliver, although it could hardly be called church music, naturally drew the faithful and the unbeliever also. St. Peter's and St. Stephen's, the Jesuits and the Cathedral, the Paulists and the Dominicans and the Redemptorists, were frequented by crowds, drawn by the splendid ceremonies, the good preaching, and the effective if operatic music. The Paulists in 1870 introduced the Gregorian chant and congregational singing. The people of that period, both Catholic and Protestant, had been accustomed to Puritan severity in religious ceremonies. The gradual but brilliant development of the ritual surprised and attracted the Catholics no less than their neighbors; and it certainly had its influence on the whole country, for with this efflorescence of ceremony there began a new era for divine worship. The churches were thronged at the Sunday Masses, and the confessionals crowded on Saturdays. The work of sanctification was arduous and effective. Besides the ordinary means of winning souls to the right path and keeping them in it, the pastors indulged in more special methods. The mission became an important instrument for rousing the sluggish and recalling the reckless sinner. The multiplication of the convent communities had placed in the field several bands of missionaries, so that it was no longer difficult for a parish to secure an annual exhortation from these trained and experienced men. The mission became and remained a most popular and effective means of regenerating a parish and making it spiritually new.

Between times the fervor of the people was kept up by the popular devotions. The celebration of the Forty Hours at that time took the lead, and indeed became a social as well as a religious feature. The priests gathered at the place of celebration, to preach, to hear the innumerable confessions, to carry out the ceremonies; the people attended in such crowds as made hard labor necessary; and in the intervals of labor the assembled clergy discussed the passing history of the Church, the points of pastoral theology, and the local conditions. The devotion to the Sacred Heart of Our Lord followed, partly to supplement and in time to supplant the Forty Hours, which by the end of the period had lost its first glory, or rather been absorbed in a second glory, since the object of both devotions is the Person of the Lord. The Sacred Heart devotion made the first Friday of every month a day of exposition and adoration, and it established a league or society to secure a systematic adherence and labor from thousands of members; a literature and an organization grew up around it, which time and experience made very effective, although the charm of spontaneity thereby suffered. The devotion of the Rosary and celebration of the month of May in honor of the Blessed Mother of God, and also the wearing of the scapular of Mount Carmel, had a very large influence among the people in arousing veneration for Mary, and were carefully encouraged by the Dominicans and the Franciscans. The time of Lent was as usual made the occasion of public services in the churches, and in particular the Stations or the Way of the Cross became most popular. The devotion was carried out with great dignity in those days, and its weekly recital, amid prayers and the singing of the Stabat Mater, of the chief incidents in the Passion of the Lord, had a striking effect on the people.

For the better instruction of the children two institutions existed, the Sunday School and the library. The former remains with us, the latter has almost disappeared, except in the larger cities and parishes, among those who believe in the usefulness of a religious press. The catechism schools were numerous, popular, and effective in preparing the children for the Sacraments, but they never attempted much beyond the point of Confirmation, until the Paulist community began on a large scale the system of carrying the child through a graded course of instruction in religion up [to] the age of eighteen, graduated him, and gave him a diploma. This system has been in use ever since in many places. The library at one time enjoyed a great vogue, and was usually an attachment of the Sunday School; and the Catholic authors of the day, like Mrs. Sadlier, Lady Fullerton, Mrs. Dorsey, Hendrik Conscience, and Abram Ryan, owed to it their wide popularity with their own people. For unknown reasons the library lost its popularity before the end of the period. Devotion was kept up also by means of parish societies, among which the sodalities of the Blessed Virgin for men and women were in high favor. Hardly a parish but had them, and on certain Sundays the members went to communion in a body, the ladies wearing white veils and the men their simple badges. The older people affected the Rosary Society. The attempt to organize societies of the young men, as much of a social as of a religious character, resulted very well in spite of ridicule and opposition, and the young men's societies grew so numerous that a national organization was formed towards the end of this period, and won substantial success. The Total Abstinence movement was the great movement of the time, however, and made a very striking display during its popular period. The temperance society was in those days as peculiar to a parish as its pious sodality; the general union of these numerous societies resulted in the usual conventions, meetings, lectures and speeches and resolutions, and also in the more stable work of rescuing the drunkards, restraining the intemperate, regulating the drinking-places, and warning the people of the grave danger to be apprehended from this source. It had its effect also upon the legislation of the day. The best men, priests and laymen, supported the movement and carried it through successfully, until more moderate and cautious use of alcoholic drinks prevailed.

The result of the careful parish organization, of the regular service, of the steady reception of divine grace from those fountains of grace, the Sacraments, showed powerfully in an enthusiasm for the faith, whose expression at least has not been surpassed either before or since that day. . . .

Archbishop Hughes found the people of standing cold and staid, and the multitude timid and reluctant; he had to fire them with his own courage, enthusiasm, and initiative, teach them their own strength and their rich opportunities, and lead the way in all enterprises. His successor was not of that temperament, and could not have led in that splendid style; but he found a more willing and enterprising set of leaders and an emancipated multitude, full of the joy of life in New York, ready of great deeds. First freed from the restraints of Europe, and again freed from the curb of Puritanism, which the war had weakened as a public force, the Catholic body had resumed its natural joyousness. Archbishop Hughes came to New York in 1838 almost in secret as far as its citizens were concerned; Archbishop McCloskey sat down to a banquet a Delmonico's, where Charles O'Conor and two hundred New York leaders welcomed him to his high place and his happy career in the metropolis. The enthusiasm and gayety of the people burst forth in the public parades, the grand religious ceremonies, and the gigantic bazaars, which provided the opportunity of displaying their strength, their numbers, and their power to themselves and their neighbors.

> John Talbot Smith, *The Catholic Church in New York: A History of the New York Diocese from Its Establishment in 1808 to the Present Time* (New York and Boston: Hall and Locke, 1905), 1:315–18, 319.

25. Prayer Life in a Rural Parish, 1870–1900

In the wake of the Kulturkampf, thirty-six-year-old William Bigot (1838–1903) arrived in the Cincinnati area in 1874 and became pastor for over thirty years of a parish whose members were chiefly farmers. Bigot's journal, written in German and translated into English, records his impressions as a missionary priest in rural Loramie (Berlin), Ohio. He records observations on American social, political, economic, and religious life. The remarks included here provide an intimate look into rural parish prayer life and practice, focused as they were on the regular cycle of the church's liturgical year, major feasts, and the calendar of saints. The mission, usually preached by a priest from a religious order, provided a regular impetus to the community's growth, education, and participation in sacramental life.

In the fourth chapter of this book I told about my first work and experience in the parish, about the organization of sodalities, about the first impression of the country and people. I also told about taking the census, its completion by trusted ones, to find out the expansion, condition and morale of the people in the far territory, so the pastor could labor joyfully and cheerfully.

All considered to pay proper attention to the division of the church year in different liturgical divisions or classifications. The three great feast days, Christmas, Easter and Pentecost, give the Christian a full knowledge of his duty to God. To prepare the Christians for the great feast of Christmas, the *Rorate* Mass was celebrated every morning during Advent. The choir sang *Rorate Coeli*, with other German songs. With the arrival of Christmas the eagerness of the children to visit the church knew no bounds. The beautiful crib, put up yearly, and the many fir trees made the place seem like a forest. The many candles and colored lights called even the not so eager ones to church. The services were always well attended, even though the farmers had to come a distance of four to six miles. The 8:30, or Shepherd's Mass, was especially for the children. The later Mass was a Caecilian Mass.

One of the outstanding parts of celebrating Christmas in our parish was the devotion to the Child Jesus. Evenings at 6:30 from Christmas until the feast of Epiphany, the patron feast of the Child Jesus Society, we had a procession through the church with the statue of the Child Jesus. The last evening a solemn blessing was given the children.

Following Christmas-time was Lent, in preparation for Easter. On Wednesday and Friday after Mass we had Lenten Devotions. For many years I had devotions for both sexes which were well attended. On Friday, after Mass, I had sermon and benediction, also the Way of the Cross. On Palm Sunday the procession, with the blessed palms and singing of the Passion, took place; this was always a big day for the parish.

The last three days of Holy Week, with their impressive ceremonies, the adoration of the Blessed Sacrament, and especially the glorious Resurrection Services on Saturday evening at eight o'clock, were well attended; for this St. Michael's became known in the whole territory. At this time the big church was filled with parishioners and many others of different faiths.

Regularly on Whit Sunday was First Communion celebration. This was done yearly with an escort of young men.

The third part of the Church year began with Pentecost, which began with a silent prayer of veneration, worship and invocation to the Holy Ghost.

The Corpus Christi Feast inspired the hearts and souls of Christians with true happiness. We had solemn procession with the Blessed Sacrament around the village; the bells ringing, the choir singing and the participation of the people added to it a splendor which was not to be seen any better in large parishes in Germany. The people built four beautiful altars, which was no trifling sacrifice.

The remaining feasts of the year, Ascension, Assumption, All Saints and Immaculate Conception, were celebrated with complete church services, just as in Germany. On All Saints and All Souls most of the people received Holy Communion.

The patron feast of St. Michael's, September 29th, was celebrated and many neighboring priests came to help celebrate. The consecration of the church, Oct. 2, was also celebrated yearly, that is within the octave of the feast, which is customary in the Catholic Church. Also some feasts that do not fall on

Sunday, such as the feast of the Three Kings, the Annunciation, the second Christmas and Easter Monday, were remembered. The people thought that on these days there should be a High Mass, sermon and benediction. Also in all German parishes Candlemas and St. Joseph's were observed.

It was a very good year regarding the attending of services, and the receiving of the Sacraments increased each year. The first communicants went every month, the second communicants retained this habit and also went every month. There were none in the parish that did not make their Easter Duty, and all went to the table of the Lord again at Forty Hours. During Forty Hours a good many priests came to Loramie to help.

The sodalities are always a good prop for the pastor, and even for the parish itself. Many things are necessary for the church, parsonage, church services and celebrations, when the pastor does not care to ask the parishioners. The sodalities always help if they know what is needed. This is very much the case at St. Michael's. Each sodality purchased an expensive banner from Lyons, France: St. Ann Ladies; Holy Mary Young Ladies; St. Lawrence Young Men; and one for the Child Jesus Society. Each has its own beautiful banner to carry in processions. The different sodalities helped with buying of the new bells and also the expensive new windows. What would a country priest do if he had no sodalities? The different sodalities remained steadfastly with the practice of procession, High Mass, sermon and Communion, also benediction on their particular feast day.

The month of May, Rosary month of October, and November, All Souls month, were very much liked by the people and were well observed.

All these different devotions must be taken care of with a Mass, since the farmers attended services less in the evening and it was not safe for the young to go home at night. It was a joy to see that, in the month of May, when the bells rang, the people would come to church from far and near.

Once the new church was finished more Missions were held to uplift the religious spirit. The first Mission took place in the latter part of May, 1882. The Rev. Jesuit Fathers Karstatter, Haverstadt and Von Gudens had the Mission. This was an event for the parish, for never before had such a Mission taken place, and all felt themselves to be fortunate to take part in this time of grace. Three times a day for eight days the church was filled. The sermons and instructions for the different groups were very distinguished. The second Mission took place in 1889, also in May. This time the Redemptorist Fathers, P. Schwartz and P. Zinnen, with their instruction and advice, delighted the people. P. Zinnen, with his winning voice, lengthened his sermon at least twenty minutes every evening, because the acoustics of the church were so exceptional; he would have liked to have gone on for hours. At both Missions the whole parish went to the table of the Lord.

Wilhelm V. Bigot, *Annalen der St. Michaelsgemeinde in Loramie (Berlin), Shelby County, Ohio in der Erzdiözese Cincinnati von 1833 bis 1903* (Sidney, Ohio: Shelby County Unzeiger, 1907), 171–74.

26. A Pastoral Letter on the Sacred Heart, 1873

Devotion to the Sacred Heart, a staple in the community's prayer life from colonial times, achieved great popularity in the post–Civil War church in the United States. The Jesuits began publication of Messenger of the Sacred Heart *in 1866, and the devotion was introduced, as an innovation, at the American College in Rome later in that decade. Eventually its popularity surpassed that of Forty Hours, and by the mid-1870s numerous books, prayers, associations, and images served to fashion and reflect the piety of the community. In some circles, especially influenced by trends in Europe and zealous loyalty to the Holy See, the devotion was described as a response to the liberal currents of the times and given a new and explicitly conservative ecclesiastical and political interpretation. The most prominent example of this trend was the 15 November 1873 pastoral letter of the New York bishops, a selection from which is given below. (For comparative emphases in this devotion, see docs. 2, 27, 66.)*

1. ... There are Catholics whose hearts do not respond to the voice of the Sovereign Pontiff; who do not receive with docility and submission the words that fall from his infallible mouth. There are those who are not obedient to their own pastors; who take for themselves the liberty of questioning, and even doubting, the truths that are delivered to them from the sanctuary. They will have their opinions; they are not to be bound down by blind obedience to their teachers. They have imbibed the spirit of the day. They would seek to compromise, if it were possible, the unchangeable Gospel and the inflexible law of Christ, to accommodate it to the pressure of the day. They are not willing to confess the Lord before men. They would hide their talent in a napkin. The glorious faith that God has given to them, a gift more precious than all the treasures of the earth, they would bury in the ground, waiting until the Master shall come to demand His own with interest. "Liberal Catholics," says the immortal Pius IX, "are the pest of the Church and traitors to the truth." Liberal Catholics are they who would seek to accommodate the verities which God has revealed to the tastes and dispositions of the age; who are willing to hide what God has spoken, as if it were possible thus to be liberal in keeping from man the glorious gift of truth, and leaving him in the darkness of his sins, where the bright rays of the Sun of righteousness that shine in the temple of Emmanuel cannot reach him.

2. The opposition of modern society to religion is an evil which flows, perhaps, from this decline in faith. It is, however, an evidence that the world is marshalling its forces for a last battle with God and His Christ. The social order, as you know full well, has its foundation in the law of God. "There is no power but that which is ordained of God," and when kings and rulers reign, they rule and reign by Divine authority; and he that obeyeth them obeyeth the ordinance of God. Modern society, while it denies the very foundation on which the social order rests, asserts its independence even of God, and claims that the people are the fountain of its authority. The right of revolution so generally held, asserts that the majority may, without any just cause, change their form of government and dethrone their rulers, no matter how legitimately they may be established. Thus the age has arrayed itself for an

attack against the Lord most mighty and the religion which is the very foundation of all social happiness. Christian society owes its existence to the Church of God. Men were emancipated from the blindness of heathen darkness by the light of the Gospel. Woman was raised from her servitude to her equal and glorious position with man, by the light that shone upon her from Bethlehem and the home of the pure and spotless Virgin. Society arose in its strength and its magnificence from the creating hand of the living Church; and the law of morals, revealed by God and taught by His Church, is not only the foundation of the social order, but also its security against error and decay. The nation and the kingdom that will serve God shall stand; the nation and the kingdom that resisteth God shall perish; for saith the Holy Ghost, "No weapon that is formed against Thee shall prosper." And yet what do we behold in this age but the attempt to go back to the days preceding Christianity, and divorce, if it were possible, society from religion. They tell us that faith has nothing to do with the social fabric, which rests on its own basis. They say, "Let religion keep to its own cloister; let kings and rulers govern according to their interests or ambition. We will restrain the Church and shackle her; we will imprison her, if necessary, if she interfere with the exercise of our prerogatives." Dearly beloved brethren, do not the same morals exist for the individual as for nations? Is man, as an individual, to be governed by one law, and, as a member of society, to be governed by another? Religion must of necessity be the teacher of those principles which are the foundations of right, and which must govern society....

3. We have, however, not only to look at the decline of faith and the opposition to God beyond the boundaries of our Zion, but we have to behold the decay of love within the Church and among men. This will plainly appear by several important marks, which are far too evident to be contradicted.

There is wanting now among us a strong personal love to Jesus Christ our Lord. This, dear brethren, is a most serious want, which will take from virtue its vigor, and from purity its power. God is the infinite beauty; all that is attractive is in Him....

Almost everywhere you see bishops and priests, religious men and women, holy servants of God, devout believers, both of high and low degree coming together in pious confraternities, in associations of prayer, in pilgrimages, and all, as if moved by one common impulse, hastening to have recourse for succor and protection to the compassionate Heart of Jesus. There they confidently hope to find a sure asylum, a safe refuge from every danger. There, also, is the never-failing fountain of infinite love and mercy — the overflowing source of every grace and blessing. Let us hasten, then, to this same Divine Heart, and we, too, "shall draw waters with joy from the fountains of the Saviour...."

The Rev. Pastors are requested to read this Letter to their congregations on the two Sundays preceding the 8th of December. On that day the High Mass will be celebrated with all due solemnity. After Mass, the Sermon will be preached, and then the Act of Consecration, a printed formula of which is sent you, will be read aloud, the people meanwhile kneeling and accompanying with their hearts the words of the Priest. The ceremony will close

Copia della Sacra Immagine del SS.™o Cuor di Gesù che si venera fin dal Mese di Maggio 1792 nella V. Chiesa del Monast.™ di S. Silvestro in Capite fatta dipingere d: una pia Religiosa di dette. Monastero.

English translation:
"Copy of the holy Image of the most Sacred Heart of Jesus venerated since May 1792 in the Monastery Church of St. Silvester in Capite, made by a pious member of this monastery."

with the "Te Deum." Where the urgency of time or place requires it, the Act of Consecration may take place at Vespers, with the Benediction of the Most Blessed Sacrament.

> "Pastoral on the Sacred Heart," reprinted in Thomas Scott Preston, *Lectures upon Devotion to the Sacred Heart of Jesus Christ* (New York: Robert Coddington, 1874), 128–32, 141, 169–70, 173.

27. An Act of Consecration to the Sacred Heart, 1874

Annetta Bentivoglio (1835–1905) grew up as the twelfth child of a prominent noble family in Rome. Educated by the sisters of the Society of the Sacred Heart both in Rome and Turin and a friend of Madeleine Sophie Barat (1779–1865), she took her religious name of Maddalena when she entered the Poor Clare convent of San Lorenzo, Rome, in 1864. Maddalena was commissioned by Pope Pius IX to establish the primitive observance of Saint Clare in the United States. She arrived in New York City in October 1875, and after being rebuffed by Cardinal McCloskey, she eventually went to Omaha, where she found her original convent in August 1878. As with many of the religious foundresses of her era, Maddalena suffered poverty, the insecurities of life on the frontier, and persecution from the leaders of the institutional church. She died in her third convent in Evansville, Indiana, on 18 August 1905. Reflecting the inheritance of the Ignatian, Salesian, and Franciscan spiritual traditions, her "Act of Consecration," dated 29 September 1874, summarizes much of the interior depth promoted by

devotion to the Sacred Heart and its relationship to both personal transforma-
tion and mission in church and society. Her document concludes with the Latin
initials for "Praised Be Jesus Christ." The "Act of Consecration" was signed by her
spiritual director, the minister general of the Order of Friars Minor, Bernardino
da Portogruaro (1822–95).

Although I am an unworthy miserable creature, still with lively confidence, I protest to my God to sacrifice myself in everything that Thy Divine Will requires, consecrating to Thee, my will, heart and all its affections and my whole self without any reserve whatever. I intend now to renew the protestations made on former occasions and with this present writing to destroy, to efface all sinful writings and objects, if any still exist.

The mercy of my God has triumphed over the unworthiness of His sinful daughter, drawing her to His Heart and transforming her into Himself by means of His Cross, His sufferings and His love; may the only chain which binds me to this earth be that of the Most Holy Eucharist, although living in exile, may I live only for the love of God, and may I leave this earth from the wound in the Sacred Heart of Jesus, and from thence without passing through Purgatory, wing my flight to the Choir of the Seraphim in Heaven, where I shall eternally praise, bless and thank God. These graces I ask also for Most Rev. Father, begging God to assist him in all his necessities, may God make him a Saint like our holy Father St. Francis, and give him health of body etc., and likewise may my Spiritual Father make me holy and may he be able to assist me in death, if it is not given me to die a martyr, which grace I desire above all other graces.

In order to give more weight to my request, I offer my petitions to my God through the hands of the Most Holy Virgin, the Blood and Merits of the Most Sacred Heart of Jesus, to this Admirable Virgin, I commend this affair, imploring her to intercede for me with God the Father and obtain for me the grace of the pardon of all my sins, His Blessing, an intimate union with the Heart of His Divine Son, an ardent love for the Holy Spirit with the perfect knowledge of God. Lastly I implore of this dear Mother her powerful and perpetual protection together with her holy Blessing.

St. Michael, my Holy Guardian Angel, St. Joseph, Holy Father St. Francis and Holy Mother St. Clare bless me and pray to God for me in union with all the Holy Franciscan martyrs. I also ask of my Spiritual Father, his blessing together with the merit of obedience to ask for what I have written submitting all to his guidance to change as he sees fit what I have written, if through ignorance or presumption, I may have written that which is not in conformity to the respect and submission that I owe God, and also the freedom to add that which he may consider more conducive to the welfare of my soul.

I hope that this document may be placed with me in the Tomb, as a testimony of the submission, gratitude and love that I owe my God, etc., etc. When I am dissolved and reduced to ashes, may these words be as so many tongues, ever occupied to the end of the world, in adoring, blessing, praising and thanking the incomprehensible, eternal and adorable Trinity.

Benedic anima mea Domino et omnis quae intra me sunt nomini Sancto ejus, et noli oblivisci omnes retributiones ejus. Benedic anima mea Domino.

L.J.C.

September 29th, 1874
Sister Maria Maddalena, Slave of the love of the Heart of Jesus
Secundum beneplacitum suum det tibi Deus petitiones cordis tuis.
Fr. Bernardino Min. Glis.

> Translation from the Italian by L.J.C. Archives of the Poor Clare Nuns, Evansville, Indiana. Printed by permission of the Sisters of the Monastery of St. Clare in Evansville, Indiana.

28. Using a Sacramental, 1876–1917

Popular in the Catholic community since its beginning, scapulars (the word coming from the Latin word for "shoulder") were small pieces of blessed cloth joined by cords which one could wear over the shoulders. Often decorated with pictures, the scapulars as sacramentals (cf. doc. 15) were signs of belonging to a devotional confraternity usually associated with a religious order. Members of these confraternities promised to lead a more intense Christian life. As a religious practice, the wearing of the scapular provided a readily accessible sign of the immediacy of God's presence and power, a reminder of the individual's participation in the communion of the church, and a material symbol of the close personal bonds formed with particular religious communities. Scapular societies increased in number in the late nineteenth century and were more clearly associated at that time with the increasing focus on the juridical power of the church to grant indulgences or remissions from punishment due to the debt of sin. Within the context of a community more aware of its social boundaries and anxious to differentiate itself from Protestant beliefs, scapulars with their indulgences also carried a strong sense of communal identity. One of the most popular confraternities was that of the Mount Carmel Scapular promoted by the Carmelite sisters and fathers. The document below reproduces a pamphlet describing the "privileges and obligations of the Holy Scapular of Our Lady of Mt. Carmel," in use from the Civil War to World War I and beyond.

I

The Holy Scapular makes us *Brothers of the Blessed Virgin,* protects us in life and secures for us a good death.

The Most Holy Virgin while giving the Holy Scapular to St. Simon Stock on the 16th of July, 1251, in Cambridge, made him the following promise, saying: *"Receive my beloved son, the Scapular of thy Order, as the distinctive sign of my confraternity. Whoever dies invested with this Scapular shall be preserved from the eternal flames. It is a sign of salvation, a sure safeguard in danger, a pledge of peace and of my special protection until the end of ages."*

Conditions Attached to This Privilege

1. To receive this Scapular from a Carmelite or a Priest duly authorized to enroll a person in the confraternity. 2. To wear the Scapular over the shoul-

ders always until death. 3. To inscribe the name of the Sodalist in the nearest Carmelite Convent or canonically erected confraternity.

The Holy Scapular consists of two pieces of woolen cloth of brown or black color, made in oblong or square form, not smaller than one square inch, joined by two tapes of any color and material, with or without any picture.

The Holy Scapular can be imposed on children before their use of reason, S.C. of Indul. 29 Aug. 1814. The imposition of the Scapular is done only once during life and the first Scapular only is to be blessed. Soldiers can invest themselves with the Holy Scapular blessed by a duly authorized Priest, saying some prayers to the B.V. Mary, and without further imposition they are members of the confraternity and gain its graces and indulgences. S.C. Ind. 4th Jan. 1908.

II

The second Privilege consists in the Promise of the B.V. Mary to Pope John XXII, saying: *"I will, as their tender Mother, descend in the midst to Purgatory at least on the Saturday after their death, and I will deliver them and bring them to the holy mountain, in the happy sojourn of life eternal."* Bul. Sacratissimo ut Culmine 3rd May, 1322.

Conditions to Gain the Second Privilege

1. To observe chastity according to each one's state in life. 2. To recite the Little Office of the B.V. Mary (Officium Parvum) it is enough to say it in English. S.C. Ind. 14 June 1901.

Those who do not know how to read have to keep the fast-days of the Church and abstain from flesh-meat on Wednesdays and Saturdays of every week, except on any Festival which dispenses the fasting. It is enough to observe the fast-days of the country in which one lives. S.C. Ind. 14 June 1901. The abstinence of Wednesdays and Saturdays for those who do not know how to read can be commuted by any confessor. S.C. Ind. 14 June 1901.

Affiliation to the Order of Carmel

Those who become members of Carmel by receiving the Holy Scapular, participate in all the good works of the Religious of this Order.

Communication of Merits and Good Works

The members of the confraternity participate, moreover, in the merits and good works of all the associated members in the different confraternities throughout the world.

Participation in the Graces and in the Numerous Indulgences Attached to the Holy Scapular

List of Plenary Indulgences. 1st. On the day of admittance into the Confraternity; 2nd. At the hour of death; 3rd. On the following feasts: Christmas, Holy Thursday, Easter, Ascension, Pentecost, All Saints, Patron or Titulary of the Churches of the Order of Carmel.

February 2 - Purification B.V. Mary

February 4 - St. Andrew Corsini of the Order of Carmel

March 19 - St. Joseph, Spouse of Mary

March 25 - Annunciation B.V. Mary

May 5 - St. Angelus of the Order of Carmel

May 15 - St. Simon Stock of the Order of Carmel

May 25 - St. Mary Magdalen of Piazzi of the Order of Carmel

June 24 - Nativity of St. John Baptist

June 29 - The Apostles SS. Peter and Paul

July 2 - Visitation B.V. Mary

July 16 - On Solemn Commemoration of Our Lady of Mount Carmel for each visit and during the Octave.

July 20 - St. Elias, Prophet, Founder, and Father of Carmel

July 26 - St. Anne, Mother of B.V. Mary

August 7 - St. Albert of the Order of Carmel

August 15 - Assumption B.V. Mary

August 27 - Transverbation of the heart of St. Teresa

September 8 - Nativity B.V. Mary

September 14 - Exaltation of the Holy Cross

October 15 - St. Terese Reformatrix of Carmel and during the Octave

November 21 - Presentation B.V. Mary

November 24 - St. John of the Cross, first Discalced Carmelite Father and during the Octave

December 8 - Immaculate Conception B.V. Mary

Third Sunday after Easter - Feast of the Patronage of St. Joseph and during the Octave Sunday within the octave of the Assumption. Feast of St. Joachim, father of B.V. Mary. Forty Hours' Devotion.

All these indulgences are applicable to the Souls in Purgatory (Clement X January 2nd, 1672).

Conditions: To gain these plenary indulgences, it is necessary to confess, communicate, to visit a Church of the Order of Carmel or the parish Church in places where there is no Church of this Order, and pray there for the intentions of the Sovereign Pontiff.

𝔒ur 𝕷ady of 𝔐t. 𝕮armel

Whosoever dies wearing this Scapular shall not suffer eternal fire.

Scapular Promise given to St. Simon Stock, July 16, 1251

Our Lady of Mount Carmel Holy Card

List of Partial Indulgences

Indulgence of 10 Years and 10 Quarantines of the following days: First, second and fourth Sundays of Advent. The Ember Days in Advent. Every day during Lent, except those mentioned below. The Vigil of Pentecost. The Ember Days in September.

Indulgence of 15 Years and 15 Quarantines third Sunday in Advent, Vigil of Christmas, Christmas Day at Midnight Mass and at that of daybreak, Ash Wednesday, Fourth Sunday of Lent.

Indulgence of 25 Years and 25 Quarantines: Palm Sunday.

Indulgence of 30 Years and 30 Quarantines: Feast of St. Stephen, first martyr; St. John, Apostle; Holy Innocents; Circumcision; Epiphany; Septuagesima, Sexagesima, Quinquagesima Sundays; Good Friday; Holy Saturday. Each day of the Octave of Easter, St. Mark and the three Rogation days. Each day of the Octave of Pentecost.

Conditions for Gaining These Partial Indulgences

It suffices to be in a state of grace, to visit on the aforesaid days a Church of the Order of Carmel, to pray there for the exaltation of our Holy Mother, the Church, the extirpation of heresy, and the union of Christian princes, and to recite before one or more altars five Paters and five Aves in memory of the Passion of Our Lord Jesus Christ.

Five hundred days indulgence for kissing the Scapular each time.

The devotion of the brown Scapular is the most popular among the devotions to the Blessed Mother of God. It helps us during life, at the hour of our death, and it releases us from Purgatory. These favors are confirmed by innumerable and authentic miracles.

Imprimatur: Cardinal J. Gibbons, Archbishop of Baltimore, 23 November 1917.

> *Privileges and Indulgences Attached to the Holy Scapular of Our Lady of Mount Carmel* (New York: J. Schaefer, ca. 1876). Printed pamphlet found in VIII, Dev. Series 5, Box 5, File 3, Archives of the Baltimore Carmel.

29. A Missionary Model of Holiness, 1880–1900

Ordained in 1869, Peter Bourgade (1845–1908) was appointed vicar apostolic of Arizona in 1885 and became the first bishop of Tucson in 1897. Two years later he became the fourth archbishop of Santa Fe. Among his papers are "model" sermons in French, probably carried with him from his home in France. "Heroism in a Cassock," the text given below, reflects the spiritual ideal of French mission seminaries of the time in the wake of the martyrdom of several Paris Foreign Mission Society priests in the Tonkin (modern Vietnam). As Bourgade learned, the ideal could apply equally well to the mission territory of the Southwest.

The city of contrasts, the fast, whirling city, the University of the Seven Capital sins, Paris, contains also colleges of Apostles and seminaries of Martyrs. In the jumble of these houses where blasphemy alone recalls God, in the midst of these schools of business, ambition and pleasure, Paris also has houses of missionaries, schools of catholic apostolate. There courses are taught on how to die for the name, the glory and the love of God.

I say to die, but that is saying too little, because it is not only the giving of one's life just once, nor even to expose it for a period of time to the hazards of a war which is bound to end. What the missionaries learn is the art of dying totally, every day and always! He wages an unrelenting war against an immortal foe, who will be only momentarily vanquished by miracles and definitively tamed but by God's strength.

To engage in this combat, the missionary must dispossess himself completely. First, he dies to his family according to the flesh; he leaves it and no longer is part of it, and most likely, will never see it again. Then, he dies to his brothers according to the spirit, to those whom he joined to share their work; he also leaves this second home and, most likely, will never reenter it. He dies to his country: he will leave for some far off land where neither the heavens nor the earth, nor the language, nor the customs will remind him of his native land; where, very often, man himself does not even look like the man he has once known, except for his vilest vices and for his burdensome misery.

When these three separations have taken place, when these three deaths have occurred, there is still another one that the missionary must face, one that will not be sudden, but slow and constant until the last hours of his days: he will have to die to himself, not only to the luxuries of life, of every need of his body, but of all the ordinary necessities of the heart and soul. Most of the time, the missionary has no fixed abode, no temporary asylum, not even a stone on which to lay his head. He travels throughout vast areas. A few Christians hidden somewhere in a vast territory, here is his parish, here is his flock. He makes incessant visits among incessant perils. If God, in the midst of such bitterness, afflicts him with the cruel trial of a long life, he will grow old in terrible destitution. He will no longer have that youthful vigor nor the first ardor of the soul that gives a certain charm to the earliness, an attraction to the danger, even a certain savor to the break of exile. Thus, he will wait until his foot hits the stone that trips him where he is supposed to fall, until his life becomes hung up on a thorn where it will remain suspended, or ends up in a shack, a hiding place deep in the woods or even a ditch on the side of the road. Because, even the cemetery, that asylum in consecrated ground, the missionary does not always have, finding that on dying, even in death he has given up his resting place.

That is missionary life. According to nature, it is incomprehensible, and it is too little to call it a slow and formidable death. Who can explain why there are always some men who are ready to consume themselves in this obscure and bloody work, men who desire this kind of life, who seek it out, who have dreamed of it since childhood and who, concealing their design from their mothers but forever nursing it, obtain from men through their determination and from God through the strength of their prayers, that this should come to pass; that is God's secret and the noblest mystery of the human soul. Until the end, there will be men of sacrifice, enlightened by a divine flame, who, with their eyes turned towards Jesus, will know perfectly what others can barely understand. To God's light, they can guess the joys of this life of immolation for God; they desire it, they can taste these joys, they want to be satiated by them, and the world has no flower leis that can hold them from running to encounter these noble irons.

Now let us enter together one of these colleges of Apostles. Four young priests are about to take their departure and tonight, a farewell party is to be given.

The missionaries take their places, standing facing the altar. The choir is singing. During the singing, first the missionaries, then all of those in assistance come on bended knees to kiss these happy feet that will carry afar the good news and the peace of the Lord. All of a sudden, an old man among them comes forward, walking with difficulty. A missionary is helping him. A tremendous emotion that escapes none of the missionaries, seizes everyone in the chapel and voices begin to crack. It is a kind of anxiety that all feel even though they don't really know why. The old man keeps coming very slowly. Once at the altar, he kisses in turn the feet of the first three missionaries. The fourth one, as though by instinct, bends down, extending his hands to prevent him from kneeling before him. Nonetheless, the old man kneels, or rather prostrates himself. He presses his lips to the feet of the young man who turns pale, he even presses his forehead and his white hair; and finally, a sigh escapes from his lips, just one, but it echoes loudly in all the hearts and I can never recall it without turning pale like I saw his son turn pale.

And now, this son is the second one who this sacrifice Abraham is giving to God. He has no more.

> Anonymous, "Heroism in a Cassock." Signature illegible. Translated from the French by Marcel G. Langlois. Bishop Bourgade Papers, Miscellaneous Notes. Archives of the Diocese of Tucson, Arizona. Printed by permission.

30. An American Model of Holiness, 1883

While many in the church moved toward a more institutional understanding of holiness, John Joseph Keane (1839–1918), bishop of the Diocese of Richmond, Virginia, suggested that the goal of "religion" was not the correct performance of external ritual. Even a good moral life was not the end but rather one of the means to a greater value, the call to a profound interior spirituality. In the following passage from his pastoral letter of 1883 he describes holiness as the life of grace which permits union with a Trinitarian God and a corresponding commitment to "do all in the name of the Lord Jesus Christ." Keane avidly promotes devotion to the Spirit and membership in the Confraternity of the Holy Ghost as paths toward holiness.

No efforts of ours, beloved brethren, could possibly do justice to the importance of the duties upon which we have addressed you. Our words are but the feeble echo of what has been taught concerning them by the Saints, Doctors and Prelates of the Church in all ages. Yet all their importance, great as it is, flows from their being means to an end of still higher importance, that is, holiness of life. You are entreated to shun whatever fosters concupiscence, in order to remove the obstacles that would hinder holiness of life. You are exhorted to the fulfillment of the important duties classed under the head of Christian marriage and Christian educating, in order to ensure holiness of life to yourselves and to your children — to yourselves by the sanctification of the marriage state, and to your children by guarding and developing in them the precious germs of faith and religion. And whatever other evil or dangerous thing we might warn you to shun, besides those which we have mentioned, and whatever other useful or essential duty we might encourage you to comply with, besides those here dwelt upon, — all would have for their object the same all-important end, holiness of life. For the highest aim that we can have in all things is the holy will of God; and, says the Apostle St. Paul: "This is the will of God — your sanctification." (I Thes. IV, 3).

Holiness of life means to a Christian, much more than morality of life. It implies indeed morality of life, for holiness without morality would be an impossibility and the pretence of it would be hypocrisy. But it also implies a spiritual superstructure of which morality of life is the foundation. Holiness of life means turning to God and clinging to God, our First Beginning and Last End, with a pure conscience, a loving heart, and a prayerful soul.

It means union with God by the grace of Christ, which renders the faithful soul a true child of God our Father, a worthy disciple and member of our Divine Redeemer, and a living temple of God the Holy Ghost. By this blessed relationship with God through the grace of Christ, morality is changed into holiness, and that sublime word of Holy Scripture is fulfilled: "The Kingdom of God is within you." (Luke XVII, 21). For this our Divine Lord has commanded us to pray, in teaching us to say: "Thy Kingdom come." We cast sin out of our hearts and lives, we "crucify the flesh with its vices and concupiscences," in order that every enemy of God's Kingdom within us may be destroyed. We perform our duties, we do good to others, we practice virtue, in order that God's Kingdom may be fully established within us, and its holy sway extended to all the actions that make up our life, and if possible to the lives of others also. We receive the Sacraments, in order that the sway of God's Kingdom within us may be made more and more complete and perfect, by an increase of the grace of Christ in our souls. This is the indwelling of the Father, the Son and the Holy Ghost, in the faithful soul, so clearly and repeatedly promised in the Holy Scripture; for not only is it taught that the Holy Ghost shall dwell in the soul as in His temple, but our divine Lord declared the same concerning Himself and the Eternal Father: "If any one love me, he will keep my word, and my Father will love him and we will come to him, and will make our abode with him." (John XIV, 23). This is what is meant by the state of grace; and it is by this union with God in time that we are to attain to union with God in eternity.

To bring one's whole being and life more and more completely under this control of grace, more and more intimately into this union with God, is the chief object of our vocation as Christians. Not to [attain] this object is to waste one's life and to miss God. To fulfil the exterior duties of a Christian life, without bearing in mind this interior sanctification which is their only end and aim, is to live unthinkingly, and shows a sad want of intelligence or of reflection. To receive the Sacraments without adverting to their internal effect of increasing in us the grace of Christ and perfecting the Kingdom of God within us, is to forget the very meaning of a Sacrament, which is "an outward sign and channel of *inward grace*," is to lose sight of the end for which our Divine Lord instituted the Sacraments, is to run great risk of making our spiritual life a mere collection of forms and externals, without internal meaning and life and soul, such as God reprobated of old when He said: "These people draw near me with their mouths, and with their lips glorify me; but their heart is far from me." (Is. XXIX, 13). "The true adorers," says our Divine Saviour, "shall adore the Father in spirit and in truth." (John IV, 23).

Therefore, beloved brethren, to live an intelligent Christian life, and such surely ought to be the ambition of every Christian, three things are required.

The first requirement is, that we should have, and should keep habitually before us, at least an elementary idea of the relation between God and our souls which is produced by the grace of Christ. It is true that the grace of God can sanctify a simple soul that is, without any fault of its own, ignorant of the work of divine grace within it. But does not common sense tell us that God would rather have us walk in the spiritual life understandingly, than blunder through it ignorantly? And does not our Lord thank His heavenly Father not only for *doing* these things in simple souls, but also for *making them known* to them? "I confess to thee, O Father, Lord of heaven and earth, because thou hast hid these things from the wise and prudent, and hast revealed them to little ones." (Matt. XI, 25).

To neglect such knowledge when it is offered to us must evidently be very displeasing to God; and it is offered to us in the greatest abundance. The sublimest source of that knowledge are the teachings of our Divine Lord and the Apostles in the New Testament. And the same knowledge is offered us, in shapes fitted to all understandings and to the ordinary ways of life, in the works of spiritual writers. Among the great number of those, we will mention only the works of Father Faber, and the "Internal Mission of the Holy Ghost," by Cardinal Manning. These books we would love to see in the hands of all who desire to live a real Christian life. Their perusal will be found full of sweetness and enjoyment as well as of spiritual profit. To read carefully and reflectingly, every day or nearly so, something concerning the spiritual life, is almost indispensable for keeping its nature and importance clearly before us, and for preserving the mind from being entirely engrossed, distracted, and taken away from God, by the multiplicity of objects and occupations around us.

The second requirement is, a firm resolution to shape one's life by this knowledge of our relation to God and our duty towards Him. The necessity of such a resolution is self-evident. Without it, our knowledge would be only for our condemnation, as servants "who knew their master's will and did it not." (Luke XII, 47). Such a resolution must be honest and earnest. It honestly shuts out from one's life whatever is contrary to God, making no compromise with the devil. And it makes no reserve, holds no part of life back from God, but honestly strives to fulfil the Apostle's command: "All *whatever* ye do in word or in work, *all things* do ye in the name of the Lord Jesus Christ, giving thanks to God and the Father through him." (Co. III, 17). This is to live according to a Christian conscience, and to realize the rule laid down by Holy Scripture: "The just man liveth by faith." (Gal. III, 11).

The third requirement is, to desire and endeavor to draw nearer and nearer to God as life goes on. This is that growth in holiness or spiritual advancement, concerning which spiritual writers hold it as an axiom "not to advance is to go back," and concerning which the Angel of the Apocalypse exclaims in the name of Our Lord: "Let him that is justified be justified still more, and let him that is holy be sanctified still more." (Apoc. XXII, 11). Fidelity to the two requirements just mentioned will ensure the accomplishment of the third: because generous and faithful effort to serve God is sure to produce the desire to love and serve him better and better; and fidelity to grace is sure to lead to greater abundance of grace, to closer and more perfect union with God, and thus as the lapse of life brings us nearer to heaven, it also brings us, as it ought, closer interiorly to God.

This, then, beloved brethren, is what is meant by holiness of life. This the meaning, and value and object of all exercises of piety and duties of religion.

This is all the work of divine grace. This is what God made us for; this is what our Divine Saviour redeemed us for; this is what the Holy Ghost lives and works in our souls for. This is what the Church exists for, what her sacraments are dispensed for. Were we to fail in turning our people's hearts and lives to this, "then would our preaching be in vain, and your faith also be in vain." (I Cor. XV, 14).

It is with this view that we have established the Confraternity of the Servants of the Holy Ghost in all our missions, that we have given to the devotion all the encouragement in our power; and that we now again earnestly recommend it to our people. We do so because convinced that the devotion to the Holy Ghost is better calculated than any other to make Christians "think in their heart," and to lead them to live interior and spiritual lives. It keeps before their minds God the Holy Ghost dwelling in the faithful soul, building up in it the Kingdom of God, and turning it into a temple of the Holy Trinity. It helps to a better understanding of the grace of Christ, and to a worthier appreciation of the dignity of a Christian and our relation with God. It deters from sin, which "violates the temple of God." (I Cor. III, 17). It rouses from lukewarmness and negligence, which "grieves the Holy Spirit of God, whereby we are sealed unto the day of redemption." (Eph. IV, 30). It is a constant incentive to advance in the love of God, that we may not be unworthy temples of Him who is the very Love of the Father and the Son. Were this not the one aim of the devotion to the Holy Ghost and the natural result of its faithful and fervent practice, we would never think of encouraging its propagation, lest, by adding another to the list of "special devotions" and "pious practices," we should be but adding to *"the letter"* without advancing *"the spirit"* of religion. For a fuller understanding of this important subject, we again refer to the "Little Handbook of the Servants of the Holy Ghost," by the Rev. Father Rawes, Moderator of the Archconfraternity in London, and to the Sodality Manual of the Servants of the Holy Ghost, of which copies can easily be procured through your pastors. We request that all pastors will occasionally explain the devotion and recommend it to their people, and that, when it is possible, they will have every month some public exercises for the members, as explained in the Manual. We again express our desire that all who have received their First Communion should be members of the Confraternity, because all need the encouragement and help to holiness of life which earnest souls will be sure to find in it....

John Joseph Keane, *Pastoral Letter, 1883* (Richmond: Catholic Visitor Printer, 1883), 15–22.

31. The Choice of a Way of Life, 1883

Katharine Drexel (1858–1955), the philanthropist who almost single-handedly supported the largest number of missions to Native Americans and African Americans in the nineteenth and early twentieth centuries, founded a congregation of women religious in 1889 to meet the needs of missions by direct service to the two groups. As she sought to discern her future she counseled with her Philadelphia friend James O'Connor (1823–90), who had been made bishop of Nebraska. In this autobiographical writing she discerns her future by bringing to bear upon her decision her intellect (weighing factors on both sides), her emotions (fears, aspirations, experience of "dryness"), her image of religious life at the time, scripture, self-knowledge, and her relationship to O'Connor.

My Reasons for Entering Religion

1. Jesus Christ has given *His* life for me. It is but just that I give Him mine. Now, in religion we offer ourselves to God in a direct manner, whereas in the married state *natural* motives prompt us to sacrifice self.

2. We were created to love God. In religious life we return Our Lord love for love by a constant voluntary sacrifice of our feelings, our inclinations, our dispositions, appetites. Against all of which nature powerfully rebels but it is in conquering the flesh that the soul lives.

3. I know in truth that the love of the most perfect creature is vain in comparison with Divine Love.

4. When all shadows shall have passed away I shall rejoice if I have given in life an *entire* heart to God.

5. In the religious life our Last End is kept continually before the mind.

6. A higher place in Heaven is Received for all eternity.

My Objections to Entering Religion

1. How could I bear separation from my family? I who have *never* been away from home for more than two weeks. At the end of one week I have invariably felt "homesick."

2. I hate community life. I should think it maddening to come in constant contact with many different *old maidish* dispositions. I hate *never* to be alone.

3. *I fear* that I should murmur at the commands of my Superior and return a proud spirit to her reproofs.

4. Superiors are frequently elected on account of their holiness, *not* for ability. I should hate to owe submission to a woman whom I felt to be stupid, and whose orders showed her thorough want of judgment.

5. In the religious life how can spiritual dryness be endured?

6. Do not know how I could bear the privations and poverty of the religious life. I have never been deprived of luxuries.

7. The attainment of perfection should be our chief employment in life. Our Lord has laid a price upon its acquirement when He says, "If thou *wilt* be perfect go sell what thou hast and give to the poor and thou shalt have treasure in Heaven and come followeth Me . . . He that followeth Me *walketh not in darkness.*" How can I doubt that these words are true wisdom, and if true wisdom why not act upon them?

7. When with *very slight variety* the same things are exacted of me day in and day out, year in and year out, I fear weariness, disgust, and *a want to final perseverance,* which *might* lead me to leave the convent. And what then!!

The above undated document accompanies the following letter written to her spiritual guide, Bishop O'Connor, whom Drexel knew originally in Pennsylvania.

St. Michael, May 21st 1883

Right Rev'd and dear Father:

As you can readily see by the bulk of this letter I have availed myself of your extremely kind permission. In presenting "my papers" for your perusal I feel that I am imposing upon time that can ill be spared from important business. And yet, I would not confide these papers to any one else. I confess, I have come to no conclusion about my vocation in writing them but I know that I cannot do better than submit everything to you whom God in His mercy has given me to lead me to Him and Heaven. I hope the matter of my "papers" may prove intelligible; I fear it may not.

I have made a novena to the Holy Ghost and have received the prayers of several very holy souls. After that I have tried to lay open my heart to you. But it is a difficult matter to know ourselves, and I trust I have not been self-deceived. If my papers are all wrong, please tell me, and in what way and I shall make as many attempts as you may require of me. If you were to tell me you thought that God called me to the married state, I should feel that a great weight were off of my mind and yet I should not in the least feel satisfied with the consequence of such a decision, namely — a low place in Heaven. Does it not appear that my own corrupt nature leads me to the married state, and the Holy Ghost prompts me to choose the better part? Again the religious life seems to me like a great, risky, speculation. If it succeeds I gain immense treasures, but if I fail I am ruined.

Please do not feel obliged, dear Father, to answer me for months, if it is not convenient for you to do so soon. I am in no hurry about the response. I think it is clearly my vocation at present, to remain an old maid. My reasons for desiring a speedy decision as to my vocation have now been removed. The gentleman who was paying me attentions has proposed, and I have refused the offered heart. I have every reason to believe that it was not a very ardent one. *No one* (not even my sisters) knows of this little affair except Papa, who gave me my free choice, saying that he desired but my happiness.

If Lise and Louise knew that I am writing to you, they would certainly ask

Saint Katharine Drexel (1858–1955)

me to send their warm remembrances. I hope we shall never forget what you were and are to us in our first great sorrow.

With a big apology for boring you with such a mass of egotistical matter, believe me entirely,

Your unworthy child in Christ,
K. M. Drexel

Archives, Sisters of the Blessed Sacrament, Bensalem, Pa. Printed by permission.

32. Catechisms and Prayer Books, 1884

Between the Second and Third Plenary Councils of Baltimore the Catholic population in the United States had almost doubled, and the composition of the leadership of the church had significantly changed. Presided over by Archbishop James Gibbons of Baltimore (1834–1921) as the apostolic delegate, the Third Plenary Council — an assembly of seventy-one bishops, archbishops, religious, and theologians — met in November 1884 and attempted to codify the juridical norms compiled in the American church since the first synod in 1791. Much of its legislation still governs the church in the United States. Its decisions respecting preaching and catechesis in the faith and the need for a national compilation (which would become known popularly as the Baltimore Catechism) and a uniform national prayer book (see doc. 40) reflected the continued concern of the prelates for the expression of correct doctrine in the prayer and practice of the community. The texts presented below contain the council's statements regarding the catechism and prayer books.

Chapter II
On the Catechism

217. The mysteries of the Kingdom of God are revealed to all by the ministry of Holy Mother Church, but especially to children and the uneducated. She strives to do this always, with all her might and effort, that they may be nourished always with the milk of heavenly doctrine. Therefore, the most holy Tridentine Synod of Bishops ordered that at least on Sundays and other feastdays care should be taken to teach children in every parish the rudiments of the faith. (Sess. xxiv., de Ref. c. 4). It is the responsibility of rectors of souls to pasture the lambs of their flock. He is completely unworthy of the name of father who wickedly refuses to share bread with his child dying of hunger. We, therefore, want the rectors of churches or their vicars to go often on Sundays to visit catechism classes, and on weekdays to parish schools, and to high schools and academies for boys and girls that are not directed by priests. Teachers who are not distinguished by the character of priesthood, whether religious or lay, are indeed of great help in the education of young people, though they do not have as their own the office of teaching the word of God. "The lips of the priest shall hold knowledge, and from his mouth they shall seek the law." (Mal 2:7).

218. We command, therefore, that rectors of souls shall have constant care for children, especially at the time they are being prepared for receiving holy communion for the first time; and that the same rectors or their vicars shall teach the catechism to those children at least for six weeks, three times every week (at least in the place where they live or at a place they can easily reach). No one shall be allowed to receive confirmation unless they have been carefully instructed about those things which concern the nature and effect of that sacrament. We exhort the Bishop who is to confer confirmation on adolescents that he himself examine, or have a priest examine those to be confirmed in regard to Christian doctrine. The rectors, furthermore, shall take pains that boys and girls be further educated in Catholic doctrine and the Christian duties for two years following their first communion.

219. It is very important that this be the whole catechism, complete in all its numbers. There are many catechisms used among us that are useless, insufficiently adapted to the understanding of children or faulty for other reasons. Furthermore, since many of our people move frequently and their children attend various schools, everyone can see that great inconveniences arise from the variety and number of catechisms circulating in these provinces. Having considered the issue sufficiently, we decree that a committee of the Most Rev. Bishops be established with these tasks:

1. To select a catechism, or, if necessary, amend one or develop a new one, according to what seems necessary and appropriate to them;

2. Once this work is finished, to send it to the assembly of the Most Rev. Archbishops who will in turn approve the catechism and have it sent to be printed accurately. Once this catechism is published, all those having the care of souls, as well as religious and lay teachers, must use it as soon as possible.

This new catechism written in English will be prepared with the goal that it serve not only to promote uniformity, eliminating those inconveniences mentioned above, but also that it be better adapted to the condition and state of our faithful. We greatly hope that it will also be translated into other languages and used by the faithful in their own language. Furthermore, since the children of German and French families and those of other nationalities often move to Catholic churches where Christian doctrine is preached in English, we recommend that adolescents who speak both languages and are thoroughly at home among the English-speaking should learn the catechism also in the English language.

Chapter III
On Prayer Books

220. Prayer books, whose number is almost infinite, are frequently composed by writers who are not experts, and stray far from the true and sound norm of prayer which the Church presents in the sacred liturgy. We therefore command that all such books be subject to examination by the synod of bishops or other learned and devout men. Printers shall not dare to publish such books, or Sacred Scripture, catechisms, stories of miracles, prayer sheets, or any books in general that explicitly treat of faith or morals unless these have first been subjected to the required censorship and bear the Ordinary's permission for their printing. Thus readers may know that nothing is to be found in them that is offensive to faith or morals. We decree the same concerning the publication of new editions of any such books.

221. It is most regrettable that many Catholics are almost completely ignorant of the rule and form of prayer. In this age of ours, in which people eagerly seek worldly things and have difficulty understanding the things of God, it is incumbent on priests especially that often, from the pulpit and in teaching catechism to children, they should explain faithfully and clearly the rites and prayers of the Church. The holy Tridentine synod has already reminded us that pastors and others having the care of souls should frequently explain those things that are read during the Mass, especially the mysteries of the most holy sacrifice itself, so that while the sacrifice of the New Law is offered by the ministry of the priest the faithful themselves may also be made participants, and thus receive more abundant graces and spiritual fruits. (Sess. xxii., de Sacr. Missae c. 8). In the same way, the same Sacred Synod ordered that each pastor should piously and prudently explain, also in the vernacular language, the power, use and rites of the sacraments, so that the faithful people might approach the reception of the sacraments with greater reverence and devotion of mind. (Sess. xxiv., c.7 de Ref.). In regard to the norm of prayer in general, it is obvious that the Roman

Breviary is the most perfect of all, since in a wonderful way it combines divine eloquence, writings of the Fathers and sacred hymns in one prayer.

It is clear to everyone how useful it would be to the faithful if selected prayers and rubrics of both the Missal and Breviary as well as the Ritual should be accurately translated in books of prayers that they could have at hand. We know that all those treasures cannot be fully assembled within the pages of a single prayer book, but it would be useful to select some of the more precious ones, so that the sacred liturgy's buds and flowers, like a garden of paradise, might be presented to the minds of readers.

222. It is well known that the prayers used by the faithful frequently suffer from defects of language and sometimes depart from the path of sound doctrine. The same prayers, either written originally in English or translated from Latin into English, frequently do not agree among themselves, and do not conform at all with the original exemplar. Therefore, we order that in the aforesaid prayer book there should be reproduced with the highest degree of accuracy exemplars of all the prayers, hymns, psalms and chants which are commonly recited in the presence of the faithful in church, and that the Bishops carefully ensure that none of the aforementioned prayer formulas should be published unless they agree exactly with the exemplar.

223. We consider that a Prayer Book prepared according to the norm above would be very useful and welcome to the faithful entrusted to Us. We have decided therefore that a committee of the Fathers of this Plenary Council shall be established, with the Most Rev. Apostolic Delegate as president, which will entrust this most important matter to men who are pious and expert in sacred liturgy, and will ensure that this work be completed as soon as possible. The group of Bishops will subject the book to rigorous examination and will then send it to the Most Rev. Archbishops, who in turn will approve the book, as we said in regard to the catechism, and will send it to press.

> Titulus VII, "De Doctrina Christiana," *Acta et Decreta Concilii Plenarii Baltimorensis Tertii* (Baltimore: Typis Joannis Murphy et Sociorum, 1886), nos. 118–22. Translation from the Latin by Brother William J. Short, OFM.

33. A Native American Rite of Passage, 1884

> *Mother St. Angela Abair wrote these reminiscences of the first six Ursuline sisters from Toledo, Ohio, sent to the Cheyenne Indians in 1884. In her reflections, she describes the events which happened to them along the way to Miles City, Montana, and the interaction between the sisters and the Native Americans and cowboys on the frontier. A four days' journey away was the St. Labre Mission, which the sisters helped found. Mother Abair's observations provide details about Native American practices and how the sisters became the pastoral agents when the local priest was traveling elsewhere. In the following selection, Mother Abair tends to a dying young girl and her family.*

Now I will tell you how some bury their dead. One day White Bull stopped at our cabin. He was on his way to the Agency for provisions. He told us that his little girl was very sick. He asked us to bring her medicine and to ask the Great

Spirit to cure her. Of his accord he stepped into the schoolroom and placed his hand on the picture of the Sacred Heart, bowed his head, said something, and then rode away. We know that little Lucy was baptized, and we could do nothing for her. However, Sister Ignatius and I put on our rubber boots, took Holy Water and a crucifix and went through mud and water to the camp. We found little Lucy alone in the tent, all painted and ready to start for the hills as soon as she would die, even the horse and *travois* were in readiness. We made all the Indians come into the tent, and we said the rosary in their language. They listened but would not look at the dying child. We used Holy Water, placed the crucifix to her lips, the blessed candle in her hand, said a few more prayers, and after a few minutes she was gone. After gathering all her things, dishes, toys, and possessions, a few squaws wrapped her in a piece of canvas and put her on the *travois*. Then we started. After walking for miles, crossing ditches, fields, and forests, the procession finally stopped on a very rocky hill. The squaws dug a hole about two feet deep, while others gathered poles and branches. When all was ready, they placed her body in the grave together with all her things, including her little pony saddle. The pony was killed later. Everything was then covered with a blanket. Next they laid the poles or little trees and branches across the grave, and another blanket was put over the poles. Then stones and mud were piled on until they had formed a mound about four feet high.

> Archives of the Ursuline Convent of the Sacred Heart, Toledo, Ohio. Printed by permission.

34. The Religious Meaning of Mortification, 1888

When she was twenty-three years old, novice Sister St. Pierre Cinquin (1845–91) arrived in Galveston, Texas, from her convent in Lyon, France. Bishop Claude Dubuis (1817–95) had visited the sisters seeking help to treat cholera and yellow fever victims in his diocese. Four years later Sister St. Pierre became the superior of the Incarnate Word Sisters, whose members subsequently provided direct services to other Texas communities through hospitals, schools for Spanish- and English-speaking children, and orphanages. Hard work and the rigors of her responsibilities led her to seek medical help in Austria, where she died at the age of forty-six. The sisters on the frontier economized in food, clothing, and work-related items in order to secure needed materials for the people on the frontier. This letter of Sister St. Pierre to her sisters and her prayer to St. Joseph reveal a homely familiarity with the saint, motivation for austerity and service, and a union with the Incarnate Word typical of many nineteenth-century pioneers.

Mother St. Pierre to Her Sisters

From our Convent of the Incarnate Word
San Antonio, Texas
February 25th, 1888

Dear Sisters,

May our suffering Savior inspire our souls with the love of mortification and penance!

This letter, our monthly messenger, will bring you the love of our religious family, and bid you to the holy season and salutary reflections of the holy season of Lent. United to our Adorable Incarnate Word in His work of redemption of mankind, let us fear more than ever every sin and keep our souls pure and animated with the desire of cooperating by our prayers and mortifications to the great end of our religious vocation, the salvation of souls. Beginning at home, I mean offering first our own soul to Our Loving Redeemer and asking Him to keep it pure and burning with the fire of true charity, we will then take the true road — the essential means to reach our aim in aiding to bring about the conversion of sinners and the salvation of souls.

We have begun here our Lent by drawing our practices of humility, and renewing our resolutions of observing more faithfully the holy prescriptions laid down for us in our rules and Constitutions, but we have taken silence more than any other to heart. If we keep silence in the right spirit, we will destroy more and more in us that worldly spirit which creeps ever into the house of God, and tries to rob His chosen ones of the love of the maxims and examples of Christ. Silence is also a great help to union with God, to salutary reflections on our great and only aim — salvation. I am sure you will unite with us and no matter where the Incarnate Word will see His daughters and Spouses, He will find them in the same spirit and zeal to love and glorify Him by imitation of His virtues, particularly in His great and Divine Silence.

We bid you also to unite with us in making with devotion, confidence, and fervor the month of our Holy Father, St. Joseph. Our devotion to him is the gift and the example of Our Model, the Incarnate Word. He trusted, obeyed and loved him as a father, and called him by this endearing name. Then, my loved Sisters, when I call on you to look at St. Joseph in a special manner, I feel that I exhort you to do what Our Only Love, the Incarnate Word, has done Himself, and, if for every Christian soul St. Joseph may be a chosen protector, for us He is the chosen one by God Himself. Being so certain of this choice when it is of Divine Authority, we can see and feel our claims on His protection and love are in every way safe, excluding all danger of particular devotion. We leave it to you, Sister Superiors, to decide what you will do and say for the monthly devotion. The works to which you have to attend and the difficulties of having proper time or place to pray may not permit a universal way of acting in our spiritual homages to our dear Saint. You may then consult God in prayer and, after reflection, decide and order what you think proper for the devotions of the month of St. Joseph in your local missions. I dare ask you, dear Sisters, to say daily one Our Father, one Hail Mary, one Gloria and one Ave Sancte Joseph for my intentions.

[P.S.]

Our R. R. [railroad] Hospitals are going as usual amply providing our Sisters with means of sacrificing themselves for God alone. There also the ingratitude and selfish nature of men give very little return for a life of devotedness. But, if the servant of God has faith and works and endures in the name of God alone, all is gained, for it is to Him we offer our services in the person of suffering humanity. Let us then take a new start in our holy purpose of living for God alone, and, strengthened by prayer and Christian considerations, let us go ahead rejoicing that God has selected us and preserves us in His holy service.

Your affectionate Mother
Sr. St. Pierre
Sup[erior]

Prayer to St. Joseph

St. Joseph, we need 60 *piastres* to pay for that horse which Sister Mary of Jesus bought; 155 *piastres* to pay Mr. Grenett; 110 *piastres* to pay Mr. Woolfson; 60 *piastres* to pay Mr. Thalteyer. We need this money at once, my good Father. These debts are contracted by you who are the owner, father, and protector of your orphanage, St. Joseph's, San Antonio, Texas. The servants of your house, those who have charge of it, are the spouses of the Incarnate Word, your Son on earth and your God in time and eternity. We are not asking you for this money in our name; we, especially I, do not deserve to be heard; but we are asking it of you in the name of your adoptive Son, the Incarnate Word, and for your own honor because you are the master of the house.

I am going to have a candle burned for you today and, having given you this missive, I hope you will reply immediately. For you there is no difficulty; what you want you can do. If you answer this appeal, I shall have a Mass in your honor offered in thanksgiving. If you do not reply, I will punish you in some way, my good Father. You have always spared me this latter pain. Please do not deceive our confidence in you. I am displeased for I have reminded you during the month about these debts and asked you to send us the money to pay them. You have not done so yet and the day of payment is approaching. Hurry! Hurry! Your honor is at stake,

Your servant and the most unworthy of your children,
Sister Pierre
unworthy religious of the Incarnate Word

P.S. In heaven there cannot be any bankruptcy; its funds and treasures are inexhaustible. Pay your debts, St. Joseph. We are asking for nothing superfluous but only for what is just and necessary.

"Letters of Mother Saint Pierre Cinquin" (copy), 264–65, 266–67. Archives of the Incarnate Word Sisters, San Antonio, Texas. Printed by permission. Not to be reproduced without proper authorization of the Archives.

35. Appeal to the Charitable on Behalf of the Colored Missions, 1890

Not surprisingly from a diocese whose two previous bishops were well-known missionaries (James Gibbons, 1872–77, and John Joseph Keane, 1878–88), the Catholics of the Diocese of Richmond were urged to take responsibility for organizing their community to finance a variety of works on behalf of African Americans. Punctuated with the pertinent scriptural lines, the following appeal suggests sev-

eral ways for Catholics, motivated by spiritual rewards which related them to each other, to African Americans, and to God, to assist their neighbors. This type of appeal, uniting prayer, good works, and community, exemplifies a spirituality common to mission-funding societies established throughout the country.

"According to thy ability be merciful. If thou have much, give abundantly; if thou have little, take care even so to bestow willingly a little." Tobit 4, 8, 9.

Our cause being God's and our need being one of necessity, arising from the very nature of missionary work, we feel justified in appealing to the hearts of God's more favored children to come to our relief. Much good has been accomplished heretofore by our predecessors in their labor among the colored people of Virginia, and the work of each shows that while the advance has been slow, still, the growth bears the impress of soundness.

From the erection of St. Joseph's Church for the colored people in Richmond, Va., up to the present time, many other features of the work have been developed. In that time around the church have sprung up a convent for the Franciscan Sisters, St. John the Baptist's Institute, schools and missions at various points in the state, and an infant asylum, whereby many souls are saved.

During that period a church with Rev. Charles Reilly, pastor; and a school taught by the Franciscan Sisters have been built at Norfolk, Va., and both are prospering.

Looking over the baptismal register, we find that, year after year, the baptisms and receiving of converts into the Church have gradually increased, and the future promises a greater harvest than the past. This growth, both material and spiritual, gives us hope and encouragement, as we enter upon this, our new field of labor, and we believe this information will be gratifying to those generous souls, who in the past have contributed of their means to establish, increase and sustain this missionary work among the colored people in Virginia.

Our missionary efforts in the beginning were heartily encouraged by Rt. Rev. Bishop Keane, and today a no less warm and sympathetic assistance is given us by Rt. Rev. Bishop Van De Vyver, who bids us Godspeed in our labors.

"Do not forget to do good and to impart; for by such sacrifices God's favor is obtained." Heb. 13, 15.

What Are Our Needs[?]

1. School salaries for our teachers, $200 per month.

2. Maintaining Sisters, nurses, and running expenses at the Infant Asylum.

3. Keeping of priests and residence, expenses traveling to and from the outlying missions, and deficits in church expenses.

4. Coal and books for schools, coal for Infant Asylum, coal for church, coal for residency.

5. Keeping of property insured and repaired.

Will you, of your charity, meet any of the above, kind friends? Besides the general expenses just enumerated, there are other incidental minor expenses which amount to considerable during the year.

"Give alms out of thy substance, and turn not away thy face from any poor person; for, so it shall come to pass that the face of the Lord shall be turned from thee." Tobit 4, 7.

How Are These Needs to Be Met[?]

Only by the charity of the faithful, upon which we depend solely. For years the good work has been kept up in this way, and the same generosity, we trust, still dwells in the hearts of our laity, who may be encouraged in their generosity by the thought, that: "Some distribute their goods and become richer; others take away what is not their own, and are always in want." Prov. 11, 24.

That charity can find expression in the following ways:

1. By remembering the Colored Missions of Virginia in your will. The legal form of making such a bequest will be sent anyone upon application.

2. By sending us donations, large or small, for the general use of the mission.

3. By sending us food, clothing and means for the Asylum, where the neglected infants are received, the foundlings cared for, baptized and made children of God and heirs of heaven.

4. By sending us money and the means to care for the infants (a great number having been received in the last few months), foundlings in our asylum. Many souls are saved by having this asylum, who otherwise would die without baptism and never see God, and our labor is that of saving souls.

5. By sending for our "Collecting (Cards) Hearts," and either become a member by punching card and giving one cent, or have five cards filled and become a Zelator. Each card calls for one dollar.

6. Last and not the least efficacious: By sending your prayers to the throne of heaven for the success of the Colored Missions in Virginia. This practice we kindly ask teachers in our schools, colleges and seminaries to occasionally recommend to their pupils.

Benefits to Us, Benefits to Souls, Benefits to Yourself

First — You free the mind, hands and feet of the priest; on the missions that his mind, relieved of anxiety about financial affairs, may be given entirely to souls; that his hands, unfettered, may be engaged in the true labor of his vocation for which they are consecrated, rather than with material affairs; that his feet may be free to lead him more frequently into the dwellings of his colored charge, and less often to seek means of support at the doors of other people.

Second — You will be consoled, especially at the hour of death, to remember that you were instrumental in bringing souls to God, who, perhaps without your aid, would never have received the light of faith, and died never to enjoy the happiness of Heaven or sight of God for all eternity. A blessing which each and every one of us desires for ourselves. "As ye would that men should do to you, do you also to them in like manner." Luke 6, 31.

What would you [be] like were you one of these unfortunates? Does not your gratitude prompt you to share with others, by all in your power, the priceless inheritance you possess — the true faith? Does not the warmth of this faith never stir your soul to have compassion on those outside the fold? Remember, too: "He that giveth to the poor shall not want; he that despiseth his entreaty shall suffer indigence." (Prov. 28, 27). And who are poorer or more worthy objects of your charity than these children of Ham?

Third — You will receive benefits during life and after death — priceless benefits — not merely a hundred-fold, but the invaluable sacrifice of the Mass, and who is there who does not need it? "Do good to the just, and thou shalt find great recompense, and if not of him, assuredly of the Lord." (Eccl. 12, 2).

Benefits without Value

1. Every week two Masses will be said for all living members, one for the deceased members and friends. A member is one who gives one punch on the card, or has one card filled.

2. The public novena of St. Joseph, including Masses from the 10th to the 19th of March, will be offered for the intentions of all who help. Send your intentions, they will be placed at the altar.

3. A novena of Masses, beginning on the 2nd of November, will be said for all deceased members and friends. Names sent will be placed in a box at the altar.

4. On the first Friday of every month the Mass of Reparation before the Blessed Sacrament exposed will be offered for the special intention of Zelators. A Zelator is one who has five Collecting (Cards) Hearts filled. "Restrain not grace from the dead." (Eccl. 7, 37). Who is the one [who] has not this dead? Ask for yourself: "Lay not up to yourself treasures on earth, where thieves break through and steal. But lay up to yourselves treasures in Heaven, where neither rust nor moth doth consume, and where thieves do not break through nor steal." (Matt. 6, 28).

During the year we have sent a number of "Collecting Hearts" to friends of the mission. Many of these have not as yet made returns, and we hope these kind friends will pardon us if we pray them to favor us with their remittance.

So pressing are our needs at present, dear friends, owing to the recent hard times, our Asylum and the growth of our work, that we are compelled to place ourselves in the light of being rather importunate with our good benefactors.

"The Apostles"

"Go therefore and teach all nations, baptizing them in the name of the Father and of the Son and of the Holy Ghost." (Matt 28, 19). A new feature has been added to our Missionary Union which gives promise of accomplishing much good. Individuals have privately sent us a quantity of old Catholic papers, books and magazines for distribution on our various missions which we visit monthly. This outlet for the zeal of our Catholic laity is now taking shape.

Some Catholic ladies in our larger cities are organizing themselves into bands of Twelve, and are called "The Apostles" of St. Joseph's Colored Mission Union of Virginia. They are rightly called "The Apostles" for most effectually do they aid in spreading that truth which our Lord commanded to be taught to all nations. These ladies elect a President, meet monthly at the different members' houses, and after their monthly meeting, the President sends us in one package, the collection of old Catholic papers, etc., made by all the members during the month. Thus while the little Apostolic bands are moved primarily by a religious motive it also has a social nature.

We are always glad to hear from such bands as "The Apostles" or from private persons who send us so valuable a help to our work as Catholic reading matter. On our trips to the different missions we take large quantities of these old Catholic papers, etc., teeming with truth ever new and they are readily accepted by those attending our services on the mission.

Let every kind reader of our appeal send us their share of Catholic reading matter. "The Apostles," as well as all who help our mission in any way, will share in the two Masses read by us every week for the living members of St. Joseph's Colored Union of Virginia.

Having set forth our cause, our need and the scope of our work, we, in conclusion, confidingly trust in God and in His generous children to render a ready response to our appeal and that assistance which will enable us, with God's grace, to push on in the conquest of souls and the reclaiming of subjects for the kingdom of Heaven. Send your donations or returns for "Collecting Hearts" by money order, check or express. "Collecting Hearts" will be cheerfully mailed you upon application.

Yours sincerely in the Sacred Heart,
Rev. Thomas B. Donovan

Archives of the Diocese of Richmond, Virginia. Printed by permission.

36. The Use of Sacred Images, 1892

James Cardinal Gibbons's (1834–1921) immensely popular catechism was based on his successful work as a missionary in North Carolina. Several requests came to have Spanish and German translations, and The Faith of Our Fathers *became a tool for information for Catholics and a means of evangelization among Protestants. "Images," the selection here, provides knowledge about an area Protestants often misunderstood and also explains the proper dispositions Catholics needed in their spiritual life. In a community whose faith was largely shaped by the statues, pictures, holy cards, and windows which portrayed the mysteries of faith, Gibbons's explanation related their secular and religious worlds and provided a visual means of identity in a burgeoning age of advertisement.*

Let us consider the advantages to be derived from the use of images.

1. *Religious paintings embellish the house of God.* What is more becoming than to adorn the church, which is the shadow of the heavenly Jerusalem, so beautifully described by St. John? (Apoc. xxi). Solomon decorated the temple of God with images of cherubim, and other representations. "And he overlaid the cherubim with gold. And all the walls of the temple round about he carved with divers figures and carvings." (III Kings vi). If it was meet and proper to adorn Solomon's temple, which contained only the Ark of the Lord, how much more fitting is it to decorate our churches, which contain the Lord of the Ark? When I see a church tastefully ornamented, it is a sure sign that the Master is at home, and that His devoted subjects pay homage to Him in His court.

What beauty, what variety, what charming pictures are presented to our view in this temple of nature which we inhabit! Look at the canopy of heaven. Look at the exquisite pictures painted by the hand of the divine Artist on this earth. "Consider the lilies of the field....I say to you that not even Solomon in all his glory was arrayed as one of these." If the temple of nature is so richly adorned, should not our temples made with hands bear some resemblance to it?

How many professing Christians must, like David, reproach themselves for "dwelling in a house of cedar, while the ark of God is lodged within skins." (II Kings viii. 2). How many are there whose private apartments are adorned with exquisite paintings, who affect to be scandalized at the sight of a single pious emblem in their houses of worship? On the occasion of the celebration of Henry W. Beecher's silver wedding, several wealthy members of his congregation adorned the walls of Plymouth church with their private paintings. Their object, of course, in doing so was not to honor God, but their Pastor. But if the portraits of men were no desecration to that church, how can the portraits of saints desecrate ours? And what can be more appropriate than to surround the Sanctuary of Jesus Christ with the portraits of the saints, especially of Mary and of the Apostles, who, in their life, ministered to His sacred person? And is it not natural for children to adorn their homes with the likenesses of their Fathers in the faith?

2. *Religious paintings are the catechism of the ignorant.* In spite of all the efforts of Church and State in the cause of education, a great proportion of the human race will be found illiterate. Descriptive pictures will teach those what books make known to the learned.

How many thousands would have died ignorant of the Christian faith, if they had not been enlightened by paintings! When Augustine, the Apostle of England, first appeared before King Ethelbert, to announce to him the Gospel, a silver crucifix, and a painting of our Saviour, were borne before the preacher; and these images spoke more tenderly to the eyes than his words to the ears of his audience.

By means of religious emblems, St. Francis Xavier effected many conversions in India; and by the same means Father De Smet made known the Gospel to the savages of the Rocky Mountains.

3. By exhibiting religious paintings in our rooms, *we make a silent, though eloquent, profession of our faith.* I once called on a gentleman in a distant city, some time during our late war, and on entering his library, I noticed two portraits, one of a distinguished general, the other of an archbishop. These portraits at once proclaimed to me the religious and patriotic sentiments of the proprietor of the house. "Behold!" he said to me, pointing to the pictures, "my religious creed and my political creed." If I see a crucifix in a man's room, I am convinced at once that he is not an infidel.

4. By the aid of sacred pictures, *our devotion and love for the original are intensified, because we can concentrate our thoughts more intently on the object of our affections.* Mark how the eye of a tender child glistens on confronting the painting of an affectionate mother. What Christian can stand unmoved, when contemplating a picture of the Mother of Sorrows? How much devotion has been fostered by the stations of the cross? Observe the intense sympathy depicted on the face of the humble Christian woman as she silently passes from one station to another. She follows her Saviour step by step from the Garden to Mount Calvary. The whole scene, like a panoramic view, is imprinted on her mind, her memory, and her affections. Never did the most pathetic sermon on the Passion enkindle such heartfelt love, or evoke such salutary resolutions, as have been produced by the silent spectacle of our Saviour hanging on the cross.

5. The portraits of the saints stimulate us to *imitation of their virtues;* and this is the principal aim which the Church has in view in encouraging the use of pious representations. One object, it is true, is to honor the saints; another is to invoke them; but the principal end is to incite us to an imitation of their holy lives. We are exhorted to "look and do according to the pattern shown us on the mount." (Exod. xxv. 40). Nor do I know a better means for promoting piety than by example.

If you keep at home the likenesses of George Washington, of Patrick Henry, of Chief Justice Taney, or of other distinguished men, the copies of such eminent originals cannot fail to exercise a salutary though silent influence on the mind and heart of your child. Your son will ask you: Who are those men? And when you tell him: This is Washington, the Father of his Country; this is Patrick Henry, the ardent lover of civil liberty; and this is Taney, the incorruptible Judge, your boy will imperceptibly imbibe not only a veneration for those men, but a relish for the civic virtues for which they were conspicuous. And in like manner, when our children have constantly before their eyes the purest and most exalted models of sanctity, they cannot fail to draw from such a contemplation a taste for the virtues which marked the lives of the originals.

Is not our country flooded with obscene pictures and immodest representations which corrupt our youth? If the agents of Satan employ such vile means for a bad end; if they are cunning enough to pour through the senses, into the hearts of the unwary, the insidious poison of sin, by placing before them lascivious portraits; in God's name, why should not we sanctify the souls of our children by means of pious emblems? Why should not we make the eye the instrument of edification, as the enemy makes it the organ of destruction?

Shall the pen of the artist, the pencil of the painter, and the chisel of the sculptor be prostituted to the basest purposes? God forbid! The arts were intended to be the handmaids of religion.

James Cardinal Gibbons, *The Faith of Our Fathers: Being a Plain Exposition and Vindication of the Church Founded by Our Lord Jesus Christ,* 42d ed. (Baltimore: John Murphy and Co., 1892), 241–46.

37. The Promotion of Devotion to the Blessed Sacrament, 1895

Eucharistic congresses had their origins in Europe when Marie Marier Tamisier (1834–1910) encouraged pilgrimages to places where Eucharistic miracles were reported. Later, her observations of members of the French Parliament, gathered in prayer in chapel and pledging to work against secularist government policies, linked the idea of devotion to the Eucharist with the reform of society. The first international Eucharistic congress met in 1881. Catholics in the United States held their first national Eucharistic conference in Baltimore in 1895, a tradition which would continue in the nine national congresses (1895–1941), diocesan gatherings, and the International Eucharistic Congress in Chicago (1926). Rallying points for Catholic identity, they grew to reflect major developments in the practice of frequent Communion, catechetics, liturgy, Catholic Action, and the relationship between Catholicism and American citizenship. The following document is from the 1895 congress. In it a pastor from a St. Louis, Missouri, parish suggests some pastoral remedies to Eucharistic practice. The document reflects the increasingly urbanized and industrialized milieu of many Catholics, especially in the eastern part of the country. His practical suggestions are based on his desire to have Catholics involved, knowledgeable, and appreciative of the Eucharist and to emphasize the leadership role of the priest in that direction (cf. 48, 50, 79, 90, 91).

[89–95] Under the circumstances of more than usual prominence, it has been said recently by one who is eminently capable of pronouncing such a judgment, that nowhere are Catholics so docile to their clergy in religious matters as in the United States. If it may be added that our clergy are earnestly and honestly doing their full duty, then is the Church here working out her mission under conditions that are almost perfect. Even if I could justly do so, I believe it would not be within my province, in the present instance, to draw a conclusion in so grave a matter, especially if that conclusion were unfavorable. Perhaps I might go so far as to utter the general warning, that while the life of the Church is eternal, her temporal perpetuity, in any given locality, depends to a very great extent upon the proper use of the Divine aid which is there given her. But, I am satisfied, the mind of those who are behind this Congress does not entertain an unfavorable appreciation of the labors of the rank and file of our home clergy, whose self-sacrificing lives are strikingly unique in the Church's history.

The conditions which confront us are new, but so is the spirit that is implanted in the American Priesthood. At least we drag no regrets from out the past, we offer no apology to the present, nor are we waiting, Micawber-like [*sic*], for something to turn up. The problem before us is not unlike that which clamored for solution when Christianity was young. Then the right idea of God was frittered away and almost destroyed by the horrible vagaries of Paganism, while today the Divinity of Christ and the mystery of the Incarnation are differentiated into so many inharmonious views as to have ceased to be essential to religion in the world's acceptation of it. We have not here the devilish cunning and brotherly hatred of Europe to contend with; calm indifference, ignorance, and specious idolatry are the obstacles we know best, and so, strange as it may seem, we are the "early Church" living over again, barring persecution. A warm devotion to the Blessed Sacrament, which is bound to be promoted through the Eucharistic League, is the one feature to be brought out better to make the picture complete, and the rapid increase of membership amongst us of late is doing this very satisfactorily.

The question assigned me involves the whole of an immense subject. Whether we consider it from a purely theological standpoint as defining the relationship between the human soul and the mystery of the Incarnation, or as a theme which shall set forth practically the ways and means to further the religious life of a community so diverse as ours is, the effort to state tersely how to promote devotion to the Blessed Sacrament among the people can be little better than tentative. The admirable division of the matter, which is shown in the headings of these papers, spares me some misgivings by limiting me to such suggestions as might come from the pews. I speak for the people, "the multitude," and I have endeavored to examine the subject with their eyes and from their stand-point. Right here I may as well admit, that when looking up matter for the present occasion, I was amazed at finding so little help from the library. It brought to my mind a remark I heard credited, some years ago, to the venerable archbishop whose bright intellect is now setting in the West: "I wish theology would be written for the people." Books, by the yard, are on the shelves to tell how walls are to be built around the Blessed Sacrament, and yet, if I have got it correctly, there were but two notable instances, barring what is said of the desert, when Christ hid Himself from the people — one when they would make Him king, the other when they would stone Him; and these were more than offset by His triumphal entry into Jerusalem, and His crucifixion.

Some of the recommendations in this paper may appear small and common, and beneath the dignity of the subject and the occasion; but I confess I drew courage to introduce them from Cardinal Wiseman's second article on "Minor Rites and Offices," in which he devotes nearly four pages to pleading for the restoration of the "truly Catholic and sound practice of ever keeping a lamp lighted before the Adorable Sacrament." Against the objection to the practice on the ground of expense he remarks: "Our first inquiry, upon hearing such a plea, naturally is, Have you really, and with practical views, calculated the expense of such an appurtenance of Catholic worship? Are you aware that a few shillings a year would defray it? We believe there is great error prevalent in this matter; and that in truth there are not many places in England where, if the true spirit and meaning of the discipline were infused, means could not be found to observe it." Passing the smile that easily arises over the incongruity of an essentially commercial people excusing so grave a neglect on the ground of a trifling expense they had not even calculated, I am emboldened to say that if the great cardinal could busy himself before the public with such homely details, surely am I justified in hinting at carelessness and abuses in the particulars which I adduce.

It goes without saying that the priest should be pious, and his piety should be genuine if he would be better than supervisor of the mere mechanism of spirituality. His duty is to stand between the people and the altar and pray, and therefore both God and man demand that his heart be in his work. Appointed both consecrator and custodian, fidelity and reverence and zeal must ever characterize his relations with the Tenant of the Tabernacle. The age in which we live is, however, so nervous in its methods, that even in the sanctuary there is exhibited occasionally a disregard of the measured majesty that should hedge its great Sacrifice. The Mass is indeed an action, but not a rapid action. Sometimes from our separated brethren comes the taunt that if we sincerely believed in the Real Presence we would spend more of our time in church; but this conclusion does not take into account human nature, nor does it put a sane construction on St. Paul's "reasonable service...." [H]urry in the sanctuary begets hurry in the pews, and hurry is not conducive to devotion. It may be said here that the eyes of the people are not directed to the altar only. The sanctuary railing keeps them at a sufficient distance to prevent that keen inspection which is oftentimes the forerunner of sharp criticism. Besides, I am sure that every parish has its sanctuary society, which contains devout members who are ever ready to give the care that secures cleanliness, if not beauty, to the immediate surroundings of the Tabernacle....

General criticism, however, is leveled justly and not seldom at the body of the church and some of its appurtenances; for an inviting church, one that is cleanly kept and well ordered in all its services, is an imperative demand today, since cleanliness and regularity are becoming more and more characteristic of our people....

[96–97] To return a moment to the idea of parish sentiment, I desire to offer a suggestion which may as well come here as later. There are voices in the air whispering the prayer for unity into every nook and corner of the world where the magic name of Leo has conjured up admiration or love. It will be heard in God's good time, but we may hasten the day by promoting peace and concord among ourselves. As a further aid to this greatly desired consummation, more churches should be called after the mysteries of the life of our Saviour. The Blessed Eucharist is essentially the Sacrament of Unity, since nothing can show forth so efficaciously the brotherhood of man as the breaking of bread at a common table of the Lord. Why not have this thought in mind when selecting names for new churches, and choose such as will keep before the people the Real Presence, or at least some other mystery connected with the life of Christ?...

[99–100] Sunday is sanctified chiefly through the Mass, which is also, at all times, one of the principal means by which we obtain divine grace; it is therefore of paramount importance that it be heard in a profitable manner.

The inattention of those who are present and the indifference of those who remain away are due in part, no doubt, to the fact that so few realize how closely united they are to the celebrant while he offers the Holy Sacrifice. It is, of course, true that by means of prayer-books virtual participation is effected with him; but in most cases this is not known or not adverted to, and much fruit is lost. Pious attention is just barely sufficient for complying with the Sunday obligation; but surely more than this must be striven after by the pastor who would preside over a live congregation. The divine drama of the New Dispensation must have actors and not spectators in the pews, otherwise it would be more interesting, and perhaps equally as profitable spiritually, to assemble the people in the school hall for a curtailed rendition of the Passion Play. Furthermore, if this were better understood, our separated brethren would not be puzzled so often over the inaudible voice, or the attitude, or the unchangeable language of the celebrant during so sacred a sacrifice.

[101] From a religious point of view our age can scarcely be called heroic. The experience of every thinking priest demonstrates the necessity of making all possible effort to remove obstacles, even the smallest, that may intervene between the people and their duty. The need of churches conveniently located is becoming more and more apparent from the increasing number of those who wish to excuse absence from Mass on the ground of distance. In many cases the excuse is not valid, but we must take people as we find them; if the mountain will not come to Mohammed, Mohammed must go to the mountain.

[102] I should add that the needs of city life are now so pressing that many Catholics are obliged to labor on Sunday, and this must be considered in fixing the hours for Sunday Masses. The convenience of the people should be consulted on weekdays also, if we would reasonably expect them to form the habit of attending the Holy Sacrifice daily. In country districts circumstances of season and place are often so unpropitious that devotion, as such, is out of the question, and the pastor will consider himself fortunate if he can keep the piety of faith from dying out utterly. This applies more particularly to the West, where many an unpretentious priest is unconsciously a hero in his own right, as he uncomplainingly does the work of the Master amidst privations that need but the perspective of history to make his sacrifices sublime.

[103–4] The practice of coming late to the Holy Sacrifice is confined, I presume, to no one locality; how to remedy it is a problem which lies within the scope of this Congress. It is not so long since many were accustomed to give scandal and annoyance by leaving church before Mass was finished; but thanks to the wise direction of our Holy Father, the prayers which are said at the foot of the altar have brought about a quiet and effective reform of this abuse. It seems a matter of regret that the space between the Introit and the Offertory is so brief, and if the Holy Spirit would suggest some means of lengthening it, I am sure earnest thanksgiving would be made by every pastor who has an easy-going congregation to manage.

What can be corrected easily, however, is the practice of making long and unnecessary announcements. Mothers who have pressing household duties awaiting them — say, for instance, children to get ready for a later Mass — will find this very trying to their devotion....

[110] If the Spirit of the church is to be seen in the accepted practice of religion, then is monthly communion to be one of the rules of life for her children today.... The monotony of doing good may indeed be felt in monthly Communion unless care is taken to have people realize that the greatest worship they can pay their Creator is to receive Him as food in this sacramental mystery, and that their act, far from being merely an individual one, unites them to the whole Church and forms an integral part of the grand oblation of knowledge, love, and service which must ever ascend to the Beneficent God....

There is no better way known, I believe, of securing [these dispositions], or the practice of making thanksgiving, or spiritual Communion, or of paying visits to the Blessed Sacrament, or of attending Benediction, than through the instrumentality of parish organizations. When the young and old of each sex are united in sodalities, they form so many classes distinct from the congregation as such, and an opportunity is thus afforded the director to select terms and considerations which are best suited to each....

[113] Wherever it is feasible, nocturnal adoration is also commendable, and so is the practice of bringing the congregation together for night prayers, which may be said during private exposition of the Blessed Sacrament. It would seem unnecessary to mention the "Forty Hours" devotion, only that in some places it languishes for want of supervision by proper authority.

J. F. Foley, "How to Promote Devotion to the Blessed Sacrament among the People," in *Eucharistic Conferences: The Papers Presented at the First American Eucharistic Congress, Washington, D.C., October, 1895* (New York: Catholic Book Exchange, 1896), 89–95, 96–97, 99–100, 101, 102, 103–4, 110, 113.

38. Litany for the Conversion of America, 1908

The "mission to America," made popular in the last half of the nineteenth century by Orestes Brownson (1803–76), Isaac Hecker (1819–1888), Walter Elliott (1842–1928), and the Paulist Fathers, found expression in a litany prayed daily at the Apostolic Mission House in Washington, D.C. The prayer became more national through its publication in The Catholic Mission Feast *(1914), published by the Divine Word Fathers near Chicago. This litany reflects both an increasing sense of nationalism and the division of history into the standard mission "eras" of the time. The prayer seeks to develop enlightened Catholics who will be diligent in the conversion of the United States, the location for the next era of mission. It is a striking example of prayer, patriotism, and zeal for evangelization (cf. 77, 83).*

Lord, have mercy on us.
Christ, have mercy on us.
Lord, have mercy on us.
Christ, hear us.
Christ, graciously hear us.
God the Father, Creator of the world, Have mercy on America.

God the Son, Redeemer of mankind, Have mercy, etc.

God the Holy Ghost, perfector of the elect,

Holy Trinity, One God,

Holy Mary, conceived without sin, Pray for America.

Holy Mary, whose intercession destroys all heresies, Pray etc.

Holy Angels, guardians of the souls of this people,

St. Michael, Prince of the Church,

St. Gabriel, glorious messenger of Our Savior's Incarnation,

St. Raphael, faithful guide of those who have lost their way,

St. John the Baptist, precursor of the Messias and great example of
    penance,

St. Peter, prince of the Apostles and supreme pastor of Christ's sheep,

St. Paul, doctor of the Gentiles,

St. Augustine of Canterbury, apostle of the English,

St. Patrick, apostle of the Irish,

St. Boniface, apostle of the Germans,

St. Anscar, apostle of the Scandinavians,

SS. Cyril and Methodius, apostles of the Slavonians,

St. Francis Xavier, apostle of the Indies and the Far East,

St. Peter Claver, apostle of the Negroes,

All ye holy apostles of the nations.

St. Francis de Sales, patron of convert-makers,

St. Rose of Lima, first flower of American sanctity,

St. Turibius, glorious shepherd of the souls of the people,

St. Francis Solano, great apostle of the Western races,

All ye holy missionaries to the American people,

Be merciful, Spare us, O Lord.

Be merciful, Graciously hear us, O Lord.

From the consequences of our sins, O Lord, deliver America.

From the spirit of pride and apostasy, O Lord, etc.

From the spirit of hypocrisy, worldliness, and sacrilege,

From presumption and self-conceit,

From schism, heresy, and all blindness of heart,

From gluttony, drunkenness, and all uncleanness,

By Thy compassion on the multitude,

We sinners, We beseech Thee, hear us.

That it may please Thee to hasten the conversion of our country, and
    unite it to the ancient faith and communion of Thy Church, We
    beseech, etc.

That it may please Thee particularly to convert our relations, friends
    and benefactors,

That it may please Thee to strengthen timid souls to be faithful to
    conscience,

That it may please Thee to give them grace boldly to take the step that
    leads from darkness to light,

That it may please Thee to inspire many apostolic vocations,

That it may please Thee to give all Thy priests a special grace for
   making converts,
That it may please Thee to fill Thy people with an ardent zeal for
   gaining souls,
That it may please Thee to inspire us all with zeal for the apostolate of
   prayer,
That it may please Thee to preserve the Catholics of this land from all
   sin of scandal,
That it may please Thee to convert the American people,
Son of God, Good Shepherd of souls,
Lamb of God, Who takest away the sins of the world, Spare us, O Lord.
Lamb of God, Who takest away the sins of the world, Graciously hear
   us, O Lord.
Lamb of God, Who takest away the sins of the world, Have mercy on
   us, O Lord.
Christ, hear us. Christ, graciously hear us.
Our Father (secretly) . . .

Let us Pray:
   Look down, O Lord, with an eye of compassion on all those souls who,
under the name of Christians, are yet far astray from Thy unity and truth,
and wander in the paths of error and schism. Oh, bring the American people
back to Thee and to Thy Church, we humbly beseech Thee. Dispel their darkness by Thy heavenly light. Remove their prejudices by the brightness of Thy
convincing truth. Take away from them the spirit of obstinacy and pride and
give them a meek and docile heart. Inspire them with a strong desire to find
out Thy truth, and a strong grace to embrace it in spite of the opposition of
the world, the flesh and the devil. We humbly pray Thee to raise up for them
Catholic friends, whose burning zeal shall instruct them, and whose holy lives
shall edify them, that all may be converted to Thy true faith, O Lord, who
livest and reignest, world without end. Amen.

The Missionary 12 (December 1908): 8–11; republished in Anthony Freytag, *The
Catholic Mission Feast* (Techny, Ill.: Mission Press, 1914), 201–6.

39. The Drama of the Passion Unfolds in the West, 1910

*In medieval times, church buildings were the location of religious dramas. In
the nineteenth century in the United States, some forms of missions given at
parishes employed dramatic techniques by constructing a large cross outside
the church during the time of the renewal. Enkindling the faith of the people
moved beyond the walls of church and home in a variety of dramas which
took place in public spaces, either indoors or outside. A form of mass media
before radio, movies, and television, these dramas appealed to the emotions
of those who participated and those who attended, Catholics and Protestants
alike. While Catholics in farm areas processed around their fields during the
rogation days, uniting land, work, and the blessing of God, public displays of
religion in cities through dramas became a comparable urban communal gather-*

ing which linked the masses with the great mysteries of salvation. These dramas were part of a national movement of public displays of various kinds, often meant to manifest patriotism or a religious theme. Boston, for example, was the scene of the 1913 Second American Catholic Missionary Congress, which met in the shadow of the 1910 "Chorus of a Thousand Voices" drama of the missions, part of a month-long Protestant mission conference in that city and attended by Catholics, as well. The following description of a passion play in the West, produced in San Francisco just a few years after its great earthquake, explains the importance of participative and visual dramas in people's faith (cf. docs. 57, 80).

The co-ordination between pictorial religion and the masses is so well established that it would be mere futility to deny that the average man is more largely influenced by what he sees than by what he hears. This truth is instinctively emphasized by children, whose memories grasp and hold the picture scenes of their nursery or school-books more firmly than any word of the printed page. If a powerful mental picture becomes suddenly visualized, that moment chisels an unforgettable niche in the thought. This faculty of visual remembrance is most apparent in the emotional and therefore plastic mind; and as an evidence of its use in the uplifting of mankind may be instanced the recent production of that mighty and majestic drama, the Passion Play, enacted at the San Francisco Coliseum, consuming four nights in its recital, and witnessed by audiences which filled the vast structure to its doors.

On the largest stage ever built west of Chicago, erected in the fashion of a central stage and two smaller flanking ones — a device adapted from the German dramas and used in the famous play at Oberammergau — the twenty-one acts of the Franciscan drama were presented. Twenty-five thousand dollars is the estimated cost of this stupendous production, to perfect which one hundred characters took part, three hundred supernumeraries aided, and a chorus of two hundred voices, led by an orchestra of forty pieces, furnished the musical setting. A net of finest piano wire was stretched from side to side of the great building, to further the acoustic properties, and scenery and costumes of historical accuracy filled in the impressive picture of Jerusalem at night, the wonderfully beautiful opening scene of the play.

This opening scene is in reality but the introduction to the drama. During the few moments of its presentation Mount Calvary, with its splendidly luminous cross in the foreground and the multitude kneeling in awe and holy reverence before it, is shown on the central stage, while on the smaller stages are portrayed the expulsion of Adam and Eve from paradise and the sacrifice of Isaac by Abraham. With the approach of the angel, dawn breaks over the city and the curtain falls.

The first act of the play proper pictures the entrance of Christ into Jerusalem, with King Solomon also entering on the left, the city in its entirety being shown on the right.

The return of the prodigal son and the dining hall of Simon form the main features of the second act, while the third is one of great solemnity and woe. In it the curtain rises on the left stage showing Tobias taking leave of his mother,

Passion Play of the West, the Crucifixion, p. 249

while on the right is seen Jeremiah lamenting over Jerusalem. As the curtain rises slowly over the center stage, the figure of Christ is revealed weeping on the Mount of Olives.

The impressive scene of the last supper and the sacrifice of Melchisedec mark the fourth act, and in the fifth, Judas sells the Saviour for thirty pieces of silver, while on the flanking stage the boy Joseph is being sold into captivity by his brothers.

Adam earning bread in the sweat of his brow, the beautiful and dramatic picture of the garden of Gethsemani, the Mount of Olives, the stoning of Naboth, Christ before Caiaphas, and Job lamenting and deserted by his friends, are the main features of the second night's performance, while the opening act of the third night shows the impressive scene of Christ on trial before Pilate, and the last scene, the Christ on Golgotha.

Ending this stupendous and wonderful presentation of the solemn scenes and incidents of Holy Week come the pictures of the crucifixion, the lonely burial, the triumphant resurrection and the sublime ascension. This magnificent and dramatic culmination, presenting the Saviour of mankind in all the agony of His tremendous sacrifice on the cross, made such an impression on the vast audience, breathless in their realization of its overwhelming import, that one great sigh arose from the thousands assembled, as if from a single throat. The most sublime sight of the ages — He Who died to save a world — was before their eyes, and, beyond that sigh of horror, the immense auditorium was silent as the rock-hewn tomb.

A great and tragic darkness overspreads the stage. An earthquake rends the ground. Deep and solemn peals of thunder weight the quivering air. The mob flees terror-stricken. The Saviour groans aloud. Death strikes the pierced body. Over the stricken face a luminous light softly glows. The light surrounds Mary Magdalen embracing the foot of the cross. A centurion, grim and harsh, thrusts a naked spear into the yet bleeding side. Joseph of Arimathea comes forward and asks the body of the persecutors. This granted, he bears the Christ tenderly away.

This Passion Play of the West is the production of Father Josaphat Kraus, of the Franciscan Order. The drama, as originally planned, was to have been a totally different affair from what it came to be at the end. Father Kraus belongs to the Church of St. Boniface and has labored for the advancement of humanity for over twenty years. He wanted to reach the hearts of men, and he conceived the idea of presenting this sublime spectacle, rightly judging that the best way of influencing mankind was by the appeal through the emotions. It was to have been produced in the parish hall, and probably not more than a score of persons outside the congregation of the church would have known anything about it. But from a small beginning sprang one of the mightiest and most powerful stage presentations that San Francisco has ever seen; a presentation that drew thousands night after night at a time when the gayest and merriest fete the city has witnessed was nightly going on, to sit awe-stricken and reverent, beholding the presentation of the story that has rung through nineteen centuries and whose power never fails. Night after night men gathered before that great and often darkened stage; night after night tears coursed silently down rough and gentle faces; night after night groans and choking sobs were heard on all sides of the crowded house; night after night men wrung each other's hands without a word of speech and went their way feeling in dumb fashion the uplifting power of Father Kraus' drama, and night after night the mighty truths there presented found an echo in many a heart to remain forever.

The actors for these sacred parts were chosen carefully. They were to approach as nearly as possible the ideal, and to this end the part of Mary, the mother of Jesus, was given to Mary Wondra, whose face and manner carried the part to the point of perfection. Miss Sophie Schilling assumed the part of Mary Magdalen, and the magnificent role of the Christ was bestowed upon James Hans, a man of deep piety and great histrionic talent, who is said to resemble strongly Joseph Maier, who played the part in the sacred drama of Oberammergau.

The musical setting for this masterpiece of Father Kraus was arranged by Father Peter Huesges, who made careful and appropriate selections from the compositions of Palestrina, Rossini, Handel, Gounod and Mendelssohn, and blended these into a score of remarkably unity and fitness. Some few of Father Huesges' own compositions of a fine and high order were interwoven into the themes chosen, and the least that can be said in praise of the musical factor is that it harmonized perfectly with the meaning and solemnity of the biblical incidents, enhancing and supporting them in a devotional and wholly satisfying manner.

> L. B. Jerome, "The Passion Play of the West," *Rosary Magazine* 36 (March 1910): 243–48.

40. A Visit to the Blessed Sacrament, 1916

Throughout the nineteenth century, massive amounts of territory had become part of the United States. Catholics from Native American, Spanish, Mexican, English, and African American heritage, and the newer immigrant populations of Europe, each with its diverse religious and liturgical practices, were now members of the "American" Catholic Church. The missionary character of the country in much of that century left Catholics on their own to navigate the religious waters among their social, religious, and economic circumstances and their Protestant neighbors. In an effort to standardize the variety of catechisms, prayer books, and devotions which were being used, the bishops at the Third Plenary Council of Baltimore in 1884 commissioned a Manual of Prayers to curb abuses in devotions and to provide a guide for Catholics' personal spiritual life (see doc. 32). The manual, published in 1888 and reprinted in 1916 (from which version this excerpt is taken), presupposes a literate population. The adoration prayer from the manual could be prayed before the Blessed Sacrament if one were in a church or could be prayed at home. The Eucharistic setting anchors a Trinitarian framework for prayer and evokes feelings of adoration, thanksgiving, sorrow for sin, openness to God's Spirit, and the overflow of those expressions into a transformed life.

An Act of Adoration to the Most Holy Trinity

I most humbly adore Thee, O uncreated Father, and Thee, O Only-begotten son, and Thee, O Holy Ghost the Paraclete, one Almighty, Everlasting, and Unchangeable God, Creator of heaven and earth, and of all things visible and invisible. I acknowledge in Thee a true and ineffable Trinity of Persons, a true and indivisible Unity of Substance. I glorify thee, O Almighty Trinity, one only Deity, my most compassionate Lord, my sweetest hope, my dearest light, my most desired repose, my joy, my life, and all my good. To thy most merciful goodness I commend my soul and body; to Thy most sacred Majesty I wholly devote myself, and to Thy divine will I resign and yield myself eternally. All honor and glory be to Thee for ever and ever. Amen.

O Heavenly Father, O most forgiving Father, O Lord God, have mercy upon me a wretched sinner, have mercy upon all men. In fullest reparation, expiation, and satisfaction for all my iniquities and negligences, and for the sins of the whole world, and perfectly to supply the deficiency of my works, I offer unto Thee Thy Beloved Son, Christ Jesus, in union with that sovereign charity with which Thou didst send Him to us, and didst give Him to us as our Saviour. I offer His transcendent virtues, and all that He did and suffered for us. I offer His labors, sorrows, torments and most Precious Blood. I offer the merits of the most Blessed Virgin Mary and of all Thy Saints. Assist me,

I beseech Thee, O most merciful Father, through the same Thy Son, by the power of Thy Holy Spirit. Have mercy on all unhappy sinners, and graciously call them back to the way of salvation. Grant to all the living pardon and grace, and to the faithful departed eternal light and rest. Amen.

O Holy Spirit, sweetest Comforter, who proceedest from the Father and the Son in an ineffable manner, come, I beseech thee, and enter into my heart. Purify and cleanse me from all sin, and sanctify my soul. Wash away its defilements, moisten its dryness, heal its wounds, subdue its stubbornness, melt its coldness, and correct its wanderings. Make me truly humble and resigned, that I may be pleasing unto Thee, and Thou mayest abide with me forever. O most blessed Light, O Light worthy of all love, enlighten me. O Joy of Paradise, O fount of purest delights, O my God, give thyself to me, and kindle in my inmost soul the fire of Thy love. O my Lord, instruct, direct, and defend me in all things. Give me strength against all undue fears and a cowardly spirit; bestow upon me a right Faith, a firm Hope, and a sincere and perfect Charity; and grant that I may ever do Thy most gracious will. Amen.

A Manual of Prayers for the Use of the Catholic Laity: The Official Prayer Book of the Catholic Church, prepared and published by order of the Third Plenary Council of Baltimore (Baltimore: John Murphy Co., 1916), 340–42.

Part 3

THE ERA OF CATHOLIC ACTION 1918–45

Introduction

The Great War, brought to an end with the signing of the armistice 11 November 1918, seemed to unleash a religious fervor and genius for organization unparalleled in American religious history (see docs. 41, 42; hereafter document numbers will be in parentheses). The next two decades would see not only a fluctuation in Protestant church attendance, at one time referred to as the "American Religious Depression," but also a revitalized evangelicalism, a marshaling of new techniques of advertising and publication for the mission of the gospel, and a resurgent anti-Catholicism.[1] To some extent, the Catholic community entered into this void created by the weakening of Protestantism as a public force and responded to the era's challenges by adopting its own brand of evangelical techniques aligned with a strong institutional presence: new methods in catechetics, missionary outreach, emphasis on scripture, a proliferation of publications, the use of the radio, and the organization of the National Catholic Welfare Conference (44, 46, 48, 51, 56). Shaped greatly by the social and spiritual vision of both Pius X in his call for liturgical renewal and a more frequent reception of Communion (*Tra le Sollecitudini*, 1903; *Sacra Tridentina*, 1905; *Quam Singulari*, 1910) and Pius XI in his plan for social reconstruction (*Ubi Arcano*, 1922; *Mens Nostra*, 1929; *Quadragesimo Anno*, 1931), the community marshaled its institutional, educational, and parochial resources under the name of "Catholic Action." A far-reaching program of spiritual revitalization ensued (43, 48, 50, 53, 54, 55, 58). The story can be summarized by noting the interpenetration of devotional, Eucharistic, liturgical, and Catholic Action themes at the innumerable national congresses and conferences which the era engendered: one international Eucharistic congress (Chicago 1926) and four national ones (Omaha 1930, Cleveland 1935, New Orleans 1938, St. Paul and Minneapolis, 1941); seven congresses of the Confraternity of Christian Doctrine (1935–1941), which played a major role

---

1. For background, see Robert T. Handy, "The American Religious Depression, 1925–1935," and Joel A. Carpenter, "Fundamentalist Institutions and the Rise of Evangelical Protestantism, 1929–1942," in Jon Butler and Harry S. Stout, eds., *Religion in American History: A Reader* (New York: Oxford University Press, 1998), 371–83, 384–96; Joel A. Carpenter, *Revive Us Again: The Reawakening of American Fundamentalism* (New York: Oxford University Press, 1997); John T. McGreevy, "Thinking on One's Own: Catholicism in the American Intellectual Imagination, 1928–1960," *Journal of American History* 84 (June 1997): 97–131.

in the promotion of lay leadership and the spread of the liturgical and biblical renewals; five national liturgical weeks (1940–45); numerous sodality conventions on the national and regional levels; four national congresses of the Third Order of St. Francis between 1921 and 1936; ten national conferences of the Laymen's Retreat League and five for the Laywomen's Retreat Movement; and different programs sponsored by the various departments of the National Catholic Welfare Conference (42, 48, 50, 51, 60, 61).[2] This vast organization of the church, its obvious public presence associated with specifically Catholic religious symbols such as the Eucharist, and the emergence of Catholics into professional positions as educators, nurses, bankers, lawyers, businessmen, and businesswomen generated critiques from outside the community and calls for reform from within, calls which only strengthened the broader movement for a spiritual renewal (47, 52, 55, 59). Into the gap between cultural accommodation and the need for interior depth and fidelity to the gospel and tradition stepped people whose influence would cast a far-reaching and fruitful light on the spiritual development of the community: Dorothy Day (1879–1980), Virgil Michel (1890–1938), Catherine de Hueck Doherty (1896–1985), Paul Hanley Furfey (1896–1992), and Thomas Merton (1915–68) (48, 53, 55, 59).[3] With very different theological orientations, two periodicals argu-

---

2. See for examples and background, C. F. Donovan, comp., *The Story of the Twenty-Eighth International Eucharistic Congress Held at Chicago, Illinois, United States of America from June 20–24, 1926* (Chicago: Committee in Charge at Chicago of the XXVIII International Eucharistic Congress, 1927); "The Eucharistic Congress," *Emmanuel* 36 (November 1930): 283–309; "Gleanings of the Eighth National Eucharistic Congress," *Emmanuel* 44 (December 1938): 354–73; *The Confraternity Comes of Age: A Historical Symposium* (Paterson, N.J.: Confraternity Publications, 1956); Gerald P. Fogarty, SJ, *American Catholic Biblical Scholarship: A History from the Early Republic to Vatican II* (San Francisco: Harper and Row, 1989), chaps. 10 and 11; annual printed programs of *National Liturgical Week;* Keith F. Pecklers, *The Unread Vision: The Liturgical Movement in the United States of America, 1926–1955* (Collegeville, Minn.: Liturgical Press, 1998); Sister Mary Florence [Wolff], SL, *The Sodality Movement in the United States 1926–1939* (St. Louis: The Queen's Work, 1939); Daniel A. Lord, SJ, "Sodality Moves Apace with Needs of the Times, Its Slogan for Centuries: 'To Christ through Mary,'" *America* 61 (23 September 1939): 558–60; Alden V. Brown, *The Grail Movement and American Catholics, 1940–1975* (Notre Dame, Ind.: University of Notre Dame Press, 1989); *Grailville: Women in Community, 1944–1994*, entire issue of *U.S. Catholic Historian* 11 (fall 1993); Steven M. Avella and Jeffrey Zalor, "Sanctity in the Era of Catholic Action: The Case of St. Pius X," *U.S. Catholic Historian* 15 (fall 1997): 57–80; Paul A. Martin, ed., *Fourth Quinquennial Franciscan Third Order Congress, Louisville, Kentucky, October 6, 7, 8 – 1936* (St. Louis: Office of the National Secretary, 1937); B. A. Seymour, "The Retreat Movement in the U.S. up to Now," in *Proceedings of the Third National Conference of the Laymen's Movement* (Detroit: Sacred Heart Seminary, 1930), 4–7; Jude Mead, CP, "Historical Background of the Lay-Retreat Movement in the United States," in Thomas C. Hennessy, SJ, ed., *The Inner Crusade: The Closed Retreat in the United States* (Chicago: Loyola University Press, 1965), 133–60; see also the successive editions of *Catholic Action,* the monthly published by the National Catholic Welfare Conference.

3. The bibliography on these individuals is immense, but see as beginning points: Brigid O'Shea Merriman, *Searching for Christ: The Spirituality of Dorothy Day* (Notre Dame, Ind.: University of Notre Dame Press, 1994); William D. Miller, *All Is Grace: The Spirituality of Dorothy Day* (Garden City, N.Y.: Doubleday, 1987); Sandra Yocum Mize, "Dorothy Day's *Apologia* for Faith after Marx," *Horizons* 22, no. 2 (1995): 198–213; idem, "Unsentimental Hagiography: Studies on Dorothy Day and the Soul of American Catholicism," *U.S. Catholic Historian* 16 (fall 1998): 36–57; Jeremy Hall, OSB, *The Full Stature of Christ: The Ecclesiology of Dom Virgil Michel* (Collegeville, Minn.: Liturgical Press, 1976); *Worship* 62 (May 1988): entire issue; Lorene Hanley Duquin, *The Life of Catherine de Hueck Doherty: They Called Her the Baroness* (New York:

ing for a reform of religious life, *Sponsa Regis* (1928) and *Review for Religious* (1942), attempted to address the same issue of interiority and the problem of overinstitutionalization.

With the advent of the depression, an even deeper devotional life, which participated in a new sense of national identity, entered into the community's practice; St. Jude, Our Lady of Perpetual Help, Our Sorrowful Mother, and St. Anthony replaced the older, more ethnically centered, and neighborhood-based local practices (49).[4] This new devotionalism, different from its nineteenth-century counterpart, was combined with a strong feel for the importance of intercession, knowledge of invisible companionship, the need to bear the sufferings of others, and practices which gave meaning to life through participation in the sufferings of Christ (44, 45, 46, 56, 57).[5] Here was a community on the move, full of vitality and action, with a variety of movements not always in agreement but united in a strong sense of institutional, corporate, and personal identity and purpose.[6] Here were the prayer and practice of the American Catholic community between the wars. As the reader examines some representative documents, the following trends in particular should be noted.

1. In some respects the spiritual revival encouraged by the end of the Great War resembled similar occurrences in the post–Civil War period (20, 21, 23, 24). Public displays of the faith coupled with new organs of affiliation followed

---

Alba House, 1995); Bruce H. Lescher, "Paul Hanley Furfey: Insights from a Spiritual Pilgrimage," *Records of the American Catholic Historical Society of Philadelphia* 107 (fall–winter 1996): 39–64; Michael Mott, *The Seven Mountains of Thomas Merton* (Boston: Houghton Mifflin, 1984); for a new interpretation of the period, see Eugene McCarraher, "American Gothic: Sacramental Radicalism and the Neo-medievalist Cultural Gospel, 1928–1948," *Records of the American Catholic Historical Society of Philadelphia* 106 (spring–summer 1995): 3–23.

4. See especially the works of Robert Orsi, *The Madonna of 115th Street: Faith and Community in Italian Harlem, 1880–1950* (New Haven, Conn.: Yale University Press, 1985); idem, *Thank You, St. Jude: Women's Devotion to the Patron Saint of Hopeless Causes* (New Haven, Conn.: Yale University Press, 1996); idem, "The Fault of Memory: 'Southern Italy' in the Imagination of Immigrants and the Lives of Their Children in Italian Harlem, 1920–1945," *Journal of Family History* 15 (1990): 133–47; John M. Huels, OSM, "The Popular Appeal of the Sorrowful Mother Novena," *Marianum* 38 (1976): 191–99; Timothy Kelly and Joseph Kelly, "Our Lady of Perpetual Help: Gender Roles and the Decline of Devotional Catholicism," *Journal of Social History* 32 (fall 1998): 5–26.

5. For a beginning analysis of the problem of suffering, see James Terence Fisher, *The Catholic Counterculture in America, 1933–1962* (Chapel Hill: University of North Carolina Press, 1989); Robert Orsi, "'Mildred, Is It Fun to Be a Cripple?' The Culture of Suffering in Mid-Twentieth-Century American Catholicism," *South Atlantic Quarterly* 93 (summer 1994): 547–90; idem, "The Cult of the Saints and the Reimagination of the Space and Time of Sickness in Twentieth Century American Catholicism," *Literature and Medicine* 8 (1989): 63–77. However, the motivations and activities of someone like Clary Tiry (see doc. 45) might modify some of the conclusions of these groundbreaking historians, and the theology of the "victim soul" needs a much greater examination. For a good presentation of the broader context and meaning of "being a victim," see Joseph Kreuter, OSB, "Twenty-Five Years of Sponsa Regis (1928–1953)," *Sponsa Regis* 25 (October 1953): 29–33.

6. Studies which are very valuable in seeing the unifying elements but whose scope does not address the diversity of the spiritual currents are William M. Halsey, *The Survival of American Innocence: Catholicism in an Era of Disillusionment, 1920–1940* (Notre Dame, Ind.: University of Notre Dame Press, 1980); Philip Gleason, *Contending with Modernity: Catholic Higher Education in the Twentieth Century* (New York: Oxford University Press, 1995).

the traditional development in the community. The eras are worth comparing for some parallel trends. Yet the mid–twentieth century brought on a high level of organizational technique, mass communications through publications and the radio, and a stronger sense of a national church symbolized in the permanent structure of the National Catholic Welfare Conference. These new organs of community exchange and formation gave to the present era's prayer and practice a distinctive flavor and, in some measure, as a reaction, encouraged an even deeper thirst for interiorization: exteriority and interiority complemented each other within one Catholic "system of the sacred" (41, 46, 47, 48, 58, 61). The church as institution and the church as mystical body coexisted. This combination would grow to tensile breaking point in the post–World War II era.

2. A strong emphasis on professionalism and the development of a prayer and practice associated with a "state in life" (priest, religious, laity, healthy/ sick, rich/poor, married/single/religious) or gender (male/female) or occupation (teacher/worker/student) developed as the church emerged into prominence and took on the class and role visage of society at large (42, 43, 45, 46, 53, 56, 58, 59, 61). At the same time, the model of holiness associated with Catholic Action, emphasizing as it did the unity of the Mystical Body of Christ, the shared call to mission, the fundamental sacrament of baptism, and participation in the Eucharist, argued for an equalizing and leveling universality (46, 48, 54). Stratification and democratization went hand in hand. Devotionalism, by requiring the presence of the cleric and placing everyone along the same spectrum of intercession, also exemplified both the hierarchical and communal features of Catholic identity (45, 49, 57), as it had in an earlier era (16, 24).

3. This postwar period saw the growth of the catechetical, liturgical, and biblical movements on a large-scale basis in the community (43, 48, 51, 53, 54, 58, 60, 61). To some extent these represented a different type of prayer and practice than those associated with the highly devotional retreat movement (42) or the Eucharistic promotion of frequent Communion (50). Yet, at this time, in the parish, the school, and the national convention, the two views interacted and fed off of each other.

4. A significant trend in this period is its great idealism reflected both in a theology of the "victim soul" and in numerous recurring themes: (*a*) a preoccupation with the heroic sanctity of the martyr (made only more evident by the persecution of the church in Mexico); (*b*) the desire to make reparation for the sins of the world; (*c*) the need to bear suffering with patience, charity, and a sense of mission; and (*d*) the search for a "totalitarian Christianity" (44, 45, 59).

41. Postwar Social and Spiritual Reconstruction, 1919

American Catholics, one-sixth of the U.S. population, were estimated to have comprised about 35 percent of the army during World War I. The Knights of Columbus, a fraternal organization founded in 1882 and embodying the har-

mony between religious liberty and Catholicism, had joined with the National Catholic War Council to coordinate the church's relief efforts during the Great War. When the hostilities ceased, both groups embarked on a huge effort of demobilization and reconstruction, and numerous commentators spoke of a widespread religious revival taking place. The war and idealism of such leaders as Woodrow Wilson had aroused a sense of mission, organization, and commitment to the establishment of a new moral and spiritual order, a social gospel, which would inspire countless efforts during the 1920s and 1930s (cf. docs. 20, 24, 62, 87, 88, 90). In this Lenten pastoral letter, John Joseph Cantwell (1874–1947), an Irish-born immigrant, protégé of Archbishop Patrick Riordan (1841–1914) of San Francisco, and newly appointed bishop of Monterey–Los Angeles, summarizes much of the social and spiritual "call to arms" pervading the era.

To the Reverend Clergy, Diocesan and Regular; to the members of the Religious Communities, and to the well beloved faithful of the Laity committed to our care: HEALTH AND GREETING IN THE LORD.

DEARLY BELOVED BRETHREN: It is in accordance with venerable custom that Bishops, anxious to recall to the minds of the faithful of their diocese such truths as appear most fitting, address to them a pastoral at the approach of the Lenten season. This most excellent custom we may not despise. Rather should we place ourselves in harmony with it, especially at a time when we have many reasons to be grateful to God, and to bless His holy Name.

One year has passed — the first since our coming among you. With deepest gratitude we return thanks to Almighty God for a record of great spiritual and material progress made possible through the whole-souled support of a devoted clergy and a faithful laity....

The most titanic conflict the world has ever seen, the consuming flames of which swept from one nation to another, until all the world was afire, has at length come to a close. The fearful carnage is ended. Peace, so universally desired, so much besought of Heaven, is in sight. What a relief to know that those engines of war which for four unbroken years have brought death to millions of human beings, which have dealt destruction to thousands of peaceful cities, which have engulfed in irreparable ruin treasures of art and monuments of antiquity, which have laid waste the most fertile and beautiful provinces of Europe — what a relief to know that these fierce monsters of hell have ceased at length to roar and to "spit forth their iron indignation." The bloody mists of battle have disappeared. Once more the sun of peace has triumphantly burst forth over a sad and broken world.

God in His kindness has given us peace, and not peace alone, but, as our President has so well said, "the confident promise of a new day as well, in which justice shall replace force and jealous intrigue among the nations." A new day shines about us, in which our hearts take fresh courage, and in which we look forth with blessed hope to greater duties.

A social order different from the old shall rise from the ashes of this world conflagration. There is, on every side, talk of readjustment, economic, political, social, educational. Reconstruction has become the watchword of the world. It sums up the various problems with which nations and peoples shall have to grapple in every sphere of human activity. It tells of conditions that are no more, and suggests new and untried outlines of the social order. Never, we venture to say, have such tremendous responsibilities weighed upon a passing generation.

It is not a question of re-establishing a balance of power, which, though it might make war impossible in an exhausted world, would leave the nations conscripted to military service, and hearts aflame with suspicion, jealousy and hatred. The task now is to create, as it were, a Brotherhood of the World. The splendid lessons of duty, service, sacrifice, which peoples have learned through the long night of the direful struggle, must be conserved. Rich and poor, the weak and the strong, must understand that no man can reach his highest development so long as he lives to himself alone. Nations and individuals must hear the message that God is Love, that the supreme law of the world is Christ's new commandment that we should love one another even as also He loved us.

The Church was established by Jesus Christ that it might proclaim the message of Love, infinite and eternal, as the law of a life that alone is worth living. The Church, therefore, must take no mean part in solving the great problems confronting our country during the present era of social reconstruction. Every effort must be made to promote the well-being of the masses and to bring about a solution of rising questions in conformity with Christian principles.

The world has used many antidotes in an effort to counteract the poison that is eating into the very marrow of the social fabric. Materialism has had its day, and has passed without honor. The achievements of science have not developed a panacea for the ills that afflict the world. Cultured independence of thought and action have had their trial. They too, have been weighted and found wanting. Democracy is now in the pride of place. But, dearly beloved brethren, a mere change of government or of rulers will not transform the hearts of men, nor guarantee universal peace and prosperity.

New duties and responsibilities, therefore, rest heavily upon the spiritual leaders of our Catholic people. In the re-establishment of civic order and the arts of peace, in the restoration of a Christian temper and spirit, in the creation of wise reforms never more desirable or opportune, in the wise guidance of their own peoples through menacing storms, the leaders of Catholic thought and action will need our prayers, our confidence and, above all, our generous cooperation.

What part, then, are Catholics to take in this nation-wide task of reconstruction[?] What are our duties at the present hour[?] Verily, is our place with the workers who strive to rebuild the very framework of society[?] Verily, is our task to see to it that a newer and better world shall arise from the ruins of the old, that society shall be builded on Christian principles, and draw its vitality from the very life of Christ[?] Our ideas may not, indeed, always prevail; but fear of failing would not justify us in standing aside when our fellow citizens are unselfishly striving for the better things. In these anxious days when work is ready to our hands, it is not for us to stand idle in the market

place, and act recreant to our religion and to our country, by failing to give
our fellow citizens the best that is in us in the great work of reconstruction.

Our duty then it is, and glorious is the task, to bring the vision of the Bride
of Christ, the Catholic Church, that has come down to us from two thousand
years, before millions of our countrymen, countrymen who are asking for
light. "There is balm in Gilead, and the anointing there." Our duty it is to
show our fellow citizens that Catholicism is not uncivil, but eminently social
with a message unto every generation. We must throw all our energies into
the various social activities. The spiritual and moral resources of our Holy
Church, the mighty weight of her moral laws, definite and unchanging, her
indestructible and well tried principles, are at the command of the nation, and
to co-operate with church and country is the duty of every faithful Catholic.

Catholics, therefore, should not stand aloof from movements that aim at
the social betterment of the community of which they are a part; but, rather,
actively participate in public life. Isolation in matters that make for the common good would be most prejudicial to our people. We Catholics have, indeed,
a message to deliver, and never have we had more willing listeners than in this
hour of strain and suffering. To create and spread Christian opinion in social
matters, should be the aim of our activities. This is the greatest asset we can
contribute to the vast work of reconstruction. The scope of our Pastoral does
not permit us to dwell upon the manifold problems which reconstruction will
bring before the country. Our aim, now, is rather to awaken the sense of responsibility, stir up the sleeping conscience, and give to our Catholic men and
women the stimulating thought of co-operation.

We Americans seem at present to be at the height of our power and glory.
But there are, unfortunately, forces of dissolution at work within us. The
pauperization of labor is in evidence. Wealth has become vastly more concentrated and more selfish. An oligarchy of capital controlling the wheels of
industry, and almost beyond the power of law, would bargain with labor as
a commodity and treat as chattels free-born men. It would be far better that
the whole industrial system should be disrupted than that individuals should
be brutalized, and should perforce leave our factories and our yards with faces
haggard, and discontent and bitterness in their hearts. A time there was when
the cobbler who at his door, had joy in his heart and music on his lips.

No wonder then that ominous rumblings of discontent are heard amongst
our working classes, that there is an impassioned spirit of unrest everywhere,
an unrest that augurs no good. . . .

The Church of Christ has ever been, as the ages bear testimony, the best
and the most unselfish friend of the working man. It has ever been her endeavor and it is her purpose today, to do all that in her lies, to remove between
capital and labor all recrimination, hostility and misunderstanding. It is her
mission to inaugurate and perpetuate the exchange of mutual love, confidence
and good will. Christ must reign in the world, for from Him alone comes the
only life that is worth living. "Seek therefore the Kingdom of God and His
justice, and all things will be added thereto."

This is as it should be. Ever since her Divine Founder, the Redeemer of mankind, handled the tools of an artisan in the carpenter's shop at Nazareth, He has shed a halo around the brow of the workingman. Christ it was who lifted up the son of labor to equal dignity with other men by proclaiming the brotherhood of man with man, and the fatherhood of God over all men. Christ it was, and His Bride, the Church, who broke the manacles of servitude to which in days of paganism labor had been reduced. Christ it is, and His Church, who in all future times will teach and uphold the everlasting principles of justice and of charity, that alone can bring labor and capital together in love and harmony, and establish between them the relation of peace and amity.

As the Church has been the truest friend of the workingman, so she has been, in all ages, the most loyal friend and the loving protectress of God's poor. By principle and tradition, the Catholic Church is a living source and centre of charity. Her vital doctrines demand works of charity as the essential evidences of inward faith. Her most loyal and devoted children have ever consecrated their energy to works of charity. Her most glorious monuments, strewn along the rivers of time, and marking her passage through the nations, are the homes of charity. The Decrees of her Councils, the Letters of her Pontiffs, the lessons of her theological and ascetic writers, all urge and command charity....

It is encouraging and consoling to note the general forward trend in effective charity. It is very gratifying to see so many volunteer workers from all walks of life giving generously of their time and money to relieve distress and infirm conditions of the poor. It is inspiring to meet laymen and women whose hearts are full of tender sympathy for the afflicted, and whose souls are aflame with zeal for the salvation of others, who never turn away from the petition of the truly needy, who hating sin, are touched by the plea of the sinner, and are willing to give all their goods, if that were necessary to save a single soul.

There is no doubt that Christian Charity, in the fullest sense of the word, is exercised and carried on by the various charitable institutions of our Diocese in an eminent degree. All strive to do their very best, with their limited means, to alleviate the many forms of want and misery. Yet it is, likewise, true that not all our Catholic people are sufficiently interested in Charity work, that the many have forgotten the Scripture's admonition: "Give alms out of the substance and turn not away thy face from the poor." (Tobias iv, 7), and the prophet's exhortation: "Redeem thou thy sins with alms, and thy iniquities with works of mercy to the poor." (Daniel vi, 24). There is no doubt, moreover, that the full measure of charitable work accomplished under the guidance of the Church is not adequately appreciated or realized by the general community.

The precept of charity binds all men to give to those who are in need. We all are obliged to give alms to the poor if we would have a claim on God's love and His blessings. "He that hath the substance of the world, and shall see his brother in need, and shall shut up his bowels from him: how doth the charity of God abide in him[?]" (I John iii, 17). In the poor and sick, Christ appears personified. Their own merits or demerits are lost to view; their faces shine with the beauty of Christ; their words of gratitude are the words of Christ: "Amen I say unto you, as long as you did it to one of these my least brethren, you did it to me." (Matt. xxv, 40).

Charity to the poor is so precious, that, if Christian people fully realized it, they would give alms for the very joy of giving. We have the Scriptural warrant that it is a "more blessed thing to give than to receive." (Acts xx, 35). And if this precept were universally known and its moral binding force felt by all of the wealthy class, there would be no lack of funds to relieve the material wants of all the deserving who are in need.

The work of Catholic charity in any diocese takes the first place among our responsibilities. There should be, then, a fuller co-operation on the part of all, priests and lay people, a deeper interest, a warmer sympathy and a larger measure of generosity towards the poor and destitute. We bespeak, then, the generous assistance of all people for the different charitable institutions of the diocese. We make a plea for the destitute sick in our hospital, for the fatherless and the motherless, for the aged and the incurable. What we particularly desiderate is that our influential laymen and women who have been blessed by God with an abundance of worldly things, arouse themselves to a fuller sense of duty, and grasp the opportunities to improve and better the conditions of their less fortunate brethren. They should remember that not only in life should they be mindful of the poor, who are called God's poor, but when they come to dispose of their worldly possessions in their last will, they should be especially kind to those who are in need. This is the full expression of true charity, a charity that covers not only "a multitude of sins," (I Peter iv, 8) but solves a multiplicity of problems.

And now, Beloved Brethren, let us conclude with the sacred words of St. Paul to the Corinthians: "He that soweth sparingly, shall reap sparingly; and he who soweth in blessing, shall also reap in blessings. Everyone as he hath determined in his heart, not with sadness or of necessity; for God loveth a cheerful giver. And God is able to make all grace abound in you; that you always, having all sufficiency in all things, may abound in every good work.... The grace of our Lord Jesus Christ and the charity of God and the communication of the Holy Ghost be with you all, Amen." (II Cor. x, 6–9; xiii, 13).

John Joseph Cantwell
Bishop of Monterey and Los Angeles
9 March 1919

John Joseph Cantwell, *Pastoral to the Clergy and Laity of the Diocese of Monterey and Los Angeles,* 9 March 1919. Located in American Catholic Pamphlet Collection, Rare Books and Special Collections, The Catholic University of America, Washington, D.C.

42. The Spiritual Retreat for Women, 1922

One of the most significant organizations to emerge from World War I was the National Catholic Welfare Council, established in September 1919. Its Department of Lay Activities was, in turn, organized into the National Council of Catholic Women and the National Council of Catholic Men. The women's branch became very active in social reform, and in the following selection, titled "The Soul's Vacation," its president, Gertrude Hill Gavin, shows an awareness of both the developing middle class and the changing social profile of the Catholic woman, two major forces shaping twentieth-century prayer and practice (see docs. 63, 64, 76, 77, 87). Gavin's plea builds on the foundations established in the nineteenth century (see doc. 11) and argues for the need to practice the disciplines of retreat and solitude in order to maintain a spiritual center. The document reveals the postwar cultural roots of two of the largest and most influential spiritual reform movements of the mid–twentieth century, the National Laymen's Retreat League (1926) and the National Laywomen's Retreat Movement (first conference sponsored in 1936). The two branches would eventually form Retreats International in the wake of the Second Vatican Council (see doc. 89).

What will the American woman of today do with the privileges and freedom which have become hers? Will these new possessions develop a finer type of womanhood or will the newly acquired power make woman forgetful of her real mission here on earth? If we are to face these questions fairly and answer them truthfully, we must admit that the conditions in America today threaten to break down the ideals and standards upon which true motherhood is based. The sons and daughters of tomorrow can only be as fine as the women of today. Only when we think in terms of posterity, do we as Catholic women accept the grave responsibility which is ours.

With each succeeding year, life becomes more complex and more hurried, allowing less time for reading, thinking, and meditation. We may argue that women are doing more today than ever before and are giving more careful thought to the real things of life. The educated woman is well read in the classics; she is not considered well informed unless she has read the current issues of at least a dozen accepted periodicals; she must not only read her own town paper, but should be familiar with the columns of the New York and Washington press. She must keep up with the interests of her husband, guard the welfare of her children and direct her home.

Seeking Peace for the Soul

True, the modern woman is doing more and is crowding her life with many things, but how much closer is she coming to those things which really count? How much time is given to the question of questions — "God and my soul?" Who but our Blessed Lord Himself can answer this question? The woman of today is going through a period of readjustment which at times strains her patience to the very limit. Her soul is tired and troubled. Where can she find peace and calm and contentment? Where indeed but in Him to whom the secrets of the soul are revealed. The heart which longing for Him with insatiable longing has sought to satisfy its hunger with material things and worldly joys. But how shall His voice be heard amid the clamor of the world? Since He led His Apostles "apart and explained all things to them" so too must she who today would hear that voice, go apart from the world and, in solitude, commune with Him. In that solitude she will learn to know God, and through this knowledge will come a greater love. In the light of this love no service He asks will seem too great.

At no time has it been more necessary that an opportunity for such retirement be offered to Catholic women. In different parts of the country, retreat houses have been established, but as yet there are too few. It is most fitting that Washington, the nation's capital, should be among the cities which offer such a wonderful source of spiritual recuperation.

The Mount Carmel Retreat House at 200 T Street is one of the picturesque spots in Washington. Twenty minutes on the electric car brings us to the lovely old estate formerly known as Eckington Manor. The house which was designed for Mr. Joseph Gales, editor of the "National Intelligence," by the eminent artist, Charles King, retains all the atmosphere which marked it in the days when social, political and literary gatherings were held in the spacious rooms. The wide portico welcomes the guest to the hospitality of a southern home which was enjoyed by Lafayette, Calhoun, Clay, Webster, the Lees and many other famous figures of history. The light, airy rooms look out on ten acres of ground with glorious almond trees, blossoming bushes, and old-fashioned gardens.

"The Soul's Vacation" is the manner in which Father George T. Schmidt describes a spiritual retreat. It would be impossible to find a more ideal setting for bringing souls closer to God than that chosen by the Discalced Carmelite Fathers. In his address delivered at the opening of the house, Rt. Rev. Thomas J. Shahan, rector of the Catholic University, said:

Bishop Shahan's Comment

"Let us hope that we shall see, from this time forward, a continual stream of souls seeking this place that they may know God's will and gain the power to do it." The philosophy of the last century, Bishop Shahan explained, was the philosophy of materialism. It was cold, heartless and cruel. It has pervaded the whole world, but is evidenced especially in this country where it is reflected in a spirit of vulgarity and leisure. "Thank God," said the Bishop, "there are springing up places such as these in our country where women can retire for a while and reflect on the fact that life can be made to count for more than the falling of a leaf or the dropping of a bud."

Not only does the Retreat House offer the privilege of the spiritual exercises of the retreat, but visitors to Washington, who bring letters of recommendation from their pastors, may find accommodations there for any length of time. This is another addition to the many attractions of a visit to the nation's capital. Many women traveling through the country will undoubtedly be glad of the opportunity of stopping at this lovely old spot and there, in the silence, let the soul find its vacation.

The peace and joy which will come from this visit with God will enable them to go back to their daily tasks with renewed strength and vigor. And just as our Blessed Lord stilled the tempest, so in the quiet of the retreat house will He send to the soul that peace which the world cannot give.

> Gertrude Hill Gavin, " 'The Soul's Vacation': What the Spiritual Retreat Movement Means to Our Catholic Women," *National Catholic Welfare Council Bulletin* (June 1922): 20–21.

43. The Apostolate of the Choir Singer, 1923

Reform in the liturgy in the United States came from several directions. One of them was the St. Cecilia Society, of Germanic origin but founded in the United States by John Singenberger. The society's intention was to reform liturgical music, return to a Renaissance style, and encourage the singing of Plain Chant. The reform contrasted with the operatic music in Sunday liturgies in large cities (cf. docs. 23, 24). The journal of the society, Caecilia, edited by Singenberger for many years from its inception in 1874, worked from the principle that the dissemination of appropriate church music was a primary agent in the reform of the current practice. Each issue included a piece of original music. The journal continued into the 1950s, and the following selection, titled "The Choir Singer: An Apostle," shows how it attempted to develop a spirituality for the choir member's public deportment, role in forming community, and participation in the liturgy.

As the example which the conscientious Catholic church singer gives is capable of effecting much good in his practical, everyday life, thus also that which he gives in the church itself. One thing cannot be denied: the singer more easily falls into the danger of failing in due reverence in church than the other attendants at Divine Service. These enter the house of God, go quietly to their respective places, and thus they can occupy themselves with their God with calmness and devotion, without being solicitous for anything else. The liturgical functions at the altar, the chants, the devout deportment of the others, everything stimulates their devotion. Besides, they kneel in the nave of the church and are observed by many, a circumstance which for a conscientious Christian is of itself conducive towards forcing him to give a good example, primarily to avoid giving disedification to his neighbor. The singer, on the contrary, is not observed by anyone; this exterior element of reciprocal edification falls away from him entirely. It sometimes happens that at the performances it becomes necessary to speak a few words, and to this comes the rather unholy question if "all's well"; and if the singers are not on their guard, there is a constant danger of becoming careless for all those who are daily employed in the service of the church. These dangers are known to every singer; he should, therefore, be possessed of a high degree of self-control, and endeavor on account of, and in spite of these dangers to conduct himself in the organ loft as though, to use the words of the Apostle, he were "a spectacle to angels and men." At all events he stands in the august presence of his Redeemer and his God, and celebrates the holy mysteries with the Saviour through His representative — he is numbered, as it were, among the disciples who were so near the Master at the Last Supper, and "sang a hymn" with Him!

As the director in his deportment in the choir ought to be a model and example for the choir members, the singers should likewise edify one another; and this is indeed apostolic labor. When the Mass has commenced every singer must know exactly what is required of him during the entire service, be it that these communications were previously made at the rehearsal, or that they are written upon a blackboard for all to see. The singer must always "be ready" so that the director will not be obliged to wait. During the pauses which usually occur in a high Mass, no one is allowed to speak or to leave his place to find a convenient corner in which to rest. The singers might use these pauses for their own private devotions. The rosary does excellent service and ought to be in the hands of every singer. The translation of the Missal is likewise a good companion; when there is nothing to be sung, he could read the translation of the next chant.

One of the most beautiful means of doing apostolic work by way of giving good example is the general holy Communion of the choir members. I have in mind the choir of a church in one of our metropolitan cities, which, apart from the Easter duty, approaches the holy Table in a body at two other times in the year. The Pastor upon these occasions, reads the early Mass for the singers, the altar is adorned more elaborately than usual, and, whereas on other Sundays simple folk-songs are rendered, the choir sings Latin motets until the Elevation, and then the members approach the Communion table in closed ranks before the other communicants. The unusual solemnity of the Mass, the execution of figured music, the closed ranks of the singers, all of this makes a deep impression upon the congregation; it shows the meaning and importance of the choir in its true light, and this beautiful example often induces many another member of the congregation who has been remiss in his duties to approach the Holy Table once more. It is really remarkable that there are so many church choirs that have not yet adopted the beautiful custom of a general holy Communion. Although each individual singer receives holy Communion at various times in the year, and this they probably all do, the *feast* of the general Communion is a new, firm and spiritual bond which unites the members more closely and gives their work a higher degree of sanctity. If the various societies in a congregation receive holy Communion in a body so many times in the year, why should not the choir, which stands in a closer relation to the church and the liturgical functions than any other religious association? This beautiful custom is conducive towards preserving the distinctively ecclesiastical character of the choir, it strengthens peace and harmony among the members, and makes them capable of fulfilling their office in the manner so beautifully described by Amberger: "Whoever glorifies the sublime mysteries of the church with song does not perform a human office; he should, therefore, endeavor to imitate the celestial strains with which the angels and saints celebrate the mysteries of the heavenly Jerusalem." If all the members of a church choir do this, will they not be doing apostolic work in the congregation in which they exercise the sublime office of the angels and saints?

Another means of doing apostolic work is fidelity to duty. At the present time nearly all of our choirs but with few exceptions are "volunteer" choirs, that is, they are not paid, but they sing solely for the honor of God. Most of the members of these choirs are men who work all day, and in the evening, after the labors and fatigues of the day, bring the sacrifice of attending the rehearsal; and besides, all this in a choir where people criticize very severely, while excellent performances are taken as a matter of fact. This spirit of generosity displayed by so many singers should of itself make an impression upon every thoughtful member of the congregation and cause him to consider that every human being is required to do his share towards promoting the greater honor and glory of God.

When a singer has become possessed of this spirit of sacrifice, great conscientiousness and regularity in attending the rehearsals and Divine Service, he will gradually become conscious of the fact that, having been blessed with a good voice, a gift of God, while discharging the duties of his office, he is filling obligations of the most sacred character; and this will likewise exert a beneficial influence upon all those in the congregation who have a little understanding of self-sacrifice, conscientious discharge of duty, and fidelity in the service of God.

The greatest spiritual advantages, however, accrue to the singer himself through the blessed hope that God does not allow the least thing to pass unrewarded that is done in His service with a good intention.

> R. B., "The Choir Singer: An Apostle," *Caecilia: Monatsschrift für Katholische Kirchenmusic* 50, no. 10 (October 1923): 37–38.

44. The Example of the Saints, 1925

In the midst of the postwar revival, American Catholics sought to relate their idealism to the men and women who had gone before them and who had been publicly recognized by the church as exemplars of holiness. In an era when the church was to find itself persecuted in Russia and Mexico, heroic sanctity would become the model of the Christian life. The beatification of the Jesuit martyrs (21 June 1925) symbolized the recognition in the universal church of the spiritual "coming of age" of the church in the United States. In the same year John Gilmary's Shea's 1884 Little Pictorial Lives of the Saints *was reprinted; the work, excerpted below, included the newly declared models of sanctity who had formed the church in the United States. Blessed Isaac Jogues and companions were canonized in 1930; the serious promotion of the cause of Kateri Tekawitha (beatified 1980) and also the Franciscan martyrs of North America began, and the apostolic delegate Ameleto Cicognani published his work* Sanctity in America *in 1939. The promotion of the models of the immigrant church developed in subsequent decades: Frances Xavier Cabrini (beatified 1938, canonized 1946, see doc. 56), Rose Philippine Duchesne (beatified 1940, canonized 1988), Elizabeth Seton (beatified 1963, canonized 1975), John Neumann (beatified 1963, canonized 1977, see doc. 13), and Katharine Drexel (beatified 1988, canonized 2000, see doc. 31).*

The beatification ceremonies of June 21, 1925, by Pope Pius XI established the first calendar of martyrs for North America, for the following holy Jesuit missionaries have received the title "Blessed:" Isaac Jogues, John de Brebeuf, Noel Chabanel, Anthony Daniel, Charles Garnier, Gabriel Lalemant, priests; and Rene Goupil and John Lalande.

Blessed Issac Jogues was born at Orleans, France, January 19, 1607. After entering the Society of Jesus, he was appointed professor of literature at Rouen, and later was sent as a missioner to "New France," now Canada. His zeal for converting the Indians led him amid continual hardships to penetrate as far as Sault Ste. Marie. As they were extremely superstitious and attributed the blighting of the crops or the advent of sickness to the presence of the missionaries, the latter were in constant danger of death. One time he and some companions were captured near Three Rivers, New York. Blessed Goupil was slain, and the others after severe tortures were condemned to death. But while preparations for their slaughter were in progress, they escaped, and Jogues returned to France. Though several of his fingers were mutilated, the Pope gave him permission to say Mass. In a few months, he returned to Canada and as a delegate arranged peace with the Indians. On his subsequent arrival among them, however, the crops were bad and the blame was put upon him. They stripped and slashed and finally tomahawked him, October 18, 1646, at the town of Auriesville, New York, now a popular place of pilgrimage. Shortly after his death 3,000 Huron Indians were converted, much to the distress of the Iroquois. The latter therefore seized his remaining companions and, after torturing them with arrows, boiling water and hot irons, put them to death.

Reflection — Some are especially called to work for souls; but there is no one who cannot help much in their salvation by holy example, earnest intercession and the offering of actions in their behalf.

John Gilmary Shea, *Little Pictorial Lives of the Saints* (New York: Benziger Brothers, 1925), 635.

45. The Meaning of Suffering, 1927

Within the context of a growing awareness of sickness and disease, the persecution of the church in Mexico, and the economic depression following the 1929 crash, the interpretation of suffering, the focus on martyrdom, and the action of becoming a "victim soul" became consistent themes in the spirituality of the Catholic community during the late 1920s, 1930s, and 1940s. In an age of increasing organization and ecclesiastical bureaucratization, the individual believer also became concerned about the meaning of his or her role and significance in the spiritual economy of the church. Clara Tiry (1894–1972), as an asthmatic, thought she was unable to be active in local parish activities. She was often homebound. Inspired, as were many during this period, by the recently canonized Thérèse of Lisieux (1873–97), Clara inaugurated an extensive apostolate which joined prayers and sufferings to the needs of the global church. In 1927 she compiled Comfort for the Sick, and the fruitfulness of her apostolate manifested itself in her extensive correspondence, especially with priests around the world, and the newsletter she edited. In addition to prayers related to health, sickness, and suffering, her prayer manual discussed such topics as the gifts of God, trials and gifts of the sickroom, devotions, the example of the saints, and the sacraments. The following selection from one of her writings presupposes a notion of church as a communion of people whose suffering love influences one another (see docs. 4, 19, 34, 46, 75, 88). By uniting the isolated person with others in similar situations, membership in the association provided personal dignity and companionship.

How the Sick Can Be Apostles!

Dear Sufferer:

In your hours of solitude, loneliness and inactivity you no doubt have often thought how gladly you would leave your bed to go forth into the world like the Apostles and strive through patient labor to win souls for the Sacred Heart if only health would be given to you. Being confined to the bed or room you have felt yourself useless, perhaps considered yourself a burden to those around you.

You too, dear friend and sufferer, can be an Apostle, you can help Jesus to save and sanctify souls. St. Therese, the Little Flower of Jesus, says that more souls are saved by suffering than by preaching. Therefore, you need not leave country or home, nay, not even your room or bed to accomplish this great work.

How can you be an Apostle? By the patient bearing and offering of all pain and suffering in union with the bitter sufferings which Jesus endured for our redemption. The hours of pain and suffering are hours of grace, filled with precious coin that can purchase for yourself and other souls a high degree of happiness for all eternity.

The saying, "In union there is strength" can be applied to prayer and also to suffering. Therefore, in order that your sufferings may be of greater efficacy by being united to those of others, you are invited to join the noble band of sufferers of the Apostolate of Suffering. The knowledge that you are not alone in your misery, that thousands of others are walking along the same thorny path, will be an incentive to you to follow more bravely in the footprints of the Suffering Savior.

The Apostolate of Suffering

Object. The object of the Apostolate is to unite all the sick, infirm, crippled and defective — priests, religious and lay people — into one large family, where the example of one will encourage the other; that by their combined sufferings offered for the intentions of the Apostolate they may help to spread the kingdom of Christ here on earth.

Aim. The Apostolate aims to bring spiritual sunshine into the lives of its members; to instill into their hearts a love for suffering and a filial resignation to God's Holy Will. Through the "Our Good Samaritan" sent to them four times during the year they are kept in touch with the progress of the Apostolate, and are given such spiritual reading and prayers that will promote their spiritual welfare.

Dues. Membership dues are only 25 cents a year or $1.00 for four years. Each member receives a certificate containing the daily offering.

Spiritual Benefits. Thirty Holy Masses are offered for the members each month. Also a Holy Mass on sixteen special feasts during the year. Send in your name and dues for membership, and thus participate in the spiritual benefits and the prayers of all the members.

The Apostolate of Suffering

National Office: 1551 North 34th St., Milwaukee, Wis.

Miss Clara M. Tiry, Secy.

Very Rev. Dr. A. J. Muench, Spiritual Director

Enclosed find _____ for _____ year; _____ 4 years.

Very sincerely, yours, Name _____

Street _____ City and State _____

Clara Tiry Papers, Apostolate of Suffering Collection, Archives, Archdiocese of Milwaukee. Permission granted through the courtesy of the Apostolate of Suffering, 7452 Harwood Ave., Wauwatosa, WI 53213.

46. A Geography of Prayer, 1927

In many congregations of women religious, when the sisters were sent to teach or nurse, they were "on mission" from the motherhouse, even if their assignments were just a few blocks away. Those at the motherhouse or "headquarters" who provided food, housekeeping, and other services, however, did not have a sense that they were in mission. At the same time, the 1917 codification of Canon Law tightened up the structures of religious life and made them more regularized and centralized. During the mid-1920s, as congregations were rewriting their community constitutions to fit that pattern, one congregation developed an imaginative response which gave all of the sisters a sense of universal mission in which even daily mundane actions received global spiritual significance. The following "geography of prayer" is taken from the Directory of the Sisters of St. Francis of Assisi in Milwaukee. *Two years after "Missionaries, Sisters All!" (the document presented below) was published, the congregation had its first mission overseas, in Shandong Province, China (cf. docs. 63, 75, 93).*

Missionaries, Sisters All! — Out for a Rich and Golden Harvest. We all want to do great things for the good God; that is why we came to the Convent, that we might have more chances and greater chances of doing much for Him and souls. But, it is often said that community life offers so few chances of doing anything worthwhile for God, — there is nothing more than a monotonous round of little, often irksome duties, day in and day out, duties that distract rather than lead us nearer to Him.

It is for us to make them worthwhile! It is for us to use them to bring us close to Him, into His very Heart.

His call for missionaries today is as strong as in the days of the Apostles, — there is Africa with its millions, and China and India and the Islands with many, many millions more! And we here, in our little kitchen, or classroom, or sewing room. Let us convert each into a small mission field. It requires only the touch of the magic wand, the spirit of Faith.

Let the kitchen, for instance, be some poor little village in China, with souls, big souls and little souls, young and old, waiting for spiritual alms. Every step in the kitchen, every pot and pan and kettle washed, every egg beaten, every broom handled, — every single hand's turn, can be united to the works of the Infant Savior which He performed at Nazareth helping His Mother. These are our alms saving heathen souls. Our Fairy Godmother is the Blessed Virgin; lay these poor little gifts at her feet, with the plea, "Mother, they are for Jesus and Souls, make them beautiful." And she will add the brilliant white luster of her own pure soul, her own merits to our poor works, and presto, — we have done something great for souls.

The following may look like strange geography, but if Faith can move mountains, surely it can do something so simple as moving China into our kitchen, Africa into our classrooms, or Japan into our laundry. But above all, with the Grace of God, we hope it will enable us to make everyday, commonplace duties golden opportunities of showing ourselves zealous, Franciscan missionaries according to the heart of our Holy Father St. Francis.

MISSION FIELDS

Chapel	Indian and Negro Missions in U.S.
Kitchen	China
Refectory	India
Bakery	Philippine Islands
Laundry	Japan
Cellar	Fiji Islands
Coolers	Iceland
Vegetable Garden	Arabia
Community Room	Siberia
Dormitory	Russia
Classroom	Africa
Study Room	Alaska
Music Room	South Sea Islands
Library	Turkey
Printing Shop	Korea
Studio	Peking, China
Reception Rooms	Island of Molokai, Home of the Lepers
Tailor Shop	South America
Infirmaries	Wuchang, China (Our own mission to be)
Mending Room	New Guinea
Embroidery Room	Armenia
Shoe Shop	Liberia, Africa
Lavatories	East and West Indies
Attic	Labrador
Greenhouse	Greenland
Garden	Hawaiian Islands
Bee Hives	Borneo
Chicken House	New Zealand
Barn	Brazil

The corridors that lead to the different parts of the house, and the walks from the building to another building, may be the mountain passes, roads, and stormy seas often filled with great danger for the missionary.

And the missionaries' helpers? One day join your works with the merits of the Blessed Mother, another day with our Holy Father St. Francis or with your own Patron and Guardian Angel, and still other days with great missionaries like St. Francis Xavier, St. Patrick, St. Boniface, St. Peter Claver, St. Francis Solanus, or St. Theresa of Jesus, the Little Flower, or St. Madeline Sophie Barat. But everyday and in every way work for the missions!

"Missionaries, Sisters All!" in *1927 Directory,* pp. 26–29. Courtesy of the New Assisi Archives, Sisters of St. Francis of Assisi, Milwaukee.

47. A View from the Outside, 1928

Throughout the history of the Catholic community in the United States, its prayer and practice have been perceived in various ways by other citizens of the country (see docs. 23, 52, 73). In the middle decades of the twentieth century, the institutional and numerical growth of the church, the leadership style of numerous consolidating bishops, the regularization encouraged by the adoption of the Code of Canon Law, *the intellectual reaction to the modernist crisis at the turn of the century, and the inherited tradition of anti-Catholicism combined to fashion a popular and very negative image of the church as an inherently authoritarian, antidemocratic, and nonevangelical presence in society. As can be seen in the following passage, this fairly common critique, which culminated in Paul Blanshard's (1892–1980)* American Freedom and Catholic Power *(1949), drew a clear relationship between Americanism, gospel principles, and democracy. A similar type of reaction to "institutional worldliness" would emerge from within the community in some Catholic spiritual writers of the 1930s (see doc. 59).*

How glorious might the Church have been had her popes and bishops resisted lust for power and wealth! Never was the Church so magnificent as in the first three centuries of existence. Then her members were held together, not by the fear of papal authority, but by the sacred bond of brotherly love. In that long period the bishop of Rome and his fellow bishops were Christlike in the simplicity of their lives. Money to them meant little else than means to help the poor. Bishops, in those days, were good shepherds of their flock. They were, it seems, gentle, unassuming men who strove only to imitate the meek Redeemer. But with power came arrogance and with arrogance came dogmatism. Thus the system grew.

Modern popes, who have been great and good men, are the victims of this system. They have been, for the most part, men of God, filled with zeal for the cause of Christ. It would not be easy for one of them to introduce any great change in the policy of the Church. For this a modern Hillenbrand would be required, a man with a world vision of love and brotherhood, a man who could cast off the shackles of traditionalism and cry out, "Back to the simplicity of the Gospel!" Then Christlike life would be the concern of the Church, human life, the more abundant life. To achieve this the Church must needs adopt the words of Christ for her motto: "The truth shall make you free...."

In this great movement, the whole organization of the Church must change in spirit. The old idea of obedience must pass, together with their idea of authority. Obedience must come to mean love and reverence, not fear, for superiors. Authority, on the other hand, must come to mean the benign influence of love and service....

This is the spirit which animated the Apostles, the first bishops of the Church. How different is the spirit of later-day bishops, especially those in America! In no other country of the world, perhaps, has the hierarchy preserved the spirit and the methods of feudalism as have the bishops of the United States. It was a dark day for the church when her bishops became feudal lords....

A Catholic bishop is still given his title, Your Lordship. At ordination the newly made priest kneels, as he once knelt before his feudal lord, his two hands held between the hands of the bishop. Then the bishop says: "Dost thou promise me and my successors reverence and obedience?" The answer follows: "I promise." In these later days the oath against modernism is generally demanded after ordination just as it is required of seminary and university professors at the beginning of each academic year.

The newly ordained priest has now bound himself to reverence and obey his bishop. Little does he dream of the future humiliations this step may entail. "Of all the tyrannies the worst is that which can thus (as in feudalism) keep account of its subjects, and which sees, from its seat, the limits of its empire. The caprices of the human will then show themselves in all their intolerable extravagance and, moreover, with irresistible promptness." (*History of France,* vol. I, p. 232) The bishop feels that he is responsible to God for the lives of the priests who have promised to reverence and obey him. Not satisfied with the reverence and obedience shown by devoted children to their parents, he demands those external signs of fealty and honor which the feudal lord required of his serfs.

When the priest, or any of the faithful, greets His Lordship, he must kneel before him and kiss the episcopal ring upon his hand. For this act of submission he is granted, each time, an indulgence of fifty days. A certain American bishop of the Middle West is very insistent upon this point of ecclesiastical etiquette. One day a young priest came suddenly upon the bishop, and in his excitement forgot his manners and simply said: "Good morning, Bishop." His Lordship flew into a pious rage and shouted: "Is that the way to greet your bishop? Get down on your knees and kiss your bishop's hand and learn to show due reverence for your superior!" It must not be supposed, however, that this bishop, who is so zealous for his own honor, is necessarily oblivious of his duty toward God. It is entirely possible that he went to his chapel afterward and thanked God for having permitted him to teach this obstinate priest a sound lesson. Maybe he prayed for the soul of the erring one. For, indeed, the bishop feels that he must at least help to bear the burden of all the priestly consciences in his diocese.

...On occasion, too, the bishop helps the priests to keep his conscience. When the episcopal visitation takes place, the priest is given a blank form to fill out. Here he must state whether he said his daily prayers, made his meditation, [went] to confession regularly, and the like. He is required to answer many other questions which touch the intimacy of his own private life. If he thus confesses, in writing, he is liable to ecclesiastical censure. It must be said, in justice, that many bishops do not observe this ordinance.

...But it was not always thus. In the early Church, before the monarchical episcopate came into being, Christ's ministers still retained His meek and humble spirit. Like their divine Master, they considered themselves servants of the people. "He that is the leader, [let him become] as he that serveth. I am in the midst of you, as he that serveth."

...Christians made by law or authority have never brought much honor to the name of Christ. It is notable, too, that the Church's power passes, largely, with the passing of those tyrannous rulers who lent their powerful arm to the propagation of her dogmas. Wherever democracy has prevailed there has ever been a marked weakening of Catholic ecclesiastical power. With liberty and enlightenment heresy and unbelief run apace. This is not unnatural, since the Church has so often been identified with the absolutism which oppressed the human race for centuries. Besides, it is this absolutism which is still practised in the Catholic hierarchy. In its religious code there is no more freedom of thought, nor more personal liberty, than there was in feudalism. There is no more kinship of spirit between an ecclesiastical potentate today and his followers than there was between a feudal lord and his serfs. Fear, physical fear, bound the serf to his lord. Fear, moral and religious fear, prompts the Catholic to kiss the foot or the hand of his ecclesiastical ruler.

...If Christ had intended to establish a Church fashioned after the kingdom of the Caesars, He would certainly have called Herod or Pilate, not the poor fisherman Peter to be its first head. If He had intended to found a school of theological science, He would have called some of the Greek or Roman philosophers, whose teachings have since been adopted, to watch over its early destinies. But Christ said: "Suffer the little children and forbid them not to come to me, for the kingdom of heaven is for such." His only thought was to unite humanity in one great brotherhood of love. He wished only to destroy the spirit of arrogance and despotism which prevailed and to lead men to love one another....

"The Incubus of the Temporal Power: The Catholic Church and the Modern Mind," *Atlantic Monthly* 141 (April 1928): 542–44, 547, 548.

48. The Popularity of the Liturgical Movement, 1928

The Benedictine Virgil Michel (1890–1938) founded the magazine Orate Fratres *(later, as of December 1951,* Worship*) in 1926, a date usually taken as marking the institutional beginnings of the liturgical movement in the United States. Many other people, working in different parts of the country, were also involved, most prominently Mother Georgia Stevens (1871–1946), who had*

*already pioneered work in liturgical music at the College of the Sacred Heart,
Manhattanville, New York City; Martin Hellriegel (1891–1981), the chaplain of
the Sisters of the Most Precious Blood, O'Fallon, Missouri; Gerald Ellard (1894–
1963), Jesuit educator and influential promoter of the movement; William Busch
(1882–1971), professor of church history at St. Paul Seminary, Minneapolis; and
the women leaders of the Grail Movement, who gathered for retreat during
Holy Week, 1941. A little-studied aspect of these better-known developments
is the popularization of the liturgical movement through the school system (see
doc. 51) and its convergence with the youth sodality organization headed by
the Jesuit Father Daniel Lord (1888–1955; see doc. 74). In the spring of 1927,
in Chicago, ninety-seven delegates representing twenty-two local Catholic high
schools met in the first student-sodalist convention held in the United States.
A series of leadership schools began in the fall of 1927, and the following August, 1,310 delegates (66 priests, 7 brothers, 221 sisters, 760 girls, and 256 boys)
gathered in St. Louis for the first Students Spiritual Leadership Convention. In the
following letter the Jesuit Father William Puetter of St. Louis describes the great
impact of the Missa Recitata, a dialogic celebration which was a significant departure from the dominant practice of simply "hearing" the Mass on the part of
the laity (see doc. 23).*

St. Louis University
St. Louis, Mo.
St. Januarius
September 19, 1928

Rev. Dom. Virgil, OSB
The Orate Fratres Press
Collegeville, Minn.

Reverend dear Father, Pax Christi!

I do not know how to apologize for this delay. I had intended to send you
the news of our convention as soon as things happened. But the truth is that
things did happen so fast in those days that I had no time for extra work
whatever.

However I shall try to give you all the details now. On Friday, Aug. 17th,
at nine o'clock amid the ringing of the bells of St. Francis Xavier's and a
tremendous thunder storm the Solemn High Mass began. There were over a
thousand delegates in the church, boys and girls, and Sisters and many priests,
from Los Angeles, from New York City, from New Orleans, from St. Paul,
from Rhode Island, and Oregon, and California and Washington, and from
Florida and Texas, West Virginia, from New Jersey and Wisconsin and Minnesota they were assembled there to ask God's blessing on the work they
came to do. As Fr. [Daniel] Lord said in his sermon during this Mass: "We
came to pray, we came to work, we came to plan for God." With that the
Convention had the note which was to mark [it] through the three days. The
delegates were undoubtedly the best of our youth in this country: their conduct, their speeches, their piety, their frequent Holy Communions, the piety
boys showed while serving some of the 87 early Masses for the visiting priest

delegates was all indeed a source of inspiration to us who were here at the University to work and prepare for the Convention.

The Solemn Mass from a liturgical point of view was what I desired and really hoped it would be. Everything we did in the sanctuary, or on the stage in the auditorium, in the dining hall, in the exhibit room, all was to be a model and example to the visitors so that they could return to their own cities and schools with correct ideas and high ideals. The Solemn Mass was such: correct, devotional, and perfect in all the details of the ceremonies of the celebrant, deacon and subdeacon, and acolytes and thurifer. Our acolytes were from Kansas City, from New Orleans and from Chicago. The celebrant was from Saint Louis, the deacon from Kansas City, and the subdeacon from New York. St. Anthony's Choristers from this city sang the Mass: Gregorian Mass.

On Saturday we had our first *Missa Recitata*. A small pamphlet had been prepared for the Convention only. We had no rehearsal or practice before, however, Fr. Lord told the Conventionists what was to be done at Mass the next day, briefly and clearly he told them that they were expected to use the pamphlet, follow the leader, and pronounce the words clearly and pause at the asterisks. And finally he insisted on the idea: we will celebrate the Sacrifice together with the priest. Fr. Keith offered the Mass, two New Orleans boys served, and with the leader in the pulpit the Mass began. (I enclose a copy, reluctantly, because the *Imprimatur* was not printed on this copy by mistake of the printer.) Seventy priests were in the sanctuary, using the pamphlet and following the Mass, and the congregation responded splendidly. I cannot say much about myself, because the view and impression one gets from the outside is better. I was on the inside of the experiment. But the comment made by others was universally favorable. Priests, Sisters, and delegates all expressed their enthusiasm. In the speeches and talks during that day, since that was Liturgical Day, frequent reference was made to the *Missa Recitata*. Thus far we have received requests for about 6000 copies of *Missa Recitata*. The pamphlet is now being revised. In fact I sent the revised manuscript to Fr. Hellriegel last evening for his suggestions.

Saturday was Liturgical Day and Blessed Sacrament Day. Problems were discussed there that would naturally bring in much on the Liturgy. One sad need I realize, is a good English book on Liturgy in the form of a Catechism, I believe. And then something that will bring out the idea that Holy Communion is part of our grand Sacrifice of the Mass and not a private devotion. However, we shall get there sooner or later. From the thoughts that were uttered on the Convention floor one could see how ripe the field is and receptive the soil for intimate participation in the Sacred Mysteries and the Prayers of the Holy Church of God. This day was a splendid preparation for the Communion Mass on Sunday morning.

Sunday morning at 8 we had *Missa Recitata* again. This time Fr. Hellriegel celebrated, assisted by his acolytes from O'Fallon. He wore his green bell vestment and you may be sure the impression was even better than that at the Solemn Mass and on the previous day. Most of the delegates received Holy Communion at this Mass: about 1000 of them. On the preceding day the Mass took 33 minutes, on this day with five priests distributing Holy Communion, it took 47 minutes. That was a surprise to me; I thought that the Mass without Communion would take 60 minutes at least.

In the afternoon at 4:30 the church bells again rang: this time to call the Convention to a close with Solemn Benediction of the Blessed Sacrament. The congregation sang. Under Fr. Lord's personal direction you may be sure that they sang well. It is not often that our church hears such a magnificent hymn of praise and thanksgiving.

This is in brief an account of our convention activities. I do not exaggerate when I say that judging from the things others are saying and have been saying to us, we can say that we thank God for the blessing he has given to our poor endeavors to bring this Convention to do great good in souls of our American youth. We thank God for it all. And personally I am convinced now that the *Missa Recitata* is the ideal and only method for our students. They like it; they love the Mass for it; and they appreciate more and more what the Mass is for them. I am now working on a Prayer Book for High School students which will be in press by the end of the month. I am sure that this book would have been out three years ago if I could have found a way of satisfying me about the *Missa Recitata*.

The revised edition of *Missa Recitata* is changed very much. There I follow the division of the Mass as it is in Eucharistia, and in *Die Betende Kirche*, that is, more or less. I synopsize the Canon in a different way, and I have added the Te Deum to the thanksgiving.

You may use this account as you like, but do not use it as it is now. Use the facts and the thoughts only, not this letter as it is. Please do not pass the *Missa Recitata* on to others out of your community. I shall send you copies of the new book as soon as it is off the press. I mention your work at Holy Mass every day. May God bless you and your noble work.

Sincerely yours in Christ,
William Puetter, S.J.

"Gerald Ellard," Z-24, in Virgil Michel Papers, no. 48. Courtesy of St. John's Abbey Archives, Collegeville, Minn. Printed with permission.

49. Devotions in Troubled Times, 1930

The 1930s and 1940s have been referred to as the "heyday" of Catholic devotionalism. Certainly, numerous newsletters, prayer books, novena pamphlets, holy cards, and the increased merchandizing of statues, medals, and shrines gave strong indication that the religious sensibility of the Catholic community was searching for intercession and a way to create bonds, both visible and invisible, between earth and heaven. In many ways, this devotional culture built on the foundations of the immigrant church (see docs. 10, 15, 16, 20, 24, 28); in other ways, it marked a new departure. Many local devotions now went national, taking advantage of the new means of communication in religious periodicals; as ethnic neighborhoods began to break up and the society became more mobile, these mass practices gave expression to new spaces of urban and American Catholic unity. In the practical order, devotions became opportunities for "fund-raising" for the increasing network of Catholic parishes and schools. Devotion to St. Jude, Our Lady of Perpetual Help, St. Anthony, and Our Sorrowful Mother achieved phenomenal success from 1930 to the early 1950s. The following selection describes the beginnings of devotion to St. Anthony in Louisville, Kentucky. The author refers to the new mobility of the people and carefully notes the devotion as a leveler in the context of shared spiritual and material poverty.

Never before has the city of Louisville, Kentucky, seen anything like it — this string of novenas which is being conducted at Saint Boniface Church in honor of Saint Anthony of Padua. For forty-five weeks, hundreds, really thousands, have come to the shrine of the well-loved Saint and placed their petitions in his care. The Monday evenings and the Tuesdays have been set apart as pilgrimage dates by men and women of all sections of the city and vicinity.

The Reason

But why? "If miracles thou fain wouldst see..." The news has gone out in all directions that good Saint Anthony is answering prayers here, at this Franciscan church, in a way that is remarkable. People have come to expect great things from their novenas at his shrine; and when they do receive an answer, they are anxious that all their friends and acquaintances should know about it and be in turn encouraged to put their own needs before the Wonder Worker. But, after all, there is no reason to be surprised at this, for it has ever been thus; wherever Saint Anthony really became known, he has given favors lavishly and brought human hearts nearer to their God. And now, that he has become well known in Louisville, faithful Christians here are sure that he can and will help them if it be for the good of things; they have learned to look up with the highest confidence to this gentle Saint, who has come down to us through seven centuries holding the Child Jesus in his arms and giving bread to the poor.

The Pilgrims

So they come, from everywhere, and their numbers go on increasing. Many of them — very many — are clothed in the garments of poverty, asking this Franciscan friend of the poor for the things they need: for work, that they may be able to feed and clothe themselves and their babies; for charity in the hearts of such as are blessed with this world's goods to have pity on their distress. Others that come are dressed in the silks of fashion, but nevertheless begging for bread — for the bread of enlightenment, of consolation, of spiritual peace. But perhaps the greatest number belong to that large army of Catholic souls who feel the need of help from Heaven in their daily tasks and trials and who realize that Saint Anthony is a valuable friend to have at any time, even though for the moment they are in no special want: they too are asking for bread, the daily bread of God's graces; and they are reaching for larger portions of faith, hope, and charity.

And some of them are sick or crippled in body; others, sick at heart with sorrow or wounded to death by sin; still others there are who keep on begging

St.Anthony who
didst merit to hold
in Thy arms
the Infant Jesus.
Pray for us.

*Saint Anthony of Padua
Holy Card*

for favors, not so much in their own behalf as for relatives or friends who cannot or will not come to beg for themselves; and some come just for love of the Saint and the Child he holds forever — all looking up to the kindly Friar like the beggar at his feet, looking up with the light of faith in their eyes and a new love of God in their hearts.

There are very many men among Saint Anthony's clients, too; grey-haired men, who have found out the meanings of life through hard experience, now asking this holy Man to help them pass the rest of it in safety; and young men, who are just starting out on the road, but who already see the advantage and the necessity of strong and holy help. They come and pray with a fine devotion and a deep sincerity — these Catholic men; and they put to shame those worldly wise who claim that piety and religion are only for old women (God bless the old women!). "How many men there are here!" "Isn't it good to see all those young men at prayer, so interested and devout?" Remarks like these are frequently heard when the novenas are the topic of conversation.

By automobile, by street-car, they come, or simply on foot; in good and bad weather, on hot days and cold, through the snow and the rain and the slop of a busy city. Nothing else seems to matter to these men and women except getting to the shrine. And what sacrifices they are making week after week will only become known when the Book of Life is thrown wide open on Judgment Day and the deeds of God's heroes and heroines are read to the world.

Prayers Answered

Surely that Saint who has such firm hold on human hearts deserves to be called "the People's Saint." Everybody seems to know him, and certainly, every one who knows him will love him and pray to him. And it is the experience of seven hundred years that wherever and whenever you find devotion to him in a flourishing condition, you will also find that he is generous in answering the people's prayers.

It is not at all surprising, then, that here at Saint Boniface Church, where an uninterrupted series of novenas is in progress, they are telling of numerous favors richly answered. It would indeed be a matter for real astonishment if such a manifestation of faith and piety as is going on here were left unrewarded. God's love for Saint Anthony and St. Anthony's love for the faithful are far too great to allow high trust to be confounded. What has been occurring in this church during the past forty-five weeks has proved to be taking Heaven by storm and bursting open its gates, thus letting a rush of blessings fall down upon hungry souls and hungry bodies. "Ask, and it shall be given you: seek, and you shall find: knock, and it shall be opened to you" (Mt. 7:7) — oh, there has been asking here and seeking and knocking and also perseverance!

As one of Heaven's treasure-keepers, "the People's Saint" can well afford to be generous to his faithful ones. Often he gives them just what they want, at times even more than they dared to expect. During each and every week of these eleven months the Fathers of the monastery have received thirty, forty, fifty, and more written acknowledgments of particular favors Almighty God had granted through the intercession of this lover of humankind. Men who needed food and clothing for their families have unexpectedly been offered employment; lost and stolen articles have quite suddenly been returned; families and friends long estranged have been happily reconciled; peace has come to some in trouble and light to others in their darkness; souls away from God for months and years and starving to death have been led back to feed once more upon the Bread of Angels; and, that may be considered as a very special fruit of these weeks of prayer, there has been given to those of good will a great and consoling sense of conformity to the will of God.

Conformity to God's Will

The last mentioned favor has come to be recognized by our good men and women as an invaluable grace and necessity in times of need. It has made them see through the fact that if Saint Anthony does not give them exactly what they are asking for, it must be because of some fault of their own or simply because the thing requested would not be for their good; and it has brought home to them that God and His Saint have too much affection for their friends to give them what would harm them in the least. For this reason many of the petitions placed at Saint Anthony's feet read something like this: "...help us pay our rent if it be God's will"; "...bring me out of this trouble if it is for the good." And who can say what special graces have been granted to those whose prayers apparently remained unanswered?

"Novena to St. Anthony," *St. Anthony Messenger* 37, no. 10 (March 1930): 446–47. Reprinted by permission of St. Anthony Messenger Press, 1615 Republic St., Cincinnati, OH 45210; 800-488-0488. All rights reserved.

50. The Practice of Frequent Communion, 1930

Pope Pius X's decrees on the frequent reception of Communion and the re-ception of Communion at an earlier age for children (1905, 1910) brought the sacrament into liturgical prominence (cf. docs. 16, 37, 40). In the text below, written a quarter-century after Pius's decrees, Paulist Father Joseph McSorley (1874–1963), retreat director, pastor, and one of the most astute popularizers of contemplative prayer, raised the question of whether a change of practice effected a changed interior life for Catholics. He synthesized a theology of Eu-charist in the language of incorporation and union, suggesting that "hidden saints" were all around. American Catholic involvement in mission, more priestly and religious vocations, and the growth of many Catholic societies evidenced this infusion of new life into the community. This model of holiness, a type of spiritual democracy, contrasts with that of the heroic martyr (see docs. 34, 44, 59), which tends to highlight holiness for an elite group. It would foreshadow many subsequent developments (see docs. 53, 79, 90).

Church historians look upon a century as a reasonably small unit of measure-ment. Others of us, however, clinging to a more individual viewpoint, regard twenty-five years as a considerable lapse of time. Since, therefore, the decree of Pope Pius X on Frequent Communion will have been operating a quarter century on the twentieth of this month, we are led to reflect just now on the changes wrought in Catholic life up to date by the publication of that famous document.

Apparently there has been, as yet, no serious attempt at an exhaustive pre-sentation of the increase in the number of Communions since 1905. Such a study would be an extremely interesting and enormously useful contribution to our knowledge. But it would require an almost prohibitive amount of time and labor, for it should investigate not merely the number of Communions in the two periods before and after the year named, but such other relevant cir-cumstances as fluctuations of population, ages of communicants, organization of propaganda in schools and pulpits, and the like.

However, I am now less concerned with statistics which are not avail-able, than with general impressions shared by all. The present seems a fitting moment to review, at least in a cursory sort of way, the more obvious re-sults of the decrees, *"Sacra Tridentina Synodus,"* published in 1905 for the double purpose of correcting certain prevalent misconceptions about the conditions required for a worthy Communion and of persuading the faithful to the practice of frequent, and when possible daily, reception of the Body of Our Lord.

So far as the general situation is concerned, probably no one will gainsay the following two statements:

First: Since 1905 there has taken place a notable increase in the frequency with which the faithful receive Holy Communion.

Secondly, not only the actual practice, but also the mental attitude of the Catholic people has been revolutionized. Whereas a generation ago daily Communion was looked upon as the privilege of a select few — members of religious communities or near-saints — that practice is now understood to be the inalienable right of every Catholic, on the sole condition of freedom from mortal sin and a right intention.

A rather interesting illustration of the spirit now prevalent among Catholic young men properly trained may be found in Georgetown University's report that for the past fourteen years more than fifty percent of the students have been receiving Communion daily. Of the 150 Catholic students at the U.S. Naval Academy, we are told, about one-third go to Communion each week. The custom of the Notre Dame football squad is a matter of common knowledge; and in the fascinating Report of the Prefect of Religion of Notre Dame University we find that among the 2900 Catholic students the average reception of Holy Communion was four times a week.

But without going further into the inviting field of study concerning the average rate of daily Communions among different classes of Catholics, let us turn to the consideration of certain commonly known facts.

It seems reasonable to begin by recalling that to Catholics the reception of Holy Communion implies actual incorporation with Jesus Christ, an embrace of the soul and God. To the uninitiate this very idea is startling. In fact a persuasive argument for the divine origin of the Church might easily be constructed from her proven ability to bring a world of men to the unquestioning acceptance of Holy Communion as a truth of faith and to the eager desire of it as an actual experience. Freedom from grievous sin being presupposed, Holy Communion effects a contact of spirit with Spirit, a union more complete, more unreserved than any other possible to man. On the part of the Divine Lover, there is gracious and generous giving; on ours grateful, humble, loyal return. With Him, it is a lifting up, purifying, ennobling of the soul; with us an appeal for pardon and aid, a self-dedication, a grasping of His outstretched hand, a bending of the knee in worship, a touching of God Himself with reverential lips. And the desirability of frequent reception of Communion becomes obvious, as soon as we realize that each new Communion is a renewal of intimacy, a re-enforcement of affection, a confirmation of the mutual pledges already given.

Bearing in mind these implications of Holy Communion, we now recall as the salient point of the decree its proclamation that every individual Catholic, of whatever rank or condition of life, is, by the desire of Our Lord, daily invited to the Holy Table. The decree adds a further command that pastors, confessors and preachers shall frequently and vigorously exhort the faithful to the daily reception of Communion. In other words, with a solemnity and urgency not to be paralleled, every Catholic in the world is reminded over and over again of this standing invitation to approach God, of this daily opportunity for the supreme spiritual experience of life.

To men of good will already united to God in bonds of obedience and love, there is thus given an effective reminder of their duty to deepen and to intensify their consciousness of God and to fix fast their hold on Him. To the wicked, the negligent, the sluggish, the decree sounds forth a warning, which reechoes in their souls every time they see a worshipper approaching the altar. Sinners dislike to be reminded of their duties or of their neglected opportunities; but now, less than ever, can they escape these daily reminders and suggestions, unless they altogether forsake the company of Catholics and literally keep outside the Church. For each of these Communions, now multiplied beyond all calculation, is a notification of the uninterrupted obligation of the human soul to seek God. Ever present to both saints and sinners, He offers reconciliation to the offender, a higher degree of holiness and happiness to the faithful disciple. The disloyal are reminded of their treason, are summoned to surrender on most generous terms, are warned solemnly of the danger of delay.

No one can measure the power of this mighty force surging constantly into the consciences of men, swaying them away from evil and towards God. The total result of the decree, therefore, must necessarily escape even the man who can calculate the numerical increase of Communions. For the external fact suggests only dimly and inadequately the whole influence on the spiritual life of Christendom, and the tremendous impulse for good which reaches even outside the walls of the visible church.

The decree has functioned also, as an emphatic reminder to the laity of their vocation to holiness. Too often lay people have the conviction, or at least the lurking suspicion, that aspirations to perfection are the monopoly of persons consecrated to God by a special state of life, priests, for instance, and members of religious communities. The inertia consequent upon such a mental attitude forms a very serious obstacle to the proper spiritual progress of the people of God. What more practical, more convincing, more final way of disposing of this difficulty than the authoritative announcement to men and women living in the world that they have received a divine invitation to daily Communion and all it involves!

May we not reasonably suppose that in proportion as souls realize their daily call to Holy Communion, they also understand that they are called to the pursuit of perfection and to imitation of Our Lord? May we not even assume that their fervent use of the privilege of daily Communion, insofar as possible to them, will also be the measure of their spiritual progress? The decree seems to teach this, where it says: "it is impossible but that daily communicants should gradually emancipate themselves from even venial sins, and from all affection thereto." This result, of course, does not imply a sort of magical operation; nor even a mechanical effect. It is dependent upon the contribution of mind and will made by the communicant; for Holy Communion will "produce a greater effect in proportion as the dispositions of the recipient are better; therefore care is to be taken that Holy Communion be preceded by serious preparation and followed by suitable thanksgiving."

The success of this pursuit of holiness is guaranteed, on the conditions laid down. The soundness of that guarantee may be determined by an acute observer following the career of those who practise daily Communion and are faithful to the graces received. He will be able to attest many an instance of people actually lifted out of sin and impelled steadily along the paths of virtue by their daily contact with the Lord.

The decree on frequent Communion and the later legislation of 1910 on the Communions of children must have had no little bearing on the supply of priestly and religious vocations. When all is said, a surprisingly large number of young men and women come forward each year to dedicate themselves to the service of religion. To the critical outsider it seems nothing less than a standing miracle that the Church is able to obtain these tens of thousands of replacements for her spiritual army. For they are the children of a world crowded with opportunities of selfish gratification, whose inhabitants at times seem to be all running wild in pursuit of pleasure. Now who would venture to deny a connection between the Church's perennial supply of spiritual volunteers and the habit of frequent Communion characteristic of the younger generation!

Once upon a time a poet lingered in a country churchyard, meditating on the unrevealed beauty and courage and genius in the souls of the simple peasants buried there. So does a priest often dream of angelic innocence and Christlike goodness hidden under the plain exteriors of ordinary men and women in any gathering of God's people. There they are, heirs of a glorious, heroic tradition, kindred to saints whose images grace the sanctuary and whose names are known to the farthest limits of the civilized world, simple husbands and wives, fathers and mothers, sons and daughters. They are generous, patient, honest, pure. They embody faith and trust in God; they live charity; they preach the Gospel of good example; they reproduce the image of Christ; they count themselves least; they bear the cross patiently; they would readily suffer death for the faith.

The fact that these hidden saints are all about us often serves to console a heart saddened by the world's disloyalty to God. No doubt it has been kept a fact and has been made all the more a fact in these times by the decree which reintroduced the practice of frequent Communion into ordinary Catholic life. Very little keenness is required to perceive the striking coincidence, shall we not call it the providential connection? — of the publication of the "Sacra Tridentina Synodus" and the beginning of that new freedom in morals which is probably the most significant social phenomenon of our day. History records no other period when liberty, especially the liberty of women and young people, was more comprehensive, more widespread, and — when it degenerates into licence, — more sure of immunity. Can it be mere accident that, contemporaneously with the growth of this new social liberty, we have seen the development of a new freedom of access to the Holy Table? These young people who live at such dangerously close quarters with pagan friends, who have such amazing familiarity with sin, have also in large numbers established a custom of approaching the altar with a readiness which startles when it does not scandalize their elders. There may be another side to that. Of course, there is necessarily another side: for no good thing escapes the possibility of abuse. But I for one like to see in this juxtaposition of two very striking phenomena a providential relationship. May it not be perhaps a fresh proof of God's readiness to give us our daily bread not for the body alone, but also and chiefly to satisfy that greater hunger of man which can be appeased by nothing less than the possession of Himself?

All in all, then, we have much reason to be grateful to Pope Pius X for the issue of the decree on frequent Communion. Using rather a bold figure, someone has likened that act of the Holy Father's to a surgical operation, saying that he ordered a transfusion of blood from the Body of Our Lord into the weakened, enervated bodies of the faithful. It seems an apt enough illustration; for the activity of the Catholic people during these recent years can best be explained as due to a divine renewal of vitality. Confining ourselves, for the moment, to a consideration of our own country alone, we find much here that is noteworthy. Not to enumerate the details of expansion along ordinary lines — the multiplication of parishes, churches and schools — one thinks quickly of developments suggested by the mention of Foreign Missions, the Catholic University, Church Extension, the National Catholic Welfare Conference, the Knights of Columbus, the Holy Name Society, the Catholic Daughters of America.

Thus even after only a partial fulfillment of the duty of training the people enjoined by the Holy Father, the result looms magnificently large. Perhaps what the Church needs now more than anything else is that every leader shall emulate the example of those whose zeal for the extension of frequent Communion has already become a proverb.

Joseph McSorley, CSP, "The First Twenty-Five Years of Frequent Communion," *The Missionary* 44 (December 1930): 408–10. Reprinted with permission of the Paulist Fathers, Washington, D.C.

51. Learning to Pray by Doing, 1930

The standard text for parochial grade and high schools of this period was a version of the Baltimore Catechism *(see docs. 1, 32). Memorization of questions and answers, explanations on the chalkboard, and stories from Bible history fleshed out the academic component of religious education. In* The Mass: A Laboratory Manual for the Student of Religion, *pioneer educators Raymond J. Campion and Ellamay Horan (1898–1987) suggested a further way of acquiring religious knowledge: the "hands-on" method, influenced somewhat by John Dewey's practical approach to education. The manual, excerpted below, combined active involvement for students, scripture passages, knowledge of the liturgical year, and the use of scripture and liturgy for reflection upon one's daily life. When aligned with the organization of the school system and the in-*

creasing popularity of programs of Catholic Action (see docs. 53, 54, 74, 76),
these pedagogical methods represented a significant change in Catholic prayer
and practice.

Foreword

The purpose of this manual is to assist the junior and senior high school pupil
in the study of the Mass. It is an aim of Catholic education to give not only an
intelligent attitude towards the Mass itself, but also to help the pupil appreciate
the Holy Sacrifice and participate to the fullest in its sacred action. This work
book has been so designed that the boy or girl may get from working with it:

1. An intelligent attitude toward the Mass itself, its history, and its acces-
   sories.

2. An appreciation of the tremendous action that takes place during
   the Mass.

3. An ability to assist at the Mass intelligently.

4. Ways and means of using the Mass most effectively as the core of his
   spiritual life.

5. An ability to follow with the Church her liturgical year.

The Mass may be used in the junior and senior high school years with any
of the texts in current use and with any course of study in which *The Mass* is
present in the curriculum.

Teachers will find in this work book desirable material to use in supervised
study periods, in instruction by the unity method, in measuring achievement, in correlating English composition with the study of Religion, and in
promoting self activity on the part of the pupil....

Unit III

Exercise V. Using the Missal

"Remember thou keep holy the Sabbath Day."

1. Write below a letter to a friend who is attending a non-Catholic school
   and explain to him how to use the Missal that you have sent him as
   a gift.

Unit IV. The Ecclesiastical Year

Date assigned _____ Date due _____

"No one knoweth the Father but the Son and he to whom it shall please
the Son to reveal Him." St. Matthew, XI, 2.

Exercise I. The Ecclesiastical Year and Holiness

1. Write an explanation of what you understand by the statement that the
   study of the ecclesiastical year is a way to grow in holiness....

Exercise III. Living the Gospel

"Show O Lord, Thy ways to me, and teach me Thy paths. Direct me in Thy truth and teach me: for Thou art God, my Saviour: and on Thee have I waited all the day long." Psalm, XXIV, 4–5.

The purpose of this exercise is to help you discover some of the lessons contained in the portions of the Gospel assigned to the different Sundays of the year. Using a Missal, or a prayer book containing the Gospels for Sunday, read one Gospel at a time and record in the outline form below: (1) The liturgical name of the Sunday. (2) The event described in the selection of the Gospel read. (3) The lesson one might learn from that portion of the Gospel.

SUNDAY	EVENTS DESCRIBED	PRACTICAL LESSON

Raymond J. Campion and Ellamay Horan, *The Mass: A Laboratory Manual for the Student of Religion* (New York: William H. Sadlier, Inc., 1930), foreword, 73, 79, 97. Used with permission.

52. Roman Catholicism — a Liberal Appraisal, 1931

From the very beginning of the Catholic Church in the United States there appeared different approaches among church leaders and community members to the traditions, prayers, and practices of the church (cf. docs. 8 and 14; 24 and 25; 26 and 30; 65 and 66). In the mid–nineteenth century, one Anglican observer had referred to the differences between those of the school of John Carroll and those of a more "Roman" persuasion. At the turn of the new century, media had witnessed the opposition within Catholicism between "Americanizers" and "conservatives." Catholic commentators in the early twentieth century noted a similar split. Here, in this passage from the prominent Unitarian magazine The Christian Register, *the author notes two forces at work in the church in this country and in the process sets out to detail some of the spiritual resources Catholicism offers to people. The author's positive assessment contrasts sharply with the more typical critique of the church's institutional power (see doc. 47).*

What of the future of the Roman Church? Will she remain belated? Two forces are at work within Catholicism. One force tends to keep the Church static; the other to liberalize thought and practice.

Some Catholics believe that they see evidences of a strong liberal movement developing within the Church, especially in America. Father Barrett writes that the Church is "in the throes of a childbirth of an un-medieval up-to-date Catholicism." Ex-Governor Smith, Catholic layman, renounced some of the most fundamental principles of Catholicism when he declared several years ago, "I recognize no power in the institution of my Church to interfere with the enforcement of the law of the land.... I believe in the public school as one of the cornerstones of America." Yet no Catholic authority, even in Rome, brought him to task.

It may transpire that this increasing liberalization will result in a schism. Centuries ago, East broke with West. In Luther's day, North Europe broke with South. Perhaps in the not distant future, liberal Catholics will break with reactionary Rome. Perhaps, on the other hand, the miracle may happen and Catholicism as a whole will readjust her ideas and practices to the tendencies of the time. That has occurred in the past; it may happen again.

The true liberal is interested in Roman Catholic shortcomings and evils primarily in order that he may separate the chaff from the wheat and find in Catholicism elements which will enrich his own religious life.

What values has Roman Catholicism for us?

We may learn from the Catholic the importance of tradition. The reactionary commits the intellectual sin of looking only at the past and of belittling the future. The intellectual radical sins by looking only to the future and thus belittling or ignoring the good of bygone times. We can no more divorce ourselves from the past than a tree can break loose from its roots and continue to live. The liberal may well listen to the Catholic, G. K. Chesterton, when he writes: "Tradition may be defined as the extension of the franchise. Tradition means giving votes to the most obscure of all classes, our ancestors. It is the democracy of the dead. Tradition refuses to submit to the small and arrogant obligarchy [sic] of those who merely happen to be walking about. All democrats object to men being disqualified by the accident of death. Democracy tells us not to neglect a good man's opinion, even if he is our groom; tradition asks us not to neglect a good man's opinion, even if he is our father."

Again, the Catholic can teach us that reverence is indispensable to fullness of life.

This age has many virtues, but reverence is not one of them. Catholics reverence many things that the liberal cannot — for example, relics, holy places and the Pope. But the Catholic also teaches reverence for God, for beauty, and for one's own inner spiritual self. Such reverence is the very basis of temperateness, self-control and moral cleanness. No force in the world is more potent against Bohemian self-indulgence and self-degradation than is Catholicism. The collapse of the Roman Church today would mean the moral collapse of multitudes tomorrow. "They are kept in check by fear," some say. Probably that is true, but only in part. Reverence also is a vital factor.

Roman Catholicism also inculcates the habit of worship and prayer.

Dean Brown of Yale tells of visiting early in the morning the Cathedral at Milan. Outside the great central door were market baskets filled with produce. The owners were within, kneeling for a few moments of silence and adoration. He watched them as they came out — their faces full of serenity and peace.

The Roman Catholic knows, too, that there must be regularity of prayer and worship if these are to enrich personality. He also is aware that the inner life can be cultivated much as one fosters bodily health — through discipline and exercises. The true Catholic has learned the value of relaxation, concentration and contemplation.

The true Roman Catholic has learned, likewise, the habit of self-sacrifice. During the Great War, I said to an English army officer, a member of the Anglican Church, "You tell me that you served three years at the Front. What chaplains were most self-sacrificing, most ready to endanger life in serving the men of their regiments?" He answered without hesitation, "The Catholic chaplains." Thousands of priests and sisters, thousands of Catholic missionaries walk in the footsteps of St. Xavier, Father Damien and Junipero Serra, declaring by their lives, "I came not to be ministered unto, but to minister."

53. The Liturgy and Social Reconstruction, 1935

From its very beginning in the United States, in the wake of World War I, the liturgical movement took on a distinctive character as a program not simply of spiritual renewal but also of social reconstruction. In his student days Virgil Michel had written on Orestes Brownson (1803–76), the nineteenth-century Catholic philosopher and social reformer, and in 1921 the young Benedictine penned a programmatic article "The Mission of Catholic Thought." In articles, conferences, retreats, pamphlets, and letters he addressed the role of the laity, the position of women, the economic principles of St. Thomas, the relationship between love and sacrifice in the Christian life, and the moral condition of society. In this short letter to a young student, Michel refers to some of the European sources of the liturgical movement, shows its ecumenical breadth, and describes the practical revival of the Mystical Body in the liturgy as a model of human society. His explanation correlates well with the philosophy which Paul Hanley Furfey (1896–1992) presents to his young students of sociology at the Catholic University of America (see doc. 55). This relationship between liturgy and social justice would differentiate the American liturgical movement from its European counterpart (see docs. 76, 91).

St. John's University
Collegeville, Minnesota
Nov. 27, 1935

Dear Father Martin,

I just got your very interesting letter this afternoon. It is really a shame for me to answer it at once, since I have two unanswered letters of Fr. Osmond's with me. But he will have to understand that business comes before pleasure.

I think you should grab the chance at once to write your M.A. thesis on Liturgy and Sociology, provided only that [Paul Hanly] Furfey understands that there is practically nothing done on the subject, and that you will have to do individual creative work rather than much research work. You'll not very readily get a subject suggested again for an M.A. that will require so little mechanical research work. I'd grab the subject at once after a talk to Furfey in which he tells you about how large a thesis will be a minimum.

About the German sources you happen to be all wrong. There are none that Fr. Godfrey or I know of, save perhaps a book on very general principles [on the Mystical Body]. There is a little more in French — but all in all the subject has hardly been treated at all. So you can break ground of your own. I know for sure that Fathers Jaspar and Hellriegel had no books as a basis for their wonderful pamphlet except Guardini's *vom Geist der Liturgie*, which is being published anew in English as part of a new book Sheed and Ward are getting out this winter (whole book is Guardini).

I would suggest that you get at the work by reading in the proper liturgical literature about fifteen or twenty minutes a day regularly. As soon as some thought strikes you put it down on a slip of paper. Especially if connected thoughts come, or sketches, or correlations between the liturgy and sociology, put them down at once. You could do the same whenever you are studying or reading in sociology. If you get the objective firmly in your subconscious, you'll find many suggestions coming to you during the day. Always put them down black on white at once, and review your slips once a week. You'll be surprised how the thing will accumulate. And you'll have a real original work to write in summer with all the thoughts gathered.

Of course, the liturgy does not offer a detailed scheme of economic reconstruction, or anything of that kind. But it does give us a proper concept and understanding of what society is like, through its model of the Mystical Body. And it puts this concept into action in its worship and wants us to live it out in everyday life. The liturgy furnishes admirable basis for education along social lines, has much to do with proper family life, etc. The notions of the nature of society and societal organization, hierarchy of order, individual and social responsibilities, mutual duties and rights between individuals and groups and between groups and groups, and between parts and whole, proper notion of authority as service, rank on the basis of merit (also social merit), doctrine of Communion of Saints, common treasury of the faithful, etc., there are all sorts of points of correlation. And all such points should be also points of inspiration drawn from the liturgy for sociology. I feel sure that the thing will grow on you day by day in a most joyous manner. And the best of it is that there is not a vast amount of reading to do. You cannot depend on compiling the opinions of others, it must come from yourself.

As to sources, I suggest the above Guardini book, then my own LIFE IN CHRIST, which I think indispensable, then Beauduin and Caronti of the Popular Liturgical Library, and some of the pamphlets, such as the Liturgical Movement, etc. Some time I can look up our periodical index of liturgical articles, and if anything worthwhile is there, we can send the books on to you. I just found out that there was an article on "Liturgy and Sociology" in the April 1935 *Blackfriars*, which must be in the Dominican House of Studies if not in the C[atholic] U[niversity] Library. There is an Anglican book out by Fr. Hebert, SSM, entitled "Liturgy and Society" which may have something. It is published by Faber and Faber (London). The book may be in the

Congressional Library. Or you might inquire at the most High-Church Anglican Rectory in Washington. Perhaps they also have the review *Christendom*, of which I'll send you a copy in two weeks.

So there you are! I do hope you'll undertake it, because it will mean the least amount of hack-work for you. Just get your mind set in time, and the whole thing will grow automatically. As soon as you have some main ideas, let us know, and we'll examine them here in conclave assembled.

Best wishes to you on everything. God bless you.

Yours in St. Benedict,
Virgil [Michel], OSB

Michel-Schirber Z–27, Virgil Michel Papers. Reprinted by permission of Saint John's Abbey Archives, Collegeville, Minn.

54. The Spiritual Foundations of Catholic Action, 1935

Catholic Action, a program for the renewal of society and the "participation of the laity in the apostolate of the hierarchy," articulated by Pope Pius XI in 1923, served as the unifying philosophy for many of the renewal movements of the 1930s and 1940s (see docs. 48, 51, 58, 61, 62). Spawning study clubs, permeating national assemblies, mainstreamed by numerous groups of laity in Third Orders, pushed and supported by the National Catholic Welfare Conference, and eventually developing into more specialized action groups of farmers, workers, and students, this philosophy and spirituality of Christian life focused on membership in the Mystical Body of Christ and the organized mission of the church in society. One of the earliest and clearest articulations of its spirituality, the following article makes notable departures from the previous models of holiness in the immigrant church (see docs. 14, 17, 26). Moving away from juridical and legal categories of thought, focusing on the role of grace (not sin) in life, shifting the emphasis toward everyone's share in baptismal rebirth, defining marriage as the elevation of two mortals "to be co-creators" of God's adopted children, and making the trinitarian life the central foundation of belief, this explanation of Catholic Action carried far-reaching implications for the future prayer and practice of the church.

The thirty-three years of the earthly career of our Lord Jesus Christ constituted a splendid synthesis of contemplation and action. Especially in the three years of His public life do we see a beautiful proportion of prayer and activity. Rapt communion with the eternal Father preceded and fortified Him for all the acts of His sacred ministry. Gethsemane's elevation of heart provided the insuperable strength for the sacrificial act of the cross.

Logically, therefore, the Angelic Doctor teaches us that the ideal Christian life is characterized by contemplation superabounding in action. The *"alter Christus"* is he in whom a life of contemplative charity overflows in a life of charitable action.

Every great movement of apostolic action which has advanced from the evolving processes of the Church's history is rooted deep in the rich soil of Christ's doctrine.

With these thoughts in mind it is pertinent to examine three grand interrelated conceptions of Catholic dogmatic truth which may well form the spiritual foundations of Catholic Action and the full comprehension of which would lend tremendous impetus to this current crusade for personal and social sanctification.

The first concept, the significance and dignity of which we wish to consider, is the life of grace in the individual soul.

Many Catholics, and even many well-intentioned Catholics who are endeavoring to engage efficaciously in Catholic Action, have but a very vague conception of the character of grace and, concurrently, of the nature of sin. If they completely grasped the central basic verity that grace is supernatural life, surging life, the very repletion of which demands expressive fructification in supernatural acting, then, the grandeur of Catholic Action would compel an impetus in this apostolate which would be the glory supreme of the Mystical Body.

The present widely prevalent ideas on the character of grace and sin are attributable, in great measure, to certain current methods of catechetical instruction. As youthful catechumens many of us were taught (and the identical method is still in vogue) that the sacramental effect of Baptism symbolized by the purifying pouring of water was the cleansing from our soul of the mark of original sin. This latter phenomenon was pictured as a sort of viciously black ink-stain that permeated the naturally immaculate parchment of our soul. Baptism was a magic eradicator which restored the soul to its ordained whiteness. To the challenge that this material metaphor was relatively accurate and commensurate with the limited capacity of puerile minds, we shall assent, adding, however, that such a similitude also gave birth to the grossest and gravest of misunderstandings of the great realities....

Even from the standpoint of educational psychology, would it not be as easy to give a more integrally true idea of the divine character of grace? We could state that as man has the physical life of the body and the intellectual life of the mind, so, also, he is destined to have the supernatural life of the soul. Apt illustrations from ordinary life should make the comprehension of this hierarchy sufficiently easy for the least tutored of minds. Original sin signifies that the soul is paralytic; it is without life but endowed with the potency for life. Baptism is the miraculous cure of the spiritual paralytic; it is the awakening from the spiritual sleep of death. Baptism is the granting to the soul of the supernatural Christ-life, which is not due to any human efforts but is the gratuitous gift of the infinitely good God. Baptism completes mortal man's being according to the destiny of his Creator — it culminates the hierarchy of life. The newly liberated creature now has physical life, intellectual life and supernatural spiritual vitality....

This revolutionary reorientation of the Catholic's conception of grace, as life and not as sinlessness, should prove of profound importance. It is the parallel in the highest realms of spiritual reality and intellectual comprehension to that positive outpouring of Christian vitality that is called Catholic Action.

What is the mission of Catholic Action? Is it not the dynamic radiance of the Christ-life which is poured abroad in the Mystical Humanity in the exuberance of charity "by the Holy Spirit who is given to us"? Is it not the positive communication of the sanctified life of the extended Word Incarnate?

Catholic Action is the dynamic expression of consciously positive life. To discover and reveal its vast potentialities, the right understanding of grace, the basis of Christian life, is requisite. Catholic Action is meant to be the external manifestation and conveyance of the interior Christ-life of supernatural grace.

True Catholic Action is the fruition of sanctifying grace. It is a truism of Catholic theology that grace is an essential prerequisite for meritorious and efficacious activity. Its place therefore in the programme of Catholic Action is self-evident.

The clear and accurate comprehension of grace as the formal inflow of Christ-life should certainly promote this deliberate and alert meriting of grace *ex opere operantis*. Such mystical reciprocity with Christ and the Mystical Christ at the holy Sacrifice of the Mass and in the reception of the sacraments is the basis for active and intelligent participation in the liturgical life and such, too, is the indispensable foundation for that metaphysical solidarity of souls, the logical issue of which is corporate worship of the external Father by and with and in the mediatorial Christ Jesus.

A further practical fruit of the correct concept of grace is a vivid realization that the sacraments are channels of special graces marking the growth and progress of our supernatural life. Baptism is understood as the grace of spiritual regeneration whereby we are initiated into the divine life of grace. "We are buried together with Him (Christ) by Baptism into death; that as Christ is risen from the dead, so also we may walk in newness of life."

Confirmation is a strengthening of spiritual life, a stabilization in original grace, an invigorating influx of Christ-life, the plenitude of which renders our souls vibrant with a richly mature and militant Christianity. The Eucharist becomes intelligible as the perfect nourishment of our soul — the divine Food nurturing, sustaining, fortifying, replenishing the divine life. The sacrament of Communion, the sacrament of charity, is supremely the sacrament of the Christ-life of grace because it is Christ Himself, body and blood, soul and divinity. "He that eateth My flesh and drinketh My blood, abideth in Me and I in him." [John 6.5,6] The sacrament of Penance heals our wounds, cures our spiritual diseases and restores our souls to the perfection of the integral Christ-life. Extreme Unction is a powerful influx of the life of grace the reaction of which sometimes returns bodily health but, primarily, revivifies the soul in faith and hope and charity in preparation for the final onslaught of Satan. Matrimony is the sacrament which raises human partners, associate members of the Mystical Body, into a special union destined to issue in a human and miniature representation of the society of the blessed Trinity. It is the sacrament designed to consecrate the vocation of preparing new souls for supernatural life. It is the natural counterpart of Christ's union with His Mystical Body whereby two mortals are elevated to be co-creators of God's adopted children. Finally, Holy Orders is the sacrament providing for the promotion of sanctifying life. It is the sacrament perpetuating Christ's eternal priesthood whereby the continuation of the Christ-life of grace is guaranteed and assured of application.

The practical consequences of this apprehension of truth can be further illustrated by a few examples. With such a truth grasped should not the apostolate of Catholic Action as manifested in the retreat movement receive zealous promotion? For the retreat movement is a training school of sanctity, a medium for the perfection of the Christ-life of grace. Considering the grandeur of grace, moreover, would any Catholic parent deny his child a Catholic education? Catholic education's ideal is to perfect nature with the supernatural culture of sanctifying grace. Again, what Catholic would remain indifferent to the great Liturgical Movement which exalts the sacramental mediums of Christian vitality and purposes a universal return to the well-springs of spiritual life? . . .

The second great truth, the full knowledge of which forms a potent inspiration for the apostolate of Catholic Action, is the Pauline doctrine of divine adoptive filiation. According to St. Paul, the positive Christ-life of grace which finds its first influx into our soul at Baptism and which is nourished and enriched by the reception of the sacraments, by prayer and charity during the course of the Christian career, is in reality but an inauguration by participation into the beatific life of the blessed Trinity whose communicate love-life is our destined eternal happiness. . . .

The positive life of grace interpreted in terms of divine adoptive filiation raises the apostolate of Catholic Action to otherwise unthought of levels. It becomes the action of the coordinated and collaborating sons of God. No longer is Catholic Action a series of monotonous activities; it is the creative expansion of "other Christs" communicating the life of divine charity, the infinitude of which reposes in the bosom of the eternal Father.

Under such circumstances, what Christian worthy of the title can excuse himself from the apostolate of the missions, which is such a prominent feature in the Catholic Action movement? The missions are the cradles of future Catholicity, the nurseries for rearing and cultivating sons of God. Furthermore, if we appreciate our heritage in being called to be the sons of God, who of us can abstain from advancing the Catholic press, which is the herald of the gospel of divine adoptive filiation? Which one of us, finally, can be so callous as to neglect the liturgical life, which represents the prayer of the sons of God grouped in corporate contemplation about Jesus, the eldest Son, in glorification of the eternal Father?

The third great truth of our faith which should be considered in this study of the spiritual foundations of Catholic Action is the doctrine of the Mystical Body of Christ. Since however this doctrine has repeatedly received extensive treatment in the pages of ORATE FRATRES, it will be sufficient for my purpose to point out some of the practical conclusions to be drawn from it, regarded in its relation to Catholic Action.

Certainly the reign of Christ in the kingdom of Christ, the enthronement of peace and the Prince of Peace would be more deliberately hastened by organized Catholic Action if the internationalism and universalism of the

Mystical Body were completely apprehended: "That there might be no schism in the body; but the members might be mutually careful one for another."

Catholic Action understood as the expansive life of the Christly organism could never be apathetic to brethren suffering in Spain, Mexico, Germany or Russia for: "If one member suffer anything, all the members suffer with it. . . . Now you are the body of Christ, and members of member."

The Mystical Body as the basis of Catholic Action is, finally, the key to social reconstruction as explained by the sovereign pontiffs. Who, understanding the doctrine of the Mystical Christ, would prosper the strife between capital and labor? Who, with such an understanding, would tolerate the vision of another war? Who would preach Chauvinistic nationalism in the face of the unity of Christ, the internationalism and supranationalism of the organic Mystical Humanity? For "Ye are all one person in Christ Jesus." Catholic Action of the Mystical Body is the communion of grace, the collectivism of the communion of saints, the democracy of divine adoptive filiation presided over by the Prince of Peace, and the universalization of its charity is the foundation of all enduring economic rehabilitation and social reconstruction.

John J. Griffin, "The Spiritual Foundations of Catholic Action," *Orate Fratres* 9 (September 1935): excerpts from 455–64. Printed with permission.

55. A New Social Catholicism, 1936

During the 1930s small groups of Catholic Christians, committed to social reform and founding their programs on a return to the simplicity of the gospel call to "love of neighbor," formed in various parts of the United States. On 1 May 1933 the first edition of Dorothy Day's (1879–1980) Catholic Worker was published. In Washington, D.C., Paul Hanley Furfey (1896–1992) and Mary Elizabeth Walsh adopted a lifestyle of "gospel literalism" with its emphasis on interracial justice and identification with the poor. Later in the decade, in 1938, Catherine de Hueck Doherty (1896–1985) would establish a Friendship House in Harlem. In the following letter to Norman McKenna of Christian Front, Furfey outlines the basic spiritual principles underlying many of these movements. He elaborated on this vision in his influential book Fire on the Earth *(1936).*

The Catholic University of America
Washington, D.C.
October 30, 1936

Mr. Norman McKenna
1371 Teller Avenue
Bronx, NY City

Dear Mr. McKenna:

We are writing to you and to a few others to ask your advice about a project we have in mind. The project is, in brief, to hold in Washington next spring a "Colloquium on the New Social Catholicism" — or perhaps better a "Colloquium on the *Revived* Social Catholicism." For this movement which we have in mind is "new" only in the sense that it represents a return — with a new loyalty — to the traditional social doctrines and methods of the Catholic Church.

In order to evaluate this proposal, it will be necessary to define the *New Social Catholicism.* We are using this term to designate the new spirit and the new lines of Catholic social thought which have become apparent all over the world in the last five years or so. Such periodicals as the *Catholic Worker, Liturgy and Sociology, Christian Front,* and *Social Forum* exemplify the sort of thing we have in mind. Again, the social thought of people like Fr. Gillis, CSP, Rev. Dr. Phelan, Fr. LaFarge, SJ, Dom Virgil Michel, OSB, or the leaders of the new Catholic agrarian movement seem to reflect the same principles.

It is hard to give an entirely satisfactory definition of the New Social Catholicism, but possibly the most characteristic principles of the group mentioned above might be summed up somewhat as follows:

1. In developing a Catholic social theory the data of divine revelation are incomparably more important than the data of scientific sociology. The plain meaning of the New Testament must not be attenuated in order to make it more palatable to the twentieth century. The keynote of this movement, therefore, is faith.

2. In the reformation of society, political methods are important and are by no means to be neglected; but much more important are such spiritual means as the sacraments and prayer. The liturgy is an excellent form of spiritual social action.

3. Social reform must be personal. It is not enough to try to reform others by legal coercion. We must emphasize the Christian social virtues in our own lives.

4. We must live the doctrine of the Mystical Body of Christ by show-ing charity to all groups. We must neither hate the rich nor fawn upon them. Our social movement must recognize no distinctions of nationality, color, or social class.

It seems to us that the leaders of this new movement have been working in isolation or in small groups with only occasional inter-group contacts. Would it be useful if about thirty of these leaders were invited to meet for, say, a three-day colloquium in Washington after Easter, or perhaps even sooner[?]

If such a group were to be called together it seems to us that the meeting itself should be governed by the principles of the New Social Catholicism. We should try ourselves through the duration of the meeting to live an ideal social life. The meeting should not give an opportunity for self-display. It should not be held in the luxurious surroundings of a first-class hotel. We propose then the following procedure:

1. The meeting would be held at *Il Poverello* House. This is a house in a poor Negro district of Washington which is used as the headquarters of the Washington Campion Group. Miss Sellew of the Catholic University

Faculty lives there and so does one Negro family. A few of the participants could stay at the house over night. Meals could be served during the meeting. About fifty people can meet at once in the parlors of the house. This would limit the size of our group — a desirable result.

2. The program would emphasize group discussion. Each session might last an hour and a half. We would begin with three or four papers strictly limited to two minutes each. Then there would be an hour for discussion. With such a small group the discussion could be very intensive. By having short papers each participant could receive the opportunity to deliver one paper. This would avoid an undesirable emphasis on "star" performers.

3. The participants should be selected solely or the basis of their ability to contribute something. Some of these participants may be well-known Catholic leaders; some may be relatively obscure. No one must be selected simply to add to the program the prestige of a famous name.

4. The liturgical life should be emphasized. Each day should begin with the chanting of a Solemn Mass. At least part of the Divine Office should be sung or recited each day.

5. By keeping the group small we could spend the entire day together, eating our meals in common. We propose further that we divide the housework among ourselves and do it during two or three one-hour periods of manual labor. This would help us to approach the study of social problems in a proper spirit of humility.

The program might be arranged somewhat as follows:

First Day: Principles

> The Mystical Body of Christ
> Satan as a Social Force
> Liturgical Social Action

Second Day: Problems

> War and Peace
> Minority Groups
> The Disabilities of the Wage Earner

Third Day: Techniques

> Art Forms as Propaganda
> The Catholic Agrarian Movement and Cooperatives
> The Example of the Saints

It might prove very valuable if the formal papers, together with a synopsis of the discussion, were published in book form at the conclusion of the meeting. Such a book might serve as a handbook of principles for those interested in the New Social Catholicism.

We are anxious to have your judgment (1) on the advisability of such a meeting, (2) on the best date for it, (3) on possible participants, and on any other points which occur to you.

Very sincerely yours in Christ,

Louis Achille	Martin Schirber, OSB
Joachim V. Benson, MS SS T	Gladys Sellew
Paul Hanly Furfey	Mary Elizabeth Walsh

by Paul H. Furfey

Copies of the letter were sent to: A. J. Coddington at Liturgy and Sociology; *Dorothy Day at* The Catholic Worker; *Dom Virgil Michel; Richard L. G. Deverall at* The Christian Front; *John LaFarge, SJ; Gerald B. Phelan at the Institute of Medieval Studies, Toronto; Smith Sullivan at* The Social Forum, *Ottawa; James Gillis, CSP, at* The Catholic World; *and Howard Bishop.*

Paul Hanly Furfey to Norman McKenna, 30 October 1936. McKenna–Furfey Z–26. Virgil Michel Papers, no. 55. Reprinted with permission of St. John's Abbey Archives, Collegeville, Minn.

56. Cardinal Mundelein Extols Frances Cabrini as a "Real Christian Heroine," 1938

The popularity of radio for entertainment and news suggested an analogy of the communion of saints for Chicago's George Cardinal Mundelein (1872–1939), who sent the following message on the air waves from Vatican City Radio to American Catholics on the occasion of the beatification of Frances Xavier Cabrini (1850–1911). Just as radio broadcast waves, unseen, connected millions with the cardinal's voice, so too Catholics obtained a glimpse of the connection between the unseen but real world of the communion of saints and their own lives. Catholics in the United States could now be in communion with someone close to them, an American immigrant. The model of rugged holiness the cardinal painted in describing Mother Cabrini's life bears many of the hallmarks noted in documents 29, 44, and 63 but emphasizes a holiness of action.

Friends, in the Apostles Creed, which is the symbol of faith for all Christian Churches, there are these words: "I believe in the communion of saints." Even as a small boy, when first studying the little catechism, this sentence intrigued me and held my attention.

It seemed so consoling to think that I had some one in Heaven belonging to me to whom I could talk and who could help me by his prayers so close to God. It seemed to me just as consoling that I had some one even closer to me by ties of blood perhaps in purgatory to whom I could be of assistance, to whom I could bring aid now that he needed it, and I was taught, as I now believe, that neither in Heaven nor in this entrance hall of Heaven, this place of purgation, is there any such thing as ingratitude, and thus in either case would the ultimate benefit accrue to me.

Perhaps in those early days it might have been difficult to understand how it was possible for us to communicate our prayers and our intimate thoughts

Saint Frances Xavier Cabrini

to the Blessed Above, but surely now when at this minute millions who are
thousands of miles away across a vast expanse of land and water, millions
who have never seen me are listening to every word that drops from my lips,
the very breathing of my lungs, surely now we better understand how very
possible, how very real is the communion of saints.

The consciousness of all this was brought home to many of us today. We
have just concluded, under the great dome of St. Peter's, a very solemn and a
very beautiful ceremony. By the supreme authority vested in him as Christ's
vicar Pope Pius XI has solemnly declared, that Mother Frances Xavier Cabrini
has been accorded her place among the blessed in heaven.

From the ends of the earth to which she sent them have come her daughters, the members of the religious family she founded. From distant lands
have come the friends who knew her in life and from every city in Italy have
come the citizens who are so proud of this saintly woman who followed their
emigrants into all the lands beyond the seas.

As the head of a great diocese in the Western world I have come for more
than one reason. I knew Mother Cabrini very well, first in the East, in New
York, the place of her first missionary endeavor, later on in Chicago, where

she made three different foundations. I was the last one to whom she spoke outside the nuns of her own community. I celebrated the Pontifical Mass at her funeral and gave the final Absolution at the end.

I remember as if it were yesterday the content of our first conversation. I turned to Monsignor Bonzano, who accompanied me, and said, "A very extraordinary woman."

There are many in New York, Chicago and other cities who remember her well. There are many, too, who admired her courage, her resourcefulness, her intense love of her fellow-man. She dedicated her life to a special phase of missionary work. She recognized the fact that there were souls to save at home, even as in the more romantic fields of China and India, and so she followed her countrymen and countrywomen who left home to seek bread and shelter as well as more abundant opportunities for their children in newer lands.

They were very poor, they were unlearned, they had only their labor, the sweat of their brows, the strength of their bodies to offer. They came in great numbers, lost mid strange surroundings. They drifted into the more squalid quarters of the great cities. But few, very few, of the priests in those parishes spoke the only tongue they knew. They were in danger of drifting away from the faith, the faith of their fathers. Some of them did.

Mother Cabrini went after them. She penetrated places where even the police were afraid to go: That was her apostolate. To those poor souls she dedicated her life and the community she founded. Missionaries of the Sacred Heart she called them. Wherever they went she followed her people. From the Atlantic to the Pacific she planted hospitals, schools, orphanages and homes for them. Absolutely devoid of means, she erected these fine institutions and paid for them all in the short space of a man's lifetime.

As great a miracle [is] this, almost as [great as] the multiplication of the loaves and fishes, the Lord performed through this favorite daughter so devoted to Him, the little woman of the frail body and stout heart.

To further her work, to link her institutions more firmly to the country, to show her country men the road to opportunity for their children, she became an American citizen, and thus she belongs to us. She became the first of our people to receive the second highest honor the church can bestow on one of her children, to be numbered among the blessed in heaven.

Many of us are still immigrants or children of immigrants. It is fitting, it is encouraging, then, that a foreign-born and naturalized citizen be the first to be raised to the honors of the altar, to become a national heroine, a patron of the male as well as the devout female sex.

Did I say heroine? In these days when we hear so much about heroes in the great war, war-like preparations, pre-war propaganda, we are apt to forget that peace has its heroes as well as war.

When we contemplate this frail little woman, in the short space of two-score years, recruiting an army of 4000 women under the banner of the Sacred Heart of Jesus, dedicated to a life of poverty and self-sacrifice, fired by the enthusiasm of the crusaders of old, burning with the love of their fellowmen, crossing the seas, penetrating into unknown lands, teaching them and their children by word and example to become good Christians and law abiding citizens, befriending the poor, teaching the ignorant, washing the sick, all without hope of reward or recompense here below — tell me, does not all this fulfill the concept of a noble woman?

Can we find in our history a truer or finer example of the real Christian heroine than the Blessed Mother Frances Xavier Cabrini? And, as I conclude this brief tribute to this saintly woman for the great army of her admirers in the United States, it is with the hope as well as the prayer that having said the last blessing over [her] lifeless remains as well as the first prayer to her in St. Peter's at her beatification, that her great soul may be there to welcome me when the doors of eternity open for me and conduct me into the mansions of our Heavenly Father.

> "Cardinal Mundelein Calls Blessed Frances Cabrini 'A Real Christian Heroine,'" *The New World* (18 November 1939): sec. 1, p. 2. From the radio broadcast from Vatican City, 14 November 1938. Reprinted with permission from the Archdiocese of Chicago, Joseph Cardinal Bernardin Archives and Records Center.

57. The Way of the Cross, 1939

The Stations of the Cross, choreographed in the version made popular by the Redemptorists for decades, provided a complete kinesthetic experience. Ideally, the assembly walked with the priest from station to station, imitating and identifying with Jesus' journey to Calvary. In the process, an affective aspiration of love, compassion, and repentance was encouraged. Meditation on the passion occupied the mind, and resolutions of "sin no more" attracted the will. The repetitive nature of the prayers ingrained the experience in the memory, which enabled the "way" to be carried back and extended to one's home. The popularity of the Stations of the Cross as a devotional exercise in the Catholic community during the depression and war indicates that it focused attention on Jesus' own human journey in identification with all of humanity. This Christocentric devotion, very different from the rural outdoor processions of the nineteenth century (see doc. 25) or from the passion play enacted in San Francisco in 1910 (doc. 39), complemented other depression-era novenas and prayers dedicated to the saints (doc. 49). Still another form of devotion to the passion would develop in the 1960s (doc. 80).

Foreword

This Manual has been compiled for the convenience of our Retreatants. It is arranged strictly according to the Order of Exercises followed at San Alfonso and contains all the prayers recited in unison by those attending the retreat.

Let us hope that our Retreatants will find it useful also as a book of devotion for themselves and their families at home and attending church.

May it serve to keep alive the spirit of the Retreat and be a constant reminder of the happy hours spent at the Retreat House under the very roof with Christ, the Lover of our Souls.

Stations, or Way of the Cross

The Stations represent places and scenes of the sufferings of our Lord on His way to Mount Calvary, and of His death and burial. A Plenary Indulgence may be gained each time the Stations are made. An *additional* Plenary Indulgence may be gained (a) Any day you make the Way of the Cross and receive Holy Communion; (b) Or after making the Way of the Cross ten times, you receive Holy Communion within the month following. Conditions to gain these indulgences:

1. To be in the state of grace; 2. To go from one Station to the other as far as the convenience of the place permits; 3. To meditate on the Passion of our Lord. These indulgences can be gained also for the souls in Purgatory. Those who are sick, or in prison, or at sea, or otherwise prevented from going to church, may gain these indulgences by saying devoutly, with a contrite heart, while holding in their hands a crucifix blessed for that purpose, the OUR FATHER, the HAIL MARY, and the GLORY BE TO THE FATHER, each fourteen times, and at the end of these the same three prayers, each five times in memory of wounds of Our Lord; and then again one OUR FATHER, one HAIL MARY, and one GLORY BE TO THE FATHER, for the Pope.

Preparatory Prayer
(To be said kneeling before the altar)
(Priest and Men)

In the name of the Father, and of the Son, and of the Holy Ghost. Amen.

My Lord Jesus Christ, Thou hast made this journey to die for me with love unutterable, and I have so many times unworthily abandoned Thee. But now I love Thee with my whole heart, and because I love Thee, I repent sincerely for having ever offended Thee. Pardon me, my God, and permit me to accompany Thee on this journey. Thou goest to die for love of me. I wish also, my beloved Redeemer, to die for love of Thee. My Jesus, I will live and die always united to Thee....

Sixth Station
Veronica wipes the face of Jesus

PRIEST: We adore Thee, O Christ, and we bless Thee.

Genuflect

MEN: Because by Thy Holy Cross Thou has redeemed the world.

PRIEST: Consider how the holy woman named Veronica, seeing Jesus so afflicted, and His face bathed in sweat and blood, presented Him with a towel, with which He wiped His adorable face, leaving on it the impression of His holy countenance.

MEN: My most beloved Jesus, Thy face was beautiful before, but in this journey it has lost all its beauty, and wounds and blood have disfigured it. Alas, my soul also was once beautiful, when it received Thy grace in Baptism, but I have disfigured it since by my sins; Thou alone, my Redeemer, canst restore it to its former beauty. Do this by Thy Passion, and then do with me what Thou wilt.

Our Father. Hail Mary. Glory be, etc....

Tenth Station
Jesus is stripped of His garments
PRIEST: We adore Thee, O Christ, and we bless Thee.

Genuflect

MEN: Because by Thy Holy Cross Thou has redeemed the world.

PRIEST: Consider the violence with which the executioners stripped Jesus. His inner garments adhered to His torn flesh, and they dragged them off so roughly that the skin came with them. Compassionate your Saviour thus cruelly treated, and say to Him:

MEN: My innocent Jesus, by the merits of the torment Thou hast felt, help me to strip myself of all affection to things of earth, that I may place all my love in Thee, who art so worthy of my love.

I love Thee, O Jesus, with my whole heart; I repent of having offended Thee. Never permit me to offend Thee again. Grant that I may love Thee always; and then do with me what Thou wilt.

Our Father. Hail Mary. Glory be, etc.

The Redemptorist Fathers, *San Alfonso Retreat Manual* (West End, N.J.: San Alfonso, 1939), foreword, 57, 64. Permission is granted to Orbis Books, Maryknoll, N.Y., to use for publication the above cited texts, 23 August 1999. Reprinted with permission, Redemptorist Fathers, Redemptorist Provincial Archives, Baltimore Province, Brooklyn, New York.

58. A Student Plan for Catholic Action, 1941

The Catholic Students Mission Crusade, founded in 1918, was a vigorous component in the spiritual life of thousands of high school, college, and seminary students, especially between 1930 and 1960. Its threefold focus was prayer, study, and action on behalf of the missions. The crusade published its own magazine, ran its own radio station, and organized national and local conferences and other mission-related activities for young people. Its efforts were successful largely because of the strong infrastructure of the Catholic school system, where sisters and brothers assisted and encouraged the young students. By the 1940s the shift had occurred from discussing the interior elements of Catholic Action to identifying a more structured emphasis on the role of the laity as supportive of the work of the hierarchy. Sister Rosaria's plan, presented here, was published in the magazine sponsored by the National Catholic Welfare Conference.

At a mission exhibit recently held in Detroit, Michigan, many visiting sisters registered the opinion that our Catholic high school students are not doing as much as they could do to further Catholic Action through the Catholic Students' Mission Crusade. The general thought was that the main reason for this lack of interest and response was that most of the students were not thoroughly acquainted with the Catholic Action program or how to go about organizing the Crusade in the schools.

It was suggested that there be prepared a brief outline giving Catholic high school teachers and students a knowledge of how to go about preparing and organizing for Catholic Action, under the direction of the hierarchy. Thus, we are privileged to present herewith the accompanying outline, reprints of which will be made available by the NCWC Publications Office.

Objectives:

1. Development of a sense of personal responsibility for the defense of Catholic principles and for the spread of the Faith.

2. Formation of leaders through Mission Action so that they may become active leaders in other organizations of Catholic Action in their own parish when they leave high school.

I. Study and Preparation Prior to Organizing the Mission Crusade

    A. The way to Catholic Action

        1. The first promoters of Catholic Action (Apostles and those who gave aid and assistance to the Lord)

        2. Catholic Action in the Sixth Century (St. Benedict)

        3. In the Thirteenth Century (St. Francis of Assisi)

        4. In our own time (Twentieth Century) laymen contributing

        5. Study texts from sacred Scripture (Luke 8:2–3; Acts 4:33–35; Phil. 4:3)

    B. What is Catholic Action?

    Pius XI defines Catholic Action as a participation of the Catholic laity in the apostolate of the hierarchy.

        1. Analyze definition

            a. Participation

            b. Catholic laity

            c. Apostolate of the hierarchy

        2. Essential elements of Catholic Action

            a. Mission for the salvation of souls

                1) One's own spiritual development

                2) That of our neighbor next

            b. Apostolate of the laity

                1) Initiative should be in the laity

                2) Must have the same purpose as the Church

      c. Formation of conscience

         1) Solid piety

         2) True knowledge of things divine

         3) Lively zeal and unstinted loyalty to the hierarchy

      d. Good example and zeal in defending the Faith

      e. Obedience to the laws of the Church

   3. Apostolicity

      a. Formation of the habit of daily prayer, work and sacrifice

      b. Unceasing effort to spread Faith among those outside the Church

   4. Means employed

      a. Daily contacts

      b. Written word

      c. Programs

      d. Study clubs

      e. Lay retreats

      f. Suggestions and encouragement for private reading

C. Basis of Catholic Action — Liturgy

Defined as the socializing factor in the most perfect of perfect societies — the Catholic Church. Another definition. It is the whole collection of the official services of the Church used in public worship

   1. Effects of

   2. Work of

D. Motivating Catholic Action

   1. Guiding principle — love of Christ

   2. Becoming active members in the Mystical Body of Christ

   3. Taking part in sacred ceremonies

   4. Making offerings

E. Organization of Catholic Action

   1. Actual affiliation under the direction of the hierarchy

   2. Branches of the CSMC High School Senior Units

II. Organizing Mission Crusade and Promoting Catholic Action After Preliminary Study

A. Organizing crusade

   1. Organized on a diocesan basis by the Diocesan director

   2. Branches of the CSMC High School Senior Units

    B. Requirements for affiliation

        1. Charter

        2. Membership cards

        3. Manual for Unit Directors

    C. Privileges after affiliation

        1. Spiritual benefits

        2. Participation in rallies

        3. Conventions

        4. Honor Clubs

    D. Obligations of Crusaders

        1. Fulfillment of pledge (viz. prayer, study, sacrifice)

        2. Contributions of membership offerings

        3. Making of periodic reports

III. Program of Mission Crusade

    A. Education and action

        1. Education

            a. Detailed study

            b. Training for sacrifice

            c. Stress need and importance of American contributions at the present time

    B. Mission prayer

        1. Promote spiritual activity through frequent reception of the Sacraments

        2. Offering of Mass once a week for the success of the missions

    C. Mission sacrifice

        1. Material support

            a. Crusade to direct its member Units to send contributions to the missions of their choice

            b. Contributions to be sent through the offices of the Diocesan Mission directors

            c. Have projects that have been approved by the Bishop receive first consideration

        2. Personal service

            a. Cultivation of vocations for the missions

            b. Advertising the missions through radio talks, etc.

D. Mission study through the following educational program

1. Projects

2. Simple programs

3. Mission plays

4. Debates

5. Discussion club courses

6. Review of mission literature

7. Printed posters publicizing missionary happenings for display on the school bulletin board

8. A list of timely topics for special assignments classes of English and religion

E. Discussion clubs

1. Study of individual countries and special mission questions

2. Study of home missions

3. Round Table discussions

4. Insistence upon practical application of the information acquired

F. Lectures, plays, debates and other activities

1. Illustrated mission lectures

2. Lectures by missionaries and promoters of missionary work

3. Mission plays from colorful pageants down to simple plays that can be presented at assembly meetings

4. Mission debates on mission questions that are debatable

G. Other activities

1. Display of mission scrap books

2. Collect Catholic papers, pamphlets, magazines, books from members of the parish for redistribution in home and foreign missions

3. Collect holy pictures, stamps, tin-foil, etc. for the missions

4. Visit a nearby home Indian or Negro mission and make a survey of the needs

5. Visit indifferent Catholics in the parish as part of the missionary apostolate

6. Subscribe to mission papers and magazines

7. Make linens for home and foreign missions

H. Special activities

   1. Sponsor one annual benefit entertainment in the missions

   2. Attend rallies held under the auspices of Diocesan Directors

   3. Attend national conventions and report on the work of the
       convention

Sister Rosaria, PBVM, "Student Crusaders for Catholic Action," *Catholic Action*
23, no. 5 (May 1941): 13–14.

59. The Divine Ideal of Holiness, 1942

*Father John J. Hugo (1911–85), a priest of the Diocese of Pittsburgh, attended
the retreat of the Canadian Jesuit Father Onesimus Lacourture (1881–1951) in
September 1938. The experience transformed his life, and he embarked on a
life-long journey of preaching the gospel word to others. His most famous re-
treatant was Dorothy Day, who recounts the impact of Hugo's retreats on her
in her autobiographical work* The Long Loneliness. *The Pittsburgh priest published frequently in the* Catholic Worker, *and the following excerpt, titled "The
Two Rules," presents the stark nature of his presentation of the following of
Jesus. In a country where Catholicism was seen as a public institutional force
and the practice of the faith seemed minimalistic to some, Hugo's use of scripture and his focus on the forgiveness that comes from Christ and the destiny of
creatures to be "like God" provided a strong foundation for the intense Christian commitment of many people. Advocating adoption of the heroic ideals of
the age (see docs. 44, 45, 55), his radical presentation led to charges of excessive rigorism, and the "retreat," as it came to be known, became the subject of
some controversy.*

"We are dying of complacency and insipidity, of vulgarized and minimized
truths, of a religion reduced to our own standards." These words of Jacques
Maritain are not merely an opinion; they are rather a statement of fact. If
Christ is in truth the Prince of Peace — and it is the Holy Ghost that says
He is — then all the turmoil and unhappiness in men's hearts must be there
only because they have not lived fully in accordance with the truths of the
Gospel. Further, the discord and distress of the whole world must likewise be
due to the fact that men have rejected, or insufficiently realized, the teachings
and promises of Christianity.

What is the diminished Christianity that leaves the world open to oppres-
sion by hatred and evil? What are the marks by which we may recognize the
lessening of the Christian ideal? It is especially necessary for those engaged in
the apostolate to know this. Ice cannot diffuse that; those who wish to help
enkindle the fire that Christ came to cast upon the earth must themselves be
aflame. Certainly they must at once reject any minimized version of Christian
teachings. If the world today is to be cleansed and Christianized, nothing less
than fire will do. The religion that is needed now is what Rosalind Murray, in
The Good Pagan's Failure, calls totalitarian Christianity.

Now the mark of diminished Christianity is this: those who live by it take as their aim the absolute minimum of Christian morality. No doubt they are sincere in their desire to be Christian; they are careful to regulate their conduct by Christian standards; but not less careful to choose the minimum standards. Doing this much, they consider that they have done enough, that indeed they have done all that can be expected of them. Religion has its place and God His rights; they are scrupulous that this place and these rights be acknowledged, but equally scrupulous that God does not invade the domain of their private activities, which are governed by self-interest and the desire to get the most out of life. Those who go beyond this minimum, demanding that the whole of life be regulated in reference to God, are regarded as extremists. Such extremists, if dead, are called saints; if alive, then fanatics and even lunatics.

Minimum Ideal

The nature of the minimum ideal is clearly shown in the rule of conduct that goes with it. This rule can be expressed either positively or negatively; in its positive form it runs: "Stay in the state of grace: as long as you are in the state of grace, you will be saved." Of course it is true that those who die in the state of grace will be saved, but it is also true that the state of grace is not an end, but a beginning; not a maximum, but a minimum; not the most that God will accept from us, but the very least. Grace is given to the soul that it may grow in holiness. The process of growth, which may be compared to that which goes on in all living things, begins in baptism. It ends when the Christian has become fully matured, a saint. The sanctifying grace that enters the soul at baptism is the grain of mustard seed, "the least of all the seeds," which, when it is carefully tended, grows up until it becomes "larger than any herb and becomes a tree, so that the birds of the air come and dwell in its branches." The Christian who is satisfied with "staying in the state of grace" is like a farmer who does not tend his trees and gets great satisfaction from the fact that they neither develop nor bring forth fruit.

State of Grace

The state of grace is compatible with a certain amount of worldliness and self-interest; without destroying grace, one can, up to a certain point, enjoy the things of the world and pursue natural satisfactions. When this fact is taken into consideration, the minimum rule undergoes a slight but significant development. It becomes: "Enjoy the things of the world; get as much as you can out of life — only preserve the state of grace." The minimum rule thus opens up the way to a practical paganism; it enables men to live like pagans while holding on to the bare essentials of Christianity. Although claiming to be followers and imitators of Christ, those who live by it take as their actual norm of conduct the maxim of the rich fool in the Gospel condemned by Jesus: "Eat, drink and make good cheer."

Mortal Sin

In its negative form this rule becomes: "Since mortal sin alone causes grace to leave the soul, it is necessary only that you avoid mortal sin; avoid mortal sin and you will be saved." No one could question the truth of this proposition; only it is an inadequate statement of the truth. It causes men to aim at the absolute minimum of Christian morality; it is a diminished Christianity. Moreover, like all partial truths, it is misleading. When we console ourselves for our lack of fervor by the thought that we at least are not in the state of mortal sin, we are like a man grievously sick, who, instead of sending for a doctor, consoles himself with the reflection that at least he is not dead. No doubt he is not dead, but he is not alive either — not alive in the sense that he can take a vigorous part in the affairs of living men. Meanwhile, if he does not take care of himself, he will soon be dead in the proper sense of the word. Now the man who can say of himself that he is not in the state of mortal sin, but can say no more, is in a similar way. He is not dead; but neither is he alive in the sense that he can live vigorously and fruitfully, bringing forth the words of holiness and spreading Christianity. And he, too, unless he begins to take care of himself will soon be dead completely.

Encourage Paganism

The rule of diminished Christianity, in its negative form, is also an opening, and even an encouragement, to practical paganism. One can be worldly without at once falling into mortal sin. The rule therefore becomes: "Enjoy the things of the world, only avoid mortal sin." Thus, by taking the minimum of Christianity as a maximum ideal, one is easily led to a way of life entirely opposed to that recommended to us by St. Paul in the maxim of practical conduct that he proposes to us: "Mind the things that are above, not the things that are on earth." (Col. 3,2)

Something Lacking

In a word the minimum rule of Christianity reduces Christian practice to the level of paganism. In the introduction to his book on the Holy Ghost Father Leen writes: "But apart from this (i.e., apart from the fact that the Catholic 'holds to certain defined religious truths and clings to certain definite religious practices') there is not any striking contrast in the outward conduct of life between Christian and non-Christian in what is called the civilized world." No wonder that Christians are unable to overcome the forces of paganism. They have not the heart to work against or fight against an enemy with whom they have so much in common.

More Than the Minimum

Even if we leave out of account worldliness in thought and conduct (which is the mark of the gross, uncultivated pagan), and confine our attention to the positive element in the minimum rule, it is obvious that its observance would not raise us much higher, if any higher, than the level of the good pagan, the righteous natural man. For the good pagan, as described by the great philosophers, is one who lives according to reason, who practices the natural virtues, shuns vice, and observes the natural law. In a word, he practices virtue and avoids sin. This is the maximum of the good pagan. It makes no difference that there are few, if any, pagans who realize this ideal; the point is that it is a natural ideal, entirely within the range of reason. Therefore, the Christian who seeks only to avoid grave sin has adopted a norm of conduct that, of itself, is not better than that followed by the good pagan. A natural life at its best is a diminished Christianity; and it can be called Christian at all only when it is joined to grace. It is the absolute maximum of the good pagan; but it is the absolute minimum of the Christian. Jesus was not yet satisfied with the rich young man who had avoided serious sin from his youth: "One thing is still lacking to thee...."

To Do Evil Stronger

It should be noted in passing that the ideal of the good natural life is difficult — rather, impossible of achievement *in practice* by those who live merely in accordance with their natural inclinations. The threefold concupiscence spoken of by St. John have [sic] given these inclinations a marked turn towards evil; so that those who live according to the desires of fallen nature will surely sin. "Those who live according to the flesh shall die," St. Paul writes, without qualification and in a tone of complete finality. (Rom. 8,13) This means that the minimum rule set up by the diminished Christianity, although it is theoretically sufficient, will fail *in practice* to raise men even to the minimum. It would be interesting to know what happened to the rich young man after he had refused the pressing invitation of Jesus.

Totalitarian Christianity

Now let us look at the other kind, totalitarian Christianity. It was the kind preached by Jesus. You will look in vain for so much as one place in the Scriptures where Jesus preached the minimum. He always demanded the maximum: "Be ye perfect as your heavenly Father is perfect." He placed before all men an absolute, divine ideal of holiness. St. Paul of course followed His master in this teaching; he wrote: "Be imitators of God." (Eph. 5,1) And St. John (I Jo. 1,6): "He who says he abides in Him, ought himself to walk just as He walked."

This is totalitarian Christianity: the pursuit of holiness, divine holiness. All men are called to it, and the whole plan of God for men can be summarized by saying that God wills all men to have it. "This is the will of God, your sanctification." (I Thess. 4,4)

Totalitarian Christianity likewise has its characteristic rule. It is this: "Thou shalt love the Lord thy God with thy whole heart, and with thy whole soul, and with thy whole mind." *Ex toto corde tuo:* the name "totalitarian" is not only timely but altogether precise. The tepid Christian, satisfied with a diminished Christianity, follows the rule of sin: avoid sin but love the world. The totalitarian Christian follows the rule of love; he seeks to give God a total heart.

Rule to Follow

There is no doubt which rule we should follow. It is only slaves who serve their master, not to please Him, but out of fear of offending Him. "Now you have not received a spirit of bondage so as to be again in fear, but you have received the spirit of adoption as sons, by virtue of which we cry, '*Abba!* Father!'" Because we are sons, we ought to follow the rule of love — what son does not love his father? Alas, that so many Christians should obey as slaves.

Rule of Love

The rule of love begins where the rule of sin leaves off. Those who live by the latter achieve at best absolutely the lowest degree of righteousness acceptable to God. Those who live by the rule of love start here; their least is to love God above every creature, then they traverse infinite gradations of charity, seeking to love God with all their hearts. The peak of the pagan's achievement is the beginning of the Christian's effort. The absolute maximum of the natural man is the absolute minimum of the true Christian. That is why the Christian who lives by the standard of the good pagan is practicing a diminished Christianity.

Yet one who is accustomed to view the avoidance of sin as the very acme of spiritual effort will perhaps wonder how he is to go any further. The answer is: by love. Now that he has satisfied the demands of divine justice he can go on to return the divine love. Like the rich young man he says: "All these things I have kept ever since I was a child; that is, from childhood I have sought to avoid transgressions of the commandments." And to such a one will come the same reply as of old: "One thing is still lacking to thee; sell all that thou hast — and follow Me." That is, in addition to observing the commandments of the natural law, which was also the ideal of the good pagan and the good Jew, he must go on and renounce all the goods of the natural order and follow Jesus by love.

Counsels and Precepts

I understand of course, that poverty is a counsel and not a precept; that all Christians, therefore, are neither bound nor advised to take the vow of poverty. But the words, "Follow me," which are an invitation to love Jesus, are for that reason a precept, as St. Thomas Aquinas points out, and are therefore addressed to all, and the same saint teaches that an interior renunciation of all natural goods, by way of preparation of heart, is likewise required of all, even of those who do not or cannot take the vow. Every Christian, therefore, besides renouncing sin, is called also to renounce the love of all earthly things, in order that he may give the whole of his heart to God.

Love Means Preference

The reason for this renunciation is not hard to discover. Love means preference. A man shows his love for his wife when he chooses her in preference to all others, even the most excellent and attractive. If he prefers her only to filthy and offensive creatures, then his love for her can scarcely be called great. Similarly, if we prefer God only to sin, which is the foulest of all creatures, then we can scarcely claim to have a deep love for Him. To show our love for God, we must be able to prefer Him to what is most beautiful and attractive. To possess Him, we must be ready to relinquish all things whatsoever. This is why Jesus asks us to love Him over land and parents and children and even life itself. It is why, to those who fail to choose Him unhesitatingly, to the highest goods, He addresses those dreadful words, "No one, having put his hand to the plow and looking back is fit for the Kingdom of God." (Lc. 9,62)

Sacrifice

The measure of love is sacrifice. Those who wish to live by the rule of love must live by renunciation. Jesus proved his own love for us by His death on the cross. "Greater love than this no one has, that he lay down his life for his friends." (Jo. 15,13) He expects the same of us: "Walk in love, as Christ also loved us and delivered himself up for us, an offering and a sacrifice." (Eph. 5,2) No one who refuses to prefer Jesus above all things, by complete detachment from the goods of this world, can claim to love Him fully. There are some who say that they desire to love God and will not hear of renunciation. Let them not be deceived: the price and the measure of Christianity is sacrifice. The Christianity without the Cross, so popular in our day (it is the same as the diminished Christianity that we have been speaking of), is also a Christianity without love. That is to say, it is really not Christianity.

John J. Hugo, "The Two Rules," *The Catholic Worker* 9 (May 1942): 1–2. Reprinted with permission.

60. "A Surge to the New Testament," 1943

An increased interest in the reading of the scriptures had begun to develop in the Catholic community in the 1930s. When the Episcopal Committee of the Confraternity of Christian Doctrine published a new English edition of the New Testament in 1941, a real revival with far-reaching impact on Catholic prayer and practice began to take place (see docs. 65, 67, 70, 76, 78). The committee established a "Biblical Sunday" to be celebrated each year, and the organization of the church's parish and school system was brought to bear upon the popularization of the reading and understanding of the scriptures. The newly formed Catholic Biblical Association (1936) was asked to disseminate sermons, study guides, and reading lists throughout the country. The following excerpts from the news releases for Biblical Sunday 1943 indicate the extent of the movement, the prevailing approach of the chairman of the committee, Bishop Edwin V. O'Hara (1881–1956), and the sample sermon which was issued for popular use.

For Release: March 17th–20th.
Faithful Turning to Scriptures for Strength and Courage

The Catholic Biblical Association for its Lenten period New Testament reading program, has distributed 1,500,000 reading lists.

Distribution has been effected through Parish Churches and educational institutions besides the splendid cooperation of the Catholic press. The reading of selected and appropriate passages from the New Testament has added literal spiritual supplication, which in the words of the Apostolic Delegate Archbishop Cicognani, is "the great remedy given to the faithful in America by their Bishops."

The faithful are taking to scripture reading with an enthusiasm and zeal never heretofore evidenced in America. Biblical Sunday on Septuagesima Sunday February 21st, was the keynote of a surge to the New Testament.

Reports from Bishops and priests throughout the country indicate that America's 22,000,000 Catholics are appreciating the Book of God more and more. Personal reading, with the aid of the Catholic Biblical Association's new volume, "A Commentary on The New Testament," is becoming more widespread.

Undoubtedly one of the finest explanations of The New Testament was that given by His Excellency Charles D. White, Bishop of Spokane: "I would not have you regard The New Testament as merely a family volume, any more than I would advocate a family prayer-book or a family rosary. Each member of the family old enough to use a prayer-book or a rosary should have both for himself. Each member of the family should also have his own copy of The New Testament. Do not place it on an obscure shelf. Keep it before you in your room, in your office. Take it with you on your travels. Read some portion of it daily. Meditate upon what you have read and apply it to yourself. Secure a copy for your personal use...."

For Release: March 24th–27th.
Bishop Lauds Use of Bible in "Today's World"

"The bible teaches the unity of the human race: that all men are of one stock.... The denial of this truth is the immediate cause of this war." With these words as his keynote, did the Most Rev. Edwin V. O'Hara, Bishop of Kansas City, advocate the greater use and reading of "The Sacred Scriptures in Today's World."

Speaking over a national hook-up of CBS stations recently, His Excellency as Chairman of the Episcopal Committee of the Confraternity of Christian Doctrine, gave a stirring explanation of the use of the Holy Book in modern living.

"Holy Scripture," Bishop O'Hara said, "has a message for the healing of the nations today. It proclaims the supremacy of God's law. It declares the dignity and eternal destiny of the human person. It asserts that all men are brothers one to another. It maintains the supreme value of freedom."

Throwing back their lie, the eminent prelate denounced Nazi "Aryanism" as an "Obsession." "The supremacy of a race," he said, "which sees in its own sons the 'pride of human kind' has been the boast of every imperialism. It is a heresy condemned in the most searching judgment of Pope [Pius] XII in his Encyclical letter to the nations."

Quoting the ageless words of the Vatican Council, Bishop O'Hara said: "'The books of the Old and New Testaments are held by the Church as Sacred — because having been written by the inspiration of the Holy Ghost, they have God as their Author'."

In his role as chairman of the Episcopal Committee, Bishop O'Hara has been the guiding spirit of The Catholic Biblical Association, in all its work.

A profound scripture scholar, he has lauded the Lenten Biblical program of the Association.

The suggested daily Lenten readings from The Revised New Testament for the week of March 28th to April 3rd are: — The Centurion's Servant, The Widow's Son, Luke 7, 1–7; The Baptist's deputation, Christ's Witness concerning John, Luke 7, 18–35; The Penitent Woman, Luke 7, 35–50; Blasphemy of the Scribes, Jesus and His Brethren, Mark 3, 20–35; Parable of the Sower, Matt. 13.1–23; The Weeds, the Mustard Seed and the Leaven; The Treasure and the Pearl, the Net, Matt. 13, 24–52; Jesus at Nazareth, Luke 4, 16–30.

Suggested Sermon on the New Testament,
To Parish Priests for the Third Sunday of Lent

The theme for the Sermon suggested by the Catholic Biblical Association for the Third Sunday of Lent is: "The Gospels Give Us the Light of the World"; based on the quotation from Eph. 5,8: "Walk, then, as children of light."

God is the Lord of light and throughout the Bible His operations are called "giving light," enlightening. The pages of the Old Testament announce the coming of a Savior who will be a Light for the Gentiles; the Sun of Justice (Mal. 4,2).

God wants in these days of darkness witnesses to the light. Like the Baptist, let it be said of each of us: "This man came as a witness, to bear witness concerning the light, among men through other men. We must radiate and reflect Christ."

How can we learn to radiate Christ better than in the school of His Gospels? If we assiduously study and patiently read the narrative of His life, we will be able to say: "What was from the beginning, what we have heard, what we have seen with our eyes, what we have looked upon and our hands have handled:... the Word of Life... we announce to you,... in order that you also may have fellowship with us, and that our fellowship may be with the Father, and with His Son, Jesus Christ" (1 John 1, 1–3).

Of us Christ will say: "You are the light of the world" (Matt. 5, 14), and like the Apostles we will encourage the worldlings "to open their eyes that they may turn from darkness to light and from the dominion of Satan to God" (Acts 26, 18).

For reward, Jesus, "the Root and the offspring of David, the bright morning star" (Apoc. 22, 17), will give Himself forever to us, the victorious Christians who have seen and accepted, followed and reflected the Light (Apoc. 2, 28).

Catholic Biblical Association, News Release, March 17th–20th, March 24th–27th, NCWC, File Folder B, Biblical Sunday 1941–49, 10/13, Archives of the National Catholic Welfare Conference, Archives of The Catholic University of America. Printed with permission.

61. A Program for the Christian Family, 1944–45

The family in Catholic social thought had always been perceived as the basic unit of society, and throughout the twentieth century the stability and permanence of the family, its prayer life, the gender roles within it, and the institution of the sacrament of marriage were presented as important components in teaching and catechetics. In the 1920s the academic study of the sociology of the family came of age, and during the next decade both Protestants and Catholics waged campaigns on behalf of the sanctity of the family. Catholic writers objected strongly to the academic endorsement of divorce, the exclusive focus on the personal relationship between husband and wife that relegated the consideration of the children to secondary status, and the possible infringement of public agencies on the private rights of domestic life. In 1931 the Social Action Department of the National Catholic Welfare Conference established the Family Life Bureau to coordinate a national effort on behalf of the family. The approach was primarily educational. Although its influence was limited, the Family Life Bureau was complemented by the parallel emergence in the 1940s of other family-oriented efforts at revitalization and postwar reconstruction – the Cana Conference Movement (1943–44), Integrity magazine (1946), and the Christian Family Movement (1949; see docs. 76, 79) – all of which initially grew from a Catholic Action base. The following program adopted by the Archdiocese of San Francisco for 1944–45 makes use of a Family Life Bureau booklet and develops a whole spirituality for the family by emphasizing prayer, participation in the parish, frequent Communion, charity, good reading, and the virtues of self-denial and courtesy.

For 1944–45
Recommended to Organizations and Groups
of the Archdiocese

The theme of the program suggested by His Excellency, the Most Reverend John J. Mitty, is "The Catholic Plan for the Family." In developing the theme, much assistance will be obtained from the papers read at the Conference on the Family held at the Catholic University of America on February 29, March 1 and 2, 1944 under the auspices of the National Catholic Welfare Conference. These papers have been published in a booklet entitled *The Family Today, A Catholic Appraisal,* which may be obtained by writing to the *Family Life Bureau, National Catholic Welfare Conference, 1312 Massachusetts Avenue, Washington 5, D.C.* In the following outline references are made to this booklet.

In the program there are two topics to be discussed each month: 1. *Practice in the Home;* 2. *Subject of Discussion.*

1. *Practice in the Home.* The program chairman should select one member of the group to discuss the particular "practice" in a brief statement not to exceed five minutes. The members of the group will then discuss the practical ways of putting the practice into operation in their own homes. The discussion should be brief.

2. *Subject of Discussion.* The program chairman should select competent persons within or without the group who are able to present the subject to be discussed each month. Splendid results have been obtained when the person who presents the topic is a member of the group and not a visiting speaker. This procedure is especially valuable in developing leadership among the members. It also leads to more informal and consequently more profitable discussion.

Theme for the Year
The Catholic Plan for the Family

October

1. Practice in the home: Morning and evening prayers (prayers of children and parents).

2. Subject of discussion: The Christian Teaching on Marriage and the Family. *The Family Today,* pp. 11–17.

   Questions:

   1. What do you mean by natural marriage?

   2. What is Christian marriage?

November

1. Practice in the home: Grace before and after meals.

2. Subject of discussion: The Family, State, and Church. *The Family Today,* pp. 146–50.

   Questions:

   1. What is the place of the family in modern states?

   2. What is the Catholic position concerning the relationship of the state to the family?

   3. What are the possible areas of conflict between the state and Church in regard to the family?

December

1. Practice in the home: Frequent Communion by all members of the family (monthly Communion of parents with Parish Sodalities and Confraternities, the Holy Name Society, etc.; monthly Holy Communion of working sons and daughters, of children of high school age).

2. Subject of discussion: The Parish and the Family. *The Family Today,* pp. 135–40.

   Questions:

   1. Can you give a definition of the Catholic parish?

   2. How is the family related to the parish?

January

1. Practice in the home: The virtue of temperance.

2. Subject of discussion: The Community and the Home. *The Family Today,* pp. 141–46.

   Questions:

   1. What is the responsibility of the community toward the family?

   2. How can the Catholic aid the welfare of the family by serving in organizations and committees working toward the common good?

February

1. Practice in the home: Charity in thought, word, and deed among members of the family.
2. Subject of discussion: Mothers in Industry. *The Family Today*, pp. 61–67.
   Questions:
   1. Is being a mother a part-time occupation?
   2. What is the so-called emancipation movement?

March

1. Practice in the home: Self-denial (observance of the spirit of mortification during Lent by all members of the family).
2. Subject of discussion: Mixed Marriages. *The Family Today*, pp. 107–15.
   Questions:
   1. What is the extent of mixed marriage?
   2. What influence has mixed marriage on children?
   3. How can the rate of mixed marriage be retarded?

April

1. Practice in the home: Courtesy.
2. Subject of discussion: Divorce. *The Family Today*, pp. 115–26.
   Questions:
   1. What is the Catholic teaching on divorce?
   2. Is divorce increasing?
   3. What is the effect of divorce on children?

May

1. Practice in the home: Good reading.
2. Subject of Discussion: Education for Purity. *The Family Today*, pp. 38–44; 60–61.
   Questions:
   1. Who should instruct children regarding sex?
   2. Should the schools assume this responsibility?
   3. How should instruction concerning sex be given?

Supplementary Reading: Consult *The Family Today*, pp. 159–160.

"Program on the Christian Family for 1944–45," in "Circular Letters," Archives of the Archdiocese of San Francisco. Printed with permission.

Part 4

FRUITION OF EARLY REFORMS
1946–79

Introduction

As had been true in the past two periods, cessation of a mighty war wrought both a revival of religion and an upswing in the economy. Church attendance was up for Protestants, even as "imperial" Protestants realized that they no longer held hegemony. In the Catholic community, the number of people responding to vocations to priesthood, religious life, and contemplative orders grew considerably, as did lay missionaries. Catholics had risen economically, socially, and professionally, but, as the prominent Jewish sociologist Will Herberg (1901–77) noted, they often acted as though they were still beleaguered immigrants. They appeared to live a "split-level" existence, separating business, politics, and public aspects of life from "religion," thus engaging in the very process for which they critiqued the secularists (see doc. 73; hereafter document numbers will be in parentheses). In the Cold War atmosphere of the 1950s, many Catholics rallied against "Godless Communism," as the most radical figure, Senator Joseph McCarthy, hounded and indicted fellow Americans in the "Red Scare," even as he addressed Holy Name Societies. Fear of a Communist takeover and the need to atone for the crimes of war and the horrors produced by the atom bomb raised calls for communal and personal reparation (72), expressed through October rosaries, May processions, and public gatherings for prayer.[1]

Catholics were among those who built new homes in the suburbs; they succeeded educationally and achieved relative economic security. The era of the immigrant church had passed.[2] Between the 1940s and the end of the

---

1. Works which provide a background and overview of the prayer and spirituality issues raised in this period: Gary Wills, *Bare Ruined Choirs: Doubt, Prophecy, and Radical Religion* (Garden City, N.Y.: Doubleday, 1972); Robert Wuthnow, *The Restructuring of American Religion* (Princeton, N.J.: Princeton University Press, 1988); idem, *After Heaven: Spirituality in America since the 1950s* (Berkeley: University of California Press, 1998); Anne Winston-Allen, *Stories of the Rose: The Making of the Rosary in the Middle Ages* (University Park: Pennsylvania State University Press, 1997); Keith Pecklers, *The Unread Vision: The Liturgical Movement in the United States of America, 1926–1955* (Collegeville, Minn.: Liturgical Press, 1998); Leo Ward, CSC, *Catholic Life, U.S.A.: Contemporary Lay Movements* (St. Louis: B. Herder, 1959); Timothy Kelly, "Suburbanization and the Decline of Catholic Public Ritual in Pittsburgh," *Journal of Social History* 28 (winter 1994): 311–30.

2. For significant background on this transformation, see Andrew Greeley, *The American Catholic: A Social Portrait* (New York: Basic Books, 1977).

1950s, the lives of middle-class women were made easier through automation and time-saving devices, such as the electric washing machine and dishwasher. While the traditional ascetical practice of penance had emphasized the importance of sacrifice, highlighting the wartime values of thrift and rationing (64b), a new era of the disposable and planned obsolescence required a different motivation and more subtle discernment (69, 84). Electronic media became visual, and religion came "packaged" into people's living rooms with the advent of television. By the mid-1950s, many middle-class homes of Protestants and Catholics alike viewed Bishop Fulton J. Sheen's (1895–1979) *Life Is Worth Living* series or Patrick Peyton's (1909–92) *The Rosary Hour* (68, 72).

In the wake of the war, African Americans were also mobile, moving to northern cities and to California in search of work. Catholic ethnic neighborhoods dispersed, and the racial tensions which had been brewing for years erupted violently in the 1960s. Sit-ins and rallies, disregard for norms and authority, a recognition of the gap between the real and the ideal, and uneasiness about increased diversity in the United States created volatile disruption and disturbance of the established order. Questions arose as to the feasibility of any institution meeting contemporary social problems. Hostile responses to the Vietnam War left the country divided. Catholics' collective identity appeared shattered. Traditional religious practices were shifted to the streets to engage the social issues of the day (80, 84, 91).[3] The early 1970s carried over the atmosphere of the preceding decade, and a new politicization of Catholics appeared, especially as Afro- and Hispanic-consciousness blossomed into the formation of national Catholic conferences for each of these groups.

Unquestionably the watershed event for all Catholics in this period was the Second Vatican Council, which brought to fruition many of the movements which had begun earlier in the century. The ecclesiological theme of the Mystical Body, so prominent in 1940s and 1950s Catholic Action, became nuanced as "family of God" and "people of God." This last image, which emphasized the development of spiritual gifts for all and the importance of growth in the spiritual life, was perhaps the most characteristic theme, at least through the 1980s, as identified by the Notre Dame study of American parishes in that decade.[4] The theme of "people of God" undergird the major pastoral framework for the tremendous number of liturgical changes which took place in a relatively short time. In 1979, the Rite of Christian Initiation of Adults was once again restored, thus highlighting the common priesthood of all believers and providing a model of postconversion formation for the rest of the church.

In some parts of the country, Catholics had moved from a "Catholic enclave" to embrace, or, at least, tentatively reach out to, other religious com-

---

3. The transformations are well covered in John T. McGreevey, *Parish Boundaries: The Catholic Encounter with Race in the Twentieth-Century Urban North* (Chicago: University of Chicago Press, 1996); David O'Brien, *Public Catholicism* (New York: Macmillan, 1989); Leslie Woodcock Tentler, *Seasons of Grace: A History of the Catholic Archdiocese of Detroit* (Detroit: Wayne State University Press, 1990).

4. Mark Searle, "The Notre Dame Study of Catholic Parish Life," *Worship* 60, no. 4 (1986): 312–33.

munities. Only a few liberal American Catholics had attended the 1893 World Parliament of Religions, whose leaders hoped the display of the power of "religion" could stem the tide of secularism and materialism. Seventy years later, the Second Vatican Council's documents on mission and ecumenism painted a more amicable picture of world religions, acknowledging the Spirit present among all peoples, even before the advent of Christianity. This more positive appreciation of common spiritual elements in all religions had been presaged in small ways through missionaries like Maryknollers Francis X. Ford (1892–1952), James Keller (1900–1977), and Marie Marcelline Grondin (b. 1909) (62, 75).[5] By the 1970s not only had the Catholic Church begun to realize itself truly as a diverse church culturally, but prayer itself drew from more global dimensions, including those from Latin America and Eastern religions (85, 92, 93). Parishes and dioceses supported Asian immigrants after the close of the Vietnam War and put "ordinary" parishioners in touch for the first time with people whose religious constructs were deeply imbedded in Buddhist, animist, and Confucianist traditions. The global church was now living in the United States.

The reader will note at least four important movements related to prayer and practice which reflect the mobility, gender role changes, and ecclesial transformations in the period.

1. The strong emphasis on the home and family as a locus of prayer and spirituality. The family was thought of as a "little church," and the parish was identified as a "family" (74). The family rosary (68), the reading of the scriptures at home (65), mission circles (77), the enthronement of the Sacred Heart (66), the Christian Family Movement (76, 79),[6] and the Paulist-sponsored ecumenical *Living Room Dialogues* took place in people's homes. While all valued the family, each group had sometimes conflicting understandings of the relationship of the members of the family to each other and the role of clergy in the new configuration of the family.

2. The desire for a more intense prayer life can be observed in the move to address the tension between action and contemplation (63, 68, 75, 87, 88, 89, 92),[7] the reflective, prayerful study of scripture at home and school (65,

5. Angelyn Dries, OSF, *The Missionary Movement in American Catholic History* (Maryknoll, N.Y.: Orbis Books, 1998); idem, "The Missionary Critique of American Institutions: From Catholic Americans to Global Catholics, 1948–1976," *U.S. Catholic Historian* 17 (winter 1999): 59–72.

6. For important background on the general movement and the impact of gender and social issues on change, see Jeffrey M. Burns, *Disturbing the Peace: A History of the Christian Family Movement, 1949–1974* (Notre Dame, Ind.: University of Notre Dame Press, 1999).

7. This topic loomed large in discussion among American Catholics in the 1960s and 1970s. See, for example, Jordan Aumann, OP, "Activism and the Interior Life," in Louis J. Putz, CSC, ed., *The Catholic Church, USA* (Chicago: Fides Publications, 1956), 274–93; Andrew Greeley, "Popular Devotions: Friend or Foe?" *Worship* 33 (October 1959): 569–73; idem, "Culture, Contemplation, and the Religious Revival," *The Critic* 18 (April–May 1960): 17–18, 77; idem, "Changing Styles of Catholic Spirituality," *Homiletic and Pastoral Review* 67 (April 1967): 557–65; idem, ed., *Spirituality for the Seventies*, entire issue of *The Critic* 29 (September–October 1970); Mary Hester Valentine, SSND, ed., *Prayer and Renewal: Proceedings and Communications of Regional Meetings of the Sister Formation Conferences, 1969* (New York: Fordham University Press, 1970), which shows the role of the Sister Formation Conference in the revitalization of prayer, especially

70), the rise of new religious movements such as Cursillo ("a little course in Christianity"),[8] the establishment of houses of prayer (87), the reformulation of the retreat movement (89),[9] and pentecostal Catholicism (86).[10] Measured against the devotional style of the previous decades, there was indeed a "piety void" (81, 82), but the changing theological and social complex of the entire community was clearly engendering new types of devotional affiliation and expression.

3. The post–World War II church profited from important developments in scripture study: the Catholic Confraternity of Christian Doctrine (CCD), organized nationally in 1935,[11] the formation of the Catholic Biblical Association (1936), the publication of the Confraternity Edition of the New Testament (1941), and the encouragement given to study the original languages in Pope Pius XII's *Divino Afflante Spiritu* (1943).[12] Practical programs to educate and form Catholics in scripture were produced by the CCD in coordination with the Catholic Biblical Association (60, 65, 70) and the Christian Family Movement, organized nationally in 1949 (76).

4. The engagement of the liturgical movement with social justice and its coalescence with the *resourcement* in scripture gave the American Catholic community's prayer and practice a distinctive orientation in the 1960s. Changes in liturgy, begun earlier by Pope Pius X (50) and encouraged by the papal encyclical *Mediator Dei* (1947), supported the previous work of Virgil Michel, Martin Hellriegel, and others who sought to make the renewed lit-

for women religious; Margaret Rowe, "Current Trends in Prayer," *Spiritual Life* 17, no. 3 (fall 1971): 172–85, which indicates the movement toward transcendental meditation, Christian yoga, and neo-Pentecostalism; Jean Leclercq, "New Forms of Contemplation and of the Contemplative Life," *Theological Studies* 33 (June 1972): 307–19; Walter J. Burghardt, "Without Contemplation the People Perish," *America* 127 (22 July 1972): 29–32; *A Spiritual Life Handbook,* entire issue of *Chicago Studies* 15 (spring 1976); "Spirituality for the Seventies"; *The Rebirth of Spirituality,* entire issue of *New Catholic World* 219 (March–April 1976); Robert M. Hamma, "The Changing State of Spirituality: 1968 and 1993," *America* 169 (27 November 1993): 8–10; Wuthnow, *After Heaven,* describes the shift from a spirituality of "dwelling" to a spirituality of "seeking," wherein people look less to organized religion than to the eclectic selection of sources found within various religious traditions.

8. Marcene Marcoux, *Cursillo: Anatomy of a Movement: The Experience of a Spiritual Renewal* (New York: Lambeth Press, 1982); Anthony Soto, OFM, "The Cursillo Movement," in Thomas C. Hennessy, SJ, ed., *The Inner Crusade: The Closed Retreat in the United States* (Chicago: Loyola University Press, 1965), 191–207.

9. See, for examples and comparisons, Hennessy, *Inner Crusade;* Roy J. Howard, *A Liturgical Retreat* (New York: Sheed and Ward, 1959); Gerald C. Treacy, SJ, "The Beginning of the Retreat Movement in America," in *Proceedings of the First National Conference of the Layman's Retreat Movement in the United States of America* (Philadelphia: Laymen's Weekend Retreat League, 1928), 13–20.

10. Josephine Massingbird Ford, "Pentecostal Catholicism," *Concilium* 79 (1972): 85–90; Kevin and Dorothy Ranagan, *Catholic Pentecostals* (Mahwah, N.J.: Paulist Press, 1969); Edward D. O'Connor, CSC, *The Pentecostal Movement in the Catholic Church* (Notre Dame, Ind.: Ave Maria Press, 1971).

11. Mary Charles Bryce, OSB, *Pride of Place: The Role of the Bishops in the Development of Catechesis in the United States* (Washington, D.C.: Catholic University of America Press, 1984).

12. Gerald P. Fogarty, *American Catholic Biblical Scholarship: A History from the Early Republic to Vatican II* (San Francisco: Harper and Row, 1989); Carroll Stuhlmueller and Sebastian MacDonald, eds., *A Voice Crying Out in the Desert: Preparing for Vatican II with Barnabas M. Ahern (1915–1995)* (Collegeville, Minn.: Liturgical Press, 1996).

urgy a school of prayer and guide to life for Catholics (51, 53, 55, 79). The gradual introduction of English into all the sacraments (71, 79, 90), physical changes in church buildings, and the expansion of liturgical roles were not without pain, however. The experience of the Xaverian Brothers (78) and the Agnesian Sisters (93) represents the search, confusion, internal conflicts, and eventual reclamation of a religious identity which many parishes and religious congregations undertook.[13] We see examples of the intertwining of the liturgical, scripture, and social justice movements in the prominent scripture scholar Barnabas Ahern's talk to the women of Chicago in 1951 (67) and in the bishops' 1975 explanation of the Eucharist in relation to the hungers of the world (91). Within ten years after the close of the Second Vatican Council, however, the conflict over implementation of the changes and the place of the church in society would surface into well-organized oppositional movements.[14] Issues of gender, race, and justice came together in styles of Catholic prayer and practice and became the tinder box for new developments.

62. A Postwar Revival, 1945

During and after World War II there were increased calls for the "spiritual awakening" of the masses. The Catholic Action model of holiness and the shift toward the sacrament of baptism had already given increasing distinction to the role of the laity in church and society. Now, the example of Nazi Germany, increased knowledge of the role of the United States in world affairs, and the continued impact of new European trends in theology and spirituality spurred many in the American Catholic community to push for "intercreedal cooperation" and a concerted attack on modern secularism. The specter of a worldwide atheistic Communism began to shape the contours of an American democratic missionary apostolate. One of the first to articulate an overall vision that would shape the years to come was Maryknoll Father James Keller (1900– 1977). His May 1945 article, excerpted below, caused a small sensation in the Catholic community and was quickly reprinted with a run of thirty-seven thousand. Summarized in more popular form in the January 1946 Catholic World, and again in a small pamphlet, the article gave the name "Christopher" to anyone who brought Christ to people who did not know him. In 1946 Keller began to publish his bimonthly bulletins, Christopher News Notes, *which grew in circulation from four thousand to forty thousand in 1946 and by 1954 reached eight hundred thousand people. His was a missionary method with ecumenical overtones, an outreach to all sectors of society; the movement achieved even greater popularity with Keller's* You Can Change the World: The Christopher Approach *(1948) and* Three Minutes a Day: Christopher Thoughts for Daily Living *(1949).*

---

13. George Fisher, "Liturgy USA: A Status Report," *U.S. Catholic* 32 (July 1966): 6–17.

14. See as background Timothy Kelly and Joseph Kelly, "Our Lady of Perpetual Help, Gender Roles, and the Decline of Devotional Catholicism," *Journal of Social History* 32 (fall 1998): 5–26. For the oppositional styles that grew out of this period see McGreevey, *Parish Boundaries;* John Seidler and Katherine Meyer, *Conflict and Change in the Catholic Church* (New Brunswick, N.J.: Rutgers University Press, 1989); and compare Father Dennis Geaney, OSA, "How U.S. Catholic Readers Pray," *U.S. Catholic* 42 (October 1977): 6–7, with William Dinges, "Resistance to Liturgical Change," *Liturgy: Journal of the Liturgical Conference* 6, no. 2 (fall 1986): 67–73.

What about the Hundred Million?

Out of the 140,000,000 persons in the United States it is estimated that not more than 40,000,000 at most practice any formal religion. This leaves a vast mass of 100,000,000 individuals in our country who are living off the benefits of Christianity, but who are becoming less and less conscious of the great Christian fundamentals that make possible their present way of life. It is quite obvious on all sides that millions are gradually losing sight of the great Christian ideals that have bolstered our civilization for centuries, for example, the concept of a personal God, the divinity of Christ, the Ten Commandments, the sacredness of the individual, and the sanctity of marriage and the home. If this trend goes far enough, many believe that it will open the way for the speedy rise of a new paganism that would eventually remove the United States from the society of Christian nations.

But, thank God, there is a very hopeful side to this picture. This trend has not developed to the degree that it is incapable of remedy. The majority of these 100,000,000 Americans are fortunately still blessed with an abundance of common sense. They are certainly neither anti-religious nor atheistic. They are endowed with an unusual sense of fairness and are often generous to a fault. They may be prejudiced at times, but this is seldom due to malice. It is because they do not know. They are truly interested in fair play for all men of all nations. These and many other similar traits are found only in peoples with a Christian tradition.

An Obligation and a Privilege

The great majority who practice no religion can be helped. They should be helped. They are our brothers and sisters in Christ. As trustees of the fullness of Christianity, we have an obligation to them as we have a responsibility to those of our own flock.

The task of bringing Christ to all men is incumbent upon all Catholics who, by the very nature of their beliefs, are held to share them with others, even at the cost of great personal sacrifice.

It should be a great privilege for us to have a part in leavening this great mass of unbelievers in our land. If we don't, others certainly will — others whose direction is not toward the tried and true things of Christian civilization, but definitely against them. While we stand by and do little about the slow but sure trend away from the fundamentals of religion on the part of the 100,000,000, others are at work night and day to win them away from Christ as speedily as they can.

Accompanying this unfortunate trend, whether as cause or result is not important, is the subtle undermining of our social fabric by atheism. All of us know the increase in skepticism among so-called intellectuals. Where there was formerly one college instructor not firmly grounded in Christian doctrine who declared it hard to square scientific inquiry with faith in a personal God, there are possibly thirty today. Their skepticism, naturally reflected in their students, is now beginning to catch up with us. An increasing number of young people are being adversely affected. To date, insofar as religion is concerned, the net result seems to have been, for the masses, an impetus in the direction of agnosticism, if not downright atheism.

Add to the force of honest doubt the influence of the malignant, controlled propaganda against belief in God which is being spread by experts in deception, highly organized, and cleverly efficient, and we can hardly wonder at the subtle undermining of all religious foundation.

The Catholic Church in the United States is doing a very creditable job in protecting and fostering its own members. It is showing a healthy gain in numbers; the faith is cherished. But unless the Church takes a very active role in leavening the mass outside its fold, and in keeping alive a consciousness of the deep fundamentals of Christianity, is there not a likelihood that such an anti-Christian sentiment will be built up because of materialism and an active promotion of practical atheism that persecution of all religion is bound to follow?

Many feel that in our country we are gradually drifting into the same danger as that which beset the Church in Germany. A Catholic layman writing about the great setback the Church suffered in that country gave an interesting explanation. He pointed out that during the early days of the Nazi movement the Church was getting stronger and stronger — but only within her own sphere. Priests were interested and active in their work for souls. The laity also showed a deep concern for religion. They went to the sacraments more frequently. Churches were crowded. But little was done to protect the mass of people outside the Catholic Church from the false philosophy of Nazism.

The more the cancer developed, the more the Church withdrew into an isolated position. Eventually the mass, without any leadership or guidance in basic fundamentals, became infected with the poison of the new idea. Religion survived, as it always has and will, but not without a terrific shock....

The Positive Approach

The vast multitude in the United States who practice no religion live in a "no man's land." It is nobody's particular business at present to reach them. The leavening of this mass of 100,000,000 souls awaits the attention of those who are entrusted with the fullness of Christianity. Until it becomes our special responsibility to make a continued effort to bring Christ to them, they will probably get little or no attention. Possibly the very continuance of American democratic ideals depends upon what the Church does for this multitude.

This situation is acute, the time is ripe for us to assume a positive strategy. In the Confederate general's famous words, the battle goes to the leader who "gets there fastest with the mostest." What will happen to us if we do not switch from the defense to a more active offense?

If we become really serious about this problem — if we become determined to do more than merely theorize or pass resolutions — we'll have to make some radical adjustments.

For this work of the leavening of the mass to be effective on a long-term basis, it must become part and parcel of the normal, routine life of the diocese and of the parish, since they are the fundamental channels established by the Church to communicate God's grace to all men, be they Christian or pagan.

No one can question the grand job now being done by the 38,000 priests of the United States. But they themselves would be the first to say that a specialized training is needed for this type of work....

Movement Can Be Started Now

Until it is possible to give priests such training, however, something can and should be done immediately to meet not only the present need but that which is bound to come in the post-war period. The actual movement could be started without delay with only a group of priests working under some Archbishop or Bishop who would guide them and keep them in safe waters. This group could work out formulas of approach and techniques that could be used to advantage at once in leavening the mass. When these principles are reduced to a practical form it would be easy for priests and a select group of the laity to begin putting them into effect immediately.

A possible name for such a movement might be "The Christophers," since all those connected with the movement would be in a very literal sense "bearers of Christ." Its one great objective would be to bring Christ to all in our land — whether they be in the crowded cities or in the most remote and sparsely settled areas — who either do not know Christ or are opposed to Him. But at the same time it is highly important that all who would endeavor to be such bearers of Christ should first of all make sure that they themselves are filled with the spirit of Christ — that in a very literal sense they are "other Christs." These two great purposes of the movement are well summed up in the words of His Excellency the Apostolic Delegate, Archbishop Cicognani: "This is our supreme mission — to live the truth of Jesus Christ and to show it forth to others!"

If such a movement is established, it would seem wise that it should be dedicated to all phases of the task of bringing Christ to all peoples in the United States, and be prepared for anything and everything that would involve leavening the great mass of more than 100,000,000 Americans not now being contacted by the Church.

Laity Further Stimulated for Concerted Action

The work of this new mission movement for our country would be very much concerned not only with priests, but also with developing ways and means for the laity to become, under their own Bishops and diocesan priests, enthusiastic apostles in leavening the mass. If thousands of priests are needed for the leavening of the mass in our country, tens of thousands of lay persons must be found to act as auxiliaries. Throughout the country there are probably available right now at least 50,000 such persons who have both the ability and the zeal needed for the task of bringing Christ to the 100,000,000 in our nation who practice no religion. All that is needed, besides the help of God, is to arouse their interest in the vast opportunities right at our front door, organize them in their own diocesan units, and direct them by qualified priests acting under their Ordinaries....

There are many channels through which lay people may work to preserve the Christian tradition that makes a country like America possible. Foremost for immediate consideration might be (1) education, (2) communications, (3) personal influence in the community, (4) labor and government.

The First Channel: Education

Probably the most important task ahead is to develop among young Catholics through education a greater sense of the good that they individually can do if they are deeply convinced that they possess the truth which can bring peace and happiness to mankind.

The present wonderful work of Catholic schools and colleges should in no way be underestimated. It is generally admitted, however, that we are turning out few leaders. In talking on the subject with deans, teachers, and students in Catholic schools in many dioceses we have found that they readily admit that something is missing. They say that the general trend is to overlook emphasis on the far-reaching influence each student can exert for good in whatever surroundings he may happen to be, on being a bearer of Christ to those who know Him not, on devoting time and effort to the spread of truth with even half the zeal shown by those who are working to scatter error.

The present educational program, they frankly say, is limited to instilling in the student the belief that his first, and practically his only business is to save his own soul. Not much is said about his obligation to "sanctify others as he would sanctify himself," except in terms of giving money or material help to the poor. It seldom even occurs to him that he has within him that truth for which men are yearning or that many with whom he daily rubs elbows will never in their lifetime partake of that truth if it is not in some small measure communicated to them by himself.

The result is that, with few exceptions, the Catholic college or high school graduate is not a leader. He is a good citizen and the backbone of the Church, concerned with taking care of himself here and saving his soul for the hereafter. He misses tremendous opportunities for good that could also be the means of deep satisfaction and strength to himself, and all the while the forces of iniquity are busy spreading poison on every side....

The Second Channel: Communications

Opportunities are endless for infusing Christian philosophy into the main stream of American thought through the medium of communications. At present we avail ourselves of only a few such opportunities and are not even conscious how many others exist. This is no reflection on any of us. It has not been sufficiently impressed on us that we have a serious responsibility to share the truth we possess with all mankind.

We take pride in our excellent Catholic publications. But at most our journals reach only a tiny fraction outside our own body. A fine example of the aggressiveness of atheistic forces in this field is the fact that the communists have over one hundred publications in New York City alone, the majority directed outside their own body!

In all that has to do with writing and visual presentation, we should take great care to know the norms of form that are acceptable to the general run of people. So often we make the mistake of presenting a lofty message in a form that appeals only to seminarians and nuns and a small group of religious-minded people. But it is absolutely out of tune for the great majority — for the very ones who need our message most.

One of the editors of *Readers Digest* told us that they would welcome more Catholic articles but that stories with a religious theme are usually written in such a sugary fashion that they cannot be used. Editors do not ask us to compromise in our substance, but they rightly insist on a presentation that is acceptable to the majority of their readers.

Basic Catholic teachings could also be woven into editorials and articles dealing with family, education, government, property, wealth, surplus, labor, capital, etc. This would need careful study and well-developed technique.

There is a great demand for children's books. It would be easy for young Catholic writers to specialize in this field. They could gain a substantial income while at the same time conveying Christian ideas through their books.

The most popular books today are the comics. Sixty million of them are sold each month. Comics leave such a definite impression on young people that the Army and Navy are now using them in preference to the movies and radio in order to put over their message. In writing comics it would be easy to give a Christian twist to thought and language. For anyone gifted in this type of work and anxious to do good on a large scale in forming the thoughts of others, this one field alone offers tremendous possibilities.

In the field of literature, high and low, we have advantages that no other group possesses. As one non-Catholic writer put it: "You Catholics have something to write about." Even though we could not and should not label everything "Catholic," yet we should be able to impregnate many short stories, articles, books, and comics, with Christian themes....

The Third Channel: Personal Influence in the Community

Comparatively few Catholics may be engaged in such highly specialized pursuits as writing, lecturing, stage, movies, or music. But every lay person can discover opportunities right in his own neighborhood by which he can exert a power for good, whether he lives in the largest center or the smallest crossroads. Suppose there were only ten persons of real influence in a community. A practical technique could be worked out so that some one person, priest or lay, would establish and maintain a friendly relationship with each of the ten, not for any social reasons, but for the sole purpose of keeping that person continually conscious of the great Christian fundamentals.

Imagine the far-reaching results if it were possible to have each one of the most influential individuals in each diocese constantly but tactfully contacted by some priest or qualified lay person. It can be done, if the lay apostolate becomes the business and responsibility of some special group of priests of the diocese.

An occasional Catholic doctor or lawyer who has caught an idea of the great possibilities for furthering Christian principles in the pursuit of his profession has rendered invaluable service in communicating Christian fundamentals to patients and clients in a tactful yet effective manner. The apostolate carried on by these few could easily be extended to thousands in similar professional positions if they were individually taught the method of imparting to those outside the faith the simple elements of the faith they themselves possess.

Not long ago a newspaper report said that several members withdrew from some civic enterprise in Harlem because of the presence of a few Communists on the board. That was just what the Reds were hoping for. When the Catholics withdrew, they left the entire enterprise in the hands of the very ones who they thought should not even have a partial control. The first situation may have been difficult, but certainly the second one became far worse.

One layman worked for years to prepare the way for the Legion of Decency. Two officials of one of the largest news distributing agencies in the country have been important factors in keeping off the market many objectionable pieces of literature. . . .

The Fourth Channel: Labor and Government

Perhaps one of the most fruitful fields awaiting the attention of Christian influence is that of labor. Although our Catholic theories in this field are sound, unfortunately in the mind of the laboring man they are little more than theories. Something more is needed and the people know it. There's no way to fool them. They know that Christians who champion the cause of labor are few and far between.

On the other hand, the laboring class is being shamefully exploited by professional agitators, missioners of discord, themselves often of criminal association and background. Just the same, these leaders have captured the laboring man's imagination, because while we have talked they have acted — obtained better wages, better living conditions, and even if hypocritically, have pleaded the cause of the humble throughout the world. . . .

Even if Communism and all other sinister forces disappeared overnight, our responsibility would still be a terrific one. We would still have an obligation to help the 100,000,000. The challenge of the increasing paganism in the United States is a serious one for us, one that is bound to involve generations yet to be born. But it is a challenge that we can successfully meet. We have God Himself behind us.

But our success, under God, will be in direct proportion to the number who "go" as Christ commanded us to "go." If there are only a few messengers, if only a few of the clergy and laity "go" to leaven the great mass of humanity in this country now outside Christian influence, then we may eventually face a worse swamping than we have ever known. A serious setback at home would mean an even more serious setback in our efforts to Christianize the world.

The strong movement contemplated here would thus benefit not only our own 100,000,000 but would help to protect all that American Catholics are now doing and planning to bring Christ to all mankind.

If we "launch out" in great numbers, if we build and plan and venture with the daring, courage, and faith that Christ expects of his followers, we may be the means of salvation to untold millions.

> James Keller, "What about the Hundred Million?" *American Ecclesiastical Review* 112 (May 1945): 321, 322–23, 326, 329, 332–34, 338–40, 344–45, 346, 348–49. Printed with permission.

63. Mary, Model of a Woman's Spirituality, 1949

Prayers, sermons, and devotion to Mary often touted traditional "feminine" virtues allied with homemaking and childcare. Dr. Anna Dengel (1892–1980), foundress of the Catholic Medical Mission Sisters, as early as 1921 had pressed for professional medical roles for women religious to heal "the unspeakable suffering of women" worldwide. In her talk to the sisters at their motherhouse near Philadelphia, Dengel presented Mary as a model of "modern" virtues: decisions made at the expense of popularity with others, a balance between action and passivity, and strength to sustain work in the midst of new directions in mission to women. Her presentation, given below, which reflects the altered social and economic possibilities for women in the post–World War II era, is a contemporary reflection on the scriptural foundations of the joyful mysteries of the rosary. Mother Dengel and her congregation were influenced in their scriptural and liturgical formation through Michael Mathis, CSC, who helped her write the community constitutions and who later inaugurated the Liturgical Institute at Notre Dame.

Today, the feast of the Annunciation, we should try to live with Our Lady. We must, of course, live with Christ, but with Our Lady too, especially today, and we must study and find out in what way she is our model. Few things are written about her, but it is amazing all the thoughts and inspirations that come from thinking about her often.

I want to point out a few scenes in Our Lady's life today, just a few things that affect our vocation, that will be an example to us in our own lives.

The first is the Annunciation. The angel came and proposed to Mary the greatest vocation ever proposed to any human being. We cannot imagine Our Lady having the right answer immediately if she had not prepared herself beforehand. And neither shall we be ready for anything great or specific, unless we too prepare for it. We never know what God will ask of us, so we should strive every day to prepare ourselves by doing His Holy Will daily.

I read recently how Isaac Jogues thought often about what it was to be a martyr. When we read of the terrible torments he suffered, we wonder how he was able to endure them, but since I read that book, I know the answer: it was because he prepared himself for it.

So, too, Our Lady was so willing to do something that was not easy. She knew it was something great, but very difficult — yet she trusted in God and gave her consent because it was His Will.

Then, in making the journey to Bethlehem, she expected Our Lord to be born soon, and she could have excused herself from the trip; anybody would have excused her from it, but she felt it was her duty, no matter what inconveniences she suffered.

Often we are not feeling one hundred per cent, or are not in the right mood for something or other, and we are tempted to ask to be excused from it when we could really do it with a little inconvenience to ourselves. When we do excuse ourselves, we do not imitate Our Lady. As missionaries, there will be many times when we do not feel just right, and we do either choose to give in or to imitate Our Lady and suffer a little inconvenience.

Then we have the Visitation when Mary went "with haste" to her cousin, Elizabeth; that is, she went with eagerness and joy to serve and to help. That is also something that we should be — in our spirit. We should serve others, not because it is our duty and we go with heavy feet, but because we have a desire to help and go with a spirit of joy and generosity. That is our vocation. It is *generosity* that makes life easy and joyful. To be generous means a lot; if we do not serve like Our Lady, with eagerness and joyfulness, then it is not worth very much, and it is very hard on us.

The next scene is the one that took place in the Temple. Our Lord had remained behind and Our Blessed Mother blamed Him for causing them to be anxious about Him. He answered that He had to be about His Father's business.

With us, as religious and as missionaries, it is sometimes hard for us to please our parents and relatives. We owe our greatest love and obedience to our parents, but next to God. When it is difficult to cause displeasure to our parents to do the will of God, we should recall this scene in the Temple.

And then the hidden life of Our Lady. It was the happiest and the most usual life. She had the privilege of serving Christ in the Flesh and Blood, but even in her life, much Faith was required. We serve Our Lord too. We are enrolled in His own immediate service, but we must go by Faith, which makes it much more meritorious.

And now, the Marriage Feast of Cana. She could have just sat there and let the wine jugs be empty and do nothing about it. Now there is a thing that takes a lot of simplicity and prudence — that is to know when we are butting in, and when we are being helpful. We say we cannot tell at once where the *balance* is, but we must work to find out. We should not interfere in others' affairs so as to be butting in, but when there is opportunity of being helpful, we should not pass it up with the statement, "It's none of my business." Our Lady almost forced the miracle by Our Lord, by her thoughtfulness to save the situation. There are many opportunities given in Community life to ease the situation and to save the situation.

And lastly, we have the scene of Mary at the foot of the cross. Our Lady stood in the great trial and never collapsed. It is a very great example for us.

On this feast, she looks down on us and we look up at her, in all the houses of our Society. We ask her to strengthen us and to help us grow in the things we need to become good Medical Missionaries. We ask her to let grow in our very marrow and bones the desire to do the Will of God in everything, so that we will always be prepared for whatever He asks of us. Then we ask for strength not to give in to every desire of ease, and for good common sense to know when we should give in — to be sensible about it. Then to serve others with joy, to be eager to help, then the Will of God must always come first for us, rather than to please others.

Again, we are in the service of God, in the very army of Christ. We ask, too, for the grace of helping others, and thus making community life easier and happier for all. We are serving humanity and we have the privilege of sharing in Our Lady's work, by helping in the salvation of souls. She is our Mother, and she must help us to develop these virtues her life portray[s], so that we may be good, helpful, strong, cheerful and wonderful Medical Missionaries.

> From *Talks and Writings of Mother Anna Dengel*, 25 March 1949. This talk is from the Medical Mission Sisters Archives, Philadelphia, and is reproduced here with their permission. The text is from notes of a talk Mother Anna Dengel gave to the Medical Mission Sisters in Philadelphia. She did not speak to the community from a prepared text, nor did she edit this text. Her oral addresses to the community have yet to be prepared for a wider distribution.

64. Katherine Burton Reflects on Her Conversion, 1949

Katherine Burton (1887–1969) was a writer for and editor of McCall's, Redbook, and several other popular magazines. She converted to Catholicism in 1930 and wrote many biographies of founders and foundresses of religious congregations. Intellectually and spiritually, Burton was influenced by her Anglican pastor at St. Mary's, New York City, Dr. Selden Delany, who eventually converted to Roman Catholicism. Experientially, Burton had to deal with the image of immigrant Catholics as ignorant, unenlightened, and superstitious in their religious practices. Burton's quest to "seek anchor" in a changing world order led her to the church, where she found diversity in the composition of the community and a sure knowledge of faith. The first selection below is from her autobiography, wherein Burton reflects on elements in Catholicism which affected her conversion in 1930. Several years later, Burton was approached by Father Harold Purcell to write a column for The Sign, *a Passionist magazine, of which he was the editor. Her column, "Woman to Woman," ran for many years and covered a wide range of subjects. In the second section below, Burton comments upon the practice of Lenten penance during World War II, stressing greater physical sacrifice ("giving up something") and taking time for prayer. She reasoned that if Americans sacrificed for the war effort, why couldn't Catholics sacrifice for God?*

"Seeking Anchor": From Katherine Burton's Autobiography and Reminiscences

It was also at this time that I began to admire the Roman Catholics whom I knew for their way of sticking to what they had been taught. I did not know many, but they all impressed me in the same way. There was Irene Sweeney whom I knew in high school. There was Mrs. Robinson, the riding teacher in Garden City, and there was this really well-read girl. Their mentalities and their training were different, but they all knew the answers to questions about their faith and could defend it. I also liked their way of being gay about their religion. Sometimes, in fact, when I heard them speak of the saints and Our Lady in very familiar terms, it made my still somewhat Protestant soul nervous, for they spoke as if they were in the next room, as if they were part of the family....

I was continually faced by the fact that there were people of real intelligence who had become Catholics. I could see why poets and dreamers slipped into the Church. They were not ordinary people who mended for guilds or collected funds for the heathen; they merely wandered with God and sat at His feet, as did Mary of Bethany. I could see why Alice Meynell became a Catholic: I was certain if I had had her brains and if the author of *The Hound of Heaven* had stayed at my home for weeks at a time, I could easily have been swept into that Church....

I tried to continue at St. Mary's, but the security I had known there was gone and it would not return. Besides, I was disturbed by the bitterness which some members of the congregation felt toward Dr. Delany — a bitterness justified, of course, from their point of view. I tried to go occasionally to St. Patrick's Cathedral, but I felt I did not belong there. I did not really belong anywhere. It was when I began to realize that only two roads lay before me, one pointing to agnosticism, that I decided to ask advice from someone.

I wrote to Dr. Delany first to ask him what I should do. I was finding it difficult, I said, to go back to St. Mary's and besides, as he knew, I had had many uneasy moments there long before he decided to leave.

"It is not an easy question for me to answer," came back his answer. "I might say that you should not be influenced by what I have done, but what is life but being influenced by the various personalities God flings across the orbit of our progress through space? We have to choose which personalities we shall cling to. That is where we differ from the planets. But the choice must be our own, aided by divine grace. Do not try to escape from the Anglo-Catholic-Protestant-Episcopal Church unless you simply cannot stay where you are and practise your religion there any longer. And it must be an intelligent choice."

He suggested that I be patient about it, since the art of perfection consists in going slowly: "The slapdash methods which you use so skillfully in cooking and in magazine work will never enable you to master the science of the saints. 'The kingdom of Heaven suffers violence and the violent take it by force' — but that doesn't mean that you can take it by epigram or a turn of the wrist."

The letter came to me when I was already under instruction, so I felt that my choice, though influenced by him, was after all my own.

"Woman to Woman": The Sign

We all know the type of man or woman who ostentatiously "gives up for Lent." You offer them candy or a glass of wine or a cigarette and you are confronted by what? A mere "no thank you?" Never that, but by the words, "I've given that up for Lent." No fasting in secret for them, though Our Lord Himself suggested that was a good way.

At the present time — and no doubt for some time to come — such a phrase will sound extra-foolish. Greater things than a bit of abstinence from luxuries for a stated period will have to be given up.

I have always thought the Herrick poem on Lent a superb thing, and I still agree that a Lent in the heart is more important than a Lent devoted only to externals of food and drink. But this year especially we need a Lent of the body and a Lent of the soul too. And especially we don't need people who act as if it were something rarely unselfish to be going into a church a few extra times besides the days of obligation of cutting out a small personal luxury.

Lenten Fast and Abstinence

I know a group which meets at a church every month to sew for charity. Midway in the afternoon coffee and cakes are served. It is a nice break in the afternoon's work which, however, is not exactly heavy in its scope for any of us. Last year after Lent had begun the cakes and coffee came as usual. I had just finished reading the rules for Lent as issued by the Archbishop and I was amazed all over again to see how stringent they are if really taken actually and as bidden. And there was nothing in those rules permitting cake and coffee in the afternoon even for the charitably inclined.

I think it would be a fine idea if we who are members of such circles would during Lent take the money appropriated for refreshments and send it where it would feed people who don't have afternoon meals but are lucky if they get two out of three. It could be sent to the Franciscans, for instance, for the never-ending bread line, or to the Catholic Worker, which feeds many hundreds every day.

Certainly we of the rank and file are taking Lenten rules more easily than people used to, or at least it seems so. Perhaps partly this is due to the leniency of the priests. And, since sewing circles in churches all have moderators, there must be some leniency there too.

It has been so easy and pleasant for most of us in this land of ours. But the gray days are at hand and we all have to meet them in small as well as in large ways, in little uncomfortable selflessness as well as in the great ways of sacrifice. The large ways are made for us and we must accept them. The little ways are our own and we can take or leave them. But these latter will build our morale for the larger ones.

No Small Contribution

I saw a letter a few days ago, received by a woman in defense work. It came from a very sick woman in a hospital, a chronic invalid, and it was full of worry lest too many nurses desert their posts to rush into the Army when they were needed in less exciting spots, or so many women give up charity work for the poor around them to go on war work committees. She called the work on the home front "quiet and undramatic," but hoped that women would be unselfish enough to stick to it in sufficient numbers to keep it going. She added that she was sad that she herself could do so little. "I can't do active defense work, but I can complain less about my pain and so release the nurse to look out for the other women in my ward."

It sounds like a small contribution but it is not. For it involves the sacrifice of the thing she needs most. How many of us are doing that?

Extra Time for Prayer

One other sacrifice we can make, all of us, is the way of giving up. We can give up some extra time for prayer. In fact, it might be a good idea if, in addition to giving up the refreshments, the sewing circle spent the usual refreshment period in going into a church and praying together before the Blessed Sacrament.

Years ago, during the other war, Father Vernon Johnson, then a famous Anglican preacher, later a convert to the Church, suggested such group prayer — a few here and there on their knees together, then in large groups, until the whole world would be praying. Lately I saw a similar suggestion from another English convert, Dr. Orchard, now in this country. And yesterday I heard a priest from one of our foreign mission orders preaching, asking help[,] for the work abroad now is threatened and wrecked. His face was tired with worry but his voice was brave and confident as he said over and over again in his sermon the words of Our Lord, "Go to *all* the world."

And I thought that unless we go to all the world with our prayer and pray for all the world, the little Lenten sacrifices and the large ones too won't really matter. For the world must turn to prayer — prayer for all the world, for friends and enemies, for good men and bad men, if we are all to be saved, in body perhaps, in spirit surely.

Katherine Burton, *The Next Thing: Autobiography and Reminiscences* (New York: Longmans, Green and Co., 1949), 118, 120, 131–32; idem, "Woman to Woman," *The Sign* 21 (February 1942): 432.

65. Grandma Tinley Reads from the Bible, 1950

The incipient popular biblical movement in the United States received considerable support through the increasing development of liturgical participation in the use of daily and Sunday missals (widespread since the 1930s, a commonplace in Sodality and Catholic Action study clubs) and the publication of Pius XII's Divino Afflante Spiritu (1943). In 1948 in its annual instruction, the Catholic Biblical Association suggested that a passage from the scriptures be read every day during Lent; a flyer for 1950 carried a striking picture of Jesus holding a Confraternity Edition of the New Testament with the caption "A New Testament in Every Home, The Teaching of Christ in Every Heart" (cf. doc. 70 with illustration). In the following selection, circulated by the Confraternity of Christian Doctrine as a news item in 1950, a popular writer reflects on three generations of Catholics and how the reading of the Bible ebbed and flowed in each.

"Tell me a story, Mommy," Ginny begged, in bed with the sniffles.

I looked through her bookcase. "Cinderella?"

"I'm tired of Cinderella."

"The Three Bears?"

"No. *Tell* me a story, like you heard when you were a little girl."

My mind went back — to Grandma Tinley and her absorbing stories: about a little boy named David and his slingshot; Lot and his salty wife; poor Mr. Job and his troubles; St. Paul thrown from a horse....

Best of all was Grandma's story about Ruth. I think she liked it best too. Grandma knew what it meant to be homesick; knew how it felt when, as a bride, she had left her native country to brave frontier days in the new West. Somehow, Ruth's story was Grandma's story and her words were Grandma's: "Whithersoever thou shalt go, I will go; and where thou shalt dwell, I also will dwell. Thy people shall be my people, and thy God my God."

"And just think," Grandma would always finish the story, "Ruth became the great-great-many-times-great grandma of Our Lord!"

So I told Ginny the story of Ruth. "Poor Ruth," she sighed. "I'll bet they took her clear out to Chicago. Tell me another."

We took up the story of Joseph and his coat-of-many-colors that Jacob had made for him. Just like Grandma's crazy quilt, I used to think as I fingered the patches of silk and velvet carefully pieced together. Somehow, it seemed as though Grandma, not I, were telling this story to Ginny as she sat up in bed, running her finger along the colors of her plaid bathrobe.

"Those brothers were sure stinkers," Ginny said. "Hope the cops got 'em."

Ginny got over her cold but not over her love of "those *good* stories." The older children listened in too, though these stories were familiar to them. Through the influence of the Confraternity of Christian Doctrine, Bible stories are being made more interesting in school. "They're real people, aren't they?" Mary asked.

A long time since I'd thought of those stories yet they all came back, almost in Grandma's own words — taken straight from her reading and re-reading of that big, heavy family Bible. When Grandma came to the flood, my cousins and I shivered and wondered: What if God would do that again? None of us had ever seen an ocean but we had seen the Missouri River rise with the spring floods. Papa would be Noe, I was sure, because Papa was a very good man. Grandma and the cousins and all the family would be in our ark and maybe God wouldn't mind if we took along June Davis and a couple of other friends. "Gibraltar," a bluff high above the river, would be our Mount Arrarat. We were ready. Ginny decided that *our* Mount Arrarat would be the Washington Monument!

Why, I wondered, hadn't I told Grandma's stories before? Perhaps it's modern parent training: to keep everything pallid and watered-down for our children. Maybe that's why they rebel and seek tales of primitive emotions in the comics, movies, radio and television.

In our day, my cousins and I had only Grandma's stories. We even acted some of them out — fantastic feats that would put Superman to shame, like walking on the water and Elias being taken to heaven in a fiery chariot. There were glamorous girl spies too, like Dalila giving Samson his haircut and Judith whacking off the head of Holofernes. We craved tales of violence and we found them; but they were violence against evil — against the sin of Adam and Eve, Sodom and Gomorrha — and the quick retribution that followed. There was suspense too in the struggle of Moses; in the long-drawn-out battle for the House of David; in Our Lord's 33-year trial against unbelievers.

Grandma's stories had aroused in me an interest in the Bible. When high school days came, I looked forward to a real "course," one that would go still further into this fascinating book.

It was a dull thud to find that it was to be mostly a memory course. "Genesis, Exodus, Leviticus, Numbers, Deuteronomy, Joshua..." we'd murmur on our way to class, for days on end. It took a long time before everybody knew the titles of the Old Testament Books down to "Malachi," and then we didn't do much about them — all deadly boring, shredding the text apart into a lifeless pulp of detail. We didn't catch Grandma's rollicking, running story of early days when those loyal to God stood by Him through all kinds of sufferings — the ten plagues and all the rest of it.

So the Bible and I parted company — until Ginny got that cold, and I read the text again; read it the way Grandma used to. This time, for pleasure. The children and I read parts of it together, recapturing the spirit of a woman dead more than thirty years, a woman to whom the Bible was a living, breathing story, the inspired basis for her faith.

The Confraternity of Christian Doctrine is striving today to bring to children and adults that same interest in Holy Scripture that Grandma had. All its lesson plans, from kindergarten on, have biblical references. Teachers are urged to read the Bible and show their pupils that it is not just a record of births and deaths. It's to be read — the intriguing story of mankind, from God Himself down to you and Ginny and Joe Doakes and me.

Mary Tinley Daly, *At Our House* (NC Features, 30 January 1950). Courtesy of the U.S. Catholic Conference, Washington, D.C.

66. Enthronement of the Sacred Heart in the Home, 1950s

The feast of Christ the King was established in 1924 as a way to honor the consecration of the world to the Sacred Heart, earlier recommended by Pope Leo XIII. A 1928 encyclical on the Sacred Heart, Miserentissimus Redemptor, emphasized reparation and a 1956 encyclical, Haurietis Aquas, accented a theological treatment of the teaching on the Sacred Heart. The post–World War II era witnessed a concerted effort to develop devotion to the Sacred Heart in the United States. Father Mateo Crawley-Boevey, SSCC, preached the devotion throughout the country beginning in 1940. In 1943 with over 125,000 in attendance, the Chicago archdiocese was consecrated to the Sacred Heart in a ceremony in Soldier's Field, and three years later the First National Congress of the Enthronement was held. The Family Life Bureau of the National Catholic Welfare Conference supported the dissemination of the devotion, and by the mid-1950s its popularization was ensured by a national director and numer-

ous diocesan secretaries. The 1950s version of the enthronement of the Sacred Heart combined ideas from the Christ the King motif and the Sacred Heart in order to address the segmentation of the church into distinct "roles," the problem of the disintegration of family life, and the impact of the formation of large suburban, mainly upper-middle-class parishes. The document makes clear that, while families can make an act of consecration by themselves, a priest is needed for the enthronement, which represents an explicit act of reparation on behalf of those who deny Christ's kingship in public and social life. Enthronement made Christ the real head of the family and represented both a protest against the displacement of the priest from public life and an effort to reestablish clear boundaries of authority in ecclesial and family roles. This postwar piety, similar to that argued by the New York bishops in 1873 (see doc. 26), witnessed to the increasing privatization of religion and represented a strand of devotionalism different from that of the personal and communal practices of the immigrant and depression eras (see docs. 24, 49). We see a different solution to the same problems in the promotion of the family rosary, which also suggested a spiritual means to shore up and protect family life (see doc. 68).

National Center of the Enthronement
Fathers of the Sacred Hearts, Fairhaven, Massachusetts
Enthronement of the Sacred Heart in the Home

Nature of the Work

What is the meaning of the word "Enthronement"?

The word "Enthronement" means to install or place on a throne.

Is the word well chosen?

Yes, for it brings out the fundamental idea of the crusade: to publicly proclaim the Kingship of Christ in the family and society.

"The choice of the word seems to be a happy one: it evokes by the very sound of its syllables, the idea of throne, of ceremony, of effective reign" (Most Rev. Alex. Caillot, Bishop of Grenoble, Pastoral Letter, 1918).

According to the significance of the word itself, what is meant by the "Enthronement of the Sacred Heart in the home"?

"To enthrone the Sacred Heart in the home" means to install a picture or statue of the Sacred Heart as on a throne, that is to say in the place of honor in the home.

Why should we place the Sacred Heart ON A THRONE?

1. Because He has asked us to do so. "I will bless those homes where an image of My Sacred Heart is set up and honored." 2. Because Jesus is the King of love and wishes to reign by love.

Why enthrone the Sacred Heart IN THE HOME?

1. Because the home is the center of family life, under attack today. 2. Because

the reign of the Sacred Heart in the family will infallibly lead to the reign of the Sacred Heart over society in general.

Why install His image in a PLACE OF HONOR?

Because as King of Kings only the first place in the home is worthy of Him. Because we wish to make public reparation for other families who have driven Him out of their homes.

What is understood by "place of honor"?

By "place of honor" is understood a prominent place in the principal room of the home, where the family and visitors will be constantly reminded that the Sacred Heart is the KING, the FATHER, the FRIEND of the family.

Isn't the bedroom the proper place for the enthroned picture of the Sacred Heart?

No, because it is a *private* room and not the *principal* room frequented by all the members of the family, where the family can gather for Rosary and evening prayers. However, besides the enthroned picture there certainly may be another picture of the Sacred Heart in different rooms.

Do you think that the enthroned picture of the Sacred Heart would be out of place in a room where visitors are entertained, some of them Protestants, and where parties and entertainments are held?

By no means: for the time has come for every Catholic to publicly display his allegiance to Christ the King. As regards parties, either these occasions are fitting and proper, and in that case Our Lord can preside over them as He did at the wedding feast in Cana; or else they are harmful and improper, and in that case no Catholic, even if he had the Sacred Heart hidden in some other part of the house, ought to allow them.

Is this installation of a picture of the Sacred Heart in the place of honor in the home all there is to the Enthronement?

No. It is but the beginning of the Enthronement. It is merely the solemn external expression of interior submission of the family to the dominion of Christ, and a public act of reparation.

Essential Features of the Work

What then are ALL the essential features of the Enthronement?

According to Father Mateo, the Founder of the Work, they are four-fold.

"The first of these, one which dominates the whole of the Crusade, is the social and solemn recognition by the family of the divine royalty of the loving Heart of Jesus. This is pre-eminently an act of reparation especially nowadays when there is so much social and national apostasy."

Secondly, "The act by which the social reign is proclaimed consists in solemnly setting up a picture or statue of the King of Love on A THRONE. 'As on a throne,'...as His Holiness Benedict XV put it, so that the Sacred

Heart is the 'Standard of the King,' the 'Labarum' of the family." This is done according to a ceremonial approved by the Church and witnessed by a priest.

Thirdly, "The family should kneel in front of the picture which has been set up and solemnly consecrate itself to the Sacred Heart with faith and love. This was clearly specified by the Holy Father who wrote in this connection. 'Jesus should be placed upon a throne in the home, for He is to be in reality, the King. In consequence, the family should every day gather around the throne of the Sacred Heart to offer their King a token of love and adoration.'"

Fourthly, "When the King of Love has set up His abode in a home, He must be allowed to live there as the Sovereign of the family, and all the members of the household should strive to show Him their unbounded love and confidence." This is the consecration lived, the most important feature of the work....

Consecration and Enthronement

Then the Enthronement is not merely a transitory act, a beautiful ceremony?

No, it is or should be a permanent state of life, an every day recognition of all the rights of Christ the King, by every member of the family. After the ceremony the Sacred Heart should reign as the Head, the Master, the intimate Friend of the family.

"We do not attach great importance to the name. What we are more particularly concerned with is that it should not be a mere passing consecration to the Sacred Heart, a little family ceremony that may perhaps be forgotten the next day, but that in reality Jesus should be placed upon a throne in the family and that He should abide there as its King" (Benedict XV to Cardinal Van Rossum, 16 Jan. 1919).

Then the act of consecration of the family to the Sacred Heart is only a part of the Enthronement?

Yes. The Enthronement adds something over and above the consecration, namely, recognition of the Kingship of Christ (not necessarily contained in the act of consecration); solemn installation of the image of the Sacred Heart as on a throne; organized plan to see to it that the Enthronement is lived up to.

Is there anything else implied in the Enthronement which is not contained in the simple consecration.

Yes: an explicit reparation for public acts which designedly ignore this divine Kingship in all public and social life.

Are they any other differences?

Yes. The Enthronement is an act of ADORATION, a solemn act of worship of the Divine King, Jesus Christ.

Therefore, even though one can CONSECRATE oneself or one's family to the Immaculate Heart of Mary, is it permissible to ENTHRONE the Immaculate Heart of Mary in the home?

Very definitely, no, because the Enthronement is a homage of *latria*. It says with the Church: "Thou ALONE art the Lord; Thou ALONE art the Most High!" Pope Benedict XV once asked Father Mateo during a private audience, whether he enthroned the Immaculate Heart of Mary. After Father assured him that he did not, the Pope said very emphatically, "You do well, for that would never be approved!"

Is there still another distinction between Enthronement and consecration?

Yes. The consecration of the family to the Sacred Heart can be made by any member of the family, with or without the presence of the priest, in the home or collectively in the church. The Enthronement of the family, on the contrary, must take place in the home, in the presence of the priest, by the head of the family.

The Mind of the Church

Has the church expressed its mind on this question?

Yes. The presence of the priest is so intimately connected with the aim of this Work, that the Sacred Penitentiary did not hesitate to require it to gain the indulgences. For when the following questions were put to it: "Whether, to gain the indulgences attached to this pious practice (of Enthronement) it is necessary for the priest to consecrate the family in each and every home, or whether it is permitted for the ceremony to be carried out in the church where, in the presence of the assembled families, greater solemnity and devotion may be had?" it replied "Yes to the first part, no to the second." And to the next question: "Under what circumstances is the presence of the priest to be considered an impossibility, so that the picture of the Sacred Heart, previously blessed, can be installed and the act of consecration read by a lay person?" it answered: "The decision of this question is to be left to the prudent judgment of the Ordinary of the place."

From these replies it is quite evident that it is the mind of the Church that the priest should preside at the ceremony, and that collective consecrations in the Church are not to be confused with the Enthronement. Further, the Church declares that only the Ordinary of the diocese can dispense with the presence of the priest, and consequently neither the pastor nor the curate can grant such a dispensation (A.A.S. April 11, 1918).

Presence of the Priest

Why is the presence of the priest in the home so much insisted on by the founder of the work, and by the Church itself?

Because as already explained, the Enthronement is no mere passing consecration but an official acknowledgment of the supreme dominion of the Heart of Jesus over domestic society, considered as the very foundation of civil society. Through the Enthronement then, the family performs a true social and public act, and since this act is a religious act, it is little wonder that the priest should be called to take part in it, as the official representative of the King of Love.

It is precisely because the Christian family in the act of the Enthronement performs a social act over and beyond the limits of its own domestic sphere, that the founder of the work, from its very inception, has insisted that the Enthronement be presided over by a priest.

Are there any other reasons why the priest should preside over the ceremony?

Yes. Another reason is that since the aim of the Enthronement is the restoration and perfecting of Christian life, first of families and through them of all Catholic institutions, and even of society itself, it follows that the priest should preside over any public act that has this end in view, inasmuch as this is his chief function as priest and apostle.

Moreover the presence of the priest is a protest against the exclusion of the representative of Christ from public, social, and particularly from family life. This is why Cardinal Mercier wrote in 1915: "The idea of making the priest intervene in the bosom of the family for the public veneration of the Sacred Heart is a happy one."

Finally, the ceremony of the Enthronement is a splendid opportunity for the zealous priest to acquaint himself with the circumstances of each one of his families and in their very homes talk to them as a father to his children, freely and intimately as he never could from the pulpit.

A Practical Objection

How would you answer the objection very commonly made that in large city parishes it is a physical impossibility for the pastor and his assistants to enthrone the Sacred Heart in every home in his parish or even in a large percentage of them?

There is no doubt that this is a practical difficulty and one that has to be faced. However, without trying to minimize the real difficulty presented, some suggestions may be of help in solving it. First of all it must be clearly understood that it is not the purpose nor according to the spirit of this work to attempt to enthrone all or most of the homes of a parish within a limited period of time, say a year or even two years. Since this work is of the utmost importance for the family and society, it should be laid on solid foundation.

Hence a long range program should be inaugurated. Families could be instructed on the nature of the enthronement and all it entails; a plan of action could be drawn up, whereby the parish is divided up into districts, and districts into blocks and streets, each assigned to groups, or individual promoters, who prepare the families and arrange a schedule of Enthronements. This is the procedure followed successfully in many large parishes, and is the only answer to the difficulty presented.

It might be added here, that there is a most important factor in this work that is sometimes forgotten or overlooked, and that is that since this work is an apostolate of love for the Sacred Heart, the zealous priest may expect with all confidence and trust the realization in his regard of the magnificent promises made through St. Margaret Mary to all those who devote themselves to the interests of the Sacred Heart; and in particular the 5th and 10th promises: "I will shed abundant blessings on all their undertakings." "I will give to priests the power to touch the hardest hearts." Many of our difficulties and obstacles will be surmounted very quickly if the Sacred Heart is given an opportunity to help us overcome them.

Supernatural Results

Has the Sacred Heart given any proofs that this work is pleasing to Him?

Yes, by countless facts many of which border on the miraculous. The work has spread with such rapidity throughout the world that it has been called "the crusade of Divine Providence." The promises of the Sacred Heart have been fulfilled so many times through the Enthronement that Father Anzuini, SJ, who was for many years Director of the Enthronement in Italy, could say, "Miracles of grace and conversion have been the distinctive characteristic of the Work."

> Courtesy of the Congregation of the Sacred Hearts, National Enthronement Center, Box 111, Fairhaven, Mass. Printed by permission.

67. The Mystical Body and the Mass, 1951

Several themes building in the twentieth century coalesce in the presentation which the scripture scholar Barnabas Mary Ahern, CP (1915–95), gave to several hundred women assembled in Chicago. Ahern's incarnational emphasis related scripture, the women's ordinary life, and the liturgy, where all were united as members of the Mystical Body. The vine and branches motif recalls a common unity of the family and all members of the church and the distinctiveness of each one in the myriad ways of meeting God in each other. Ahern's references to various parts of the liturgy imply that the women were using one of a variety of missals, which printed the Mass in Latin on one side of the page and in English on the other. At day's end, the women were encouraged within the sanctuary of the home to examine the day as to how closely they resembled Christ in the daily actions they performed. Ahern, later a peritus (expert) at the Second Vatican Council, was an early proponent of biblical spirituality. "We," as the connection between laity, the priest, and Christ, provided a contrasting perspective to an emphasis on distinctive "roles" in the church (see doc. 66). Ahern's talk was subsequently printed as a pamphlet.

My Dear, Good Women:

It is a great honor to be here with you today, and I count this opportunity a signal privilege. These words must sound strange; for probably you feel that your life is small and unimportant — just something all locked up within the four walls of humdrum daily duties.

The trip down here today was typical. I suppose it went like this: In the bus you sat next to another lady from the parish; and the two of you chatted about the new TV and the frigidaire you just bought; you glowed over the wonderful Sister who is teaching your Billy in first grade; and you had something sharp to say about the woman next door who is becoming quite sophisticated: "Why, she is even dropping her r's now — and I know that she has lived on Halsted Street all her life!" And so the conversation just pitter-pattered on.

Our Life as We See It

That is life for you. It is just like a merry-go-round, always on the move, yet never budging an inch from the same old circle. It is a happy life, certainly, and a peaceful one. But it is also a limited life, tied down to this family, to this small group of friends, to this particular neighborhood. Your thoughts, your love, your work — all are tightly anchored to the little house you call home. So it is perfectly natural that, after the enthusiasms of youth, we gradually settle down to regard ourselves as just a little person who will live for a few more years, make a few more friends, and then pass on to claim the reward that comes to every little person who has done no great harm and no great good.

Our Life as God Sees It

But the fact still remains that it is a great privilege for any priest to speak to you. Why? Simply because God sees your life in a way so utterly different. There are five hundred women here today; each is different in age, different in appearance, different in background. But to God you are all ever so much alike. When He looks on the group here, He feels an unutterable joy in recognizing in each one of you the features of His beloved Son, Jesus. A few moments ago, I was speaking with several of our members. The tone of voice in each one was different; each had her own special point of interest, her own attitude; no two of us — thank heaven! — are quite the same. God, too, was listening to us; but in every voice He heard what we missed — the soft, sweet accent of the voice of Jesus....

Christ Lives in Us

"All you who have been baptized in Christ's name have put on the person of Christ. There is no more Jew or Gentile, no more slave and freeman, no more male and female; you are all one person in Jesus Christ" (Gal. 3:27–28).

With these simple words St. Paul tells us that Christ does have a Mystical Body in which He is always living. Yes, the very Son of God lives His own life in a special way in each one, sharing with us the thoughts of His mind and sweetening our hearts with His own love. He Himself has given us His word for this. For at the Last Supper, in that beautiful prayer of His to the Father, He concluded with these whispered words, "Father, I have revealed thy name to them; so that the love thou has bestowed upon me may dwell in them, and I, too, may dwell in them" (Jn. 17:26).

Let us put it this way. A woman here has a beautiful tree in her front yard. Everyone who passes by is struck by its lush green foliage and its perfect shapeliness. But now go up to the tree; look at it closely, and you will see that no two branches are the same. Each has its special curvature, its special coloring. Yet that whole tree is living of the same life; the same vital sap flows through root and trunk and branches. So it is with ourselves; we are five hundred here today, all of us distinct personalities; yet it is the same Christ who lives His own life in each and every one.... Yes, each of us is a branch; and He is our life.

Practical Examples of Christ-Life in Us

Our Blessed Lord counts so much on each one; He desires earnestly to live in us and to work through us. Let us see this in practice. There is a mother here who has three lovely children. Our Lord has made her their mother, because He intends to do through her a work He can do through no one else. Her prayer, her words, her motherliness — these are the means He will use to form in her little boy a priestly vocation, to prepare her little girl to be a model Catholic mother, and to give her new little baby the grace of Baptism that will bring it to heaven when He calls for it two years from now.

There may be with us today another woman whose heart is heavy with sorrow because of a husband or son who has gone astray. He is drinking, and has given up the practice of his faith. He is a burdensome cross on the whole family. But in all this Christ is working out His own purpose. He has put this woman into this home, just that He may do through her a work He can do through no one else. Each day He energizes her with His own spirit of prayer and unselfish devotion that, little by little, He may win back this wayward soul to Himself....

This is our life as Catholics, as members of the Mystical Body of Christ; we are the branches, and He is the life of all. No matter how ordinary our life may be, Christ lives in us; this is our great glory. And so it can never be merely I; it must always be We — Jesus living and acting through me. You wash dishes and prepare the meals; you teach your little ones and correct them; you love your husband and try to make home pleasant for him; ... all this is Christ living through you in a way that He can live in no one else. "All who have been baptized in Christ's name have put on the person of Christ" (Gal. 3:27)....

Holy Mass in the Life of the Mystical Body

It is just at this point that we come face to face with our compelling need for Holy Mass. It is right here that we feel the full impact of Holy Mass on the daily life of Christ's Mystical Body. For Holy Mass is the wisdom and the power of God; it is the wisdom of God teaching us how Christ must live in us; it is the power of God strengthening us to carry out our ideal.

Ever since we were little tots we have believed that in every Mass our Lord offers Himself to the Eternal Father just as He did on Calvary. This statement is true. But there is something more; we, too, have our part to play. On Calvary, our Lord alone was offered in sacrifice; but at Holy Mass He is no longer alone, for we are united with Him. He draws us to Himself that we, the members of His Mystical Body, may be offered up with Him. Yes, in each Mass Christ lives in us in a new way and lifts us up to the very throne of God that through Him and with Him and in Him we may adore, love, and thank the Blessed Trinity and ask for all we need.

Holy Mass Is Our Sacrifice

So the Mass is our Sacrifice, Christ's and mine. Is not this the meaning of the Mass prayers? Read these carefully and notice how often the word WE recurs. For instance, there is that beautiful prayer at the Offertory, when the priest bows low and, in our name, whispers the words, "In the spirit of humility and with a contrite heart may WE be received by Thee, O Lord; and grant that the sacrifice which WE offer this day in Thy sight, may be pleasing to Thee, O Lord God." Yes, it is WE — Jesus, the priest, and ourselves — who are being offered up. . . .

The Ordinariness of Holy Mass

But see how simply it all takes place. Our Lord uses just the ordinary things of daily life, and through these He works out His infinite Sacrifice. Look, here are the hands that offer Holy Mass; these hands of mine are just like yours — the hands you use to prepare supper and wash the dishes and comb the little one's hair. And these are the lips that utter the dread words of Sacrifice, "This is my body," "This is my Blood"; they are just like your lips — the lips with which you pray and sing, the lips you use to tell your husband and little children how much you love them. How simple it all is: Jesus uses our ordinary gestures and motions and words to work out His own great Sacrifice. . . .

How to Assist at Holy Mass

There is a definite spirit, then, that should be ours during the celebration of the Mass. One thought should dominate our mind and fill our whole heart as we kneel before the altar: in this sacrifice I am united with Christ and offered up with Him to the Eternal Father. This close union with Christ enriches me with His power, so that now I can adore and love God as I have always wanted to; now I can make reparation for all my sins and obtain all the graces I need. For in Holy Mass God unites us to His own beloved Son; "must not that gift be accompanied by the gift of all else?" (Rom. 8:32).

And so, whether you use the Missal, or the Rosary, or just kneel there in silent prayer; this really makes no difference. The matter of importance is that each one should use whatever means helps her best to realize that Jesus is living in her and offers her with Himself to the Father. . . .

Living the Mass

So it is that every Holy Mass gives new life to the members of Christ's Mystical Body. Just enter into the spirit of the Mass and you will find that it prepares and strengthens you to let Christ live His life in you all the day long. For He does have a real work to do through you that He can do in no one else. He has put you into your own little home; He has enclosed you in your own little circle. But never forget; all this has its divine purpose; this is His quiet, sweet way of coming down into the lives of your husband and children, your neighbors and friends. Through you Christ will draw all these souls to Himself; for in you they will see not only a wife, a mother, a friend, but another Christ living His own life: this is the sublime truth of the Mystical Body. . . .

Conclusion

Yes, in the sight of God, we are all other Christs. And so, at the close of each day, take your little crucifix into your hands. Look lovingly on Him and think of His sweet kindness and forgiving charity, His tireless patience and utter submissiveness to the Will of His Father. Remember how He loved us all and poured out every drop of His Precious Blood for each and every one of us. Then ask yourself —

Am I truly another Christ?

Do I let Him re-live in me these beautiful virtues?

Tonight, can I say more sincerely than ever before, "I am alive; or rather, not I; it is Christ that is living in me" (Gal 2:20). May the Good God give all of you grace to fulfill this ideal.

> Barnabas Mary Ahern, CP, *The Mystical Body of Christ and the Mass* (Chicago: J. S. Paluch Co., 1951). Used by permission of World Library Publications, a division of J. S. Paluch Company, Inc. The document was provided by Robert Carbonneau, CP.

68. Patrick Peyton Explains the Rosary, 1951

> *Holy Cross priest Patrick J. Peyton (1909–92), an Irish immigrant, contracted tuberculosis while he was in the seminary and attributed a miraculous cure to the intervention of the Blessed Mother. At the beginning of World War II, believing that the intercession of Mary could have a decisive impact on the achievement of justice and peace, he dedicated his life to promoting a family rosary in every home. He coined the phrase, "The family that prays together, stays together." His national campaign, coinciding with Victory in Europe Day, began with a radio broadcast on Mother's Day, 1945. Peyton's pamphlet* The Story of the Family Rosary *achieved an immediate success, and by 1947 the Family Theatre radio series had begun. In the 1960s Peyton carried the crusade to Latin America, where he eventually ran into opposition from some bishops who maintained his approach to the devotion did not meet the political, social, and economic needs of their own context (see doc. 85). The first selection below summarizes the reflections of the editors of* America *magazine on Peyton's crusade. The second selection presents his catechesis on the rosary (cf. docs. 22, 63).*

"Father Peyton's Crusade"

Legends have grown up around the Rev. Patrick J. Peyton, CSC, the zealous Irish priest who began the Family Rosary Crusade ten years ago. In sober fact, however, his accomplishments have been more legendary than the folklore. In a decade, Fr. Peyton has got from 6 million families a pledge to say the rosary every day for peace. He conducts the "Family Theatre" weekly over the Mutual radio network. Three times a year, Broadway and Hollywood stars cooperate with him in a special hour-long program. Four equally impressive TV programs have been televised by every major TV network and station in the U.S. He wrote a movie that featured Bing Crosby and Ann Blyth, and authored a book, *The Ear of God,* which related the history of the crusade.

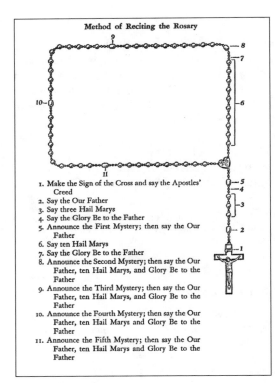

Method of Reciting the Rosary

1. Make the Sign of the Cross and say the Apostles' Creed
2. Say the Our Father
3. Say three Hail Marys
4. Say the Glory Be to the Father
5. Announce the First Mystery; then say the Our Father
6. Say ten Hail Marys
7. Say the Glory Be to the Father
8. Announce the Second Mystery; then say the Our Father, ten Hail Marys, and Glory Be to the Father
9. Announce the Third Mystery; then say the Our Father, ten Hail Marys, and Glory Be to the Father
10. Announce the Fourth Mystery; then say the Our Father, ten Hail Marys and Glory Be to the Father
11. Announce the Fifth Mystery; then say the Our Father, ten Hail Marys and Glory Be to the Father

Directions on how to say the Rosary in Patrick Peyton, CSC, The Ear of God (Garden City, N.Y.: Doubleday and Co., 1951), 181.

Rosary crusade meetings, which have reached over half a million people, have been held in Canada, the Yukon, Alaska, Australia, England and in twelve of our States. The great lesson here, apart from Fr. Peyton's personal zeal, is his mobilization of all the channels of communication to serve his apostolate. All that human ingenuity has been able to develop for the transmission of ideas is pressed into service to spread devotion to our Lady of Fatima and to bring about world peace. One man has done this because he believes passionately in his cause. Isn't it strange that all the resources of this nation and Government have not yet been able similarly to coordinate all the channels of information to tell the slave nations of the world the strength and opportunities of the free world? Is that because we do not *believe* as passionately? And is that, in turn, because the *religious* bases of democracy are lost sight of?

From *The Ear of God*

We have examined the statement of St. Thomas Aquinas that prayer surpasses other acts of religion, and the statement of another great theologian, Francisco Suarez, that he would exchange all his theology for one well-said Hail Mary. Now add to these the statement of Pope Pius IX: "The single richest treasure in the Vatican is the Rosary."

The Rosary is far more indeed than a multiplication of Hail Marys, Our Fathers, and the variable prayers that we add to it. It has an essence of its own,

Father Patrick Peyton, CSC, at one of his rallies for family prayer and the Rosary, ca. 1963. Courtesy, Archives of the Archdiocese of Milwaukee, Wisconsin

and therefore a power of its own. To this power, it is true, is added the power of the prayers it contains. But the power of the Rosary cannot be calculated by arithmetic. The only measure of its power that we have is the history of marvels it has wrought. And although many popes besides Pius IX have recommended the Rosary to us in the strongest terms, its power is attested by an authority far greater even than theirs; for we say the Rosary on the advice of Mary herself.

Why it is so powerful we can only guess. We can say it is because the Rosary is the psalter of the Redemption, the harp on which we celebrate not only the Joyful, Sorrowful, and Glorious mysteries that name its three divisions, but the whole cycle of mysteries by which God, from the time of the Fall of man, mercifully wove His reconciliation with the human race.

Or we can put it this way: the Rosary is Mary's own Way of the Cross, which is to say, her whole biography; saying the Rosary is like projecting ourselves back to the moment of her Immaculate Conception and following her through life, through the Annunciation, the Nativity, through her Son's boyhood, through His Passion; like accompanying Mary up the hill of Calvary with Jesus and standing beside her at the foot of the Cross and weeping at the real *Pietà;* and then like rejoicing with Mary at the Resurrection and the Ascension, and at her own glorification in God's love. For the mysteries on which we meditate while saying the Rosary are the soul of that great prayer. Dare one say that the soul of it is empathy? This is a word that the dictionary defines as "imaginative projection of one's own consciousness into another being." No one ever can feel what Mary felt, but the nearest we can come to sharing in the joy and pain and glory of Mary's life is when we offer up her Rosary. And when we say the Rosary in the state of grace, never on earth except at the Communion rail shall we be closer to that sad Queen.

Is this not a sufficiently logical guess why the Rosary is so powerful?

Or we can say, more simply, that it is because the Rosary is the serenade that Mary most loves, the great psalm of the race of her children, which most touches her, and which therefore moves her to carry our petitions to God. But this is not saying enough. For we know that the Rosary is pleasing also to God Himself, who has so honored His dearest daughter, His spouse, and His mother that He has established her purity as a symbol of eternal life in Him; and we know that this is why Mary has continually counseled us to say her Rosary.

The Rosary proper twines, in a garland, the two greatest prayers — the Our Father, the perfect prayer given to us by Jesus, and the lovely and mystic Hail Mary; yet the Rosary surpasses both these prayers together. It includes them and adds an original contribution from each sayer, an expression of each sayer's very nature, belief, and devotion. It is meditative prayer joined to vocal prayer, its soul an empathic participation in the greatest events in religion. Then what a wonderful device it is. It is more than prayer in the usual sense of the word: it is a kind of adventure in which we offer up a spiritual *experience*. When you look at the rosary in your hand, how simple it appears, that little string of beads, yet how far that short chain reaches, what a cosmos it encircles, how closely it binds us to God and to Mary: the single richest treasure in the Vatican — there, in your hand....

[T]he use of the Creed as an introduction to the Rosary is not only both practical and charming, but it perfects the form of the offering. But the Creed is a great prayer in itself. It has a history almost as long as the Hail Mary's and almost rivaling it in grandeur. It expresses all that the first martyrs meant when they died with its name on their lips: *Credo!* It expresses the basic doctrines for which the Church has fought, suffered, and endured through the centuries; for which Cardinal Mindszenty and other heroic men of God are suffering today; for which the Church expects to fight at Armageddon and, with God's help, to preserve in its own blood....

[Some] demur that the constant repetition of the same prayers in the Rosary is a soporific and arid experience. But when the Rosary is said with the devotion it demands, and not with a mere automatic observance of its outward forms, this is directly opposite to the truth. Assuredly, we do not concentrate on the words of the prayers — the words and their meaning are engraved on our hearts. But we contemplate the divine drama of the Redemption scene by scene, and the mysteries of the Faith that are inherent in it, and consider the virtues to be imitated, the lessons to be learned; and the words are like a sacred underscore to the performance, moving our hearts like music, assisting us to elevate our minds, so that, as we pray, our devotion increases, the scenes become more vivid, they reach out and environ us and are part of our spiritual experience. When we say the Rosary like that, it is anything but soporific — it is absorbing. To one who has said it many times it can be an intense experience. Even one who prays the Rosary for the first time with devout attention feels himself uplifted by it. And the more often we pray it, the better we pray it, the more we feel it, the closer it binds us to God and to Mary, the more graces we receive through it. That is why the Rosary has such a marked effect upon people's lives. And perhaps that is the secret of Mary's fourth promise: *The Rosary will make virtue and good works flourish, and will obtain for souls the most abundant divine mercies; it will substitute in hearts love of God for love of the world, elevate them to desire heavenly and eternal goods.*

We have called the Rosary the saga and harp of the Redemption. It is in plain fact an epic prayer. Yet a child not infrequently can pray it better than an adult. In view of the intricate theology which it contains, this may seem an odd thing to say, but it is wholly in keeping with the nature of things, for a child's faith is likely to be purer and its imagination stronger than those of a grownup. The Rosary is a song or a library, however you take it, so that a boy of nine can fill his heart with it while a scholar gropes in its mysticism. It is a sublime spiritual experience for anyone. It is a school of religion with grades from kindergarten to heaven. This is why it is a perfect prayer for a family group. And it is a prayer for all states of the soul. It has the bells of Christmas in it, the solemn tolling of Good Friday, the rising sun of Easter. It has contrition, comfort, hope, and promise. From beginning to end it is all God's love and Mary's. And the richest single treasure in the Vatican can be had for nothing in any home.

"Father Peyton's Crusade," *America* 86 (16 February 1952): 519; and Patrick J. Peyton, *The Ear of God* (Garden City, N.Y.: Doubleday, 1951), 107–9, 110, 117–18; diagram from 191. Published by permission of The Family Rosary, Inc., January 2000.

69. The U.S. Catholic Bishops Publish National Regulations on Fast and Abstinence, 1951

At their November 1951 meeting, the bishops of the United States issued two statements, one on morality and another on the persecution of the church in Communist countries. "God's Law: The Measure of Man's Conduct" was a direct response to what many perceived as a crisis in public morality in society. The previous years had seen the Kefauver hearings, and numerous allegations had surfaced of corruption in politics, collegiate sports, and the operations of the Internal Revenue Service. The statement called for integrity in education, economic life, and politics and argued strenuously against the double standard of "paying lip service to God while failing completely to honor his claims in daily life." At the same time the bishops issued new norms, excerpted below, governing fasting and abstinence in the American Catholic community. Always an important marker of social identity and cohesion, fasting from types of food and abstaining from meat helped create a sense of separateness and served as reminders in daily life of the moral norms which should govern all conduct. Significantly, while the following norms seem traditional enough (see doc. 17), they also represented a definite departure from previous practice. Embedded in the legislation was the acceptance of a "relative standard" for fasting (i.e., no longer tied to a specific quantity of food which was universal in application). While only one full meal was allowed on a day of fasting, the norms laid down that the other two meals (usually breakfast and collation) on the same day could be "sufficient to maintain strength, [and] may be taken according to each one's needs," provided they did not together equal the full meal. The confessor needed to be consulted only in cases of doubt.

To foster the spirit of penance and of reparation for sin, to encourage self-denial and mortification, and to guide her children in the footsteps of Our Divine Savior, Holy Mother Church imposes by law the observance of fast and abstinence.

In accordance with the provisions of Canon Law, as modified through the use of special faculties granted by the Holy See, we herewith publish the following regulations:

On Abstinence

Everyone over 7 years of age is bound to observe the law of abstinence.

Complete abstinence is to be observed on Fridays, Ash Wednesday, the Vigils of the Assumption and Christmas, and on Holy Saturday morning. On days of complete abstinence meat and soup or gravy made from meat may not be used at all.

Partial abstinence is to be observed on Ember Wednesdays and Saturdays and on the Vigils of Pentecost and All Saints. On days of partial abstinence meat and soup or gravy made from meat may be taken only *once* a day at the principal meal.

On Fast

Everyone over 21 and under 59 years of age is also bound to observe the law of fast.

The days of fast are the weekdays of Lent, Ember Days, the Vigils of Pentecost, the Assumption, All Saints and Christmas.

On days of fast only one full meal is allowed. Two other meatless meals, sufficient to maintain strength, may be taken according to each one's needs; but together they should not equal another full meal.

Meat may be taken at the principal meal on a day of fast except on Fridays, Ash Wednesday and the Vigils of the Assumption and Christmas.

Eating between meals is not permitted; but liquids, including milk and fruit juices, are allowed.

When health or ability to work would be seriously affected, the law does not oblige. In doubt concerning fast or abstinence, a parish priest or confessor should be consulted.

We earnestly exhort the faithful during the periods of fast and abstinence to attend daily Mass; to receive Holy Communion often; to take part more frequently in exercises of piety; to give generously to works of religion and charity; to perform acts of kindness toward the sick, the aged and the poor; to practice voluntary self-denial especially regarding alcoholic drink and worldly amusements; and to pray more fervently, particularly for the intentions of the Holy Father.

Final text approved in Washington, D.C., 1951.

Original in Archives of the National Catholic Welfare Conference, Archives of the Catholic University of America.

70. Why Catholics Read the Bible, 1952

In 1952 Protestants and Catholics alike celebrated the fifth centenary of the Gutenberg Bible. The Confraternity of Christian Doctrine in alliance with the Catholic Biblical Association coordinated a full-scale effort to promote the reading of the scriptures in the community. Through the school system, advertising, radio, press, and diocesan organization numerous programs were sponsored. "Biblical Sunday" (see docs. 60, 65) became "Bible Week," an event which would be celebrated annually into the 1960s; the confraternity sent out thirty-five thousand packets of information; special services were conducted and pastoral letters issued from coast to coast; the Dioceses of Kansas City and San Diego celebrated with special study weeks conducted at prominent schools; St. Mary's College in Xavier, Kansas, held its tenth annual Bible week; in San Antonio, the Spanish-speaking sections of the archdiocese promoted discussion texts. In the following selection, some members of the Lay Committee of the National Center of the Confraternity of Christian Doctrine present their responses to two questions: Why do Catholics read the Bible? How can we promote the sale of Bibles?

1. Most Catholics read the Bible for their own personal sanctification, in an effort to draw closer to God through a knowledge of His relationship to man from creation to redemption.

2. A national contest conducted in co-operation with Catholic newspapers each year with cash prizes might have a stimulating effect on Bible reading. The questions, based on the Bible, would differ each year. An entry blank for contestants could be inserted in each Bible after printing and before distribution to book stores. Catholic newspapers could publicize the contest and offer copies of the Bible for sale.

— Angela Burton, Grandview, Missouri

1. Catholics read the Bible because they believe in the Bible. Believe it is the Word of God through and through. No Catholic can or will deny or reject any part of it. They defend it for they know the Church has compiled it and preserved it down through the ages. They know that the Bible came from the Church backed by the Teaching Authority of the Church.

Catholics love and revere their Bible. They become familiar with the accounts of Christ's life and work and his actual words through the reading of the Epistles and Gospels which are incorporated in the daily liturgy of the Church and read during the Holy Sacrifice.

Catholics read the Bible because they are encouraged to do so by their spiritual directors as divine guidance and to gain the indulgence which is granted

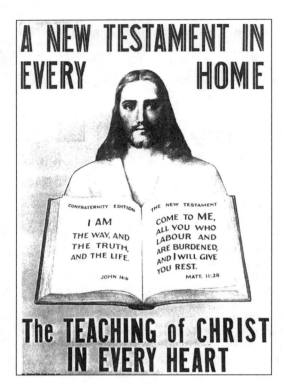

"A New Testament in Every Home," Bible Sunday 1950. Courtesy Publishing and Promotion Sources, U.S. Catholic Conference, Washington, D.C.

for the reading of Holy Scripture with reverence and veneration for at least a short period.

Catholics read the Bible as a historical document, telling a thrilling and dramatic story. The books which comprise the Holy Scriptures represent the finest labors of the great minds of antiquity.

2. Bible reading may be encouraged by the proper sales of the Bible. An appropriate and attractive display of the Book and a sales person who has a thorough knowledge of the Bible, and is familiar with the new features of the beautiful current editions now on the market, will help stimulate reading the Book after it has been purchased.

— Katherine Carroll, Houston, Texas

1. Catholics honor the Bible as the most important document ever written. God is its author, and it gives the reader a knowledge of Divinity that he cannot get in any other way. Catholics cherish the Bible for another reason: it instructs and illustrates, it inspires and nourishes.

The Church is most eager for her members to learn how to use the Sacred Scriptures, to read them devoutly, and to meditate upon them. The Church encourages private recourse to the Bible. She grants an indulgence to those who read from the Sacred Scriptures for fifteen minutes daily.

But that Catholics may read the Bible with profit, they should previously be grounded in the Faith. They need guidance that they may find in the Sacred Scriptures a source of Divine Help.

2. It is fitting, in anticipation of Catholic Bible Week, 1952, that we urge every Catholic home to possess a copy of the Holy Bible. It is desirable for every educated Catholic to have his or her personal copy of the Sacred Scriptures. But ownership alone is nothing. It's daily or frequent use that counts. Catholic schools, Confraternity classes, Confraternity study clubs, and the Catholic home itself are the best channels to direct an intelligent, profitable use of Sacred Scripture. The Catholic who does not read the Bible is deprived of a source of Divine Help in his efforts to grow in love of God and his neighbor.

— Ellamay Horan, Chicago, Illinois

1. A pattern or plan of one's life is sought by everyone. Outside the Catholic sphere where secularism has dimmed the vision of God, the pattern degenerated to an aimless following of "fads" and fashions. Among Catholics, the pattern of life is the life of Christ based on Christ's Mysteries as the Church annually unfolds them for us. Some tend to think of Christ only as the divine Person who walked the earth 1900 years ago. This is not a complete truth for, as Catholics know, He lives with us truly, though mystically, even today and continually sets the pattern for the perfect life.

Perfection is reached in the degree to which we mold our life after that of Christ. For all Catholics, who strive to do this, the Bible becomes a "textbook" of the Christian way of life. A study of this book is necessary both to understand and to appreciate this perfect pattern.

A Catholic uses the Psalms for private and family prayer so that he may praise God in his small way but yet as Christ did. He disposes himself properly for the celebration of the Great Mysteries by a study of the appropriate books of the Bible. For instance, for the fitting celebration of the Incarnation, a study of Isaias through Advent is of utmost importance. He catches a glimpse of the ineffable plan of the Redemption by the reading of Genesis and Exodus during Lent and realizes the proper spirit of mortification and penance by a study of the prophets during this season. During the time after Eastertide, he will acquaint himself with the Epistles, especially those of St. Paul, to understand the themes of growth, struggle, maturity and harvest so that he may better evaluate and map his own spiritual progress.

2. In promoting Bible reading, it seems to me better to avoid nondescript slogans which smack of "Non-Catholic" flavor and push the idea of the "textbook" of the Catholic way of life and suggest how the Bible may be used for the living and the celebrating of all the Mysteries of Christ. This may be done in the manner of a display using posters to show a number of practical ways how the Bible may be used in the preparation for all the Mysteries. This should be appealing to Catholics because this pattern of life distinguishes a Catholic from all his brothers.

— Cornelius W. Kreke, Ft. Thomas, Kentucky

1. Why Catholics read the Bible? My answer is that they do not read it; that is, aside from priests, religious, Bible students and a few "intellectual" Catholics whose interest in the Bible may be merely academic or truly hermeneutical in certain rare instances. And my conviction that they do not read it is based on experience extending over a third of a century in the very personal intimate relationship of physician to family life. A Bible on the bedside is undeviatingly a sign of Protestantism (Methodist, Lutheran or Baptist), as is a Rosary that of Catholicism. Nevertheless, the average Catholic of any intellectual level, possesses a wider range of knowledge of the Bible, either from use of the Missal, or the mere announcement of the Epistles and gospels from the pulpit, than does his Protestant brother who dwells on the Scriptures in a morass of misunderstanding and misinterpretation.

2. How to promote Bible reading through Bible sales? Probably by taking a leaf from the Protestant Bible program — the publication and general widespread distribution of single Epistles or Gospels (Matthew, Luke, Mark, Paul, etc.) in well printed and setup form. The whole Bible is too formidable a meal to present in its entirety to those who must first "peck" at it to appreciate its exquisite flavor. But how many average educated Catholics without exegetical training and background, would it be safe to turn loose on, for example, St. Paul to the Romans? Might we not be back, stealing a page from the Protestant colporteur who sold Bibles, yes millions of them — but such Bibles and such spiritual confusion! Our Catholic problem is not to "sell" Bibles — but in some way to orientate the Bible in its primary and proper relationship to the flood of devotional books to which Catholics are now spiritually and sometimes emotionally committed. When that is accomplished, "sales" will take care of themselves.

                                    — Norman M. McNeill, M.D., Philadelphia, Pennsylvania

Courtesy, Publishing and Promotion Services, U.S. Catholic Conference, Washington, D.C.

71. A New American Ritual, 1952–54

The rites of passage, or key transition experiences in the Christian life (birth, marriage, death), have always served as indicators of the tensions involved in the Catholic community's process of formation and its attitude toward society (see docs. 5, 6, 33). In the nineteenth century the concern for a common Latin ritual preoccupied many of the ecclesiastical assemblies (see docs. 7, 21). After World War II, the increasing educational standards in the community, the move to the suburbs, economic growth, and daily contacts with Protestant and Jewish fellow Americans in the civil and business communities coincided with the internal drives of the liturgical movement to argue for the use of the English language in some of the official rituals of the church. The liturgical conference held in Portland, Oregon, in 1947 supported a resolution for increased English usage in the administration of the sacraments. At their 1950 meetings the bishops had partially discussed the issue, and in 1951 the Episcopal Committee of the Confraternity of Christian Doctrine presented the importance of these changes to the hierarchy from a pedagogical point of view. A committee under the directorship of Father Gerald Ellard, SJ, prepared a new edition of the rites along with a document arguing for the changes. In November 1953, the bishops approved the revised text of the rituals and the Sacred Congregation granted permission for its use — with some reservations about the use of Latin in the form of the sacraments, exorcisms, and anointing — on 3 June 1954. The following document, a tentative brief received by the Archbishop of San Francisco in February–March 1952, provides a window on both the American reasons for the changes from Latin to English and the impact in the United States of European liturgical precedents.

The Use of English in the Liturgy
Collectio Rituum Anglicae Linguae

"*In non paucis tamen ritibus vulgati sermonis usurpatio valde utilis apud populum existere potest: nihilominus unius Apostolicae Sedis est id concedere*" (AAS 39, 545)

At the 1951 Bishops' Meeting in Washington the Episcopal Committee of the Confraternity of Christian Doctrine was charged with the task of studying the desirability of presenting a request to Rome, for the optional use of English in connection with Baptism, Marriages, the Last Sacraments and Burial, and of reporting on the same at the 1952 Meeting. The directions of the *Mediator Dei* (1947), and as interpreted by the *Collectio Rituum: I*, approved for Germany in 1950, were set down as the basis of the project....

The scope of the indult envisaged is thus limited strictly to the Sacraments and situations named, and a few attendant blessings. The proposal does not in any way concern itself with any wider question of the partial use of the vernacular at any parochial function. It bears no reference to the topic of the introduction of English into the Mass, or the Office (Vespers, Compline), or elsewhere. It *does* contemplate enriching Catholic life, for the evident good of souls, in the person and group associations involved in the situations mentioned.

In the administration of the Sacraments the Church's accompanying rites and prayers are not directed to preparing God to grant graces, but altogether directed for the better psychological preparation of the recipient (if an adult), and all the by-standers. Let us consider the situations enumerated, and first, with regard to Baptism.

Baptism

According to the 1951 *Directory*, 973,544 infant and 121,950 adult Baptisms were administered in 1950, a total well over one million Baptisms. For each administration of the Sacrament at least some few people, say five or six, were present (a group that could readily be much increased). Thus several million instances for a deep and moving *religious instruction* were present — and were almost wholly missed. In themselves the baptismal rites yield to none in their eloquent witness to Christ's redeeming and the Church's mission, but that witness must be released from the Latin barrier.

It is true that the Ritual prescribes to the minister: "He will use the opportunity afforded by the administration of the Sacraments to explain with diligence their efficacy and use, as well as the significance of the ceremonies, wherever this can conveniently be done." [*Rit. Rom.* Tit. 1,10] As applying to parochial Baptisms this is a prescription notoriously difficult of fulfillment, and not the less so, in the face of a prohibition against interrupting the procedures (for adults) to explain what is happening. [*SRC* 3492,2]

Lest, therefore, such precious chances for instruction and improvement be lost, the Holy See is permitting (in Germany and elsewhere) that the "formulae, the exorcisms, and unctions be kept in Latin, but all the rest translated into the vernacular." "Else how can he that holds the place of the layman say the Amen to thy thanksgiving, since he does not know what thou art saying?" (I Cor. 14:16).

Weddings

At a sacramental Marriage the Church gladly acknowledges that the contracting parties, man and woman, are themselves the ministers of the Sacrament. How singularly appropriate, therefore, that no unnecessary barrier of Latin hedge these contractual rites. In the *Collectio Rituum: I*, the entire rite, including the blessing of ring(s), is optionally in the vernacular, and a beautiful prayer of blessing attaches to the initial rite. For the Nuptial Blessing the Latin form in the Missal is retained, but as a substitute for the final admonition a moving prayer in the vernacular is provided. [The 1947 *Rituale Parvum Gallicae Linguae* suggests having a lector read the Nuptial Blessing in French, as the celebrant recites in Latin (p. 122).] Let [it] be recalled that the 1951 experimental restoration of the Easter Vigil provides for renewing baptismal pledges in the vernacular.

Weddings invariably draw many people to the church, not a few non-Catholics amongst them. Now, the terrible indictments of American home-life voiced by Pius XII in *Sertum Laetitiae* (1939) are still unfortunately too true. It could reasonably be hoped that if these people, especially the non-Catholics, knew what it is the Church is praying for in the Solemn Nuptial Blessing, an additional partial remedy would be provided particularly by this use of English at Catholic Marriages.

Sick-room Rites

It seems unnecessary to stress the desirability of English for the sick-room and death-bed rites. Of all life's situations where the Church, as a loving mother, would least wish a question of language to stand between the soul and its Creator, it is the crisis of a serious illness, or the still more solemn one of man's last hour.

For the administration of Viaticum (or Communion of the Sick), it is proposed,

after the *Rituale Hindicae Linguae*, that everything be optionally in English.	after *Collectio Rituum: I*, that all be optionally in English save: *Domine non sum dignus; Ecce Agnus Dei; Accipe frater*, and/or *Corpus Domini*.

For the administration of Extreme Unction, on the model of these recent Rituals, it is proposed that all be optionally in English save *"In nomine Patris..."* and the anointing forms. For the death-bed Apostolic Indulgence it is proposed that all be in English, save *Dominus noster, Per sacrosancta* and *Benedicat te.*

Burial

"At low Masses of weddings and funerals," writes Bishop Weber of Strassburg (15 February 1951), "I insist that one read at least the Epistle and Gospel: one frequently has people there who do not regularly go to church, and it is important to instruct them on this occasion." [Regulation appearing in *Bulletin ecclesiastique du diocese de Strassbourg,* reprinted in *Maison Dieu* (1951), pp. 140–145.] If His Excellency's words are true of the Mass itself, do they not apply with even greater force to the Absolution and grave-side rites? Enlightened pastoral care finds full Latin rites here to be "maimed rites" indeed, as the haphazard "home-made" rubrics constantly attest. "I keep within the letter of the law," one priest asserts, "by reading the Latin in the car on the way to the cemetery." The *Collectio Rituum: I* provides a more solemn funeral rite, a simpler one, and one for children, in all of which nearly everything is optionally in the vernacular, and the Church's eloquent mourning prayers are allowed to afford, in the vernacular, their message of hope and comfort. This illustrates what the Holy Father means by the vernacular being *valde utilis* to the people; one understands that German priests, *gratitudine commoti,* telegraphed their fervent thanks, *"ob donum novae collectionis rituum,"* as one account records. [Telegram: *Septingenti sacerdotes ex omnibus Germaniae Diocesibus ad Primum Congressum Liturgicum in urbe Frankfurt aduniti... reverentiam filialem et oboedientiam perpetuam devovent ob donum novae Collectionis Rituum: Eucharistiefeier am Sonntag* (Trier: Paulinus, 1951), p. 222.]

Has the Father of Christendom such blessings only for the Asiatic or Western European lands who look to him? Is the Holy Father himself not afraid that their "mysteriousness" will be now stripped from our rites, the sacred aura of holiness lost in translating the Latin? Is he not, rather, here going back to the even older Roman tradition that dropped the Greek when it was no more the tongue of the local congregation? *"Apud nos,"* said a fourth century apologist, *"nihil astute, nihil sub velamine, sed simpliciter unus laudatur Deus."* [Finberg, *Clergy Review* (1951), p. 1]

Are the American Bishops not fearful of asking that Rome upset a liturgical tradition so long in undisturbed possession? The best answer, we believe, is that of the Holy Father in *Mediator Dei:* "It is true that the Church is a living organism and therefore grows and develops also in her liturgical worship; it is also true that, always saving the integrity of her doctrine, she accommodates herself to the needs and conditions of the times." [*Mediator Dei,* CTS edition, p. 31: *AAS* 39, 544] Is our widespread Latin not a bond of union, and a help towards orthodoxy? Undoubtedly it is both: "The use of the Latin tongue prevailing in a great part of the Church affords at once an imposing sign of unity and an effective safeguard against the corruption of true doctrine. In spite of this (*tamen*) the adoption of the vernacular in quite a number of functions may prove of great benefit to the people. But to make such concessions is for the Apostolic See alone." [*Mediator Dei*, CTS edition, p. 32: *AAS* 39, 545]

But, it may be said, with the constant evolution of English, there could never be a fixed and definitive translation. Is there even for Holy Writ? Is it a loss that the wording of the Eight Beatitudes and the Sermon on the Mount must be, from time to time, recast into current English? Any and every translation, it is felt, will be "unfinished" and "perfectible." In the instructions of Propaganda [Fide] to India (Prot 2363/48) the advice is given to have translations made at once, and used *ad decennium* without the need of sending them to Rome for specific endorsement.

While this project is not at all regarded as a general panacea for our ills, it is of no small spiritual advantage to souls, and it is felt that the American bishops should explore, in collective appeal, the Holy Father's mind touching such indults for his millions of devoted American children.

> Collectio Rituum Anglicae Linguae, "PS 1953 Roman Ritual," with cover letter John J. Mitty to Edwin V. O'Hara, 5 March 1952. Courtesy of the Archives of the Archdiocese of San Francisco.

72. Fulton J. Sheen's Television Chalk Talks on Reparation, 1953

Fulton J. Sheen (1895–1979), undoubtedly the most well-known Catholic public figure on radio and television between 1930 and the mid-1950s, attracted an audience of various religious persuasions. Trained in Thomism at Louvain and winner of the Cardinal Mercier Prize in philosophy, Sheen sought to make Thomism practical as a force to reconstruct the modern world, which was disillusioned and torn asunder by wars and competing global ideologies. "Reparation," a theme popular in the 1928 Sacred Heart encyclical, needed to include atonement for public transgressions, as well as for personal sin. Using quasi-liturgical language, the bishop suggested a type of public ritual for America to achieve this. Quoting Lincoln, the national-savior figure, Sheen redirected the traditional religious topics of guilt, penance, and reparation toward, on the one hand, America's collective experience of disintegration and, on the other, Americans' feeling of guilt growing from increased prosperity after the war. Sheen's emphasis on global concerns in his attack on Communism and nationalism was also seen in his promotion of the "world rosary" when he was the national director of the Society for the Propagation of the Faith from 1950 to 1972. The selection below, sprinkled with Sheen's humor and wit, is one of the "chalk talks" from the 1950s television series Life Is Worth Living. *The scripts were later published with cartoons depicting his blackboard and its "angel" who erased the board.*

Our last subject was peace from a negative point of view. We warned that Russia uses peace talk as a tactic and that the danger of war increases with each overture of peace from the Soviets....

Here we are concerned with peace from a positive point of view, namely, how it is achieved in the individual and in the nation....

Suffering is related to guilt in a general way, though each individual who suffers is not individually guilty. World suffering and world crisis are also related to guilt and guilt needs reparations, or the righting of wrong.

Our modern world very seldom thinks of the relationship of a world crisis to guilt. The modern world practically ignores guilt as responsibility for the violation of a moral law. A man who disobeys one of God's physical laws, for example, that he should eat to live, after four or five days suffers a headache. It is just as vain to deny that the breaking of moral laws has consequences as to deny that the breaking of physical laws produces certain effects. Unfortunately many live amidst crises, trials, cold wars, and political disorders without any sense of guilt. They fail to see a connection between what is happening in the world order and the way we live, think, and move. This denial of responsibility reminds us of a husband and wife who went to the doctor. The doctor asked the husband, "What is wrong with you, sir?"

He said, "I eat too many cherries."

The wife said, "At the bottom of cocktail glasses."

As he blamed the sickness on cherries and not on alcohol, so too many in our modern world forget that perhaps our world headache may be due to the way we have conducted ourselves before our fellow man and before God, rather than to our political cherries.

An analogy is to be found among the egotists and the selfish, whom nobody seems to like. Failing to see that their egotism has alienated their neighbor, they accuse their neighbor of being antisocial. Instead of looking into their own hearts, they disclaim responsibility for their self-centeredness and place the blame, perhaps, on halitosis. They try using chlorophyll for thirty days, but they still are unpopular. They never shoulder the guilt of egotism, which alone would lead to a more generous attitude to others. Of such people it has been said, "They have no enemies; all their friends hate them."

Nations, too, can get in the habit of denying that their trials, the hatred of other nations, their insecurity, and the threat of Communism may be related to their moral failings. It is too superficial a justification for any nation to blame another for its crises.

Granted now that nations as well as individuals can violate God's laws, it follows that the evil that brings us to the tragic predicament must be expiated....

There is a great difference between sorrow for the wrong we did and making reparation for it. Suppose that during one of these telecasts, when my little angel came out to clean my blackboard, I stole his halo. I am sure that when my little angel took himself back into the wings, if I said, "I am awfully sorry, little angel, will you forgive me?" the angel would answer, "Sure I forgive you!" But he would say, "Give me back my halo." The return of the halo would be the proof that I was sorry for the theft.... The equilibrium and the balance of justice have been disturbed, and that balance must be restored by penance.

It is not sufficient that we as individuals make up for our own individual failings. We are also citizens of a great republic, and we have to make the expiation as a republic. This will involve some prayers and penances on our part.

REMEMBER . . .

This Unknown Communist has a SOUL

as dear to God as your own soul . . . and that Christ died on Calvary as truly for him as He died for you.

WILL YOU BE GENEROUS ENOUGH TO PRAY FOR THE CONVERSION OF THIS ONE SOUL?

If enough prayers are offered, Communism may be eliminated from the world!

Communism is Godlessness— and no Communist will ask for the Grace of conversion, but you may obtain this gift for him if you will pray.

Everyone has a Guardian Angel. Will you join in prayer with the Guardian Angel of an unknown Communist and ask for his conversion? Then when you stand before God you may meet face to face the Soul which has been brought there through *your* efforts.

Our Lady of Fatima asked us for Penance, Reparation, the Daily Rosary, Holy Communion, the Five First Saturdays, and Consecration to Her Immaculate Heart. *Do your best!*

NIHIL OBSTAT: John A. Schulien
                Milwaukee, Wis., Jan. 7, 1958
IMPRIMATUR: ✠Albert G. Meyer
            Archbishop of Milwaukee, Jan. 13, 1958

Printed with permission of
GREEN SCAPULAR FOUNDATION
Valley Stream, N.Y.

THE FRANCISCAN MARYTOWN PRESS
KENOSHA, WISCONSIN 53141
(Publ. of THE IMMACULATE Magazine)

A leaflet asking Catholics to pray for communists

It will also mean seeing that as long as human groups do not make sacrifices for peace, they will continue to settle their difficulties by war. War to egotists who deny they ever do wrong seems a smaller calamity than the renunciation of their egotism and selfishness.

National penance is a true American doctrine, as well as a profound religious doctrine in the great Hebraic-Christian tradition. Lincoln expressed this better than any President our glorious country has ever had. Maybe he knew it because he was better schooled in sacrifice and suffering. . . . Out of this life of sorrow, misjudgment, trial, and war, a great character was made. His Calvaries enabled him to have an insight into the spiritual needs of a nation that is given to but a few. On the cold, windy day of his second inaugural, he asked the American people to make some kind of reparation for their national sins:

> It is the duty of nations as well as of men to own their dependence upon the overruling Power of God; to confess their sins and transgressions in humble sorrow, yet with assured hope that genuine repentance will lead to mercy and pardon; and to recognize the sublime Truth announced in the Holy Scriptures and proven by all history, that these nations only are blessed.

And inasmuch as we know that by His Divine Law, nations, like individuals, are subjected to punishments and chastisements in this world, may we not justly fear that the awful calamity of Civil War which now desolates the land may be but a punishment inflicted upon us for our presumptuous sins, to the needful end of our national reformation as a whole people? ... It behooves us then, to humble ourselves before the Offended Power, to confess our national sins, and to pray for clemency and forgiveness.

Lincoln clearly taught that the awful calamity of Civil War was the punishment that God permitted us to have because of our national sins. Would it not be well to let ring through America today a voice like Lincoln's, summoning us to fall prostrate before God and ask God for pardon and forgiveness. We need not go to war, thus destroying our fellow man and turning poppy fields into rivers of blood. There is another way of peace, and we believe our President can lead us down that road. In his inaugural address he did not think of God as an afterthought. He began it by invoking the blessing of God. Given this consciousness of Divine protection, would it not be well to write or telegraph asking our President to declare a National Day of Prayer and Penance?[1]

The Communists are not the only ones who are guilty before God. We, too, as a nation are guilty. We have failed in some way. As Lincoln said: "It behooves us then, to humble ourselves before the Offended Power, to confess our national sins, and to pray for clemency and forgiveness."

> Fulton J. Sheen, *Life Is Worth Living* (Garden City, N.Y.: Garden City Books, 1953), 141–42, 143, 144, 145–46. Published with permission of the Archives of the Diocese of Rochester, New York.

73. Catholics as Practical Secularists, 1953

One of the most influential commentators on the American religious scene of the 1950s, Will Herberg (1901–77) penned his famous tripartite division of religion into Protestant, Catholic, and Jewish variations of a single American way of life in 1955. Two years previously, Commonweal *had run a series describing American Catholicism in which Herberg, in the piece excerpted below, anticipated his later critique. In some respects, his description of the problems of the use of religious and institutional power in a democratic society, the divorce of religion from daily life, and the separatism characteristic of the community had run like a thread throughout much of the church's history in the United States. Examples of similar problems and how they influenced prayer and practice abounded, from both internal and external sources (see docs. 26, 47, 55, 59). In the 1950s the prosperity of the community and its institutional strength made the traditional criticisms all that more sensitive. The acuteness and comprehensiveness of Herberg's observations coincided with aspirations for change from within the community itself (see docs. 67 70, 76).*

Catholicism in America today stands at its highest point of prestige and spiritual power. It is not hard to see why this should be so in this country as elsewhere in the Western world. In an age when the vacuities of "rationalism"

---

1. On 23 June 1953, President Dwight D. Eisenhower issued a proclamation to that effect. The proclamation is printed as a footnote in the Sheen text.

and unbelief have become so painfully evident, Catholicism presents the picture of a dynamic faith sure of itself and capable of preserving its substance and power despite elaborate institutionalization. In an age of spiritual chaos and disorientation, Catholicism stands forth as the keeper of an enduring tradition that has weathered the storms of the past and stands unshaken amidst the disasters of our time. In an age of social disintegration and the resurgence of every kind of narrow particularism, Catholicism speaks for and exemplifies a universalism transcending, though not negating, state and nation, culture and civilization. In an age disillusioned with the claims and pretensions of both individualism and collectivism, Catholicism is recognized as the long-time advocate of a "third way," a society built on Christian responsibility, the society defined in the papal encyclicals and the "social teachings" of the Church. Finally, in an age characterized by a total assault on the human spirit, Catholicism has distinguished itself as the "friend of man and of culture," to employ the expression of a well-known Protestant theologian....

Equally serious [among Herberg's critiques], more serious indeed in its immediate consequences, is the practical secularism that pervades American Catholic life (no more, to be sure, than it pervades American Protestant or American Jewish life, but it is of Catholics that I am speaking here). It may seem strange to charge such doughty champions of religion as American Catholics with secularism, but what is secularism but the outlook in which religion is separated from life and relegated to a purely private status, peripheral to the vital areas of economics, politics, and culture, which are held to have autonomous non-religious foundations? What is secularism, in short, but the conviction that "business is business," the affair of the businessman, just as "religion" is the affair of the priest? In this sense, secularism quite pervades the thinking of large numbers of American Catholics — a fact testified to by a familiar Catholic attitude which resents papal encyclicals on labor and industry as an intrusion of religion into a sphere where it does not properly belong.

The case of Joseph P. Ryan, the indicted president of the International Longshoremen's Association, is significant. Mr. Ryan is a Catholic and a trustee of the Guardian Angel Church in New York City. The pastor of this church is also port chaplain of New York. According to the press, he recently expressed his conception of the relation of religion to life in these words: "He [Mr. Ryan] keeps his hands off the spiritual things of my church and I keep my hands out of his business."

The same secularist doctrine has tended to obscure responsibility for political corruption and civic mismanagement perpetrated by "good" church-going Catholics; Boston, I should say, offers quite an object lesson. No one proposes that the Church directly intervene in politics or business or labor affairs, but it seems to me it ought not to be possible as it manifestly is today, to be held a "good" Catholic without regard to what one does in his business, politics, or professional life. "Spiritual things" and "business" belong together, and when they are kept apart, it is "business," the common life, that is degraded, and the Church that is devaluated and discredited.

Because of this pervasive secularism, American Catholicism often allows itself to be caught up in the narrowness and petty prejudices of its environment. European observers, Catholic and non-Catholic alike, have marvelled at the prudishness of American Catholics in matters of sex, an attitude so foreign to classical Catholic tradition. A good deal of this is probably an Irish heritage, but not entirely; the influence of American Protestant moralism is also a major factor. The slightest hint of sexual suggestiveness is pounced upon as the work of the devil, while movies, stories and advertising that quite shamelessly strive to excite pride, envy, hate, and covetousness (sins rather high up on the list) go by without a word of censure. Here American Catholics are most deplorably untrue to Catholicism.

I referred earlier to the tendency in Catholicism to smile indulgently upon men and pat them on the back, as it were. Catholicism thus comes forward as the friend of man, whereas Protestantism, with its unrelenting emphasis on judgment, sometimes appears as his enemy. But this same spiritual geniality, combined with the secularism to which I have alluded, often betrays Catholics into too easy an acquiescence in the banalities, timidities, and mediocrities of everyday life — provided they do not violate the conventional decencies. The utter mediocrity of so much American Catholicism is to me a most shocking thing. How many times have I heard an intelligent and deeply sensitive Catholic say deprecatingly: "Oh, you can't expect too much of them; after all, they're only human..." — as if to be human meant to be commonplace and mediocre! Why is American Catholicism so uncreative, when compared with European? Why does it show so little appreciation of the great cultural treasures of its own tradition? There are many reasons, but I suggest that one of the most important is a deplorable readiness among many American Catholics of culture and intelligence to compromise with stupidity, stodginess, and mediocrity, so long as they keep within the bounds of "morality."

Mediocrity is reinforced by the tendency toward separatism and seclusiveness that is characteristic of much of American Catholic life. I refer not primarily to the vast network of special Catholic institutions and agencies, from academic associations and church schools to singing societies and sports clubs, which parallel the general community institutions; these mostly serve a useful purpose. What I have in mind rather is a kind of "secessionist" spirit that keeps the Catholic busy about his own Catholic affairs and leaves the business of the community, except politics, of course, largely to non-Catholics.

My university lecturing schedule and other interests brought me to a considerable number of cities and towns in various parts of the country during the past two years, and everywhere, I think, I found the same situation and heard the same complaints. "Oh, they're very nice," Protestants and Jews would say when I asked about the Catholics, "but they're never around; they keep to themselves and don't take part in things. They've got their own concerns. ..." It is this same attitude perhaps that accounts for the strange indifference of so many Catholic educators to the problems of public education: their own special Catholic problem they feel they have solved, at least in principle, through the parochial school; the public school, even though it is attended by the great bulk of American children and Catholics are frequently quite influential in its administration, does not seem to strike them as a particular concern of theirs.

This feeling is undoubtedly in good part a carry-over from an earlier time when Catholics were indeed excluded from general community life; a good deal of it too may be traced to the logic inherent in the system of dual institutions that has been built up, but much of this attitude, it seems to me, is the indirect consequence of a deliberate policy of secluding Catholics in order to protect them from "contamination." I have heard this policy explicitly defended on more than one campus, though it is certainly not the rule at American colleges today. It seems to me unfortunate on all counts: it is utterly ineffective; it leads to a kind of social and intellectual isolationism which fosters narrowness and stagnation; and it is manifestly prejudicial to the position of Catholics in American life. Catholics are no longer aliens and outcasts in America; they have not been for some time — and they ought to cease acting as if they thought they were.

Will Herberg, "A Jew Looks at Catholics," *Commonweal* 58 (22 May 1953): 174, 176–77. © 1953 by the Commonweal Foundation. Reprinted with permission.

74. The Parish Is Our Family, 1953

In 1914, when the College of Saint Benedict, St. Joseph, Minnesota, was founded from its roots in a nineteenth-century academy, the Sodality of Our Lady was already an established organ of the students' spiritual life (for parallels, see doc. 22). Electing officers once a year, meeting every Sunday in the chapel, reciting the Little Office of the Blessed Virgin Mary, and occasionally collecting money for the mission, the sodality's fortunes had waxed and waned with the times. In 1931, under inspired leadership and now well connected with the national sodality movement (see doc. 48), its committees were reorganized to provide a strong and vital role on the women's college campus. Its history mirrored the broader community's growing interest in the Eucharistic and liturgical movements, Catholic Action, and social outreach (see docs. 50, 51, 53, 54, 55). A small school for leadership which would provide the base for the popular movements of the 1960s, the sodality organization declined after World War II, but the following selections from a larger document, dated May 1953, and composed by the sodality members themselves, indicate the growing convergence between the theology of the Mystical Body, its application in the liturgical movement, the vision of the parish, and the need for mission and social reconstruction.

Introduction

The parish is our family. This is more than a catch-phrase! It is a truth which is derived directly from the realization that the Christian family founded on Christian marriage is a symbol of a similar but greater reality, the Church, the Family of God. For Christ so loved the Church that He made it His Bride and allows its members to become one with Him and with each other by sharing His supernatural Life with them.

Now the parish is that Church in miniature. It is the Church, concrete and tangible to us in our daily lives. It is the Church, a living, functioning organism — not an organization to which we "belong" but a *life* which we *live!* It is in the parish that the love of Christ for His Spouse, the Church, is realized and made fruitful. It is here that the truest family life, of which the Christian family is a symbol, becomes reality.

Once this is understood, the more obvious similarities of family and parish life are clearly seen: the birth of new members, the growth of the children, parental authority, the nourishment at a common table, and other aspects of our daily living together. As everyone in a natural family loves and lives the "full" family life, so too will we of the Family of Christ be one in all our parish activities (weddings, baptisms, funerals, novenas, card parties, church cleaning days, financial difficulty, celebration of the patronal feast of parish and pastor, and others without number).

This booklet has been prepared to present this "community" aspect of our parish life. It offers nothing new; it suggests nothing more nor less than a full parish life in Christ. Armed with the truth of the Mystical Body in our understanding and in our practice, we can do a great deal for the cause of Christ in our own surroundings and in more remote contacts. Living this doctrine fully, we will preach Christ to those who do not know Him. Seeing us in our Christian family life, all will know that we are followers of Christ in the same way in which Christians were recognized of old — by their love, one for another.

The similarities between family and parish life are presented in the following pages. Starting with a principle of comparison, a brief explanation is given followed by suggestions and specific ways in which each idea might be brought into our parish life. Each thought ends with a prayer from the Missal. It has been suggested that some definite time schedule be planned for the consideration of these pages. The topics might be read and meditated upon, one each day, perhaps in Lent or Advent. This might be possible at a family meal or in the instruction of the children. The prayer which is given would make a fitting conclusion for this discussion.

May those who use this little booklet be prompted to live the full and vital parish life in true family spirit!...

We Unite in Worship

The unity of the parish family radiates from the altar, around which the priest gathers with his children. Here takes place the sacrifice of the Mass, the renewal of the union between Christ and His Church. Christ, knowing the need of His people to worship God and to expiate for sin, left us his own Sacrifice sacramentally renewed at each Mass. It makes present the graces He merited on the Cross. "If you wish to hear Mass as it should be heard, you must follow with eyes, heart, and mouth all that happens at the altar. Further, you must pray with the priest the holy words said by him in the name of Christ and which Christ says by him." (Pius X)

Only Active Participation Is Fitting

There are Missals for every age level, unfolding the treasury that is the Mass.

The "jangle" at collection time need not disturb us. Formerly, at the offertory Christians presented food, particularly bread and wine. This was their way of showing that they knew that in every Holy Mass they must offer themselves with Christ. Today our money offering is ourselves — the fruit of our labor.

On Sunday and on greater feasts the pastor must offer a *"missa pro populo"* for his parish. How good if the family is there!

To arrive late or leave early is to miss the point — the Mass is the only thing that really matters.

> We further beseech thee, O Lord,
> to receive this oblation
> of our service and of thy entire family.
> Provide that our days be spent in thy peace.
> Save us from everlasting damnation
> and cause us to be numbered
> among those whom thou hast chosen. . . .

We Are Not Provincial

Our interest has become very local — just the bounds of our little parish. But this has been merely for the sake of making these ideas tangible. Our parish is the Mystical Body of Christ in miniature (as our families are on a still smaller scale) but all the world is the Mystical Body of Christ, really or potentially. The bond of unity which we see most clearly in the family, the basic unit of society, which we extend to our parish, state, and nation, applies to the whole world which, on various levels, is a union of many families.

Christ prayed to His Father "that they may be one as we also are." This must become our prayer and our apostolate.

We Have a World Interest

We pray for those families in the world who do not know Christ. We pray for vocations for laborers who will bring the Mystical Body, the Family of Christ, to its full size. We help finance the missions; we'll find it wise to contribute to parish collections for the missions or to some one worthy cause for which our help is asked personally.

We Start Our Real Work in Our Own Little Parish

Charity begins at home and our best contribution to the cause of Christ is the establishment of truly Christian homes and living parishes. We will not be satisfied until our parish has become one in which the members are united in love with one another and with Christ.

> Do thou, we beseech thee, O Lord,
> by the intercession of blessed Mary,
> ever a virgin,

> defend this thy family
> from all adversity;
> and graciously protect those
> who with their whole hearts
> prostrate themselves before Thee.

Sodality of the Blessed Virgin, College of St. Benedict, St. Joseph, Minn., *The Parish Is Our Family*, 22-6B-2 f.8. Permission to use granted by the Order of St. Benedict, St. Benedict's Monastery Archives, St. Joseph, Minn.

75. Women's Apostolic Spirituality, 1956

Great numbers of women chose religious life as their vocation in the first half of the twentieth century. By 1956, almost 160,000 sisters were serving the church and society, mainly in teaching, nursing, catechetics, social work, overseas mission, and the contemplative life. Combined with an alignment of the congregations' constitutions, accomplished for the most part by the early 1930s, the structure of the women's prayer life and work often created what sociologist Audrey Kopp would later call a "split-level" life. An important factor in the renewal in religious life was the development of the Sister Formation Movement (1954–72). The example of the Maryknoll Sisters in China suggests that attempts to change the emphasis and location of ministry (the "direct apostolate" of evangelization), by egressing traditional institutional work and prayer structures, required an intensive interior prayer life, focus on Jesus Christ, and study of scripture. Sister Marie Marcelline Grondin, a Maryknoll sister from Westbrook, Maine, recounts the sisters' work in Maryknoll Bishop Francis X. Ford's (1892–1952) vicariate in Kaying Province, where she had worked for over fifteen years. She had been the director of the Chinese novices and had later been imprisoned in China. The selection is also one of many examples where mutuality between women and men in mission redounded to the good for them and for society.

The Direct Apostolate

When we [the Maryknoll Sisters] came to Hakka-Land [in China], for the work of a direct apostolate back in 1934, six of us were stationed in the mountain village of the Eastern Rock. Here we all became as children again, learning the Chinese language. After an interval of hardy study, Bishop [Francis X.] Ford came to our mountain home and gave us his first retreat. The subject matter of the retreat was very much along the lines of Dom Marmion's, *Christ, the Life of the Soul*. It was our spiritual foundation — simple lines, focussed on God, through Christ, Our Lord. Our lives and our apostolate were given their point of departure and were orientated to Christ — Christ in us and Christ in others, actually or potentially. Two more retreats, given in 1940 and 1945, were equally basic in character, Bishop Ford deriving much of his inspiration from Catholic Dogma and Scripture. One retreat, given in 1942, was based on the verses of the sequence, *Veni Sancte Spiritus*. During this retreat, Bishop Ford spoke as one whose prerogative and obligation is ex officio to know and to preach the Holy Ghost; the retreat proved to be truly a Pentecostal event in our lives. A last retreat, given us in 1950, was built around the Apostles' Creed; it was a masterly exposition of all the beautiful truths that are contained in our Creed, centering about Father, Son and Holy Ghost, and directed towards the extension of the Holy, Catholic Church and the Communion of the Saints. One retreat, given in Chinese to the Sister-Catechists, seemed to round out the spiritual theology that we learned at the school of Bishop Ford; this retreat was exclusively on the subject of Our Lady; it gave us his ideals for our life and apostolate, as embodied in the feminine mould of Our Lady, the model of womankind, and as Bishop Ford referred to her, the First Sister-Catechist.

It was our privilege to become familiar with Bishop Ford's spiritual thoughts also through the means of recollection day conferences, that he would give periodically whenever we gathered at our center.... "As I have so often remarked to you," he would say, "the Church's liturgy is a sure guide for our devotions and a divinely appointed channel of grace for us." He would then lead our thoughts and consideration along the paths of the ageless prayers and ceremonies of the Church, and show us how we as missioners must derive inspiration and strength for the daily living of our apostolate.

Bishop Ford often called to our attention what a wealth of doctrine was to be found in the simple, ordinary prayers that we taught the Christians. He wanted us to probe the depths of fundamental truths — the simple truths that we were to teach to others, without side-tracking to unessential devotions. He would tell us that one could present our whole Faith through the explanation of the Christians' few daily prayers — the sign of the Cross, the Lord's Prayer, the Hail Mary, the Apostles' Creed. He exemplified this teaching in his own preaching.... [His] retreats were the spontaneous outflow of his own spiritual abundance; they were frequently given with but short preparation, because Bishop Ford would often accept the task of becoming retreat master when others were unable to reach us because of abnormal conditions of war or for other reasons....

The spiritual education that Bishop Ford gave us over the years was basic spirituality, common to any type of spirituality. Being essentially a missioner, however, Bishop Ford interpreted his spiritual doctrine in the light of our life in the missions and of our particular apostolate with souls. This apostolic spirituality became to us like an unerring compass, showing us the best way to God and to souls. Such a basic spirituality with its consequent interior life actuated in each of us, was clearly to Bishop Ford's mind the *sine qua non* condition of our apostolate.

Of Bishop Ford it could be said most truly that his spiritual life was wholly apostolic. During a Holy Hour on one occasion — it was during the Chinese New Year celebrations — when superstitions and pagan ceremonies were going on all around us, he prayed somewhat in this way: "We offer to Thee, O God, the worship of these people. Accept all their acts as though intended for Thee. They would offer it themselves, if they knew of Thee."

In this, our day of general persecution, how natural for us to follow Bishop Ford's method of prayer, as we say the Office! Identifying ourselves with those to whom we are sent as missioners — the non-Christians as well as the Christians, the free as well as the persecuted that we had to leave behind [in China], the Chinese priests now in chains and shackles, the Chinese Sisters carrying on bravely in the big underground struggle [—] we can say, to paraphrase only Psalm 141:

> I cry to the Lord with a loud voice, with a loud voice I beseech the Lord.
> I pour forth my anxiety before Him, and in His presence I declare my distress....

Such an apostolate "into the world" [i.e., living in people's homes, going out to the people, rather than having the people come to the convent] is not, however, without requiring sacrifices of many sorts, even sacrifices of the spiritual kind. In the case where souls can be reached and instructed only in their homes, it becomes an essential requirement of the apostolate that the missionary Sister at times make prolonged stays in villages, thereby foregoing even the reception of Holy Communion. The missionary Sister must also give up on such occasions whatever spiritual exercises as gravitate about the Blessed Sacrament in the tabernacle of chapels and churches. The spirituality of the Sister-Apostle must be adapted to these requirements of work with souls. It must be of such nature that it will measure up with spontaneous charity to these exigencies; it will even thrive and grow stronger on these deprivations, which might appear to be a paradoxical statement, yet really is not so, for God will see to it that she is not the loser by working in His vineyard — He, Who is never outdone in generosity.

Mass heard and Holy Communion received spiritually bring effective peace to the soul, a fact that we perhaps do not appreciate as much as we should. God speaks intimately to the soul, through the pages of Scripture and Divine Office, and He is always found indwelling "at home," if He is sought during daily visits that replace the visits to the Blessed Sacrament. Bishop Ford used to advise us to practice recalling the indwelling of the Blessed Trinity, through such actions as whenever we incline at the *Gloria Patri,* or make the Sign of the Cross. It was a means of "tempering" us for such periods when the divine Indwelling would be our sole Refuge, but our ever strengthening and sure Consolation.

The Sister-Apostle who carries out her prayer life, unostentatiously but fully, in the homes of catechumens or of Christians, definitely brings graces, not only to herself but to the home who shelter her as well. First of all, there is a certain atmosphere created, which everybody is anxious to respect. The little children are better than convent bells calling to religious exercises. "Sh!...Sister has to pray!" Almost invariably, a quiet hush will gradually fall over a household, which is already comparatively noiseless, being without victrola, radio or television. Then, those who are not busy with farm work or house chores, whether young or old, catching the spirit of the hour, will start looking around for their rosaries. Within a short time, it becomes a common sight to see the five-year-old Rice-Glory, standing close to Grandma, sitting by the doorstep, both holding on to the same rosary, while Lily-Fragrance, the baby toddler, plays contentedly on the floor at their feet. An older girl or boy will be sitting in a corner or standing by a side door overlooking the front pond, also saying the rosary or thinking of what is going on in Sister's room.

Evening meal brings young and old together. Then, after the lull following the daily bath and so forth, the neighbors begin to come for the instruction that is scheduled when Sister is around. Night prayers come next and everyone is renewed in the reverent atmosphere of worshipping God.

The spiritual sacrifices of the Sister-Apostle have been changed into the goal of life — eternal life.

Sister Marie Marcelline Grondin, OP, *Sisters Carry the Gospel* (Maryknoll, N.Y.: Maryknoll Publication, 1956), 40–41, 45, 46–47. Reprinted with permission, Orbis Books, Maryknoll, N.Y.

76. The Christian Family Movement and the Mystical Body, 1957

The awareness in the Catholic community of a distinctive lay spirituality and apostolate had grown in conjunction with the spread of Catholic Action and the emergence of the people into prominent professional positions in business, education, medicine, law, and politics (see docs. 42, 55, 62). One of the primary concerns of the laity and the hierarchy was the development of the family as a social and spiritual institution (see doc. 61). In June 1949, fifty lay delegates and twelve priests from around the country met to create a national coordinating structure for the diverse married men's and women's groups which had been steadily growing since World War II. Predominantly middle-class at its base, the Christian Family Movement (CFM), as it came to be known, gathered couples together in homes to discuss their life of faith and its relationship to current social problems. By 1952 the movement had spread to ninety-seven cities, and its membership steadily grew throughout the decade with thirty-two thousand couples by 1957. A peak was reached in 1964 with almost fifty thousand couples. CFM combined many different elements which had been developing in the community: renewal in scripture, focus on the liturgy, social action, concern for the family, and the theology of the Mystical Body. Entitled For Happier Families *(1949), and later known as "the little yellow book" because of its cover, the basic introductory manual for participants guided young couples toward an inductive, participative, and experientially based spirituality through a basic methodology of observe, judge, and act. The following selection is taken from the fifth, revised edition of 1957.*

Meeting 1

Prayer: Come, Holy Ghost, fill the hearts of Thy faithful and enkindle in them the fire of Thy divine love. Send forth Thy spirit, and they shall be created. And Thou shalt renew the face of the earth. Let us pray. O God, who by the light of the Holy Ghost dost instruct the hearts of Thy faithful, grant us by that same Holy Spirit ever to love and cherish what is right and just, and constantly to enjoy His consolations. Through Christ, our Lord. Amen.

Scripture (15 minutes):

Ask for a volunteer to read this short passage from the Scripture.

John 4, 31–34. Doing God's Will

Meanwhile, his disciples besought him, saying, "Rabbi, eat." But he said to them, "I have food to eat of which you do not know." The disciples therefore said to one another, "Has someone brought him something to eat?" Jesus said to them, "My food is to do the will of him who sent me, to accomplish his work."

The leader should ask questions of the group. He should not call on an individual to answer. After asking a question, the leader should not worry or start to ask another question. The silence shows the group that CFM wants the members to be responsible for the discussion. Anyone should feel free to start the discussion or participate in it at any point. This first meeting should be shorter than future meetings to allow time for questions.

1. Do you think Christ was using the word "food" with the same meaning the Apostles were? Explain.
2. Why did Christ emphasize that it was more important to do the will of God than to eat?
3. How do you go about doing the will of God each day?
4. How can we become more aware of the will of God each day?

In CFM the members of the group agree on an action that is a simple resolution which puts the Scripture into everyday practice. The action need not be the one in the book but it should be simple enough for everyone to do it. For example:

Suggested Action:

The offering of ourselves at Mass, or morning offering, recalled at natural breaks in the day.

Liturgy (15 minutes):

In the Scripture part of the meeting we acquire a better knowledge of Christ and His teachings. In the liturgy part of the meeting we shall study the meaning of the Church and its worship so that we can participate more deeply. The Liturgy parts of the first fifteen meetings are taken from the manual compiled by Father James Anderson of San Diego, California. The book is called "This is YCS" published by High School YCS, Chicago. For additional reading on the Mystical Body, references are made to the booklet, "Heaven's Beginning" by Gerald C. Treacy, SJ, Paulist Press. This is a simplified edition of the encyclical of Pius XII, "The Mystical Body of Christ." It is strongly advised that these passages be carefully read. The last ten meetings of the Liturgy concern the Mass. The text is the Encyclical by Pius XII, "The Sacred Liturgy."

Christ Institutes His Mystical Body — the Church

The Church — Christ's Mystical Body

From the very beginning, Christ had in mind the idea of developing the Church. Remember, the Jewish religion was to last only until Christ came.

The Church would *have* its buildings and its organization. But the Church was to *be* Christ continued in time.

Christ knew that His days on this earth would end. He wanted to continue all He started so that people could *get* and *retain* a share of the God-life (grace). He decided to continue His work — teaching, loving, praying, working — with and through a new body. We call it His Mystical Body.

Christ continues to do through His Mystical Body, the Church, what He did with His physical body 1900 years ago.

Why "Mystical"?

This new body of Christ is called a "Mystical" Body. It is not just an idea in our minds; it is not imaginary. It is a *real* body with real, "living parts." It is not a "body" like a club. Club members are just united by the same purpose: e.g., helping orphans, sewing linens. It has a real life which unites the "parts" (members) together in a real way. We have no other body like it, so we give it a name. We call it a "Mystical" Body. (For supplementary reading consult paragraph 5, "Heaven's Beginning," Gerald C. Treacy, SJ, Paulist Press).

1. Why did Christ create this new body called the "Mystical" Body?

2. What is the basic difference between the Church and any club or social organization?

3. Why is this Body called "Mystical"?

Social Inquiry (45 minutes):

The natural place for a family group to start is in the neighborhood. To observe does not imply to snoop. In CFM it means a friendly awareness of those about us. This interest in your neighbor is not just curiosity. You must know your neighbor to love him.

Observe:

1. What do you consider your immediate neighborhood? (The area which has a direct everyday influence on you and your children.)

2. How many of these neighbors can you address by name?

3. Are you well enough acquainted with them to know how many are in the family, the names of children, the schools they attend?

4. Have you ever visited with the parents of your children's friends?

Judge:

1. Should we know our neighbors?

2. How well should we know them? What is the Christian attitude toward neighborliness?

3. What is the Christian standard for deciding what people to associate with?

Hints: *The discussion on the observe and judge questions will point out something that can be done to improve family life on the topic of the inquiry. This is the inquiry action. It should be practical and simple. The best actions result when everyone contributes a suggestion. If a couple does not like a suggested action they should speak up.*

Suggested Action:

Learn the names of your immediate neighbors.

Write down the ACTION adopted by the group:

Hint: *Write down the action so that you can refer to it tomorrow and start to carry [it] out. Host couples could see that everyone has a pencil.*

Preview of Next Meeting:

Fix the time and place for the next meeting. The leader should ask someone to read the observe question for the next meeting. Discuss how you might get the facts necessary to have a good discussion. It is good to rotate leadership once or twice around the group before choosing a permanent leader.

Chaplain's Remarks (3 to 5 minutes):

Before the closing prayer the chaplain is invited to make some encouraging remarks. He might comment about the meeting relating it to their spiritual growth.

Prayer (See inside back cover)

Chaplain's Blessing:

After the prayer the couples kneel, and the leader asks the *chaplain* to give his blessing.

Note: Simple *refreshments* help the members to get better acquainted. No more than coffee and rolls.

> *For Happier Families: An Introduction to CFM* (Chicago: Coordinating Committee of the Christian Family Movement, 1957), 21–24. Reprinted with permission of the Christian Family Movement, Ames, Iowa.

77. Mission Circles Tabulate Their Work, 1959

Financial support for missions at home and overseas was provided partially through local mission circles, which were organized most frequently by women. By the 1920s, circles were blossoming and providing a social outlet for middle-class women to meet in each other's homes and to take responsibility for prayer and action beyond one's parish. Typical of the groups was the St. Francis Mission Circle, inaugurated in 1946 by Clara Westropp (1884–1965), cofounder of the Women's Federal Savings Bank in Cleveland, Ohio. The circle provided assistance to the Jesuit mission in Patna, India, where her brother, Henry, worked. Two hundred and twenty-six circles of ten to twelve women in each circle were meeting in the Cleveland diocese by 1954. Their 1960 pamphlet noted, "Whatever any group is able to do is worthwhile, because good cannot be measured by our human standards nor can the Divine Mercy be limited by our human terms." Sacrifice and charity gave value to the gift. The energy and resources of these groups provided the foundation in 1964 for the establishment of the

Cleveland Mission in El Salvador. Jean Donovan and Sister Dorothy Jean Kazel, OSU, were two missionaries Cleveland sent to Central America, where, in 1980, they were murdered, along with Maryknoll sisters Ita Ford and Maura Clarke. The following document is a form used by the circles to record their financial data.

Secretary's Monthly Minute Report

Secretaries of all deaneries are kindly requested to keep accurate monthly accounts of all shippings and donations to missionary assignments on minute sheets ruled according to the following form:

Circle No. _____ Secretary _____
Deanery _____ Address _____
Mission Assignment _____

Our Circle has completed the following work: 1959

	January to June	July	Aug.	Sept.	Oct.	Nov.	Dec.	Year's Totals
Sacred Heart Badges								
Rosaries								
Scapulars								
Statues								
Medals								
Altar Linens								
Priests' Vestments								
Babies' Layettes								
Boxes of Food								
Boxes of Clothing								
Medical Supplies								
Books								
Magazines								
Greeting Cards								
Cancelled Stamps								
Tax Stamps								
Amount Sent through Propagation of Faith Office								
Other items:								

Secretaries: Please fill in this report and send it to the St. Francis Xavier Mission Association: 320 Superior Avenue, N.E., Cleveland 14, Ohio, immediately after your December meeting.

78. Making Community Prayer More Liturgical, 1965

From the very beginning, religious orders had played a significant role in the development and spread of the liturgical, scriptural, and catechetical movements in the United States. Internally among their own members and externally through parishes, retreat houses, sodalities, and schools, women and men religious supported the larger church's efforts and fostered the use of missals, participation in the dialogue Mass, inductive methods of learning, and the reading of scripture. After the issuance of the 1958 Instruction of the Sacred Congregation of Rites on Sacred Music and Sacred Liturgy, a 1959 survey of forty-eight major religious communities indicated that thirty of them promoted active participation in the liturgy (eighteen noted its impossibility because of the disfavor of the chaplain or lack of an organist or time); twenty reported plans of instruction in colleges and schools. In 1959 the provincial of the Sacred Heart Province of the Brothers of Saint Francis Xavier, an institute dedicated to teaching on the primary and secondary levels, appointed a committee to study the "question of making our prayers more liturgical." This would eventually involve saying the breviary in English and extensively revising the devotional schedule which had dominated community life. After the opening of the Second Vatican Council (October 1962) and particularly with the issuance of the Constitution on the Sacred Liturgy (4 December 1963), the brothers worked hard to build on their experience and institute a far-reaching program of renewal. Written from the perspective of the religious laic brother or noncleric, the following document gives evidence of much broader currents also present among women religious and laity: the long preparation influencing the implementation of the conciliar changes in prayer and practice; the grappling with change itself and the search for an explanation; the focus on equality, rights, and participation; and the types of renewal programs which characterized most religious and diocesan groups.

Statement of Principles upon Which Schedule of Prayers Is Based

The discussion of liturgical prayer and of its place in the life of the Xaverian Brother has reached a state in the American Provinces, at least, where its value need no longer be defended. Papal teaching in recent times, from *Mediator Dei* (1947) onwards, has clarified the place of this prayer in the life of the Church of the present century. The discussion among our Brothers now centers on what practical effects it should have on our religious lives. What place should it have in our community and private prayers? This essentially is the stage that has been reached.

The history of this development in our American Provinces is surprisingly brief. It began, as might be expected, with the interest and active encouragement of a few. But their enthusiasm and interest is now shared by a very large number of Brothers — and all of this growth has taken place in less than ten years!

As we know, the movement began in Europe, was nurtured there especially by the Benedictines, and brought to the Midwest United States by this Order. Here it flourished locally until it burst upon the nation only within the last generation. This movement was (and still is) slower in developing on the East

Coast, where the predominantly Irish and southern European immigrant had been untouched by it in his homeland and even less in his adopted home. Anyone can understand, therefore, why our American Provinces, restricted as they have been to the coast states, felt so little of this renewal.

But the seed had been sown by *Mediator Dei,* and our Brothers of necessity had to learn about the implications and demands of this papal document. And it was through higher education, Xaverian College and the universities (some have pointed to the contact with clerics in the process of this education), especially in the field of religious education, that the acquaintance was made.

Therefore, it is no reflection upon our Founder, his early disciples, [or] our early American Brothers to state that we are more conscious and informed about the Church's liturgy. The Holy Spirit had not deigned to make his presence felt in this specific area in the Church of their lifetimes. And natural barriers, such as that of language, the gradually increasing "clericalization" of the liturgy, lack of the early Christian emphasis on the liturgy in religious education, etc., all contributed to obscuring the connection between liturgy and life during the past few centuries. Nor is there any reflection on the personal holiness of our early Brothers. Their lives bear testimony to this. The Holy Spirit was at work in the Church in spite of men's lack of understanding of what Vatican Council II calls "*the* primary and indispensable source from which the faithful are to derive the true Christian spirit" (*Constitution on the Sacred Liturgy,* #14). But God has determined to give us in these days one more means of glorifying Him and sanctifying ourselves. To neglect it knowingly would render us liable to severe judgment by God and future Xaverians. Above all, to invoke the teaching and practice of the Founder and early Xaverians in this matter should appear to all to be doing something, which they, as men devoted to the needs and spirit of the Church, would be the first to protest against.

Officially, the liturgical renewal received great impetus from the *Instruction of the Sacred Congregation of Rites on Sacred Music and Sacred Liturgy* (1958) and, of course, from the *Constitution* (1963). In the case of these recent documents, the effect they have had on our Brothers has come from both the secondary and college level of education. High school textbooks and current catechetical developments have introduced the subject of the liturgy more and more into religion classes. Through their teaching of this subject to others, the Brothers' knowledge and appreciation of the liturgy have grown. At our scholasticate and in university theology courses, the Brothers have been impressed with the place of the liturgy in the life of the Church and of every Christian.

The flowering of all this can already be seen in such things as participated Masses in our chapels, sung Masses on Sundays in more and more of our houses, liturgical committees in both provinces to aid the Provincials in implementing the recommendations of the Church, and in many other ways. Anyone familiar with the liturgical activities in our novitiates, scholasticate, and Spiritual Advancement Program knows how much the American Xaverian Brother is a part of the liturgical revival of the Church. In such a context, it would not be irrelevant to mention that our Founder and Xaverian predecessors would be happy to see how our Brothers have responded to the teaching and guidance of the Church.

The movement is also making itself evident in areas besides the Mass. The great store of theological and liturgically orientated expositions of the sacraments are having practical effects on our life. This is true of our understanding of the sacraments of Baptism and Confirmation and in the use of Penance and the Eucharist. Evidence of this was found in the 1964 conferences for the annual retreat. The knowledge and appreciation of liturgical music are growing. Para-liturgical devotions like the Bible Vigil have already been introduced into our communities, and teachers are using Biblical prayers and readings as part of their religion classes.

To give firmer roots to all of these developments, on the Provincial level the inservice lectures of last year, which included two nationally prominent liturgists, extended this year to at least one formal lecture on the use of this body of knowledge in high school teaching. Furthermore, in response to a request from a considerable number of Brothers, the Provincial inaugurated a series of talks and open discussions in the Maryland area on the subject of liturgical prayer. The results of this latter project are already evident.

So much for the background. As was said at the beginning, the stage has been reached in our Provinces where the discussion of liturgy and liturgical prayer can be carried on intelligently, soberly, and very profitably. Some preparation was needed for this, and it was supplied by the Church, the Xaverian educational and formation programs, under the leadership of those on the Provincial level, and finally through the interest and enthusiasm of an ever-increasing group of Brothers who see the value of this renewal to the life of Christian perfection.

One may ask how does liturgical prayer, the Divine Office, fit into all of this scheme. The obvious answer, of course, is that it could not help but do so. Liturgical prayer is an integral part of the sacred liturgy; it is included in any systematic study of the subject of the liturgy. It is a separate section in the *Constitution* (chap. IV). To treat the liturgy without discussing the Office would be to distort and mutilate the teaching of the Church. So the concern of the Brothers for the place of this prayer in their lives is a natural result of their total interest in and knowledge of Church teaching. And what a compliment it is to the Congregation that such a vital issue as this is a topic of interest! Again, the Brothers have kept pace with the teaching and mood of the Church and are asking the proper questions at the proper time. Of course, the topic entered the public forum and became of particular concern after the last Provincial and General Chapters and as a result of the questionnaire of 1962. All of these developments give clear evidence of the providential guidance of the Holy Spirit, working on prepared and receptive souls.

The stage has been set for a discussion of liturgical prayer in terms of theological principles. *Ad hominem* arguments, flip answers, resort to the imputing of less than honorable motives — all these may be excluded from our serious spiritual and educational discussions. They have not place among us as intelligent, well-educated, religious sons of the Church, especially when the subject is of such importance and dignity.

Five Year Report of the Provincial Council of the Sacred Heart Province on the Question of Making Our Prayers More Liturgical, 15–17. Xaverian Brothers, Sacred Heart Province, Baltimore, Md. Courtesy of the Archives of the University of Notre Dame, Notre Dame, Ind.

79. An Early Survey on Liturgical Change, 1964

While the Xaverian Brothers (see doc. 78) were working to institute liturgical change, the Christian Family Movement was conducting a nationwide exami-nation on the "reform of the liturgy" through its annual inquiry booklet (see doc. 76). Long attuned to the importance of the liturgy in life, participants from across the nation sent numerous suggestions for changes to the national office, now charged with compiling the results in a survey. The values of intelligibility, participation, ecumenical sensitivity, and the priesthood of all believers took center place. The first changes in the Eucharistic liturgy became operative in Advent 1964, and two years later, national surveys conducted by U.S. Catholic and the Bishops' Commission on the Liturgical Apostolate indicated that many of the reforms suggested in the CFM inquiry were representative of a much broader section of the Catholic community, prepared as it was through pervious programs associated with Catholic Action (48, 51, 53, 54, 70, 74). The following selection, titled "How the 'People of God' Want to Worship," summarizes the results from the CFM survey of 1964.

"The liturgy must arouse in our people a real and intimate involvement in the life of the Church. The lay person must encounter Christ in the Liturgy so that he can become like Christ." This is a quote from one of the 58 reports that form the basis of this article — suggestions for liturgical reform by CFM [Christian Family Movement] members across the continent.

Background

Meeting 12 of the 1963–64 Inquiry Program proposed a parish study night on the Reform of the Liturgy. Having come to appreciate the value of worship as an aid to living a personal apostolic life, CFM members were asked to turn their attention to the form of worship as they had known it. In doing so they were following the lead of Vatican II where determined efforts to revitalize the Liturgy had recently been distilled into the now famous Constitution on the Sacred Liturgy.

This close look at the existing forms of worship was to seek to answer the same questions that confronted the bishops at the Council:

How can the Mass and Sacraments be better understood and ap-preciated?

How can they better nourish our spiritual and apostolic lives?

How can lay participation be more meaningful?

Each parish group was requested to list, in order of importance, those changes in the Liturgy that they would like to see introduced. These lists were submitted to CFM headquarters where a composite report for the National Bishop's Committee or its committee for the Liturgy was prepared.

Looking back now, a few months later, one can see how closely CFM was attuned to events taking place at the Council. It is interesting to note, too, that the current inquiry book dates back to July 27, 1963, in its final form. The parish study night outlined by meeting 12 was scheduled to be held sometime between February 24 and March 8, 1964. It was not until December 4, 1963, however, that Pope Paul VI promulgated the Constitution on the Sacred Liturgy. This meant that there was not much time or opportunity to digest the Constitution before the study night.

Bits of information were available through the ordinary news channels, of course, but full knowledge of the Constitution's contents was not widespread. Thus, it was a source of satisfaction to clergy and laity alike to see how many changes suggested in these reports — from a good cross section of U.S. and Canadian Catholics — have been fully anticipated by the Constitution. The Holy Spirit is indeed operating on all levels of today's Church.

Fifty-eight reports were received from parishes as widely separated as Sacramento, Calif., Providence, R.I., Ontario, Canada, and Miami, Fla. More than 2000 persons took part in the survey. The following are the changes in the Liturgy which these laymen feel would be most beneficial.

More Vernacular

Ninety per cent considered use of the vernacular the most important step towards more meaningful participation in the Liturgy. Overriding themes seemed to be:

"We want to worship in a language we can understand."

"We can repeat Latin, but cannot think in Latin."

"It is difficult to explain the use of Latin to Protestants, because we do not understand it either."

Some advanced that the Mass, Sacraments, and sacramentals (blessings) be conducted entirely in the vernacular. Others desired partial retention of the Latin. Holy week and funerals were singled out as services that would especially profit from a greater use of the vernacular.

Face the People

Highly favored was Mass facing the people, the use of a lector and commentator, a homily on the Mass, and more singing, particularly of hymns. If these suggestions were to be spiritually fruitful, it was noted time and again, the celebrant would have to make adjustments in his accustomed tone and his pace in reciting the prayers.

Make It Simple

The trend of the reports was definitely towards simplicity, avoiding duplications in the recital of Mass prayers by priest and by people. Requests for fixed dates for movable feasts, for a standardized missal, and for elimination of pulpit announcements, reflected the same yearning for the simple and uncluttered.

Some mentioned fewer statues and better taste in religious art. In addition it was suggested that less feasts of saints and more ferial days would serve the liturgical year more fruitfully.

Tell Us What It Means

Many laymen feel the need for further education on the Liturgy, if the spiritual value of coming reforms [is] to be fully realized. Some hope they can be instructed on a weekly basis and desire the same for their children. Others favor the use of a commentator at Mass. Others suggested that the priest himself might do some explaining when, for example, he performs a baptism.

The Sense of Community Worship

These reports evidenced a growing awareness that at worship we are the whole Christ, Head and members, joined together in praise of our common Father. Some requested an expression of unity at the start of Mass to help us realize our oneness in Christ. Others thought the homily might be directed to this same end. Still others thought the restoration of the kiss of peace among the faithful would help fill the same need.

A greater use of laymen as lector, deacon, sacristan, or as members of the diocesan liturgical commission would emphasize the fact that the layman does have an active role in the worship of the Mystical Body. This community consciousness extended to other Christians as evidenced by requests for interfaith gatherings and opportunities for common prayer.

The Mass of the Catechumens

Some proposed that the prayers at the foot of the altar be eliminated. Others would like to recite the *Confiteor* aloud together with the celebrant in English. After an Introit procession it was suggested that the whole first part of the Mass, the service of the Word, be conducted from a lectern facing the people, reserving the use of the altar until the Offertory. It was thought desirable to vary the scripture lessons far more than has been the custom, including more readings from the Old Testament.

The Mass of the Faithful

Suggestions were made that the Offertory procession be reinstated. Many were in favor of permitting communicants to place a host in the ciborium and then having their gifts carried to the altar at the Offertory. Some called for [the] collection to be similarly carried to the altar to signify the giving of oneself.

Since the layman does have an active role in the offering of the gifts to God, some hoped that the offertory prayers might be said aloud by the people. Two suggestions were made concerning the Canon of the Mass; one was the explicit wish that the words of consecration be said aloud in English, and the other called for a revised listing of Saints in the Canon to include the more recently canonized. Some asked that the Last Blessing be made more meaningful by omitting the Last Gospel, or deferring the Blessing until the Last Gospel is finished.

The Sacraments

In general, people asked that the ceremonies be made more meaningful. The social or community aspect should be emphasized, and if possible, the sacraments should be conferred at Mass. God-parents should be made more aware of responsibilities assumed towards the newly baptized.

Confirmation should stress more the personal commitment to God: it might do so if administered in the late teens. Careful instruction should make it clear to the confirmed that they are the assistants of the Bishop in bringing Christ to all men. More frequent, less massive Confirmation classes were requested.

Many expressed the desire to receive Holy Communion under both species, at least on special occasions.

Many parents voiced the wish to participate more fully in preparation of children for First Communion. Others like the idea of a Family First communion.

It was suggested that the formula for the Sacrament of Penance be revised so the penitent need not be saying the Act of Contrition while the confessor is saying the words of absolution. The need for more direction from the confessor was cited as well as penances more suited to the nature of the sins confessed. Some asked that the social nature of the sacrament be emphasized on occasion by having general absolution, or at least preparatory prayers, said in common. It was felt that Confession should be much simplified for small children.

Revision of the marriage ceremony was strongly suggested. One report proposed that the couple face each other when receiving the sacrament.

Summing Up

In summary, these reports evidenced the fact that Catholic education, the work of the clergy on all levels, and of apostolic lay organizations have combined to produce an enlightened laity, capable of appreciating the Liturgy and anxious for the opportunity to draw closer to the Mysteries contained in the Liturgy.

Some comments: "Because we feel this is so vital to our religious life we are greatly concerned that the Constitution on the Liturgy be implemented immediately and comprehensively." "We are prayerfully looking forward to seeing these changes made in our parish as soon as possible." "Thank you for the opportunity of expressing our opinions. Truly we live in momentous times and are thrilled to think that our opinions may have even a little effect in furthering this work."

We would like to think that the reports, we feel, are representative of Catholics throughout the nation. We can conclude that the type of leadership needed to make the Liturgy come alive to all Catholics will be on hand.

The apostolic aims of CFM members will find its [*sic*] most fruitful expression in leading other lay people to Christ in the Mass and Sacraments.

Rev. Robert Dougherty, "How the 'People of God' Want to Worship," *ACT* 17, no. 9 (July–August 1964): 3–5. Reprinted by permission of the Christian Family Movement, Ames, Iowa.

80. The Way of the Cross Moves to the Streets, 1965

The commemoration of the events in the life of Jesus in the form of shrines or "stations" became common in western Europe by the fifteenth century. In imitation of pilgrims who walked the places of the Holy Land, Catholics contemplated the significance of the event through walking around the church and pausing for prayer before fourteen small wooden crosses erected along the wall. The subject matter and the number of stations varied over time. While Franciscans were influential in the spread of the devotion, many U.S. Catholics prayed the stations via the Liguorian approach (see doc. 57). The following document, written against the political and social turmoil of the 1960s, suggests that a modern Way of the Cross was unfolding in the presence of U.S. Catholics, if they could but see the presence of the suffering Christ right in their towns and cities. Compared to the reenactment of events in San Francisco's passion play (see doc. 39), the events leading to Calvary were dramatized in the lives of real people.

Millions of times each year, we Christians follow our Leader around the walls of our churches or through monastery gardens as He trudges His way to Calvary. Saints have written inspiring meditations, artists and sculptors paint and carve graphic presentations, and Christians respond with heartfelt prayers of sorrow and love. Yet, whether we make the stations in the cold with bleeding knees or from padded kneelers in a well-heated church, it's so easy to recognize Christ and follow His steps when He's carved in marble or painted in oils.

When He is sentenced to death, we tell Him that we should be sentenced, not He. When He takes His cross, we tell Him that we want to help Him carry it. When He falls, we tell Him we're sorry for our falls into sin. When He meets His mother, we tell them we're sorry for our part in this grief-filled encounter. We feel sure that if we were standing on a street corner in Jerusalem we wouldn't look the other way like Simon of Cyrene did but we would be a Veronica-on-the-spot, ready to give Our Lord a helping hand. When Christ is stripped, we ask Him to strip us of all attachment to sin and when He's nailed to the cross, we ask Him to join us to Himself and never let us be separated from Him. When He dies on the cross, we acknowledge that it is we who should be dying for our sins. We ask Mary to receive us into her arms as she holds the dead body of her Son. And finally, we promise to bury our sins behind the rock of the sepulcher.

Yet in all this we're thinking of the historical Christ who lived and suffered and died some nineteen hundred years ago. But do we ever make the way of the cross with the Christ who's suffering and dying today? We walk along Christ's path where His blood had been dry for many centuries. But do we ever follow the warm, moist footprints of His blood freshly drawn from the veins of our brothers? Or do we vow with Peter, "I know not the man"?

But how can we miss the Man! He's still being unjustly sentenced, still falling under the cross, still being stripped of His human dignity, still dying and being buried. How many years must we brush shoulders with Him, kick dust on His bloody footprints, step over His prostrated body, and walk by His cross, as if it were only another billboard? How many times will we have to break with Him before we realize that it was with Him that we were walking along the path to Calvary, the road to Emmaus, the streets of Selma, Alabama, and the trails of Viet Nam? "Was not our heart burning inside us as He talked to us on the road?"

Let's look right through the walls of our church and see Christ as He lives and walks the stations just outside.

Look at Him standing in the courtroom docks throughout the world. He's being tried on trumped-up charges of treason for being about His Father's business in Hungary and Poland and China. Because He can't raise bond, He's being kept in jail for months on end awaiting trial in Chicago, New York, and Los Angeles. He's being unjustly arraigned before a magistrate in the grocery store courtroom of some one-horse town. He's being convicted, not for what He did but for what He is, as He stands a few shades darker than His jurors in the courts of Mississippi, Alabama, and Louisiana. Do we know the man? It's He who said, "Whatever you do to these, you do to me."

Look at Him open His arms to receive the cross of caring for His deformed child. Look at Him accept the cross of old age with its dependence and pain and loneliness. Look at Him cling to the cross of His bed where He is confined for years on end. Do you know the man? It's He who said, "When I was sick, you cared for me."

Look at Him fall under His cross. He might have fallen into the gutter or slouched into a doorway on skid row. He doesn't look much like God there, but He didn't look much like God when He fell into the dirt on the way to Calvary either. In both cases, the world just stands around unconcerned and says, "Pick yourself up." Nobody condemns Him because He fell on the way to Calvary. After all, the cross was heavy, and He was exhausted by the night long trial, the scourging, and the crowning with thorns. Yet we have only condemnation and forgetfulness for Christ the alcoholic and Christ the dope addict. No, He isn't in their sins, just as He isn't in our sins, but He is in their person: they were created in God's image and likeness; they are sons of God as Christ is; many of them have become one with Him and us through Baptism, Confirmation, and the Holy Eucharist. Can we blame them alone for their fall? Do we know about their trials, their scourgings, their crownings with thorns? Do we even suspect the part we might have played in knocking them down? Christ had His divine power to pick Himself up on Calvary. These men have exhausted their human power. And what do we do to help them? We complain that they clutter up our streets.

Look at Him and His mother as they live in the slums of Chicago, or Washington, or Rio. Maybe they're on A.D.C. [Aid to Dependent Children]

Catholics demonstrating against racial discrimination and civil rights violations, 1962. Courtesy, Archives of the Archdiocese of Milwaukee, Wisconsin

or live on a couple of spoons of beans a day. Maybe there are rats crawling out of the holes in the walls; there might not be any heat or running water.

Christ's and Mary's sorrow at this last meeting must have been heavier than the cross He was carrying. Their sorrow is heavy too in the slums, and they have to live with it day in and day out.

And what do we tell them as we relax on our contour chairs listening to stereo sets? "You're a drain on the taxpayer's dollar." Do we have half the respect for them that we have for the slum lords who might be our neighbors out in the suburbs? ...

Look, Christ falls again. He has been out in the burning sun all day, picking asparagus, and He just couldn't take the heat and work any longer. He lies there in the dust for awhile before a couple other *braceros* come to help Him to His feet. He can't work any more today, so He staggers over to the shed and falls onto the pile of sacks and rags in the corner. It's almost as hot in here as it is out in the fields, but at least He's out of the sun. He hopes His wife and children are okay in the fields.

He has only been here for a few weeks now, and tomorrow He and His family will have to get into the truck with twenty other pickers and go up to Wisconsin to start working on the cherries. At least there He'll have a little shade from the trees. Year after year He follows the harvest with no place to call home.

The unions tried to organize His fellow pickers, but the growers wouldn't hear of it. A few people are fighting in Washington to help Him, but the owners have powerful lobbies bucking them there. They don't want to pay Him more or provide decent living conditions, because this would either lower profits or raise prices.

So the next time you stop for produce in the supermarket, remember Christ fell picking it in temperatures over a hundred degrees for sometimes less than a dollar an hour. And He'll probably continue to do so indefinitely, unless we realize at what cost we're enjoying our fruits and vegetables.

How are His requests answered? With police dogs, fire hoses, and billy clubs. He's down for the last time now, too weak to fight back. A basic law of human nature is that we help the weak and unprotected. So what happens? He's grabbed by the heels, dragged down the cement steps, and thrown into the waiting paddy wagon.

How long will it be before we see the light as Saul did and have the courage to ask and want to know, "Who are you?"

"I am Jesus whom you are persecuting and keeping out of your neighborhoods, shops, unions, and offices. I am Jesus whom you force to live in slums, from whom you are running to the suburbs. I am Jesus who said, 'Knock and it will be opened,' and even a law can't make you open your restaurants, and apartments, and pools, and clubs — and much less your hearts — to me."

Look at Him standing on top of the hill, stripped naked. He's running around our cities poorly clothed, and poorly fed, and poorly housed, too. He's ashamed of His poverty, but what can He do about it? He's poorly educated; His job has been taken over by a machine, and He's too old to get another. What else can He do but stand around the corner in His rags? He feels depressed because He can't provide for His family even the basic necessities of life, much less the luxuries the affluent society displays before Him. He's ashamed. But who should be more ashamed, He or the society that stripped Him?

He has been standing around in rags for a long time now, but only recently has He become the topic for discussion in plush conference rooms and around luxuriant dinner tables. Even with all this talk and writing about the war on poverty, even though a few dollars get into the poor box, even though a few old shirts and shoes are cast His way through clothing collections, how many people have ever come by the street corner to encounter Him as a person? If He spoke to us from the crucifix of our parish church, people would flock from all over the country to see the miracle, and in doing so they would continue to drive right past Him as He stands stripped on the corner.

Look at Him as He's nailed to the cross: as He's locked behind the gates of our mental hospitals which are so understaffed that they can do little to help Him and must content themselves with keeping Him out of society; as He's confined to an old people's home because the younger generations can't be bothered with Him; as He's locked in jails and forgotten by the world outside; as He's kept in displaced persons' camps; as this land of plenty which says to Him, "Give me your tired, your poor, your huddled masses yearning to breathe free, the wretched refuse of your teeming shore. Send these, the homeless, tempest-tossed to me," nails Him down with its selfish immigration laws.

Look at Him die. Oh, we all must die; nobody gets out of this world alive. But look at Him die prematurely in those deaths that are a continuing witness of man's inhumanity to man. Look as His mangled body getting cut out of that wreck on the highway because of reckless speeding or drunken driving. Look at Him in Viet Nam, Laos, and the Congo, getting cut down like weeds. Look at the preparations we're making to annihilate Him with more and more devastating atomic weapons. Look in your morning newspaper for the times He's murdered each day in gang wars, shootings, and stabbings.

Then Christ is buried. Unfortunately, this is the most living station for many of us. We don't see Christ as He lives with us, and to the extent that we don't see Him, we bury Him. Oh, we live with Him in the Mass and other sacraments; we live with Him in our prayers. But we bury Him as He is tried, as He takes His cross, as He falls, as He's stripped and nailed to the cross, and as He dies in our fellow men. If anything in this article seemed strange to you or if you caught yourself thinking, "Gee, I never looked at it like that before," to that extent you've buried Christ — not after He's dead, but alive.

But fortunately, we follow a Christ who didn't remain dead and buried. We follow a resurrected and victorious Christ. We often forget this fifteenth station — the one that makes sense out of all the others. This one will make more sense for us, the more we resurrect the buried Christ and serve Him as He walks the way to Calvary today.

I was tried and you defended me; I carried my cross and you helped me; I fell and you lifted me up; I was stripped and you befriended me; I was nailed to the cross and you set me free; I died and you helped make my death meaningful. Amen, I say to you as long as you did it for one of these, you did it for me.

Ronald Luka, CMF, "The Way of the Cross Today," *Ave Maria* 101, no. 15 (10 April 1965): 6–9. Permission for use given by Ave Maria Press, Notre Dame, IN 46556.

81. The Traumas of Change, 1965

One year after the first liturgical changes became operative in the United States (see doc. 79) and a few weeks before the end of the Second Vatican Council, the tensions over Catholic prayer and practice which would mark the following decades were already beginning to surface. The extent of English in the liturgy, scripture translations, the quality of music, the slowness or rapidity of change, and the collapse of an older devotional style all represented areas of incipient discord. In March 1965, Father Gommar de Paul (1918–), a professor of theology and academic dean at St. Mary's Major Seminary, Emmitsburg, Maryland, issued the "Catholic Traditionalist Manifesto," calling for a reassertion of the distinctive markers of Catholic identity and arguing that the liturgical changes were being engineered by a group of experts. Disagreements in these key areas of prayer and practice would grow, especially after the full implementation of the complete use of the vernacular in the Mass (1967), the official publica- tion by Pope Paul VI of the new rite (1969), and the emergence in the early 1970s of informed and cogent critics of the more radical changes in prayer and practice (e.g., James Hitchcock, The Decline and Fall of Radical Catholicism, 1971). The following passage (from an article titled "Stop Pushing!") by the lit- erary critic and popular columnist Dan Herr provides one of the earliest general assessments of developments and their reception in the Catholic community.

If you are in an oh-what-a-wonderful world mood, I am afraid this column is not for you. Not that bubbling optimism has ever been characteristic of this depository of random and rambling profundities. This month, however, I have been influenced by the third session of the 25th Liturgical Conference, recently held in Chicago. As always, it provoked thinking about basic prob- lems among those participating. My own thoughts were not as cheerful or as hopeful as I would have wished.

There was a different air about the Liturgical Conference this year. Not, as you might well expect, an air of triumphalism — "Look what we and the Holy Spirit have wrought" — but rather uncertainty, confusion, perhaps exhaustion.... Gone were the old days when goals were unmistakably clear, when the good guys and the bad guys could be immediately recognized and even the differences over techniques were minimized. There were problems then, of course. Financial problems, opposition from all sides, lack of appre- ciation, fear of despair — but these were more than compensated for by the knowledge that these were pioneers who had a vision of the Church of the future and were willing to joyfully make any sacrifice to help make it possible.

Now the Church of the future has arrived, or at least great progress has been achieved, and the old pioneer spirit, the crusading enthusiasm, the sure knowledge of objectives and how to achieve them, seems to have been lost or seriously diminished. The old rallying cries no longer provoke the same response. The leadership seems tired and indecisive; the troops confused and filled with doubts. A sad situation to witness.

•

It has always been my opinion that movements in the Church aimed at specific objectives might well begin by planning on when to go out of existence. If a movement has not achieved its goals in a reasonable amount of time, perhaps the goals are not worthy or the techniques are faulty. If the goals are achieved, it is demeaning for the group to whimper on, or to look for a new disease to conquer (in the medical-charity field, the polio situation offers a clear parallel). I never thought I would see the day when an organization actually admit- ted that its existence was no longer essential, but I was wrong. Gloriously, after nineteen years the Vernacular Society has now disbanded with the state- ment that "the major objectives of the Vernacular Society have been attained." To its everlasting credit the Society has not only won a major battle against what once seemed to be impossible odds, but in its common-sense recognition of changing needs in changing times, has become a historic model for other similar movements to consider and perhaps to emulate.

•

Is it absolutely essential that the changes in the liturgy be accepted as a package? Is hymn-singing, for example, just as vital as the vernacular and the mass-facing-the-people? Is it possible that congregational singing does not meet the needs or even the desires of 20th century Americans? Is it impossible to turn up singable hymns? Is hymn-singing while the priest is praying the mass an example of community worship or is it another version of what used to be — the priest and the people, each about his own affairs? Just asking, that's all.

•

A recent bright note in the news concerns Professor G. B. Harrison, who spoke for many of us in the last issue of *The Critic* when he pointed out that the translation presently used in the Mass is hardly what had been hoped for. An International Committee for a Common English Text has been formed and among the advisors are Professor Harrison, Godfrey Diekmann, O.S.B., and Professor P. F. Finberg. Maybe, fellows, we will soon have a translation we will be proud of.

•

It's not so much a moratorium on criticism in the Church that is needed, but rather a desist order on alarmist and extremist statements (and I'm not talking about the pathetic Traditionalist Movement, whatever its strength). One priest foresees a "crisis of faith," another warns of "the danger of schism." Rumors are spread that certain conservative leaders say they will be forced to leave the Church should birth-control regulation be changed (the implications of that foolishness are so shocking as to be incredible). Crises of one kind of another, accompanied by dire predictions, have become daily fare. Some pundits seem to think that on their slim shoulders rests the burden of the future of the Church. If everyone involved, methinks, would take himself just a little less seriously, the demand for tranquilizers might be diminished.

•

We might also pray for an end of the current wave of informal excommunication. Years ago, Catholic liberals were regularly read out of the Church by their more conservative brethren. After a blessed lapse, the epidemic seems to be with us again — only this time the charming practice is not confined to conservatives and it seems to be particularly virulent among certain Catholic editors.

•

Among those who have been most disappointed in what the Council did or did not do — and I suspect we will be hearing more from them as the Council ends — are those who demand quick and perfect solutions to problems.

Among these are the same people who discover a new, ready-made path to salvation, such as the *Cursillo,* and are shaken when the whole world does not recognize and appreciate their discovery. It is not fair to the Council Fathers to expect them to solve all the ills of the Church and the world in four sessions. Some of the problems and their possible solutions are in such a state of flux at the moment that it might be far better for the future of the Church if discussion not be frozen by a statement from the Council. It might be argued whether other problems are really the concern of the Council at this time. (One student of the Council complained to me recently: "If laymen need the Council to tell them what their role is, they are not ready for it.")

•

I wonder if sufficient recognition is being given to what might be described as a "piety void" in the lives of Catholics. For good or bad, many popular, so-called pious, devotions have been downgraded in recent years. The visits to the Blessed Sacrament, devotional confession, novenas, missions, even retreats, no longer have the force in the lives of many Catholics that they once had. And yet the new liturgy — although in most cases it has been accepted well enough — has not yet become sufficiently meaningful or satisfying to fill the void left by pious devotions. As a result, many Catholics feel a loss in their lives and are not happy about it.

•

Few will argue that to prepare future generations, changes in the Church were necessary. But for those of us who had grown accustomed to the Church as it was, one disturbing thought is hard to put out of mind: with all its faults, some of which we did not even recognize until they were denounced by more progressive thinkers, the "old" Church did produce our generation of Catholics with strong faith and generations and generations before us — produced even the fermenters of the present renewal. In continuing to plan for the future, let us insure that what we are eliminating or changing will be replaced with new approaches of at least equal effectiveness.

Dan Herr, "Stop Pushing," *The Critic* 24, no. 2 (October–November 1965): 4, 6. Reprinted by permission of The Thomas More Association © 1965 *The Critic* magazine.

82. A Postconciliar Piety Void? 1966

Private weekly or monthly confession of sins, visits to the Blessed Sacrament, recitation of the rosary, novena prayers, and attendance at missions and retreats had been part of the prayer and practice of the Catholic community from its foundation in the United States (see docs. 2, 4, 16, 24, 42, 49, 57, 68). However, the upsurge in devotional practices which had accompanied the depression and war years (see doc. 49) had begun to decline in the postwar period; the popular expressions of the 1950s, the rosary and enthronement of the Sacred Heart (see docs. 66, 68, 85), framed as they were in the context of the Cold War and the protection of a certain conception of family life, collapsed under the

impact of different social preoccupations (racism, poverty, liberation), the move-
ment to the suburbs, changing gender roles, the decline of Catholic Action, and
the mainstreaming of the theology underlying the scriptural and liturgical move-
ments (see docs. 67, 70). In the immediate wake of the Second Vatican Council
new forms of spirituality, affiliation, and private prayer had yet to be born. The
following article, by the Redemptorist assistant editor of the Liguorian, *captures*
the heart of the moment as it comments on Dan Herr's identification of a felt
"piety void" in the community (see doc. 81).

I have reflected on [the paragraph wherein Dan Herr spoke of a "piety void"]
for several days and have discussed the matter with others. The purpose of
this article is to share my reflections and perhaps open up discussion of this
topic among my fellow priests.

Mr. Herr's statement twice refers to "many Catholics:" "a 'piety void' in
the lives of many Catholics" and "many Catholics feel a loss in their lives."
He cites no empirical evidence, and I certainly can't cite any, but I have the
impression that he is right in his estimate. My experience, and the experience of a number of priest friends, would prompt me to agree that "many
Catholics" are involved.

It is noteworthy that the Catholics Mr. Herr refers to are not simply the
"anti-liturgy" people. One would expect a "piety void" in the lives of those
who are traumatized by the vernacular, fearful of the Pope's orthodoxy, and
convinced that any change at all is the work of Satan. Apparently, though, a
number of quite balanced people — people who like the new liturgy, conscientiously participate in it and even try to grasp more and more of the serious
theology behind it — are also experiencing the "piety void."

In what is perhaps an understatement, Mr. Herr says that the Catholics
who are aware of the void "are not happy about it." It seems to me that some
of them are suffering deeply and others are quite confused. Some of the rigid
traditionalists are certainly experiencing great anguish and even, in some cases,
crises of faith. It is easy enough to laugh at such people; or to pity them.
Either way, to confront them as individuals is to realize that they are suffering. Even the more balanced and progressive, though by no means as deeply
disturbed as the traditionalists, are sometimes quite uneasy and perplexed. The
current of this problem, it seems to me, runs deeper than some observers are
willing to admit.

Schools of Thought

[Among the opinions] would be two quite different schools of thought. The
first school embraces those priests who would analyze the problem along these
lines: "Yes, there is a 'piety void.' And I couldn't care less. In fact, it is a good
thing. It is a sign of maturity among Catholics. It indicates that Catholics who
have been brought up in an individualistic, formalistic, 'Jesus and I,' merit-
piling Catholicism are finally growing up. There will be growing pains, of
course, but these will pass. As the strong food of Vatican II gradually nourishes
these people, they will have no difficulty at all with a 'piety void.' "

The second school includes those who might express themselves in this way: "Yes, there is a 'piety void.' And it's a shame. The people are confused, staggering, on the ropes. And all for no reason. Though the basic liturgical renewal is good and helpful, many other changes and opinions are the work of crackpots. Our job as priests is to place even stronger emphasis on the beautiful devotions and practices that have come down to us from our forefathers. If they were good enough for the saints, they ought to be good enough for us."

Expressing the divergent opinions in this unnuanced way may seem to make a caricature of them. Such is not my intention. Allowing for shades of opinion of both sides, I feel that these generalizations are fairly representative of the feelings of many priests.

I would like to submit that there is another approach, more balanced and realistic than any of the above. But before outlining it, I want to make some brief observations on the above opinions.

The first school (and apparently Mr. Herr would agree) contends that once the liturgy becomes completely renewed and once the people are really in tune with it, there will be no "piety void." The liturgy, in and of itself, will satisfy the people. I doubt this. I do not think that even an updated and flourishing liturgy will completely remove the "piety void" from the hearts of many Catholics. It seems to me that the history of religion testifies to the opposite. There is an observable tendency for people to come up with popular devotions and practices, even when the official worship is flourishing.

To take one example: The liturgy was flourishing in the early days of the Church. There was a rich Christian liturgy surrounding the burial of the dead. Yet many popular, quite non-liturgical devotions and practices grew up around Christian burial. These developments did not indicate that the people were ignorant of or opposed to the liturgy. They indicated, it seems to me, the very natural and normal tendency of worshipping man to intertwine the excellent and the ordinary, the official and the popular, the dogmatic and the sentimental. I do not think we have seen the ends of this tendency by any means.

The second school of thought makes the mistake of trying to "freeze" popular devotions and practices. It seems to forget that *people,* after all, instigate and develop popular devotions. But people are subject to their times, undergo many subtle psychological and sociological changes. What was a popular devotion for their forefathers, therefore, might not be a popular devotion for them. Or, what is more accurate, the basic devotion or practice might remain the same, but the *approach* to it may be quite different. Modern Catholics have a different approach from their ancestors.

To get back to my *tertium quid* proposal about the "piety void," I think there should be a *renewal of popular devotions* along with the liturgical renewal. There is no good reason why zealous priests cannot work towards a liturgical and non-liturgical updating at the same time. My proposal would emphasize the following points:

First of all, it is the responsibility of every priest to endorse the new liturgy intelligently and wholeheartedly.... Obviously included in the priest's responsibility is the obligation to instruct the people, in season and out of season, on the nature and importance of the liturgy....

But secondly,... there is no need to downgrade popular devotions. There is need, rather, to upgrade them: to make them harmonize with the liturgical seasons and accord as much as possible with the sacred liturgy, so that they are in some fashion derived from it and lead the people to it; to make them more flexible and more relevant to the people of our times, more in line with their aspirations and approaches.

I see no contradiction at all between these two emphases. I think that suffering, bewildered, confused Catholics would deeply appreciate this approach on the part of at least some priests.

To make my proposal more concrete, I will comment on the "popular, so-called pious devotions" listed by Mr. Herr.

1. *Devotional Confession.* Accurately speaking, the worthy reception of the sacrament of penance is not a popular devotion at all, but a liturgical celebration. Though I do not know why Mr. Herr included devotional confession in his list, I presume it has something to do with the fact that some priests have been discouraging the practice of frequent confession. The aim of these priests, as I understand it, is to offset a routine and mechanical approach to this sacrament.

The aim is certainly praiseworthy. But it seems to me that we have the opportunity today to take a more positive and dynamic approach to the problem. The Council has promised that "the rite and formulas for the sacrament of penance are to be revised so that they more clearly express both the nature and effect of the sacrament." While this revision is going on, there is much the individual priest can do to bring out the positive significance of this sacrament: an encounter with the merciful Christ and an entering into the death and resurrection of the Savior.

Surely, the people would appreciate a pastoral updating in the practice of giving penances. There are countless devout Catholics who long for a more imaginative and meaningful approach to sacramental penances. They are devoutly hoping that confessors will soon get over the "three Hail Marys" syndrome. Suiting the penance to the sin and to the real life of the penitent would do much to offset the problem of routine and formalism.

There is, in addition, the vast field of spiritual direction. Because of the shortage of priests and the heavy demands on their time, many Catholics hesitate even to ask a question of the confessor. Though one could argue that confession and spiritual direction are separate entities and should not be mixed, one could also suggest (and with solid historical backing) that much sound spiritual direction can be accomplished on the occasion of a confession of devotion....

2. *Visits to the Blessed Sacrament.* One might argue that if there is a "piety void" here, the individual Catholic can blame no one but himself. After all, Christ is present in our Churches and the Churches are open. The Catholic who does not stop for a visit cannot blame a priest.

Or can he? Some of the sermonizing in this area has been less than dogmatically accurate, as Pope Paul's encyclical pointed out. And aside from the dogmatic aspects, there has been the insinuation that people who quietly visit the Blessed Sacrament are somehow being too individualistic in their piety and engaging in "comfortable" Catholicism. The assumption seems to be that those Catholics who make a habit of visiting the Church are the very ones who hide from the world, indulge in racial bigotry, hate Protestants, engage in shady business deals, etc.

The assumption is gratuitous. In my years as a priest, and long before, I have known many outstandingly apostolic and committed Catholics who made frequent visits to the Blessed Sacrament. These people were not "ghetto" Catholics. They were on fire with love for Christ and their fellowmen. But they savored those moments of silence in which they could rededicate themselves to Christ and remind themselves of Christ's undying love for all of us.

It is indeed a shame when mature and committed Catholics are made to feel, as even some priests and religious have been made to feel, that they are somehow un-liturgical, unprogressive and non-relevant because of their moments of prayer before the living Christ.

3. *The Rosary.* In my opinion, the rosary is deeply imbedded in Catholic life and is not about to "go away." I have never heard a major theologian downgrade the rosary. I have heard several of them deplore the formalism and legalism that has at times crept into this popular devotion. Here again, there is a golden opportunity for us priests to help Catholics form a more solidly spiritual attitude towards the rosary; to show them, in the phrase of Pope Paul, its "continuing value for modern man." If people tend to put exaggerated emphasis on the vocal prayers and on the indulgences which can be attached to each bead (and sometimes the spaces in between), it is possibly due to the failure of priests and preachers. Most basically, the rosary is a meditation on the mysteries of Christ's life....

One help in renewing Catholic attitudes towards the rosary (and there are many others) is found in a little book called *Scriptural Rosary.*... Enlarging upon a medieval custom, the booklet provides direct quotations for meditation on each decade taken from the Scriptural episode on which the mystery is based....

4. *Novenas.* It seems commonly accepted that there have been some abuses in the matter of novenas: that some people have exaggerated the "number's game," that others have developed an attitude perilously close to superstition. To the extent that this is true, it seems far more enlightened to correct the abuses than to "forbid" the people to attend novenas. One does not fill a void, even a "piety void," by forbidding things.

Some priests seem not to realize that many novena preachers have updated their approach to novenas and that several of the more popular "perpetual" or weekly novena devotions have been radically changed. The Perpetual Help devotion, with which I am most familiar, has been revised completely. With the assistance of Biblical and liturgical experts, the Redemptorist Fathers have drawn up a service that is more Biblical, more dialogal [*sic*] and more positive.

Such a service, designed to lead the people to the liturgy, is usually followed by benediction (part of liturgical worship) and provides an opportunity for confession. It can only be of spiritual profit to those who wish to attend.…

5. *Missions and Retreats.*… The modern "piety void" here is due mainly to two factors. One factor is that missions and retreats have too often been geared in the wrong direction, failing to meet the actual spiritual needs of modern people and failing to speak to them in a language they understand and appreciate. The second factor is that modern Americans, Catholics as well as others, easily become overly attached to diversions and recreations, such as bowling, pro football, golf, mystery stories, and TV. Nothing, but nothing, is allowed to interfere with their chosen pastimes.

Happily, many missionaries and retreat masters are now updating their material and their style. The chances are good that these spiritual exercises will have an enormous impact on modern Catholics, just as missions and retreats of former times had enormous impact on the Catholics of those days. Happily, too, more and more people, as they become more apostolic and more engaged in the problems of others, are finding a need for spiritual refreshment and reflection.…

The "piety void" in this area is, in my opinion, about ready to fill up. I think that the coming years will show a great upsurge in missions and retreats. As the missions and retreats become more relevant and understandable, the people will be more eager than ever to come.

To conclude: I agree with Mr. Herr that there is a "piety void." I think many Catholics, and not just the super pious, are experiencing it. I see no intrinsic reason why there *should* be a "piety void." I have offered a few suggestions as to what can be done about it.

Daniel L. Lowery, CSSR, "A 'Piety Void'?" *American Ecclesiastical Review* 154 (January 1966): 31–38. Printed with permission.

83. Richmond Synod's Directives on Ecumenism, 1966

The presence of Orthodox, Anglican, and Protestant representatives at the Second Vatican Council set a precedent for the thoughts and attitudes which were found in the 21 November 1964 Decree on Ecumenism (Unitatis Redintegratio). The Vatican II document called for a transformation of attitudes and actions between religious groups. Catholics were to work cooperatively toward common causes for the good of humanity. Prayer in common and dialogue between the Christian groups were encouraged, a turn in the tide of regulations issued by previous diocesan synods. The following year, the Paulist Fathers popularized ecumenical ideas through Living Room Dialogues, *published jointly with the National Council of Churches of Christ in the USA. The United States was also home to the Graymoor community of sisters and brothers, who, since their foundation in 1898, had been working toward a reconciliation of Christians and had inaugurated a Week of Prayer for Christian Unity, a practice which later received Vatican approval for worldwide promotion. By the 1960s a number of Catholics worked ecumenically locally, especially in the areas of social justice, notable in the 1965 Selma, Alabama, march. Bishops established national and dioce-*

san ecumenical commissions to promote prayer, action, and study. A statement from the Richmond Diocesan Synod, excerpted below, indicated that an ecumenical emphasis needed to pervade all levels of local church life and prayer. Here was a context for prayer and practice which departed significantly from previous formulations (see docs. 14, 38, 66)

223. In the seminary, in diocesan and private schools, and in CCD [Confraternity of Christian Doctrine] schools of religion, classes in religion and social sciences must be taught with due regard for the ecumenical point of view. Special care must be given to the demands of both truth and charity. The current doctrinal and historical positions of our separated brethren must be carefully studied and genuinely understood by teachers before these positions are presented or referred to in the classroom. The clergy of other religions should be invited to explain these positions to the students whenever it seems opportune.

224. Special arrangements may be made for students to tour other churches and synagogues and to have their customs explained to them, including those which stem from our common religious heritage. Invitations to ecumenical exchanges on the high school level should be referred to the subcommittee for secondary schools (the Diocesan Superintendent of Schools and the Rector of the Seminary).

225. The syllabus for the Junior Clergy examinations should be revised to include the ecumenical viewpoint and ecumenical subjects. Clergy conferences should include subjects of ecumenical import. Seminars on ecumenism should be made a part of deanery days of recollection and the annual clergy retreats when practicable.

226. Reading and study are also necessary for the development of the ecumenical spirit. In addition to the Decree on Ecumenism and other conciliar documents, priests are urged to read the timely works being published in this field by both Catholics and others....

229. The programs of the parish councils of Catholic Men, Women, and Youth should include speakers and other programs of ecumenical value. CCD Discussion Clubs and Christian Family Movement groups should plan consideration of ecumenical topics.

230. Since the concern for restoring unity involves the whole Church, faithful and clergy alike, the various aspects, goals, and principles of ecumenism should be the subject of Sunday homilies in parish churches, when the liturgical lessons of the day have ecumenical implications.

231. The Bible devotions recommended by the Constitution on the Sacred Liturgy are excellent means of congregational prayer for Christian Unity. The Votive Mass for the Unity of the Church should be celebrated occasionally when the rubrics permit. The Votive Mass for the Unity of the Church may be celebrated as a Votive Mass of the II Class once during the annual Week of Prayer for Christian Unity. The importance of prayer and the development of a spiritual ecumenism cannot be over-stressed in the achievement of the change of heart and holiness of life, which along with the public and private prayer for the unity of Christians, should be regarded as the soul of the whole ecumenical movement.

232. Books, periodicals, and pamphlets of ecumenical interest should be made available to the laity in parish magazine and pamphlet racks and in parish libraries.

> *Fourth Synod of the Diocese of Richmond Celebrated by the Most Rev. John J. Russell, Bishop of Richmond, Together with the Clergy, Religious, and Laity of the Diocese, December 5, 1966* (Richmond: Diocese of Richmond, 1966), 47–49. Printed by permission.

84. A New Approach to Penance, 1966

Because of the increased mobility of the populace and the advent of air travel during the 1960s, the bishops of the United States petitioned the Sacred Congregation of the Council for a relaxation in the laws governing abstinence in the community. General opinion overwhelmingly supported the petition, but some wondered about the "potential scandal of making a sacred discipline the object of commercial appeal." The whole situation changed dramatically when Pope Paul VI issued Poenitemini *(17 February 1966), an apostolic constitution on the importance of penance and conversion in the Christian life. While the constitution affirmed the traditional practices of fast and abstinence, it also broadened "penance" to encompass other works of prayer and charity and left the application of the norms to episcopal conferences. The National Conference of Catholic Bishops met the following November and adopted a statement,* Penitential Discipline for the Liturgical Year. *Keeping a positive tone throughout the pastoral statement, the bishops consciously moved away from the customary interpretation of making the norms binding under pain of sin and instead related the traditional disciplines of Advent and Lent to a vision of social charity and personal identification with the passion of Christ. The document (a section of which is presented here) represents a significant development in Catholic prayer and practice (cf. docs. 17 and 69).*

Beginning with the powerful lesson of Ash Wednesday, [Lent] has retained its ancient appeal to the penitential spirit of our people. It has also acquired elements of popular piety which we Bishops would wish to encourage.

Accordingly, while appealing for greater development of the understanding of the Lenten liturgy, as that of Advent, we hope that the observance of Lent as the principal season of penance in the Christian year will be intensified. This is the more desirable because of new insights into the central place in Christian faith of those Easter mysteries for the understanding and enjoyment of which Lent is the ancient penitential preparation.

Wherefore, we ask, urgently and prayerfully, that we, as people of God, make of the entire Lenten season a period of special penitential observance. Following the instructions of the Holy See, we declare that the obligation both to fast and to abstain from meat, an obligation observed under a more strict formality by our fathers in the faith, still binds on Ash Wednesday and Good Friday. No Catholic Christian will lightly excuse himself from so hallowed an obligation on the Wednesday which solemnly opens the Lenten season and on that Friday called "Good" because on that day Christ suffered in the flesh and died for our sins.

In keeping with the letter and spirit of Pope Paul's constitution, *Poenitemini*, we preserve for our dioceses the tradition of abstinence from meat on each of the Fridays of Lent, confident that no Catholic Christian will lightly hold himself excused from this penitential practice.

For all other weekdays of Lent, we strongly recommend participation in daily Mass and a self-imposed observance of fasting. In the light of grave human needs which weigh on the Christian conscience in all seasons, we urge particularly during Lent, generosity to local, national and world programs of sharing of all things needed to translate our duty to penance into a means of implementing the right of the poor to their part in our abundance. We also recommend spiritual studies, beginning with the Scriptures, as well as the traditional Lenten devotions (sermons, Stations of the Cross, and the Rosary) and all the self-denial summed up in the Christian concept of "mortification."

Let us witness to our love and imitation of Christ, by special solicitude for the sick, the poor, the underprivileged, the imprisoned, the bed-ridden, the discouraged, the stranger, the lonely, and persons of other color, nationalities or background than our own. A catalogue of not merely suggested but required good works under these headings is provided by Our Blessed Lord Himself in His description of the Last Judgment (cf. Matt. 25:34–40). This salutary word of the Lord is necessary for all the year, but should be heeded with double care during Lent.

During the Lenten season, certain feasts occur which the liturgy or local custom traditionally exempts from the Lenten spirit of penance. The observance of these will continue to be set by local diocesan regulations; in these, and like canonical questions, which may arise in connection with these pastoral instructions, reference should be made to Article VII of *"Poenitemini"* and the usual norms....

•

Christ died for our salvation on Friday. Gratefully remembering this, Catholics from time immemorial have set apart Friday for special penitential observance by which they gladly suffer with Christ that they may one day be glorified with Him. This is the heart of the tradition of abstinence from meat on Friday where that tradition has been observed in the holy Catholic Church.

Changing circumstances, including economic, dietary and social elements, have made some of our people feel that the renunciation of the eating of meat is not always and for everyone the most effective means of practicing penance. Meat was once an exceptional form of food; now it is commonplace.

Accordingly, since the spirit of penance primarily suggests that we discipline ourselves in that which we enjoy most, to many our abstinence from meat no longer implies penance, while renunciation of other things would be more penitential.

For these and related reasons, the Catholic Bishops of the United States, far from downgrading the traditional penitential observance of Friday, and motivated precisely by the desire to give the spirit of penance greater vitality, especially on Fridays, the day that Jesus died, urge our Catholic people henceforth to be guided by the following norms:

1. Friday itself remains a special day of penitential observance throughout the year, a time when those who seek perfection will be mindful of their personal sins and the sins of mankind which they are called upon to help expiate in union with Christ crucified;

2. Friday should be in each week something of what Lent is in the entire year. For this reason we urge all to prepare for that weekly Easter that comes with each Sunday by freely making of every Friday a day of self-denial and mortification in prayerful remembrance of the passion of Jesus Christ;

3. Among the works of voluntary self-denial and personal penance which we especially commend to our people for the future observance of Friday, even though we hereby terminate the traditional law of abstinence as binding under pain of sin, as the sole prescribed means of observing Friday, we give first place to abstinence from flesh meat. We do so in the hope that the Catholic community will ordinarily continue to abstain from meat by free choice as formerly we did in obedience to Church law. Our expectation is based on the following considerations:

> a. We shall thus freely and out of love for Christ Crucified show our solidarity with the generations of believers to whom this practice frequently became, especially in times of persecution and of great poverty, no mean evidence of fidelity to Christ and His Church.
>
> b. We shall thus also remind ourselves that as Christians, although immersed in the world and sharing its life, we must preserve a saving and necessary difference from the spirit of the world. Our deliberate, personal abstinence from meat, more especially because no longer required by law, will be an outward sign of inward spiritual values that we cherish.

Every Catholic Christian understands that the fast and abstinence regulations admit of change, unlike the commandments and precepts of that unchanging divine moral law which the Church must today and always defend as immutable. This said, we emphasize that our people are henceforth free from the obligation, traditionally binding, under pain of sin in what pertains to Friday abstinence, except as noted above for Lent. We stress this so that no scrupulosity will enter into examinations of conscience, confessions or personal decisions on this point.

Perhaps we should warn those who decide to keep the Friday abstinence for reasons of personal piety and special love that they must not pass judgment on those who elect to substitute other penitential observances. Friday, please God, will acquire among us other forms of penitential witness which may become as much a part of the devout way of life in the future as Friday abstinence from meat. In this connection we have foremost in mind the modern need for self-discipline in the use of stimulants and for a renewed emphasis on the virtue of temperance, especially in the use of alcoholic beverages.

It would bring great glory to God and good to souls if Fridays found our people doing volunteer work in hospitals, visiting the sick, serving the needs of the aged and the lonely, instructing the young in the Faith, participating as Christians in community affairs, and meeting our obligations to our families, our friends, our neighbors and our community, including our parishes, with a special zeal born of the desire to add the merit of penance to the other virtues exercised in good works born of living faith.

In summary, let it not be said that by this action, implementing the spirit of renewal coming out of the Council, we have abolished Friday, repudiated the holy traditions of our fathers, or diminished the insistence of the Church on the fact of sin and the need for penance. Rather, let it be proved by the spirit in which we enter upon prayer and penance, not excluding fast and abstinence freely chosen, that these present decisions and recommendations of this Conference of Bishops will herald a new birth of loving faith and more profound penitential conversion, by both of which we become one with Christ, mature sons of God and servants of God's people.

> Text of the *Pastoral Statement of the National Conference of Catholic Bishops on Penitential Observance for the Liturgical Year* adopted on November 18, 1966, in Washington, D.C., reprinted in *The Jurist* 27 (January 1967): 96–100. *Pastoral Statement on Fasting and Abstinence,* © 1966 U.S. Catholic Conference, Inc., Washington, D.C. Reprinted with permission. All rights reserved.

85. Latin Americans' Request to Update the Family Rosary Crusade, 1966

The teachings of the Second Vatican Council (1961–65) came to be a benchmark for reevaluation of American Catholic prayer and practice. The approach of the family rosary, as advocated by Patrick Peyton (see doc. 68), is an example of the critique brought to bear on devotional life. Peyton's prayer model bore several marks of the 1950s: emphasis on the lay vocation, mass movements, the use of modern media with its communal appeal to the senses and imagination, and the sociopolitical context of changing family roles and Communist threat. Peyton's Family Rosary Crusade went to Latin America in the 1960s. In March 1966, the Holy Cross Fathers, who were working for the crusade there and in the United States, met at the University of Notre Dame for ten days to discuss whether the content and form of the crusade were relevant to the needs of the Latin American church. Among the members were Mark McGrath, CSC, bishop of Panama, Robert Pelton, CSC, and Thomas Barrosse, CSC. Other persons in the discussion were Walter J. Burghardt, SJ, Bernard Häring, CSSR, Arthur McCormack, MHM, and Chilean sociologist Renato Poblote, SJ, whose graduate work at Fordham University studied the social impact of New York's storefront churches on Puerto Ricans. Renewal in the Latin American church focused on the formation of small communities of faith, rather than mass gatherings, challenges to the social-economic order, and a response to the increase of Protestant missionaries. The document presented below, titled "Has the Rosary Survived the Council?" reflects the growing interest of U.S. Catholics in Latin America and places Marian devotion in the pattern of the conciliar document Lumen Gentium, *which saw Mary, mother of Jesus, as the preeminent disci-*

ple. The men at the gathering also reflect the conciliar stress on the primacy of the Eucharist and even suggest the potential of the rosary for ecumenical prayer.

For many of the church's traditional structures, the Council has raised basic issues. The religious orders are involved in a re-evaluation of their purposes and methods. Catholic lay action is reformulating its techniques and probing its nature. The Roman Curia is being reformed. The nature of obedience is at issue. And the resurgence of interest in the liturgy has caused many to question the entire role of private devotions.

"Of course, we were worried by some ideas presented at the Council, and even more by views expressed by Catholics in the new atmosphere of open discussion encouraged by the Council," according to Father Patrick Peyton, CSC, the founder and central figure of the Family Rosary Crusade. "It became clear to my colleagues and myself that a climate could develop in which our work would be out of line with the Church's dynamic thrust."

Father Peyton decided that the Council Fathers were themselves the best qualified to advise, and for him it was easier than for most people to get their views. . . .

"There were three elements on which I sought the opinions of the Bishops when I went to Rome during the Council," Father Peyton says. "The real objective of our movement is to promote family unity through family prayer, and consequently my first concern was to find out what the Council felt about the importance of family prayer. I wanted an overall view of what the Bishops in whose dioceses the Crusade has been preached think of its methods, and what changes they would recommend. And finally I wanted guidance on whether the rosary is still today, as it has proved for over 700 years, the best form in which to express family prayer in Catholic environments."

Thanks to Father Peyton's initiatives, which were formulated and channeled in the right directions by sympathetic priests and Bishops, the Council wrote its view on family prayer into the record. "With their parents leading the way by example and family prayer," it said in the Constitution on the Church in the Modern World, "children and indeed everyone gathered around the family hearth will find a readier path to human maturity, salvation and holiness." Again, in the decree on the Lay Apostolate, it declared that "the family will fulfill its mission to be the first and vital cell of society, if it shows itself to be the domestic sanctuary of the Church through the mutual affection of its members and the common prayer they offer to God. . . . "

Having achieved a solid approval of the basic aim of the Crusade, Father Peyton recruited a leading Latin American sociologist [Rev. Renato Poblete, SJ] to poll the Bishops for their views on methods and results. . . .

Father Poblete's report confirmed that the Bishops who had experience of the Crusade were unanimous in recognizing the benefits it had brought to their dioceses. They praised the organization and the excellent use of the mass media. The audio-visual instruction during the popular mission was universally admired, as was the use of laymen in places where often their potential contribution is completely ignored. The mass rally was also recognized as having value as a public proclamation of faith.

Many Bishops, however, also had reservations. Some urged a deeper sense of theology in the total presentation, fuller integration of devotion to Our Lady and the rosary into the life of the Church, [and] a more liturgical form for the rally. Others felt that the concept of the Christian family was presented in too abstract and too individualistic a manner. They wanted more stress on the concrete conditions, often of extreme poverty and subhuman housing, in which most Latin American families live. They wanted more stress on the relations of the family to the community, of the duty of each to the other, and particularly that of the comfortable to the indigent. If this is not done, several insisted, religion can justly be criticized as constituting a pacifier of the masses and the opium of the downtrodden.

Another recurring theme was that the Crusade was too much a shooting star, a great outburst of spiritual fireworks with little lasting impact. One Bishop expressed his belief that only 10 per cent of the pledges were honored over any significant period. The effort put into the training of the local volunteers was largely wasted because of inadequate follow-up or integration into existing organizations. Some Bishops thought that they should have spent their money on less spectacular but continuing projects....

Father Peyton decided that the time was opportune to call for a full scale evaluation of the Crusade with the help of leading Council experts....

Bishop McGrath [CSC, of Panama] also supported strongly the section in the Poblete report warning against a spirituality too removed from the existential situation of the people. Speaking specifically of Latin America, he said that Catholics do great harm to religion by handing over to the Marxists the leadership in improving material conditions. This, he said, is completely contrary to the spirit of Vatican II and to the express teaching of the Constitution on the Church in the Modern World.

Father Häring caused a profound impression with an analysis of the history and meaning of the rosary and suggestions for its future. The essential element, he indicated, is the meditation on some of the major mysteries of our Faith presented in a framework of the association of Our Lady with Christ in the work of salvation.

The modern formulation into a fixed number of mysteries each with a set number of repetitions is a convenience. There is nothing wrong with it, so long as it is so understood. But, insisted Father Häring, "we must break away from magical mathematics and mechanical indulgences."

Father Häring saw the rosary of the future take many forms. Meditation on a given mystery might be introduced with an appropriate reading from Scripture followed by a moment of silent prayer and the recitation of the Our Father and one or more Hail Marys. He said that in his own experience, he had found this kind of rosary appealed to many for whom the traditional form had become stereotyped and monotonous.

A Lutheran pastor, Rev. Arthur C. Piepkorn, of Concordia Seminary, St. Louis, supported Father Häring. He had, he said, used a form of meditation on the mysteries of the rosary combined with scriptural readings in his own church, without actually labeling it as the rosary. He believed many Protestants would welcome such a prayer, and that the rosary could thus take on a more ecumenical dress. At the same time, he insisted, a change of this kind would have to be paced to the needs of each time and place. "We must never take away from people anything that performs for them a spiritual function except in terms of replacing it by something better. . . . "

The post Crusade programs being perfected do not envision the setting up of a continuing organization in each diocese to utilize the men trained for the Crusade. Instead, it is hoped to channel them more effectively than in the past into existing organizations such as the Christian Family Movement or the Legion of Mary, and to arrange for the diocese to designate an official who will on the one hand act as liaison with these organizations, and with the offices of the Family Rosary Crusade on the other. These offices will provide programs designed to institutionalize the benefits brought about by the Crusade and thus enrich permanently the spiritual life of the diocese.

The proposal to utilize sociological and theological help in order to make the message of the Crusade more existentially significant was also eagerly seized. Bishop McGrath and others urged that the sociologist for teams operating in Latin America should himself be a Latin American, and that also was approved in principle.

Even before these specialists can be found or trained as full-time workers, help will be sought from experts to revise the literature, the model sermons or homilies and the total message of the Crusade, so that it will reflect more precisely the mind of the post-Conciliar Church. This will require, for example, as Father Edward O'Connor, CSC, pointed out, that not only will devotion to Our Lady be more integrated than previously into the liturgy and life of the Church, but that our relation to Our Lady be presented in terms more in keeping with our social concepts. In a class society, it was normal for the people to present their request to those in authority through an intermediary, he said, and it made sense to express Our Lady's function in the plan of salvation as analogically a mediation. In today's egalitarian society, we prefer to go straight to the top. The Council reflected this attitude when "it insisted that Mary does not come between the Father and us." A more meaningful concept than mediation for modern man is friendship, and this was what the Council had in mind when it "emphasized the intimate connection" between Christ and Mary. The presence of a mutual friend enriches a meeting with the friend we have come to visit. As Mary is Christ's closest friend, her presence adds a new dimension in our conversations with Christ.

Among the suggestions for a more liturgical orientation for the Crusade was that the highlight of the rally should be the Mass, with Father Peyton's talk presented as the homily at the Mass. This was the procedure followed when the Crusade was held in Bishop McGrath's diocese in Panama, and the Bishop felt strongly that it should become standard procedure.

Should the rosary itself be recognized as a liturgical prayer, as Benediction of the Blessed Sacrament is? Father Barrosse, a liturgical specialist, gave an interesting response to this question. "We have fallen into the trap of giving a too legal interpretation to the liturgy," Father Barrosse said. "The liturgy is simply the prayer of the Church, of the local Church as well as the universal Church. If it is the prayer people say, it is liturgical."

Gary MacEoin, "Has the Rosary Survived the Council?" *Ave Maria* 104, no. 2 (9 July 1966): 12–14, 28. Reprinted with permission.

86. The Birth of Catholic Pentecostalism, 1967–70

In the mid-1960s many Catholic men and women had been well formed in the community dynamics of Catholic Action groups, the Christian Family Movement, the Cursillo, and the revival in scripture and liturgy. In a context where the older patterns of Catholic prayer and practice were changing (see docs. 78, 79, 80, 84) and some spoke of a "piety void" (see docs. 81, 82), they also sought for new ways of affiliating and intensifying their religious aspirations. "Seasoned veterans of Christian work" (Bert Ghezzi), they critiqued the formalism and implied secularism of older devotional habits, the gulf between faith and life (see docs. 66, 73), and discovered a deeply personal relationship with God in an experience of the Spirit. Born on university campuses, this postconciliar devotionalism became known as Catholic Pentecostalism and achieved a phenomenal growth in the following decade. By 1977 the national magazine New Covenant *reached a circulation of sixty-five thousand, the movement had spread to over ninety countries, and more than fifty thousand people from a dozen Christian traditions gathered in Kansas City, Missouri, for the first ecumenical charismatic conference. The following article, titled "Catholic Pentecostals," assesses the movement after only three years, places it in the broad context of Protestant-Catholic relationships, and notes its strong connections with the institutional and sacramental dimensions of the church. A new form of postconciliar piety had been born.*

The first manifestation of Pentecostalism among Roman Catholics appeared at Duquesne University in Pittsburgh in 1966. A group of faculty and students began to investigate the idea of baptism of the Holy Spirit and started to meet with a neo-Pentecostal prayer group. By February of 1967, four Catholics at Duquesne testified that they had received this baptism and the accompanying gift of tongues.

From Pittsburgh the movement spread to Notre Dame and then to Newman Centers at Michigan State and the University of Michigan. Within four years from its beginning the Catholic Pentecostal movement had spread to dozens of areas in the U.S. and Canada. At least 30,000 Roman Catholics now participate in prayer meetings and have received or are seeking the baptism of the Holy Spirit. They form a tiny minority of the forty-seven million American Catholics and have not attracted many adherents outside of North America; however, the spread of Pentecostalism among Catholics may prove to be one of the most significant developments of the post–Vatican II church....

Central in the life of the Catholic Pentecostal along with the Mass is the weekly prayer meeting. Held in a home or church hall, it may well last three hours or longer. The format varies but usually includes Bible reading, singing, testimonials, fellowship, speaking in tongues, and sometimes healings. Toward the end of a meeting the group extends an invitation to any who wish to ask for the baptism of the Holy Spirit. Those already so baptized pray over these individuals and participate in the laying on of hands.

Many Catholic Pentecostals testify that their involvement has also heightened their appreciation of the Mass and other devotions. They may now try to attend daily Mass although some admit that before hearing of Pentecostalism they skipped Mass altogether or attended only out of fear of sin. Pentecostals are regularly urged to set aside at least fifteen minutes a day for Bible study and additional time for meditation and prayer. One midwestern Newman chaplain — not a Pentecostal — told me he formed a kindly impression of the Catholic Pentecostals when he went to a Newman conference and discovered the Pentecostals had spent five hours in a Bible study session. "Anything which can get a bunch of college students to spend that much time on the Bible can't be all bad," he remarked.

Ultra-conservative Catholics probably would not feel at home among the Pentecostals. The former might yearn for the old Latin Mass while the Pentecostals rejoice in the freedom of the folk Mass, feel no embarrassment at the kiss or handshake of peace, and cultivate spontaneous prayer whether in English or "tongues." The Marian piety which characterizes most conservatives is rare among Catholic Pentecostals whose prayers, hymns, and general spirituality center around the Holy Spirit and Jesus Christ. Finally, the conservative might hesitate to affiliate with any religious group which does not bear the explicit seal of approval of his bishop and pastor. In most dioceses church officials tolerate but do not actively promote Pentecostalism. Catholic Pentecostalism has been attacked in the pages of *Triumph* magazine and by spokesmen for the Catholic Traditionalists.

On the other hand, the liberal Catholic might find the Pentecostals upsetting because of their tendency toward a Biblical fundamentalism. The Catholic liberal might also fear that the Catholic Pentecostals would emulate the typical classical Pentecostal and become absorbed in his own spiritual life at the expense of Christian social action. Yet some liberals such as Dorothy Day of the *Catholic Worker* have expressed sympathy for the Catholic Pentecostals, especially those who have also embraced a life of evangelical poverty.

One noteworthy accomplishment of the young Catholic Pentecostal movement has been to build an ecumenical bridge between Catholics and those Protestants once considered the most hostile toward Rome. Protestant Pentecostals have been welcomed at Catholic prayer meetings and conferences; Catholics have entered into dialogue with such respected Pentecostals as David J. du Plessis, an observer at Vatican II.

Some Catholics have joined the Full Gospel Business Men's Fellowship International along with Pentecostals and neo-Pentecostals. This organization was formed in 1953 by Demos Shakarian, a California dairyman of Armenian extraction and Pentecostal persuasion. Its chapters are generally composed of business and professional men who share the baptism of the Holy Spirit and the gift of tongues....

To an outside observer, the speaking in tongues seems to be the distinguishing mark of Pentecostalism, but the initiates see this gift in a different perspective. Many of the people I interviewed asked me to "play down" the tongue-speaking aspect of the movement. They pointed out that tongues is usually the first gift received by one baptized in the Holy Spirit but it is also ranked as the least of the Pentecostal gifts.

Almost all Pentecostals believe that glossolalia is speaking a genuine foreign language by a person who has never spoken or studied such a language. A small minority believe that the language may be a heavenly language used only to praise God.

The folklore of the Movement abounds in cases in which Pentecostals spoke languages of which they were ignorant but which were easily translated by others in the group who knew the language. Authenticated cases, however, are few and far between. The kind of meticulous investigation which must be carried out before a cure at Lourdes is declared miraculous has not been undertaken. Pentecostals usually insist that such a scientific study would prove little. They note that there are now at least 2800 languages spoken around the world and even an outstanding linguist knows only a handful. Even a roomful of linguists combining their knowledge would be familiar with only 100 or 200 languages. Besides there are the innumerable dead languages and finally the angelic or heavenly tongues. So, say the Pentecostals, a corps of linguists might well fail to recognize the tape recording of a particular "tongue," but the authenticity of the gift would remain a question mark.

Not only do Pentecostals prefer to emphasize other aspects than tongue-speaking, but they point out that many other gifts were promised at the first Pentecost. One priest moderator of a prayer group estimated that about seventy-five out of 100 participants had received the gift of tongues, fifteen had the gift of interpretation, and several seemed on the verge of receiving the gift of healing....

[Father Kilian McDonnell, OSB, director of the Institute for Ecumenical and Cultural Research at St. John's College, Minnesota] maintains: "The issue in Pentecostalism is not tongues, but fullness of life in the Holy Spirit, openness to the power of the Spirit, and the exercise of all gifts of the spirit.... Because Pentecostalism is not a denomination, not a doctrine, but a spirituality, an experience, a way of life, which has a scriptural basis, it can fit into a Roman Catholic, a Lutheran, a Presbyterian context...."

The U.S. bishops appointed a commission headed by Bishop Alexander M. Zaleski of Lansing to study Catholic Pentecostalism. The commission's first report was released in November 1969 and neither condemned nor encouraged the movement. In part the report declared: "It seems to be too soon to draw definitive conclusions regarding the phenomenon, and more scholarly research is needed." At the same time the commission acknowledged that the movement "has legitimate reasons for existence" and "a strong biblical base." Finally the bishops' commission said that "the movement should at this point not be inhibited but allowed to develop."

The brief history of Catholic Pentecostalism suggests that all observers refrain from premature judgments. The chief criterion will be whether Catholic Pentecostalism bears good or bad fruit; three or four years is not enough to decide.

The dangers in Pentecostalism are known to participants and observers alike: excessive emotionalism, a tendency to schism, unsubstantiated Biblical exegesis, the development of a self-identified spiritual elite, preoccupation with personal spiritual growth at the expense of Christian service. The rich possibilities for a deeper religious experience, ecumenical bridge building, the solution of personal problems, and a more active witness to the Gospel are also known. If Catholic Pentecostalism is truly the work of the Holy Spirit, these potentialities will be realized and the dangers avoided in the years immediately ahead.

William J. Whalen, "Catholic Pentecostals," *U.S. Catholic/Jubilee* 35 (November 1970): 8–11. Reprinted with permission from *U.S. Catholic,* Claretian Publications, 205 W. Monroe St., Chicago, IL 60606, 800-328-6515.

87. The House of Prayer Movement, 1969

The 1960s was a decade of intense activity for American Catholics, especially for women religious. Participation in marches for fair housing and racial equality and attendance at anti–Vietnam War protests went hand in hand with experimentation with new forms of religious dress and new types of ministry. Sisters had been working together in support of the renewal of religious life across congregational boundaries since the start of the Sister Formation Movement (see doc. 75). The process was affirmed when they were encouraged by the Second Vatican Council to return to the charism of their communities, a challenge which produced a splintering of some religious congregations. At the same time, questions of identity were raised, as new subgroups of religious emerged by the early 1970s in the Black Sisters Caucus and Hermanas and as sisters sought to reclaim a spirit of prayer in the midst of all that action. In fall 1965, Father Bernard Häring, CSSR, presented the House of Prayer idea to the Conference of Major Superiors of Women. The following June, in a retreat he conducted for the general chapter delegates of the Immaculate Heart of Mary Sisters in Monroe, Michigan, Häring again spoke to the concept, and the sisters' chapter passed an enactment to establish a House of Prayer. At that chapter, Margaret Brennan, who was committed to the renewal of prayer, was elected the general superior. The community became a center of information and experience for other groups who wished to start Houses of Prayer. In August 1968, 156 delegates attended a five-day conference at the sisters' motherhouse reflecting on the theme "Contemplative Living in the Contemporary World." The sisters opened Visitation House in September 1970 with eight sisters as full-time members of the House of Prayer. The selection below is from the report, HOPE (House of Prayer Experience) '69, which evaluated the summer experiences of 137 sisters in fourteen houses of prayer.

If every religious house ought to be, in some way, a house of prayer, why should we have houses especially so designated? Let us admit that the name may not be too fortunate a choice but names often are not. Parents will take great pains to find what they consider the right name for a child but on the first day of school the boy or girl gets a nickname that will stick forever. The main objection against the title "House of Prayer," is that it lends itself to an interpretation that makes it exclusive. However, it must be interpreted inclusively. After all, if you set aside a time of prayer in your daily schedule that is not meant in an exclusive way, either, as if you were not praying any other time — at all times, if possible. Thus all houses ought to be prayerful houses, but just as one sets aside special times of prayer in order to remain prayerful all the time, so one establishes Houses of Prayer in order to make all houses more prayerful.

Of course, this implies a mutual exchange between Houses of Prayer and all other Houses, about which we will have to say more later. At the moment, we have to find the specific difference which makes a house a House of Prayer. The analogy with personal prayer will help us again. What distinguishes an hour of prayer is that everything you do during that hour is completely governed by prayer, although your speaking, your silence, your singing or dancing at other times should also be prayer but may be governed by their own laws. Thus, a House of Prayer is simply one in which all activities are governed by the exigencies of prayer. Where this is true of a given mission, we need not worry about the whole House of Prayer question; and it seems that there was a time when this was, indeed, generally so. However, we must ask ourselves (and even contemplative monasteries have to ask themselves this question today): what is it that sets the pace for our daily life not only in its rhythm but in all its forms? Is it really prayer?

Service in our days has simply become so demanding in its complexity that even people who are less radically dedicated to prayer than religious are having to take time out to listen to the meaning of life or else all their purpose for engagement will suddenly be devoid of meaning. A House of Prayer, then, is a place set aside for prayerful confrontation with the Mystery that gives meaning to life while all other activities in that House are subordinated to this primary goal.

From this it will be clear that we are not talking here about a cloister. A cloister is permanent and self-contained; a House of Prayer, as it is understood here, is not self-contained but constitutes an organ of an active community — the heart-lung complex, so to say, to which the blood must return again and again in order to be activated and renewed. The community in the House of Prayer is thus not a permanent one; this would be stagnation. It is rather a gradual exchange of people coming for shorter or longer periods of renewal. This does not exclude the possibility, of course, that some may stay for an indefinite length of time, but this does not appear as a necessary condition for maintaining a continuous atmosphere of prayer in the House.

Renewal is a major function of the House of Prayer. If it is truly a place of prayer, it will, by its very nature, effect renewal. And no renewal is possible without prayer. However, prayer, celebration, is an end in itself. It need not be justified by effecting renewal. If our prayer has any other purpose than simply to pray, it is no longer prayer. In the same way, the House of Prayer will cease to be itself as soon as we try to make it serve any ulterior purpose.

Yet, when we make prayer our one and only goal there, the place will serve countless other needs unexpectedly. One of them is continuous renewal of the community.

In every individual vocation, periods of stress are apt to precede periods of growth and this is true of a whole community's vocation, too. It is during those vocation crises, then, that both the individual and the community will have to recover their identity through prayer, through silent listening to God's calling, through self-confrontation in great simplicity. Even the Lord Jesus had to go alone to the mountain during hours of crisis. And when his heart was overflowing with joy and gratitude he sought the same mountain solitude. To follow his example we need the kind of place a House of Prayer should be.

•

Responses from some of the Sisters who participated in the summer Houses of Prayer:

> I was afraid a House of Prayer according to modern ideas, would be too noisy and cluttered up with activities — way-out liturgies, records playing all day. Instead I found silence, contemplation, simplicity of prayer together and much opportunity for aloneness with God, also the joy of togetherness in community.

> I had a little secret fear that we might become a ghetto of piety. Our "outreach" was the answer to that. I know now that the House of Prayer is *not* a once in a lifetime experience. I need the support of a community of prayer.

> I have had the ease and beauty of experiencing God with others and still had many hours for my own search. I can no longer see value in completely staying behind the cloister. If our title is a Sister, Servant, then we must manifest this service outwardly to others as Christ did. However, I would consider it important not to become too involved in service.

> I had thought of the House of Prayer as more of a "lone" venture. Now I see prayerful community living as the natural outcome of personal prayer.

> I feel that some of us saw the House of Prayer as a monastic experience with little outside contact and others saw it as more open to the needs of people who came to us. I don't think this "mixture" is bad, since I really feel that we achieved some sort of balance. However, if there are some who really feel strongly about restricting outside contacts, then, in the future, it might be better to have these people in the same house.

> Attitudinal changes have freed my spirit.

Ann E. Chester, *Exploring Inner Space* (1969), 2–3, and unnumbered page.
Courtesy of the Archives of the Immaculate Heart of Mary Sisters, Monroe, Mich.

88. Revitalizing Contemplative Prayer, 1969

Perfectae Caritatis, the Vatican II decree on the renewal of religious life (28 October 1965), built on renewal efforts which had been developing through-out the United States since the early 1940s. Efforts were taking place more quietly among contemplative enclosed religious during the same era. Exposure to developments in scripture, theology, philosophy, and psychology; renewal efforts initiated by the papal decree, Sponsa Christi (1950); the influence of Thomas Merton (1915–68); and increased contact between the groups height-ened the awareness of the need for change and cooperation. In March 1967, contemporaneous with the Lay Pentecostal Movement (see doc. 86), religious women in the New York region formed the voluntary support organization of the Metropolitan Association for Contemplative Communities; other regions also started cooperative meetings, and in 1968, fifty-two monasteries responded to a questionnaire about the meaning of contemplative prayer and its role in church and society. From 17 to 31 August 1969, 135 sisters from throughout the United States met at Woodstock, Maryland. The meeting gave birth to the Asso-ciation of Contemplative Sisters, an organization which would grow by 1974 to a membership of over one thousand sisters from thirteen separate communities. The Woodstock meeting issued a consensus vision statement, Harvest in Glad-ness, and the following selection reflects some of the major areas of discussion underlying most of the spiritual movements of the postconciliar period.

Preamble

Profoundly conscious of solidarity with all men and fellowship with our brothers in Christ, we as contemplative religious women, have looked afresh at our mission in the Church. We have asked ourselves who we are so as to understand better how we might serve.

The conviction that we have a gift does not blind us to the realization that we have failed to offer it in a manner visible and credible at our moment in history.

In the deeply human and Christian experience of this Seminar we have seen our life in the light of on-going human history, a dimension which has raised more questions as to its full implications than we could hope to explore, much less to answer, at this time. Yet the challenge awakens a deeper insight into our identity and reveals a promise of more provoking discovery.

Impelled by a renewed certainty that the charism of contemplative religious life is a timely gift for our world, we press on in the spirit of a pilgrim people to actualize our present insights and to anticipate the call of the future. We are impelled by this same spirit to share the fruit of our dialogue, reflection, and prayer.

Toward a Renewed Understanding of the Contemplative Religious Life

The charism of the contemplative religious life insistently announces, through the lives of those called to live it, that all Christians, indeed all men, are called to intimate communion with God. The inner dynamism of the charism im-pels us to become the reality we announce: to actualize the Church's own covenant relation to Christ in the Spirit.

Our life-style must foster the centering of our human powers and gifts in prayer-response to the Father in Christ. In the full human and Christian perspective we also see that this life-style cannot prescind from an authentic presence in and to the world. Much more it must be transparent of its own inner dynamism, radiating the imperative of the Christian vocation.

Therefore, in this hour we seriously ask ourselves:

1. Is our prayer rooted in reality?

2. Does our life manifest empirically the inner vitality of the prayer life we profess?

3. Are the structures of our life transparent of the reality of our mission?

4. Have we confused the isolation of enclosure with the solitude which environs prayer? Has this artificial isolation cut us off from reality?

5. Should not fidelity to our traditions have brought us to a point of readiness and hope before the challenge of the future? Has it?

We affirm that the summit and source of our life is the liturgical celebration of the Paschal Mystery: that it creates and re-creates us as a unique expression and type of the Christian community which is the Church.

1. Have we given sufficient personal and communal study to the relationship between liturgical celebration and the ordinary living out of our role as a contemplative religious community?

2. Have we realized that the liturgy celebrates a relationship to the wider Christian community? Have we been open to the full implications of this insight?

3. Have we tried to bring our influence to bear upon liturgical renewal in the Church?

We affirm the public ecclesial character of our life as constituted by our religious commitment and ratified by the priestly people of God.

We cherish our call to manifest the reign of God: Christ in our midst and Christ to come.

1. Have we investigated the new avenues opened out by an evolving theology of the vows? Do we fully acknowledge the psychic devastation wrought by a mistreatment of the whole question of sexuality, detachment and penance?

2. Have we investigated the positive implications of consecrated celibacy, realistic poverty and the wholesome responsibility of obedience?

We believe that love for Christ presses us to fill up in our persons what is wanting to his sufferings.

1. Have we accepted the challenge of the hour to express our need for personal and communal penance in new and meaningful forms?

2. Has the overflow of our love for Christ made us more sensitive to the needs of our sisters and to the anguish of our fellowmen? Within the ambit of our own vocation, have we explored the means of alleviating their pain? ...

The Role of Work and Leisure in the Contemplative Life

Considering the problem and role of work in our contemplative life, we re-assert the primacy of prayer as our service to the People of God. From this premise our concern regarding work arises.

We recognize that work, as a human value, has a dignity in itself. We celebrate our communion with all mankind in sharing the condition of the working man: carrying the burden of labor, experiencing its joyful and tedious aspects, its penitential and fulfilling tensions. We see in work a broad range of possibilities for exploring and expanding our service to the world.

Nevertheless, experience makes us acutely aware that we do not have a theology of work in which prayer, leisure and work are integrated as a harmonious continuum. Too often we find ourselves faced with the problem of living the contemplative vocation amid a segmented, unbalanced and frustrating daily horarium. Frequently unrealistic work pressures aggravate the situation.

Our two most pressing needs are:

1. To confront the problem of choosing a work which is compatible with our mode of life and able to achieve a balance between time expenditure and sufficient remuneration.

2. In an attitude of genuine creativity, to search out means of integrating the indispensable parts of the contemplative vocation into a continuum which orders our values in the light of our goal.

Therefore, we want to probe for a deeper understanding of the meaning of work in relation to the meaning of leisure.

In the light of the deeper insight we have gained into the real meaning of leisure, a deep conviction has emerged that leisure is the key to this integration. It is important to realize that by leisure we do not have in mind meaningless inertia.

We understand leisure to be the basis of culture, the source of creativity. It is, in fact, a creative attitude toward life, an inner awareness and aliveness that frees and opens us to the deeper meaning of all that happens in our life. In an attitude of playful spontaneity we take the time to explore creatively our own experiences in order that they may reveal their meaning to us. We integrate our work and our prayer through leisure, since without it there can be no contemplative prayer. Thus grounded in the right balance of give and take, of openness and inner awareness, we approach our work with an attitude of celebration and responsibility.

Recommendations

1. We recommend the development of our appreciation of leisure in its true sense and for its own sake as well as for its witness value in a world that needs to learn how to celebrate before God.

2. We express a concern that work has been seen apart from our human condition and not as an integral expression of the human person. We recommend that careful attention be given to allowing sisters to develop their own gifts and talents. These gifts, these charisms, are given to individuals, not solely for themselves, but also for the good of the community. They are the source of the person's creative contribution to the community and further the group's specific goals of service to the world community. As such, they ought to be cherished and fostered by all.

3. We also recommend the exploration of new ways in which contemplative sisters can serve the world. In the area of sharing our prayer life, especially our liturgy, time must be made available for study and planning, so that our contribution here, as well as in the various art forms, may be timely and meaningful, with a consistent emphasis on quality. Space must be left for a spontaneous service which is best characterized by availability.

4. We ask that consideration be given to the sociological impact of our work-life on the world community. What should our attitude be toward living on alms exclusively, tax exemption and the possession of large properties?

5. We strongly recommend an in-depth study of the types of work available for contemplative communities and the training necessary to engage in them.

6. Finally we recommend a particularized study of the theology of work which will enable and inspire us to take our place in the universal task of man in building a better earth.

> *Harvest in Gladness: A Statement from the Seminar for Contemplatives Held at Woodstock College, August 17–31, 1969, 4–6, 11–12.* Constance Fitzgerald Papers. Courtesy of the Archives of the Baltimore Carmel.

89. The Renewal of the Retreat Movement, 1973

Since their establishments in 1926 and 1936 respectively (see doc. 42), national organizations for men and women engaged in retreat work had sponsored numerous conferences and coordinated an ever-expanding movement. From 1909 to 1929, there were approximately 55 men's retreat houses; in the next decade that number grew to 87; and by 1965, there were 176 houses serving 189,500 men. Among the women, an extensive survey conducted in 1946 indicated that in the previous year at least 745 retreats were held in thirty states with 47,625 women attending. The number of women's houses grew in the postwar period at a pace similar to the men. Shaped by the pastoral vision of Pius XI's

Mens Nostra (1929) and mirroring the devotional and liturgical practices of the broader church, retreats for the laity underwent extensive revision, decline, and then revitalization in the 1960s and early 1970s. The use of film, dialogue and group participation techniques, personal spiritual direction, the private reading of scripture, Bible services, and focus on the liturgy replaced an older devotional format (see docs. 78, 82, 86, 87). Completely new programs such as the Cursillos de Cristianidad, Marriage Encounter, the Better World Movement, and Teens Encounter Christ provided supplementary programs. In 1971 the men's and women's organizations became two separate divisions of one Retreats International. The following statement, adopted in 1973, and generated by the participants themselves, is one of the earliest attempts to reformulate the movement's orienting principles. Clearly impacted by Vatican II and contemporary social and pedagogical realities, the document also tries to establish its continuity with Mens Nostra and the theology of the Mystical Body. The footnotes are those given in the document.

Purpose of a Retreat
(Descriptive Definition and Commentary)

Introduction

The following descriptive definition of the purpose of a retreat has been in the making for over a year. The Research and Development Committee of Retreats International first felt the need for such an undertaking and willingly engineered the project.

Since Vatican II the church has seen many changes and has undergone much experimentation in the United States. In order to have a clear sense of direction for ourselves and for the retreat movement and to consolidate the efforts of Retreats International as a service organization, the committee began explorations and probings at one of its regularly scheduled meetings, January 1971, at Sierra Madre, California. The methodology used in the investigation was twofold: Research and Field Action. The research led naturally enough to tap the resources and findings of thinking churchmen across the country. Through surveys and opinion polls of the retreat houses themselves, we were able to gather the understanding and insights of men in the field.

We can honestly say the descriptive definition of the purpose of a retreat as we now have it stands as a witness to the very substantial response of involved retreat men and women of North America. It is hoped that this final draft of the purpose of a retreat will be enthusiastically received by the total membership of Retreats International at its next convention in Buffalo, New York, 1974, and so be incorporated into our code of regulations.

Definition

THE PURPOSE OF A RETREAT IS TO FOSTER AN ONGOING PROCESS OF PRAYERFUL LISTENING AND RESPONDING TO THE SPIRIT OF GOD IN THE CONTEMPORARY WORLD; TO HELP AN INDIVIDUAL TO EXPERIENCE A DEEPER COMMITMENT TO THE LIVING CHRIST THROUGH SPIRITUAL GROWTH AND DEVELOPMENT OF THE WHOLE PERSON.

"THE PURPOSE OF A RETREAT" was sought by the committee because it gives a sense of direction, or the end-result desired, while at the same time explaining something of the meaning that goes into it. This lends itself to a more pastoral application. You might say this is an imitation of the Vatican II Council which took a pastoral position, especially in the document *Gaudium et Spes* (The Church in the Modern World). Perhaps what St. Alphonsus Ligouri said of retreats can be equally applied to the documents of Vatican II, "a treasure which God has given to His church in these latter days and for which we owe great gratitude."

"TO FOSTER AN ONGOING PROCESS"[1] The very concept of retreat is rooted in needs expressed in such classic phrases as: "come apart and rest a while" (Mark 6:30–32); "leisure is the basis of culture"; "the technocrat needs constant humanization."[2]

Retreats are to create an environment in which a man can respond more deeply to the presence of God. Retreat houses cultivate such an environment in which the human spirit weighed down with the anxieties and pressures of living can take time out "not in idleness but in consideration of those questions which are of profound interest to man" in fitting surroundings.[3]

This is an ongoing process because we are men and women of our times and times are changing, have always changed. We're members of a church that is an historical reality and sees that as part of her mission she is constantly to reinterpret the meaning and values of the gospel to our age.

In like manner an individual must engage in the same ongoing process of interpreting the meaning and values of his life to himself at every stage of growth. "True spirituality is the journey within and the journey back to the outer rim of life. The journey within is, in fact, the journey into reality."[4] A retreat is an exercise in spirituality; an intensification of the Christian life process of becoming more and more Christlike.

"PRAYERFUL LISTENING AND RESPONDING" Pope Paul VI himself beautifully described the process of our creaturehood. How we, who by our discursive way of thinking and reasoning, learn to understand things better, to grasp the truth as much as we can and to respond as living beings before God. This is the dialogue approach to life that he describes so beautifully in his encyclical *Ecclesiam Suam* as God's own method of dealing with man.[5] He sent His Word who is Spirit and Truth that we might have life and have it more abundantly. God has laid expectations upon us to respond. This is what we give that is distinctively our own as creatures. And this is the focus of the process of retreat: in His very presence we learn to listen actively and to respond with mind and heart to His will in our life.

---

1. *Mens Nostra,* #6, Pius XI. *Gaudium et Spec,* #44, Vatican II.
2. *Lumen Gentium,* #9, 33, 40, Vatican II; *Spiritual Renewal of the American Priesthood,* 6, NCCB.
3. *Ecclesiam Suam,* #58 part III, Paul VI.
4. *Spiritual Renewal,* 4–5, 6–9, NCCB.
5. *Ecclesiam Suam,* #58 part III, Paul VI.

Prayer, conversation with Him who loves us, is the medium and the atmosphere for the Spirit to keep guiding us in His constant effort of incarnating Christ in each generation.[6]

"TO THE SPIRIT OF GOD IN THE CONTEMPORARY WORLD" God is everywhere; His Spirit is at work in all things. Consequently, we can expect to hear His word anyplace, anywhere, in anyone, save sin. As the church herself so the individual follower of Christ must "scrutinize the signs of the times and interpret them in the light of the gospels."[7]

"TO HELP AN INDIVIDUAL." Here we see the particular role of retreat as assisting the person in his life process before God, making a decision for Christ. It is his or her conscience before God that must be cultivated and nurtured.[8] It is not a matter of imposing values, or laws and regulations, but of seeing, hearing and taking to oneself the deeper meanings and values of life that are God given.

"TO EXPERIENCE A DEEPER COMMITMENT"[9] Providing a prayerful environment and respecting individual liberties, a retreat supports the individual in his most important task of life, deepening his commitment to Christ. Commitment runs as deep as personal choice and the measure and worth of the person is manifest in his free choices. This conversion, *metanoia,* turning to God, is the creature's greatest response — choosing to be with God as He has chosen to be with us.

"TO THE LIVING CHRIST"[10] We worship a God not of the dead but of the living, a Christ not historically past but a resurrected Christ. Our faith commitment urges us to spiritual and corporal works of mercy, to the mystical body of Christ, to the whole Christ (I Cor. 12:12f). The Spirit of Christ has been given and is within and so we fill in what is lacking of the life of Christ in these our days. Followers of His way, we are committed to be Christlike.

Religion is not just an intellectual exercise. It is a life style; a constant series of experiences with another person. This loving interpersonal relationship deepens the individual's commitment to Christ in Himself and in His mystical body.[11]

"THROUGH SPIRITUAL GROWTH AND DEVELOPMENT OF THE WHOLE PERSON"[12] As Jesus Himself, we must grow in wisdom and grace before God and man. Jesus is our model for living and no one was more fully human than He, the Word made flesh. Grace builds on nature. Natural and supernatural are not contraries but integral to each other. God Himself has endorsed our hu-

---

6. *Lumen Gentium,* #4, 34; *Gaudium et Spes,* #4, 11, 38, 54, 58; *Apostolicam Actuositatem* #4, 32, Vatican II; *Sacrosanctum Concilium,* #12.

7. *Gaudium et Spes,* #4, 12, Vatican II passim.

8. Ibid., #44.

9. *Dignitatis Humanae,* #2, Vatican II; *Gaudium et Spes,* #17.

10. *Mystici Corporis,* #81, 84, Pius XII; *Gaudium et Spes,* #1, Vatican II.

11. *Gaudium et Spes,* #22; *Lumen Gentium,* #7.

12. *Mens Nostra* #7, 8, Pius XI; *Gaudium et Spes,* #4 and Par II, Chapter II *in toto.*

manity and has lifted it up in Jesus Christ our Lord. For example, as a person grows in his faith and trust and love of others, so he develops his capacity to believe, hope and love the Father. Human growth is this process of internalization of the deepest values of a person's life — fitting labor for a retreat. All of this is a maturing process by which a person gradually develops to the full stature of Christ and lives, now no longer self, but Christ lives in him.[13]

> Retreats International Item, RI Service 00; no. 1, June 1973. Courtesy of Retreats International, Hesberg Library, University of Notre Dame, Notre Dame, Ind.

90. The Distribution of the Eucharist, 1976

The reception of the teachings of the Second Vatican Council and consequent changes in liturgical expression and catechesis on the changes was uneven from diocese to diocese. But many parishes, especially those which had active lay groups such as parish councils, the Christian Family Movement, and Cursillo groups, quickly put into place liturgical practices suggested by the council. Nationally, the Liturgical Institute at Notre Dame, Indiana, especially through its summer sessions, provided information and formation in liturgical practice for persons around the country. For those who had spent their whole lives praying in liturgical Latin, the celebration of the Eucharist in English was a momentous event. The following explanation by the U.S. Catholic bishops addresses the situation of local versions of the Anglicized phrase for "Corpus Christi." Instead of employing juridical language to address the variations, the bishops referenced the experience of the early church, Catholics' common baptism, and the relationship of the individual and community to the presence of Christ in the Eucharist. While the theology of the Mystical Body seems to disappear at least technically in the document, the bishops' explanation of the practice illustrates the fruition of the study of scripture, the early church's liturgical tradition, and the Church Fathers.

On April 25, 1964 the Congregation of Rites issued a decree on a new form for the distribution of Holy Communion. The former form Corpus Domini nostri Jesu Christi custodiat animam tuam in vitam aeternam. Amen. was said entirely by the priest. The new form Corpus Christi to which the communicant responds Amen was immediately adopted. On September 26, 1964 with the first instruction "Inter Oecumenici" the vernacular was introduced for this part of the Mass. Several queries have been addressed to this office concerning the use of this form and whether such forms as "Receive the Body of Christ" or "This is the Body of Christ" or the like may be substituted.

A salient feature in the liturgical renewal as evidenced in the conciliar documents, especially in the Constitution on the Liturgy, and in the various new rites, in particular the Order of Mass, is the role of the community. The community is not just an adjunct or an appendage in liturgical celebrations; it is part of the mystery celebrated and is involved in the action. For this reason the Council states:

---

13. *Gaudium et Spes,* #17; *Apostolicam Actuositatem,* #4, 29.

Mother Church earnestly desires that all the faithful should be led to that full, conscious, and active participation in liturgical celebrations which is demanded by the very nature of the liturgy, and to which the Christian people, "a chosen race, a royal priesthood, a holy nation, a redeemed people" (1 Peter 2:9, See 2:4–5) have a right and obligation by reason of their baptism (no. 14).

In the liturgical renewal proper emphasis has been placed on the assembly and its nature in view of the fact that all present have been baptized into Christ Jesus and have received the Spirit. For this reason many gestures and texts take into consideration the community as, for example, the greeting at Mass, which seeks to emphasize its role in the actual liturgical celebration.

The use of the phrase *The Body of Christ. Amen.* in the communion rite asserts in a very forceful way the presence and role of the community. The minister acknowledges who the person is by reason of baptism and confirmation and what the community is and does in the liturgical action. Saint Augustine of Hippo speaking on Easter Sunday (c. 410) said the following concerning the meaning of the phrase *The Body of Christ:*

Hear, in short what the Apostle, or better, what Christ says by the mouth of the Apostle concerning the sacrament of the Lord's table: "We, being many, are one bread, one body." That is all there is to it, as I have quickly summed it up. Yet do not count the words, but rather weigh their meaning; for if you count them they are few, but if you ponder them, their import is tremendous. One bread, the Apostle said. No matter how many breads were placed before him then, still they were only one bread. No matter how many breads are laid upon the altars of Christ throughout the world today, it is but one bread. What is meant by one bread? St. Paul interpreted it briefly: "We, being many, are the one body." This bread is the body of Christ, to which the Apostle refers when he addresses the Church: "Now you are the body of Christ and his members." That which you receive, that you yourselves are by the grace of the redemption, as you acknowledge when you respond Amen. What you witness here is the sacrament of unity.

The change to the use of the phrase *The Body of Christ* rather than the long formula which was previously said by the priest has several repercussions in the liturgical renewal. First, it seeks to highlight the important concept of the community as the body of Christ; secondly, it brings into focus the assent of the individual in the worshipping community, and finally, it demonstrates the importance of Christ's presence in liturgical celebrations as evidenced in the Constitution on the Liturgy (See no. 7). The use of the expression *The Body of Christ. Amen.* which dates back to the early Church and which was always preserved in the Ambrosian rite is another example of the use of *traditio* in liturgical renewal to focus attention on important concepts in Christian worship.

"The Bishops' Committee on the Liturgy Newsletter," *National Conference of Catholic Bishops* 12 (September 1976): 33–34. Reprinted with permission.

91. The U.S. Bishops Introduce the Theme of the International Eucharistic Congress, 1976

In 1976 the United States of America celebrated its bicentennial. That same year the International Eucharistic Congress was celebrated for eight days in Philadelphia, a heavily Catholic city where the liberty bell hangs. The first Catholic president, John F. Kennedy, had allayed the fears of some that the Vatican would interfere with the U.S. government, and the Catholic Church was respected for its social and educational institutions. While the efforts of some Catholics in the 1930s through the 1950s had been to "make America Catholic," the post-Vietnam era found the church confident in the public arena and ecumenically minded. The bishops' statement that outlined the platform for the international congress and indicated motivation to attend the event was titled "The Eucharist and the Hungers of the Human Family." The document, presented below, echoes many of the teachings of Vatican II with respect to the liturgy, including the idea that the Eucharist is the center of the church's life. Supported by the renewed liturgical interest in symbol, ritual, and cultural anthropology, the document highlights a holistic approach to the bread of the Eucharist and acts as a kind of meditation on the levels of significance of bread in relation to hunger. While the Catholic Church in the United States was known for its many social agencies to alleviate physical and psychological needs, reference to the Campaign for Human Development, which was started in 1970, points to a new emphasis on structural change in society.

1. At Thanksgiving, Americans join in gratitude to God for His gifts to this nation and its people. The act of giving thanks is one in which Catholics are privileged to participate in a special way in the celebration of the Eucharist. The word, eucharist, means "thanksgiving," and the Eucharist is the supreme act of thanks in which Christ offers perfect worship to the Father and gives Himself as the perfect gift of love to those who believe in Him.

2. Next August the forty-first International Eucharistic Congress will be celebrated in the United States at Philadelphia. In the intervening months we Catholics of the United States will be preparing for that great event, which will constitute a magnificent public witness to our faith in Jesus Christ, Our Lord in the Eucharist, and our love for Him. The preparation will be primarily spiritual, as we work together to renew ourselves and the Church.

3. The Eucharistic Congress gives us a special opportunity for spiritual and intellectual growth focused on the Eucharistic liturgy, which is simultaneously "a sacrament of love, a sign of unity, a bond of charity, a paschal banquet in which Christ is consumed, the mind is filled with grace, and a pledge of future glory is given to us" (Vatican Council II, *Constitution on the Sacred Liturgy*, 47). In the Congress, we are offered means to manifest publicly our faith and love for this great gift. Coming as it does during our nation's bicentennial anniversary, the Congress also affords Catholics an occasion to invite others to join them in affirming the religious and spiritual heritage of America. It renews and strengthens our commitment to the work of spreading Christ's reign of justice and charity in the world.

4. We should all seize this opportunity, not only by participating, if possible, in the Congress itself, but also by participating fully in the programs of spiritual renewal which will be offered by dioceses and parishes throughout our nation.

5. As this season is an appropriate time to begin intensive preparation, it is also a fitting time in which to recall that there are many persons in our nation and our world who experience profound hungers which crave to be satisfied. There is no one of us who does not hunger in some way, or in many ways: for, besides physical hunger, human beings have deep emotional, intellectual and spiritual hungers.

6. Pleasure, power, or possessions may temporarily quiet the pangs of some hungers. They cannot satisfy us on the deepest levels of our personhood. Only God can do that. "You have made us for Yourself, O God, and our hearts are restless until they rest in You" (St. Augustine, *Confessions,* 1,1).

7. God the Father loves us so much that He sent His only Son, to become one of us and redeem us. Jesus loves us so much that, even after His death, resurrection and ascension, He remains with us. He is, after all, Emmanuel, "God with us," but now through His living, sanctifying Spirit. We now encounter Him in new ways: in other human beings; in any place where people gather in His name (Mt. 18:20); in the inspired words of Holy Scripture; in His Church, particularly her liturgical celebrations; in the person of His minister; and especially in the sacraments, preeminently the sacrament of the Eucharist.

8. In the Eucharist, which is Jesus really present, God satisfies our deepest hungers. The Sacrifice of the Mass is Christ's supreme act of reconciliation. "Truly partaking of the body of the Lord in the breaking of the Eucharistic bread, we are taken up into communion with Him and with one another. 'Because the bread is one, we though many, are one body, all of us who partake of the one bread' (I Cor. 10:17), 'but severally members one of another'" (Rom. 12:15) (Vatican Council II, *Dogmatic Constitution on the Church,* 7). The Eucharist is indeed the Sacrament of Unity, "by which the unity of the Church is both signified and brought about" (Vatican Council II, *Decree on Ecumenism,* 2).

9. The theme of the Congress, "The Eucharist and the Hungers of the Human Family," reminds us that men and women hunger not only for food, but also for God, not only for bread in this life, but for the Bread of Life itself: for Christ, really present in the Eucharist, really received in Holy Communion, leading us to the Father. The eight days of the Eucharistic Congress will be devoted to eight separate human "hungers" and the relationship of the Eucharist to them.

10. (1) *Hunger for God.* If we lack God, it matters little what else we have. Estranged from God, we are estranged from our own destiny and fulfillment. Human life absorbed in itself is diminished and lacking in purpose. The Eucharist is a special means given to us by Jesus for overcoming our estrangement from God. It is as Christ tells us: "The man who feeds on my flesh and drinks my blood remains in me, and I in him" (Jn 6:56).

11. (2) *Hunger for Bread.* Many persons today are physically hungry. Certainly the solution to starvation and malnutrition requires increased production and improved distribution of food. But it also requires "a concerted act of solidarity" by the nations and peoples of the world (Synod of Bishops, 1974, *Statement on Human Rights and Reconciliation*). Our sharing in the Eucharist inspires us to such solidarity, as well as to actions which express it; for sincere celebration of the Eucharist "must lead to various works of charity and mutual help" (Vatican Council II, *Decree on the Ministry and Life of Priests*, 6).

12. (3) *Hunger for Freedom and Justice.* The quest for human freedom and justice is not something optional for Catholics, nor is it a small part of the Church's mission. Participation in the struggle for freedom and justice is a duty for each one of us, as it is a central element of the Church's mission of redemption and liberation. In the Eucharist we find the source of our deepest commitment to the loving service of our brothers and sisters. It is especially timely for us to reflect on these facts at this season of the year, when we are called upon to express our solidarity with the poor and powerless of our nation through the Campaign for Human Development.

13. (4) *Hunger for the Spirit.* In considering this theme, the Eucharistic Congress will focus in a special way on religious vocations and the need for religious commitment by the clergy and religious of the world. It is most appropriate that this be done in the context of the Eucharist, for it is the special role of clergy and religious to give witness to the transcendent, God-centered nature of human life and striving, which the Eucharist supremely expresses: this is no "perishable food but... food that remains unto life eternal, food which the Son of Man will give you" (John 6:27).

14. (5) *Hunger for Truth.* Jesus proclaimed that He is "the Way, the Truth, and the Life" (John 14:6). We know, therefore, that knowledge of truth in the act of faith means more than just an intellectual understanding of abstract concepts. It also means commitment to a Person. Our most direct and profound encounter with this Person who is Truth occurs in the Sacrament of the Eucharist. Here grace strengthens both our acceptance of what faith teaches and our loving commitment to the Person who stands at the center of faith.

15. (6) *Hunger for Understanding.* Our times experience the tragedy of estrangement between nations, races, classes, churches, and even generations. Children feel that they are not understood by their own parents; parents feel the same with respect to their children. The need for reconciliation is clear. How better achieve such reconciliation than at the Table of the Lord; for "the liturgy in its turn inspires the faithful to become 'of one heart in love'" (Vatican Council II, *Constitution on the Sacred Liturgy*, 10).

16. (7) *Hunger for Peace and Love.* In an era of tension and violence, the limits of human instruments for peace are all too evident. Christ is our peace, and Christ Himself in the Eucharist provides us with both our model and best hope for peace. For it is He "who made the two of us one by breaking down the barrier of hostility that kept us apart" (Eph. 2:14). It is here, in the Eucharist, that "all education in the spirit of community must originate" (Vatican Council II, *Decree on the Ministry and Life of Priests*, 6).

17. (8) *Hunger for Jesus — The Bread of Life.* All men and women hunger for Christ, consciously or not. It is the Lord, worthily and maturely received in Holy Communion, who brings about our loving unity with one another and with Him. Without the Eucharist our lives in all their dimensions would be lacking in something essential; in the Eucharist we find means to conquer our weakness and tendency to sin and to live according to God's will for us. "Let me solemnly assure you, if you do not eat the flesh of the Son of Man and drink his blood, you have no life in you. He who feeds on my flesh and drinks my blood has life eternal, and I will raise him up on the last day" (John 6:53–54).

18. The mysterious reality of the Eucharist — "My flesh is real food and my blood real drink" (John 6:55) — is a puzzle to some, a scandal to others. It has always been so. After Jesus promised the Eucharist, "many of his disciples remarked, 'This sort of talk is hard to endure! How can anyone take it seriously?'... From this time on, many of his disciples broke away and would not remain in his company any longer" (John 6:60–66).

19. But for those who believe in Jesus' teaching, because they believe in Jesus Christ Himself, the Eucharist is, among all His gifts to us, the most cherished and the cause of our deepest gratitude. After some of his disciples had left Him, Jesus asked the Twelve: "Do you want to leave me too?" Simon Peter answered — for them and for us. "Lord, to whom shall we go? You have the words of eternal life. We have come to believe; we are convinced that you are God's holy one" (John 6:67–69). Let us pray that the Eucharistic Congress will help all of us to renew our faith, hope, our love, and our gratitude for the great gift of Our Lord and Savior Jesus Christ in the Sacrament of the Eucharist; and to recommit ourselves, in union with Him, to the task of responding generously to the hungers of the human family.

> "The Eucharist and the Hungers of the Human Family: A Pastoral Statement Issued by the National Conference of Catholic Bishops, November 20, 1975," in Hugh J. Nolan, ed., *Pastoral Letters of the United States Catholic Bishops, Vol. IV, 1975–1983* (Washington, D.C.: National Conference of Catholic Bishops, United States Catholic Conference, 1983), 77–80. Reprinted with permission.

92. Spiritual Sources Gathered from Mystics of East and West, 1977

> *The extent of institutional change and the social flux of the 1960s encouraged many in the Catholic community to turn inward to find a still point of identity (see docs. 86, 87, 88). The end of the decade witnessed a growing exposure to Eastern techniques of self-reflection and self-knowledge (transcendental meditation, yoga) and a resurgence in the publication of classic works of Western mysticism. Cistercian Studies and Studies in the Spirituality of the Jesuits both began in this era. "Mysticism" and "contemplation" for the first time in the history of the community no longer carried the popular connotations of a dangerous and esoteric elitism. Within a few years, the popular work of Jesuit, Benedictine, Carmelite, Cistercian, and Franciscan preachers in retrieving their tradition and books by Thomas Merton (Contemplative Prayer, 1969), Ruth Burrows (Guidelines for Mystical Prayer, 1976), George Maloney (Inward Stillness, 1976), and William McNamara (Mystical Passion, 1977) symbolized*

the emergence of a real "mystical revival" in the Catholic community. The following article, titled "Seeking the Wisdom of the Mysterious West," from the New York Times for 4 December 1977, summarizes this significant shift in the spiritual sensibility of the community.

Spurred by the current wave of interest in Eastern religion — particularly in the areas of meditation and mysticism — Western churchmen have begun searching their own traditions for spiritual disciplines that may have been neglected or forgotten. Signs of the rising attraction to mystical resources in the West include a large increase in the number of "houses of prayer," a sharp upturn in male candidates for religious orders, growing numbers of the laity seeking prayer retreats and ballooning sales of books by such Christian mystics as Thomas Merton and St. Teresa of Avila.

The content of these opportunities for spiritual growth differ greatly. A retreat may involve mostly silent meditation or quiet periods interspersed among such activities as Bible study, singing and common worship. The goal is uniform, renewal of the relationship with God.

The degree to which mysticism is explicitly emphasized also varies. Mystical experiences are usually described as moments in which the person feels uplifted and often at one with the universe. In this state of consciousness, many report a sense of ecstasy and say that time and space are perceived differently than in everyday life.

Because such an experience is believed to be so intensely personal, it is not thought capable of being programmatically induced. At best, proper spiritual discipline is believed to enhance the possibility of the experience.

The differences between Eastern and Western mysticism are subtle, but a comparison usually begins with two distinctions. First, Eastern practice concentrates on emptying oneself of thoughts and illusions, in order to uncover the pure state of Being, while Western discipline focuses on aspects of Christian tradition, especially the example of Christ, in order to fill the soul with God's spirit. Second, the East places greater stress on the connection between the physical means of meditation and the spiritual end.

Though few may be willing to dedicate themselves full time to contemplation, many who now follow the Western pathway seek to integrate more spirituality into their daily lives. Within Catholicism, most of the 98 "houses of prayer" listed in the directory of retreat centers — an increase of 25 percent in the last year — are filled every weekend with laity and clergy. They range from Queen of Peace Oratory in Denver, Colo., which includes provisions for 30-day "spiritual exercises," to Our Lord of the Adirondacks in Ellenburg Center, N.Y., which offers both contemplative and charismatic programs.

Book sales and scholarly trends also indicate the emerging pattern. For example, Doubleday reports that sales of its 12 books by Thomas Merton, the most noted American mystic, have combined to soar, currently running at yearly levels from 6,000 to 20,000 copies. Other popular choices are "The Cloud of Unknowing," by an anonymous 14th century mystic, and the writings of two medieval Spanish mystics, St. Teresa of Avila and St. John of the Cross.

In the academies, formal studies of Western ascetic and mystic traditions are starting to gain a foothold. Among the leaders are Western Michigan University, where a center for contemplative studies was launched two years ago, and the University of California at Santa Barbara, which this year has enrolled a new high of 300 students in the courses that include Western disciplines.

Renewed vitality in monastery life is another sign of the resurgence of spirituality. Monks have been in the forefront of looking at Christian tradition and experimenting with Eastern practice. Added impetus was provided this past spring when 40 monks and nuns representing most of the world's great monastic traditions met in Petershan, Mass., for three days to discuss common goals.

M. Basil Pennington, a Trappist from St. Joseph's Abbey in Spencer, Mass., reported in the Jesuit periodical, "America," that most leaders insisted on the "importance of the West's recovering and reestablishing its own contemplative tradition." In part, Father Pennington notes, this emphasis can be seen as "a response to the challenge from the East."

Monasteries themselves appear to be in better shape than they were a few years ago. After dramatic losses cut the size of some communities in half during the 1960s, they have stabilized and some are growing slowly.

The Abbot Primate of the Benedictines reported to the order's world congress this fall that there had been "a continued rise in vocations in almost all parts of the world." He said it was too early to assess the reasons for this growth, but added that "there is no doubt that some of the tension for survival seems to be disappearing and the question now is not whether monasteries will survive but what will be their role and contribution in the future."

One role appears to be that of providing a laboratory for testing the compatibility of mystical traditions. For example, monks at St. Joseph's have long been using techniques from Zen and other disciplines. At Our Lady of Guadalupe monastery in Oregon, many of the younger Trappists have arranged a room as a Zendo, a Buddhist place for meditation. There they meet at 2 a.m. to practice Zen as a sort of extra-curricular activity.

The trend toward mysticism is viewed with wariness and even alarm in some quarters. Many critics believe it represents escapism, excessive self-absorption and neglect of important social and political questions.

Another concern is that too much dabbling with Eastern mysticism will deter Christianity from a genuine renewal of faith that can grapple with the modern age.

"Although Westernized versions of Eastern faiths do often claim to bring salvation to the West," writes the Harvard theologian, Harvey Cox, "at this point they betray the spirit of their sources and actually worsen the Western dilemma by advertising more than they can deliver. The spiritual crisis of the West will not be resolved by spiritual importations or individual salvation."

Dr. Cox does not advocate thoroughgoing mysticism of any sort, though he meditates according to Tibetan Buddhist practice. But he shares an interest in the spirituality that is shaping a new era in the churches.

The monastery, once a walled-off enclosure that outsiders found esoteric, has become a spiritual center that has something that more people want — a life of prayer. As one monk put it, "somehow we don't seem so bizarre any more."

Kenneth A. Briggs, "Seeking the Wisdom of the Mysterious West," *New York Times,* 4 December 1977, 22E. Copyright © 1977 by the New York Times Co. Reprinted by permission.

93. The Sisters of St. Agnes Compile a Creed, 1979

Creeds represent distilled beliefs forged by communities at a time when they need to reclaim the tradition in a new way or to develop further dimensions of commonly held convictions. The Sisters of St. Agnes from Fond du Lac, Wisconsin, met together for an intensive week in Nicaragua in 1979. Since 1945 they had worked alongside the Detroit Province of Capuchins in the eastern part of the country and in Managua. The community, composed of U.S. and Nicaraguan women, reflected on their experience and struggles after the loss of several of their traditional works in a devastating earthquake, the Sandinista revolution, and the realization of differences between the mission perspectives of the sisters in Nicaragua and those of the stateside sisters. The document is suggestive of the increased influence of Latin American sources on U.S. Catholic spirituality, renewed interest in various methods of discernment (see docs. 31, 64), and the internal struggles the church experienced over a pastoral methodology when working among impoverished peoples.

WE BELIEVE:

That God has made His the cry of His people, and has been present to liberate it.

Que Dios ha hecho Suyo el clamor de nuestro pueblo, y se ha hecho presente para liberarlo.

That we ought to be conscious of the process of personal conversion that God is making in each one of us by means of the actual reality in which we are living.

Que debemos ser conscientes del proceso de conversión personal que Dios está haciendo en cada una de nosotras por medio de la realidad actual en que vivimos.

That God wishes to use us now as His instruments to help to plant, spread and share the Faith, cooperating in the transformation of the people.

Que El Señor quiere utilizarnos ahora como sus instrumentos para ayudar a sembrar, regar y compartir la fe, cooperando en la transformación de Su pueblo.

That the chapter of our history that we have begun is not the meeting, but the march to the Promised Land.

Que el capítulo de nuestra historia que hemos comenzado no es un encuentro, sino una marcha hacia la tierra prometida.

That our Christian efficacy comes from a spirit of profound prayer and contemplation.

Que nuestra eficacia cristiana se deriva de un espíritu profundo de oración y contemplación.

That we are co-responsible for the triumph of this liberating process and that we always ought to have the courage to speak in public for justice.

Que somos co-responsables del triunfo de este proceso liberador y que siempre debemos tener el coraje de hablar a favor de la justicia.

That it is the moment for giving our support to the historical process that is in the making, and that the Christian principles that are present will triumph in the revolutionary process.

Que es el momento de dar nuestro apoyo al proyecto histórico que se está formulando, y que los principios cristianos que están presentes ya triunfarán en el proceso revolucionario.

That the Lord is present in each person and that this meeting culminates in the celebration of the Eucharist.

Que el Señor está presente en cada persona, y que este encuentro se culmine en la celebración de la Eucaristía.

That the bond that unites the Sisters of St. Agnes is love.
Que el lazo que une a las Hermanas de Santa Inés es el amor.

That our testimony of poverty, obedience, and chastity be a testimony of Faith and Hope for the people.

Que nuestro testimonio de pobreza, obediencia, y castidad sea un testimonio de fe y esperanza para el pueblo.

In the rising of a new dawn for the Nicaraguan woman and we promise to accomplish it as consecrated women.

En el despertar de un nuevo amanecer para la mujer Nicaragüense y nos comprometimos a realizarlo como mujeres consagradas.

That this is the moment in which Christ's Word will come in all its plenitude.

Que este es el momento en que el Evangelio de Cristo vendrá en toda su plenitud.

South America and Central America Missions File. "Result of Meetings, November 1979." Courtesy of the Archives of the Sisters of St. Agnes, Fond du Lac, Wis.

Index

Abair, St. Angela, 93
abstinence, 213–15, 260–63. *See also* fasting; penance
African Americans, 96–100, 182
Agnesian Sisters, 185
Ahern, Barnabas, 185, 205
alcohol, 15, 20, 70–71, 262
All Saints Day, 72
All Souls Day, 72
American Catholic Missionary Congresses, 56
American Freedom and Catholic Power (Blanchard), 133
Americanism, 57, 58
American Religious Depression, the, 115
animism, 183
Annunciation, the, 192
Anthony of Padua, St., xxix, 139–42
anti-Catholicism, 2, 133
Apostolate of Suffering, the, 130–31
Ash Wednesday, 260
Asian immigrants, 183
Association of Contemplative Sisters, 273
Association of Saint Francis of Sales, 61
Association of the Perpetual Rosary, 59–62
atheism, 186–87
Augustine, St., 35, 46, 48, 53, 281, 283
Ave Maria magazine, 59

Baltimore
    First Plenary Council of, 21–23
    Second Plenary Council of, 56, 62–63
    Third Plenary Council of, 56, 90–93
Baltimore Catechism, 90, 146
Baptism
    Catholic Action and, 153
    First Council of Baltimore on, 22

language used for, 219–20
liturgical reform and, 241
in private houses, 18–19
synod of 1810 on, 18
Barat, Madeleine Sophie, 76
Bardstown, Kentucky, 32
Benedictines, xxviii, 287
Bentivoglio, Annetta, 76
Bibles, 17, 22, 215–18
"Bible Week," 215
"Biblical Sunday," 215
Bigot, William, 71–73
bishops
    on catechisms and prayer books, 90–93
    on the Eucharist, 282–85
    the Family Rosary Crusade and, 264
    on fasting and abstinence, 213–15
    First Plenary Council of Baltimore and, 21–22
    on language in the liturgy, 218–22
    on new rules for distributing the Eucharist, 280–81
    outsiders' criticism of, 133–35
    on penance, 260–63
    on the Sacred Heart, 74–76
    scripture reading and, 174–76
    Second Plenary Council of Baltimore and, 62–63
    social challenges following World War I and, 119
    synod of 1810, 17–18
Black Sisters Caucus, 270
Blanshard, Paul, 133
Blessed Sacrament
    devotion to, 103–7
    the Forty Hours Devotion and, 45–48
    the "piety void" and, 256–57
    prayer of adoration of, 113–14
    See also Eucharist

OF RELATED INTEREST

Other volumes in the American Catholic Identities Series,
Christopher J. Kauffmann, General Editor

*An indispensable resource of original documents
relating to the social and political history of American Catholics
from the Spanish, French, and English colonial beginnings to the present.*

*Absolutely must be in the library of every student of American Catholicism...
a marvelous resource for the classroom... brings alive the whole
panorama of Catholics struggling with and finding identity.*

Public Voices: Catholics in the American Context

Steven M. Avella and Elizabeth McKeown, editors
ISBN 1-57075-266-4

Catholics find their voice in the new republic, moving from outsiders to
insiders, adapting to their new homeland, staying loyal to the Catholic
vision.

The Frontier and Catholic Identities

Anne M. Butler, Michael E. Engh, SJ, and Thomas W. Spalding, CFX, editors
ISBN 1-57075-269-9

The Catholic experience in the epic adventure of expanding frontiers and
settling in a vast continent.

Keeping Faith: European and Asian Catholic Immigrants

Jeffrey M. Burns, Ellen Skerrett, and Joseph M. White, editors
ISBN 1-57075-297-4

A marvelous selection of texts provides readers an opportunity to consider
the words, review the experiences, and study the artistic expressions of
immigrants, leading the reader to appreciate what European and Asian
immigrants have brought the American Catholic Church.

¡Presente! Latino Catholics from Colonial Origins
to the Present

Timothy Matovina and Gerald E. Poyo, editors
ISBN 1-57075-328-8

Latinos preserve their Catholic traditions in the emerging culture, struggling to gain the attention of an often indifferent, sometimes hostile
church.

Creative Fidelity: U. S. Catholic Intellectual Identities
R. Scott Appleby, Patricia Byren, William Portier, editors
ISBN 1-57075-349-0

> Over against the Protestant ascendancy, American Catholics make a distinctive voice heard in the American intellectual landscape.

Gender Identities in American Catholicism
Paula Kane, James Kenneally, Karen Kennelly, CSJ, editors
ISBN 1-57075-350-4

> Women and men rub up against gender-defined roles inherited from ancient cultures and struggle to create a more egalitarian Catholic community within the larger culture.

The Crossing of Two Roads: Being Catholic and Native in the United States
Marie Therese Archambault, OSF, Mark Theil, and Christopher Vecsey, editors
ISBN 1-57075-352-0

> Native American Catholics and their quest to retain traditional identities while joining in the religious faith of those who have taken over their land.

"Stamped with the Image of God": African-Americans as God's Image in Black
Cyprian Davis, OSB, and Jamie Phelps, OP, editors
ISBN 1-57075-351-2

> African Americans experience an ambiguous welcome from their white fellow Catholics and seek a way to be both black and Catholic.

Please support your local bookstore, or call 1-800-258-5838

For a free catalogue, please write us at

Orbis Books, Box 302
Maryknoll NY 10545-0302

or visit our website at www.maryknoll.com.

Thank you for reading Orbis Books.

Maryknoll, New York 10545